The 1920s

The 1920s

Kathleen Drowne
and Patrick Huber

American Popular Culture Through History
Ray B. Browne, Series Editor

GREENWOOD PRESS
Westport, Connecticut • London

Library of Congress Cataloging-in-Publication Data

Drowne, Kathleen Morgan.
The 1920s / Kathleen Drowne and Patrick Huber.
p. cm.—(American popular culture through history)
Includes bibliographical references and index.
ISBN 0–313–32013–6 (alk. paper)
1. United States—Civilization—1918–1945. 2. Popular culture—United States—History—20th century. I. Title: Nineteen twenties. II. Huber, Patrick. III. Title. IV. Series.
E169.1.D796 2004
306'.0973'09042—dc22 2003056809

British Library Cataloguing in Publication Data is available.

Library of Congress Catalog Card Number: 2003056809
ISBN: 0–313–32013–6

First published in 2004

Greenwood Press, 88 Post Road West, Westport, CT 06881
An imprint of Greenwood Publishing Group, Inc.
www.greenwood.com

Printed in the United States of America

The paper used in this book complies with the Permanent Paper Standard issued by the National Information Standards Organization (Z39.48–1984).

10 9 8 7 6 5 4 3 2 1

For our parents,
William and Joanne Drowne,
and
Mary Huber and the memory of Paul A. Huber,
two children of the Jazz Age,
and for Genevieve

Contents

Series Foreword *by Ray B. Browne* ix

Acknowledgments xi

Introduction xiii

Timeline of the 1920s xix

Part I Life and Youth During the 1920s 1

Chapter 1. Everyday America 3

Chapter 2. World of Youth 29

Part II Popular Culture of the 1920s 49

Chapter 3. Advertising 51

Chapter 4. Architecture and Design 73

Chapter 5. Fashion 95

Chapter 6. Food and Drink 119

Chapter 7. Leisure Activities 143

Chapter 8. Literature 169

Chapter 9. Music 191

Chapter 10. Performing Arts 219

Chapter 11. Travel and Recreation 243
Chapter 12. Visual Arts 269
Cost of Products in the 1920s 291
Notes 295
Further Reading 303
Index 315

Series Foreword

Popular culture is the system of attitudes, behavior, beliefs, customs, and tastes that define the people of any society. It is the entertainments, diversions, icons, rituals, and actions that shape the everyday world. It is what we do while we are awake and what we dream about while we are asleep. It is the way of life we inherit, practice, change, and then pass on to our descendants.

Popular culture is an extension of folk culture, the culture of the people. With the rise of electronic media and the increase in communication in American culture, folk culture expanded into popular culture—the daily way of life as shaped by the *popular majority* of society. Especially in a democracy like the United States, popular culture has become both the voice of the people and the force that shapes the nation. In 1782, the French commentator Hector St. Jean de Crèvecouer asked in his *Letters from an American Farmer*, "What is an American?" He answered that such a person is the creation of America and is in turn the creator of the country's culture. Indeed, notions of the American Dream have been long grounded in the dream of democracy—that is, government by the people, or popular rule. Thus, popular culture is tied fundamentally to America and the dreams of its people.

Historically, culture analysts have tried to fine-tune culture into two categories: "elite"—the elements of culture (fine art, literature, classical music, gourmet food, etc.) that supposedly define the best of society—and "popular"—the elements of culture (comic strips, best-sellers, pop music, fast food, etc.) that appeal to society's lowest common denominator. The so-called "educated" person approved of elite culture and scoffed at popular culture. This schism first began to develop in Western

Europe in the fifteenth century when the privileged classes tried to discover and develop differences in societies based on class, money, privilege, and lifestyles. Like many aspects of European society, the debate between elite and popular cultures came to the United States. The upper class in America, for example, supported museums and galleries that would exhibit "the finer things in life," that would "elevate" people. As the twenty-first century emerges, however, the distinctions between popular culture and elitist culture have blurred. The blues songs (once denigrated as "race music") of Robert Johnson are now revered by musicologists; architectural students study buildings in Las Vegas as examples of what Robert Venturi called the "kitsch of high capitalism"; sportswriter Gay Talese and heavyweight boxing champ Floyd Patterson were co-panelists at a 1992 SUNY–New Paltz symposium on Literature and Sport. The examples go on and on, but the one commonality that emerges is the role of popular culture as a model for the American Dream, the dream to pursue happiness and a better, more interesting life.

To trace the numerous ways in which popular culture has evolved throughout American history, we have divided the volumes in this series into chronological periods—historical eras until the twentieth century, decades between 1900 and 2000. In each volume, the author explores the specific details of popular culture that reflect and inform the general undercurrents of the time. Our purpose, then, is to present historical and analytical panoramas that reach both backward into America's past and forward to her collective future. In viewing these panoramas, we can trace a very fundamental part of American society. The "American Popular Culture Through History" series presents the multifaceted parts of a popular culture in a nation that is both grown and still growing.

Ray B. Browne
Secretary-Treasurer
Popular Culture Association
American Culture Association

Acknowledgments

One of the most rewarding aspects of completing this book is the opportunity to thank the many scholars, librarians, archivists, and family members who assisted us in our research and writing. We are deeply indebted to the staff at the Wilson Library, University of Missouri-Rolla, especially Jane Driber, Marsha Fuller, Jim Morisaki, Scott Peterson, and Virginia Schnabel. They always remained helpful and friendly, no matter how tall our stacks of interlibrary loan books.

For assistance with permissions and with compiling the illustrations for this volume, we wish to thank James Goodrich, Lynn Wolf Gentzler, and Christine Montgomery of the State Historical Society of Missouri, Columbia; Deborah Patton Cline of the White Castle System, Inc., Columbus, Ohio; Vicki Russell of the *Columbia Daily Tribune*, Columbia, Missouri; Ellen Thomasson of the Print and Photograph Collection of the Missouri Historical Society, St. Louis; the Whatcom Museum of History and Art, Bellingham, Washington; the Special Collections and Archives Division of the Woodruff Library, Emory University, Atlanta; the Archives and Special Collections of the Richter Library, University of Miami, Coral Gables, Florida; the Southern Folklife Collection and the North Carolina Collection, Wilson Library, the University of North Carolina at Chapel Hill; the Still Picture Branch of the National Archives and Records Administration, College Park, Maryland; and the Photoduplication Service of the Library of Congress, Washington, D.C. Sabra Tull Meyer of Columbia, Missouri, graciously allowed us to reprint the photograph of the 1920s model kitchen.

We are also grateful to our colleagues at the University of Missouri-Rolla, especially our department chairs, Larry Vonalt, Wayne Bledsoe, and Larry Gragg, for their cheerful encouragement and support. In addition, Larry Vonalt, Trent Watts, and Buck and Helen Huber generously furnished us with books and other materials about the 1920s. We deeply appreciate the assistance and patience of our editors at Greenwood Press, Rob Kirkpatrick and his predecessor, Debby Adams. Finally, we wish to thank all of our family, especially William and Joanne Drowne, Eugene and Barbara Schutz, and Mary Huber and the late Paul A. Huber, for their unconditional love and support.

Introduction

"The Jazz Age is over," declared novelist F. Scott Fitzgerald in a May 1931 letter to his editor.[1] Fitzgerald, a perceptive social observer and chronicler of this historical period, had himself coined the phrase "the Jazz Age" in 1922 to describe the exciting, flamboyant era he saw emerge in America after the end of World War I. Just nine years later, though, as the Great Depression deepened, he eulogized this era's passing in an essay he published in *Scribner's* magazine titled "Echoes of the Jazz Age." "The Jazz Age had had a wild youth and a heady middle age," he wrote. "But it was not to be. Somebody had blundered and the most expensive orgy in history was over."[2]

Even before Fitzgerald's obituary of the age appeared, the history and popular culture of the 1920s had already begun to fascinate Americans. The same year that "Echoes of the Jazz Age" was published, Frederick Lewis Allen completed his best-selling *Only Yesterday: An Informal History of the 1920's* (1931), one of the most influential accounts of the decade. Since then, a long parade of journalists, historians, and American studies scholars has written literally thousands of articles and books, each attempting to understand and explain the enduring significance of Jazz Age culture on American life.

Few eras in American history cast such a long shadow over the nation's collective imagination and popular culture as does the 1920s. Over the years, Hollywood directors have attempted to capture the decade in dozens of movies, including films about National Prohibition and gangsters (e.g., Brian De Palma's *The Untouchables* [1987]), changing sexual mores (e.g., Elia Kazan's *Splendor in the Grass* [1961]), and adaptations of period literature (e.g., Jack Clayton's *The Great Gatsby* [1974]). Documentary filmmakers have likewise explored the remarkable lives of such Jazz Age luminaries as Henry Ford, Babe Ruth, Greta Garbo, and Charles Lindbergh, in an effort to identify their lasting contributions to our national identity. Museums, libraries, and cable television channels regularly commemorate the works of Louis Armstrong, Charlie Chaplin, George Gershwin, Alfred Stieglitz, and other influential artists of the 1920s, whose creativity and genius laid the foundations for our own music, cinema, and art. Popular singers and musicians have re-recorded numerous 1920s standards—including Willie Nelson's "Blue Skies" (1977), Harry Connick Jr.'s "It Had to Be You" (1989), and Natalie Cole's "Stardust" (1996)—that now appeal to a whole new generation of music fans. Clearly, the legacy of the 1920s continues to exert considerable influence on our popular culture today.

The ongoing academic and popular fascination with the 1920s is also reflected in the myriad nicknames that the decade has collected. Besides Fitzgerald's famous moniker "The Jazz Age," the 1920s are also remembered as "The Roaring Twenties," "The Age of the Flapper," "The Dollar Decade," "The New Era," "The Lawless Decade," "The Dry Decade," "The Age of Ballyhoo," "The Era of Wonderful Nonsense"—and the list goes on. Yet these clever descriptions often distort our understanding of the complexities and tensions that marked this tumultuous era. The Jazz Age, according to popular conceptions, ranks as one of the most glamorous and exciting decades of the American twentieth century, an era of flamboyance and prosperity best symbolized by flappers, Model T Fords, jazz bands, and bathtub gin. "To judge from some accounts," remarks historian David A. Shannon, "Americans did little else from 1920 until 1929 but make millions in the stock market, dance the Charleston and the Black Bottom, dodge gangster bullets, wear raccoon coats, and carry hip flasks."[3] But these interpretations are, at best, only superficial representations that explain little about everyday life for actual Americans during the 1920s. Like watching *The Untouchables*, attending a Charlie Chaplin film festival, or listening to "It Had to Be You," nicknames and stereotypes tell us only a small part of a vast, complicated story.

Despite the ongoing attempts by scholars, artists, and popular audiences to unravel the meaning of the Jazz Age, a wholly satisfactory explanation proves elusive. One of the difficulties perhaps stems from the continuing disagreement over the era's precise periodization. Most historians actually define the Jazz Age as encompassing the years between November 1918, when World War I ended, and October 1929, when the stock market crashed. Others, however, date its origins even earlier—to the mid-1910s—when significant shifts in mass production, women's roles, and technology accelerated the transformation of American life. Then, too, some scholars extend the end of the Jazz Age to 1933, when President Franklin D. Roosevelt launched the New Deal. For the purposes of this volume, however, we have defined the era as the literal 1920s—from the beginning of 1920 until the end of 1929—while still acknowledging that historical change seldom conforms neatly to the calendar year.

Nearly all scholars agree that most salient features of American popular culture during the 1920s resulted from a cascade of historical transformations that had begun at least by the 1890s and, in some cases, even earlier. Yet it is difficult to resist thinking of the Jazz Age as a series of unexpected surprises, as if one morning Americans awoke suddenly to find that the country had gone dry, women could vote, immigrants crowded the cities, jazz music dominated the airwaves, partyers danced the Charleston, and all the flappers had bobbed their hair. These and other defining characteristics of Jazz Age America did not spring forth fully formed in the 1920s. Nor was their appearance as sudden or surprising as we might think. Automobiles had been manufactured in the United States since the mid-1890s, for example, though admittedly not in significant numbers. Electrification of American homes and the development of gas stoves, refrigerators, and other appliances had long been under way by 1920. The temperance movement was more than a century old by the time National Prohibition went into effect in 1920, and the women's suffrage movement, which culminated in the 1920 ratification of the Nineteenth Amendment, actually originated in the 1840s. Even women's bobbed haircuts had begun to appear prior to World War I. Americans living during the 1920s participated in and were undeniably affected by these social and cultural transformations, but they certainly did not invent them.

Yet certain aspects of life during the 1920s really were significantly different, including the extent to which the United States had become an urban nation. According to the 1920 U.S. Census, for the first time in the nation's history more than half of all Americans lived in cities or towns of 2,500 or more people. This trend would only accelerate over the course of the decade. New York, Detroit, Los Angeles, and other cities experienced spectacular growth throughout the 1920s, as some 19 million rural people moved to urban areas in search of economic opportunities, modern conveniences, and amusements unavailable on the farm. The nation's booming manufacturing sector spawned a consumer goods revolution, which produced an abundance of newfangled, mass-produced merchandise that dramatically transformed daily life for most Americans. At the same time, the rise of a powerful mass media created a national obsession with celebrity, and Hollywood stars, popular singers, and professional athletes became the new American idols. All these forces contributed to the emergence of a nationwide popular culture that had never before existed on such a grand and far-reaching scale. During the 1920s, when a small-town Missouri girl danced the Charleston to a Paul

Whiteman record, tuned in to an episode of *Amos 'n' Andy*, or swooned at a Rudolph Valentino movie, she was sharing a common experience with millions of other people across the nation—an unimaginable occurrence only decades earlier. By the mid-1920s, even many rural and working-class families participated actively in this national popular culture that originated in large urban centers and then rippled out to even the most remote corners of the United States.

These social and cultural transformations, which had long been evolving, accelerated dramatically during the 1920s, but they also sparked a powerful ideological backlash. This conservative counterassault manifested itself in myriad ways, including the hysteria of the Red Scare, the resurgence of the Ku Klux Klan, the ratification of National Prohibition, the passage of stricter immigration quotas, the rise of Fundamentalism, and the furor over the Scopes Monkey Trial, to name only a handful. Millions of Americans believed that secularism, consumerism, and changing tastes in fashion, recreation, and courtship were corrupting the nation's morals and standards of propriety. This conservative reaction to popular culture ignited a series of conflicts between traditionalists and modernists. For example, Fundamentalist ministers, who condemned any notion that challenged the literal interpretation of the Bible, feuded bitterly with liberal clergy, who reconciled modern science with their spiritual worldview. Older Americans squabbled with their children and grandchildren over everything from dating and jazz to daring hairstyles and short skirts in what we now recognize as the first significant "generation gap." Of course, relatively few people were wholly traditionalist or wholly modernist in their beliefs. Rather, the tensions between old and new value systems created a confusing cultural landscape that people negotiated differently, based on their own moral principles and political ideologies. So, for example, a person who hated jazz music and bobbed hair might love automobiles and Hollywood movies and see no inherent contradiction in this position.

The complexities of Jazz Age popular culture only heighten the rewards of studying this pivotal era, and we, the authors, continue to take great pleasure in attempting to understand and explain the significance of the 1920s. This book is not, by any means, a comprehensive history of the decade, nor is it a political or economic study. Rather, it focuses on the development of some of the most prominent characteristics of American popular culture and everyday life during the 1920s. This book takes as its subject the movies, songs, pulp magazines, clothing styles, vacation destinations, soft drinks, dances, comic strips, and other dimensions of social life and recreation enjoyed by ordinary Americans. We firmly believe that these elements of popular culture offer a unique glimpse into the lives of people who experienced the 1920s firsthand. For those who seek more in-depth analyses of various historical aspects of the decade, we direct you to the dozens of fine studies listed at the end of the book in the section titled "Further Reading." And for readers of *The 1920s*, we hope that this volume provides some insight into what life was like for millions of Americans during the era we fondly refer to as "the Jazz Age."

Timeline of the 1920s

1920

Department of Justice agents arrest some 4,000 suspected communists and radicals in 33 American cities as part of what becomes known as the "Red Scare" (January 2).

The Eighteenth Amendment, prohibiting the manufacture, transportation, and sale of alcohol, goes into effect (January 16).

The Negro National Baseball League is founded (February 12).

Grand Canyon National Park is dedicated (April 20).

The Nineteenth Amendment, granting women the right to vote, is ratified (August 26).

A bomb explodes outside J. P. Morgan's Wall Street office building, killing 38 people and injuring more than 100 (September 16).

The American Professional Football Association is founded (renamed the National Football League in 1922) (September 17).

Eight members of the Chicago White Sox are indicted for conspiring to throw the 1919 World Series, resulting in the so-called "Black Sox Scandal" (September 28).

Warren G. Harding is elected the twenty-ninth president of the United States (November 2).

Station KDKA, East Pittsburgh, Pennsylvania, inaugurates regular radio broadcasting (November 2).

F. Scott Fitzgerald publishes his first novel, *This Side of Paradise*.

The Baby Ruth candy bar is introduced.

Transcontinental airmail service begins between New York and San Francisco.

1921

Charlie Chaplin's first feature-length film, *The Kid*, premieres (February 6).

The first White Castle hamburger restaurant opens in Wichita, Kansas (March 10).

Shuffle Along, the first all-black Broadway musical of the decade, opens (May 23).

A race riot erupts in Tulsa, Oklahoma, during which white mobs kill at least 85 African Americans and burn to the ground much of the black business district (May 31–June 1).

Margaret Gorman wins the first Miss American Pageant in Atlantic City, New Jersey (September 8).

Silent film comedian Roscoe "Fatty" Arbuckle is indicted for manslaughter after aspiring actress Virginia Rappe dies under suspicious circumstances in a San Francisco hotel (September 15).

The Sheik, starring Rudolph Valentino, premieres (October 31).

The American Birth Control League is founded (November 2).

President Harding signs into law the Federal Highway Act, providing states with matching federal funds to construct a national network of two-lane highways (November 9).

The Tomb of the Unknown Soldier is unveiled in the Rotunda of the U.S. Capitol (November 11).

The polygraph, or lie detector, is invented.

The Washburn-Crosby Company of Minneapolis creates Betty Crocker, a fictional model homemaker, to promote its Gold Medal brand flour.

Edith Wharton wins the Pulitzer Prize for her novel *The Age of Innocence.*

Wonder Bread is introduced.

The Eskimo Pie sells more than 1 million units during its first year on the market.

1922

*Reader's Diges*t publishes its first issue (February 5).

The U.S. Senate launches an investigation into the alleged illegal activities of Secretary of the Interior Albert B. Fall, in what becomes known as the "Teapot Dome Scandal" (April 15).

French fashion designer Coco Chanel introduces her signature perfume, Chanel No. 5 (May 5).

Abie's Irish Rose, the longest running Broadway play of the 1920s, opens (May 23).

The Lincoln Memorial is dedicated in Washington, D.C. (May 30).

Rebecca Latimer Felton, 87, of Georgia, becomes the first woman to serve as a U.S. senator, when she is appointed by the governor of Georgia to fill the remaining term of Senator Thomas Watson, who died in office; her term lasts only one day (October 3).

Archaeologist Howard Carter and his excavation team discover King Tutankhamen's tomb in the Valley of the Kings, near Luxor, Egypt (November 4).

Fruit, Garden and Home begins publication (renamed *Better Homes and Gardens* in 1924).

George Squier invents Muzak, first developed in order to calm anxious elevator riders.

Emily Post publishes *Etiquette in Society, in Business, in Politics and at Home*, which becomes a national best-seller.

Sinclair Lewis publishes his most famous novel, *Babbitt*.

The Chinese tile game of mahjong becomes a fad in the United States.

The first A&W Root Beer stand opens in Sacramento, California.

The Klondike Bar is introduced.

1923

Bessie Smith makes her first recordings, "Down Hearted Blues" and "Gulf Coast Blues," for Columbia (February 16).

Time, the nation's first weekly newsmagazine, publishes its first issue (March 3).

Alma Cummings wins the first American dance marathon, held at the Audubon Ballroom in New York City (April 1).

Louis Armstrong makes his first recording, "Just Gone," as a member of King Oliver's Creole Jazz Band, for the Gennett label (April 5).

Yankee Stadium opens (April 18).

President Warren G. Harding dies in office (August 2).

Vice President Calvin Coolidge succeeds Harding as president of the United States (August 3).

Runnin' Wild, an all-black musical revue, introduces the song "Charleston" and the dance of the same name (October 29).

Cecil B. DeMille's epic biblical film *The Ten Commandments* premieres (December 4).

John D. Hertz founds the Hertz Drive-Ur-Self Company.

Neon advertising signs are introduced.

Mars Candies markets its first candy bar, the Milky Way.

Jacob Schick receives a patent for the first electric razor.

Harold Lloyd stars in the classic silent film comedy *Safety Last*.

Reese's Peanut Butter Cups are introduced.

The nonsensical "Yes! We Have No Bananas" becomes a major hit song, to the annoyance of countless Americans.

The Bell and Howell Company introduces a 16-mm camera, marking the advent of home movies.

1924

The Computing-Tabulating-Recording Company, founded in 1911, formally changes its name to International Business Machines (IBM) (February 14).

George Gershwin's jazz concerto *Rhapsody in Blue* premieres at Aeolian Hall in New York City (February 24).

J. Edgar Hoover is appointed acting director of the Bureau of Investigation (later renamed Federal Bureau of Investigation) (March 10).

The Thief of Baghdad, starring Douglas Fairbanks, premieres (March 18).

The National Origins Act passes, restricting the annual number of European immigrants to 165,000 and prohibiting all Asian immigration to the United States (May 26).

Little Orphan Annie comic strip debuts in the *New York Daily News* (August 5).

Nathan Leopold Jr. and Richard Loeb are sentenced to life imprisonment for the kidnapping and murder of 14-year-old Bobby Franks (September 19).

Calvin Coolidge is elected the thirtieth president of the United States (November 4).

Macy's department store sponsors its first Thanksgiving Day parade.

The Kimberly-Clark Company introduces Kleenex, the first disposable facial tissue.

Flagpole sitting becomes a national fad.

Richard Simon and Max Schuster publish *The Cross Word Puzzle Book,* launching a major fad.

Wheaties breakfast cereal is introduced.

The Popsicle is invented.

The *New York Evening Graphic,* a tabloid newspaper, begins publication.

1925

Nellie Taylor Ross is elected governor of Wyoming, thus becoming the first woman governor in U.S. history (January 5).

The corpse of Floyd Collins is recovered amid a national media frenzy. Collins died after being trapped underground for 18 days in Sand Cave in Barren County, Kentucky (February 16).

The New Yorker begins publication (February 21).

The Gold Rush, starring Charlie Chaplin, premieres (June 26).

Walter Chrysler incorporates the Maxwell Motor Car Company as the Chrysler Corporation (June 26).

High school science teacher John T. Scopes is convicted in Dayton, Tennessee, of violating a state statute prohibiting the teaching of evolution in public schools (July 21).

Forty thousand Ku Klux Klan members hold a mass rally in Washington, D.C. (August 8).

The navy dirigible *Shenandoah* crashes in a storm near Ava, Ohio, killing 14 crew members (September 3).

The *WSM Barn Dance* (renamed *The Grand Ole Opry* in 1927) begins its Saturday night broadcasts in Nashville, Tennessee (November 28).

Alain Locke publishes the Harlem Renaissance collection *The New Negro.*

Bruce Barton publishes *The Man Nobody Knows,* a pseudo-biography of Jesus that becomes a national best-seller.

The Goodyear Tire and Rubber Company launches its first advertising blimp, *The Pilgrim.*

F. Scott Fitzgerald publishes his most acclaimed novel, *The Great Gatsby.*

1926

Rear Admiral Richard E. Byrd and Floyd Bennett become the first aviators to fly over the North Pole (May 9).

Western Air Express, later renamed Trans-World Airlines (TWA), begins passenger service (May 23).

Gertrude Ederle becomes the first woman to swim the English Channel (August 6).

Silent film heartthrob Rudolph Valentino dies suddenly at the age of 31 (August 23).

Magician and escape artist Harry Houdini dies at the age of 52 (October 31).

The National Broadcasting Company (NBC), the nation's first radio network, premieres (November 15).

The Book-of-the-Month Club is founded.

Langston Hughes publishes his first collection of poetry, *The Weary Blues.*

The Butterfinger candy bar is introduced.

Ernest Hemingway publishes his novel *The Sun Also Rises.*

1927

Buster Keaton's silent film comedy *The General* premieres (February 5).

The first demonstration of long-range television transmission, from a signal in Washington, D.C., to a receiver in New York City, occurs (April 7).

Aviator Charles Lindbergh completes the first solo, non-stop flight across the Atlantic Ocean (May 21).

Paramount's *Wings*, which later wins the first Academy Award for Best Picture, premieres (August 12).

Italian anarchist immigrants Nicola Sacco and Bartolomeo Vanzetti, convicted of murder in 1921, are executed in Massachusetts (August 23).

The Columbia Broadcasting System (CBS) begins broadcasting (September 18).

Gene Tunney defeats Jack Dempsey to retain his heavyweight boxing title in a match made famous by its "Long Count" (September 22).

New York Yankees slugger Babe Ruth hits his 60th home run of the regular season, a major league record that will stand until 1961 (September 30).

Warner Brothers' *The Jazz Singer*, the first feature-length motion picture with synchronized speech and music, premieres (October 6).

The Ford Motor Company introduces its new Model A automobile (December 2).

The Broadway musical *Showboat* premieres (December 27).

Kool-Aid (originally spelled Kool-Ade) is introduced.

1928

Herbert Hoover defeats Alfred E. Smith to become the thirty-first president of the United States (November 6).

Steamboat Willie, Walt Disney's black-and-white animated cartoon featuring Mickey Mouse and synchronized sound, premieres (November 18).

Peter Pan peanut butter is introduced.

Gerber baby food is introduced.

Dubble Bubble, the nation's first bubble gum, is introduced.

Kraft introduces Velveeta, a processed cheese food.

1929

The first science-fiction comic strip, *Buck Rogers in the 25th Century A.D.*, debuts (January 7).

Cartoonist Elzie C. Segar introduces a sailor character named Popeye in his *Thimble Theatre* comic strip (January 17).

Six members of "Bugs" Moran's gang, along with an innocent bystander, are gunned down in Chicago in what becomes known as the "St. Valentine's Day Massacre" (February 14).

The first Academy of Motion Pictures Arts and Sciences Awards ceremony is held in Hollywood, honoring films for the years 1927 and 1928 (May 16).

The comedy radio series *Amos 'n' Andy* premieres on the NBC network (August 19).

The New York Stock Exchange crashes on "Black Thursday" (October 24), with 13 million shares sold, and again on "Black Tuesday" (October 29), with 16 million shares sold.

The Museum of Modern Art opens in New York.

Part I

Life and Youth During the 1920s

The 1920s

1

Everyday America

According to many historians, the Jazz Age marked the birth of modern America. Since the 1890s, a modern society had been evolving in the United States, and by the 1920s, the nation was more urban, bureaucratic, and industrialized than ever before. While everyday life became more comfortable for most Americans, it also became increasingly complicated and harried. A consumer goods revolution fueled the nation's flourishing economy, and increasing reliance on new technologies and mass media transformed the daily lives of millions of ordinary Americans. These elements of "progress," however, had their downsides. Widespread ownership of automobiles, for example, improved the quality of life for many urban middle-class Americans, but traffic jams, speeding tickets, and parking problems became common hassles.

In some respects, the transformations of the 1920s spawned within some individuals a kind of cultural schizophrenia. Middle-class consumers may have enthusiastically embraced the newfangled accoutrements of modern life, from automobiles, refrigerators, and electric razors to motion pictures, radios, and stylish clothes, yet many of them also yearned for a simpler world in which their lives moved at a slower pace and they felt far less pressure to "keep up with the Joneses." For example, young women may have bobbed their hair, shortened their skirts, rouged their faces, and avidly attended "petting parties," but at the same time many of them longed to settle down to a conventional life of marriage and children. Simultaneously clinging to some traditional ideas while embracing certain modern ones enabled millions of Americans to make sense of their increasingly complex modern world.

Farm family listening to the radio, Hood River County, Oregon, 1925.
Courtesy of the National Archives and Records Administration.

THE AGE OF REPUBLICAN DOMINANCE

Three successive Republican presidents led the United States during the 1920s, and each had to confront the repercussions of a modern mass society that was expanding and changing faster than ever before. Ohio Senator Warren G. Harding, elected in 1920, had appealed to a nation weary of war, foreign policy squabbles, and progressive reforms by campaigning on the slogan, "Back to Normalcy." And "normalcy," it seemed, was just what Americans desired. Unlike his idealistic, intellectual predecessor, Woodrow Wilson, Harding was a friendly, good-natured man who liked to play poker and, it was widely reported, to drink bootleg liquor. Unfortunately, Harding's administration was riddled with scandal and corruption. Several of the political cronies he had appointed to high-level cabinet positions abused their power by accepting bribes and committing fraud. Shortly after Harding died in office, in August 1923, the details of the worst episode, the infamous Teapot Dome Scandal, emerged. Albert B. Fall, Harding's secretary of the interior, had accepted more than $400,000 in bribes to lease the government-owned oil reserves at Teapot Dome, Wyoming, and at Elk Hills, California, to private oil companies. Convicted in 1929, Fall was sentenced to a year in prison and fined $100,000.

Harding's successor, Calvin Coolidge, was a far more solemn and introverted man, and these personality traits quickly earned him the nickname "Silent Cal." Coolidge had the good fortune to preside over a nation that was rapidly expanding its industrial production and consumer wealth. A strong supporter of business and industry, he remarked famously in 1925 that "the business of America is business." Coolidge approved legislation that assisted corporations and lowered income-tax rates, especially for the wealthy. When he declined to run for reelection in 1928, Herbert Hoover, his secretary of commerce, accepted the Republican nomination and assumed the presidency after handily beating New York Democrat Alfred E. Smith, the first Roman Catholic to run on a major party ticket. Hoover's administration, begun with so much optimism and promise, soon oversaw the stock market crash of 1929 and the onset of the Great Depression—the worst economic disaster in American history. Hoover's mishandling of the crisis, coupled with his seeming lack of sympathy for the homeless and unemployed, ruined his reelection bid in 1932 against New York Governor Franklin D. Roosevelt. Despite the many differences among the three Republican presidents of the 1920s, all of their administrations strongly encouraged cooperation between government and big business, thus contributing to an era of extraordinary production and consumption.

THE RISE OF BIG BUSINESS

Although often remembered for its unprecedented prosperity, the 1920s actually began with the nation gripped in a serious economic recession. After the end of World War I, industrial productivity declined, unemployment rose, and consumer spending dwindled. But the sluggish economy rebounded in 1922, due in part to the manufacturing industries that produced automobiles, radios, and other consumer goods. Throughout the rest of the decade, industrial production nearly doubled. Meanwhile, the gross national product rose 43 percent, and in 1929 it stood at $103 billion. Purchasing merchandise on credit using the "installment plan"—once considered unwise, if not immoral—lost its stigma for millions of Americans who eagerly made a modest downpayment and then paid a few dollars a month for all sorts of consumer goods. Under these "buy now, pay later" plans, even those Americans without sufficient cash in hand could afford to buy big-ticket items such as Model T Fords, bedroom suites, pianos, and radios. Modern advertising, a nearly $3 billion-a-year business by 1929, encouraged shoppers to purchase newly invented products or ones that previously seemed unnecessary, including vacuum cleaners, electric razors, canned soup, silk stockings, mouthwash, and deodorant. Rising rates of mass production and consumer sales propelled the American economy into one of the most spectacular periods of prosperity in the nation's history.

The Coolidge and Hoover administrations' pro-business policies, combined with the unstinting support of federal and state governments, also fueled the nation's flourishing economy. In 1921, Congress reduced taxes on corporations and then, the following year, raised tariffs on imported goods. Federal regulatory agencies, which had been established during the Progressive Era to oversee and control big business, instead cooperated with these corporations. Meanwhile, the Supreme Court and the Justice Department protected businesses from unions by striking blow after blow against organized labor. Lobbyists hired by professional organizations, manufacturers, retailers, and other special interest groups intensified their efforts to gain support from legislators at every level. Not all Americans, however, reaped the benefits of the booming economy. The nation's farmers, textile workers, and coal miners did not generally share in the newfound prosperity of the 1920s. Neither did railroad and streetcar employees, since revenues generated by these forms of transportation declined with the widespread ownership of automobiles. Nor did small merchants, many of whom lost business or were driven into bankruptcy by the rise of chain grocery stores, drugstores, and department stores. Nevertheless, the overall standard of living rose for most Americans over the course of the decade, and salaries and wages increased in many occupations, even as the length of the average workweek shortened.

The individual who best exemplified America's new business ethos was Henry Ford, whose pioneering methods of mass production and labor relations transformed his company into the world's largest automobile manufacturer. Beginning in 1913, at his Highland Park Plant outside Detroit, Ford introduced the moving assembly line and applied "scientific management" techniques that minimized any wasted movement and effort by his workers. This dramatically reduced the time and cost of producing his Model T Fords, but it also made virtually every job on the line mind-numbingly monotonous and exhausting. In 1914, to combat massive labor turnover and absenteeism, Ford introduced an eight-hour workday and a so-called "five-dollar-day"—an extraordinarily high wage for the time. Workers flocked to Ford's Highland Park Plant seeking these high-paying assembly-line jobs that would actually allow them to buy their own Model Ts. Ford also created a profit-sharing program for his workers, primarily to prevent the formation of unions, and established a Social Department to inculcate workers with "traditional" moral values that he believed would make his workforce more productive, efficient, thrifty, and sober. Furthermore, Ford owned and therefore controlled all the subsidiary elements necessary for automobile manufacturing, including a steel mill, a glass factory, rolling mills, forges, railroad terminals, water supplies, and a security force. This system of vertical integration (also practiced by other major manufacturers in various industries) led to huge profits and created a model for other corporate enterprises.

SOCIAL CLIMATE

During the 1920s, the lives of most middle-class Americans improved as a result of mass production and technological advancements, but other powerful forces also influenced the attitudes and behaviors of ordinary Americans. Millions of native-born, white Americans harbored intense fears that communism would spread to America, immigrant hordes would seize their jobs, and African Americans would integrate their racially homogeneous communities. These anxieties heightened preexisting racial and ethnic tensions in the United States and led to the outbreak of repressive and often violent clashes between Americans of different races, religions, and political beliefs.

The Red Scare

Between 1919 and 1920, escalating ethnic and political tensions in the United States erupted in a wave of mass paranoia and repression known as the "Red Scare." The Bolshevik Revolution of November 1917 in Russia sparked fears that a communist coup was imminent in the United States. On the domestic front, the American economy was in recession, unemployment was high, and living costs were even higher. More than 3,300 labor strikes broke out across the nation in 1919, including a nationwide strike by steelworkers, many of whom were Southern and Eastern European immigrants. The Boston police force also went on strike, forcing Governor Calvin Coolidge to enlist the state militia to protect the city and prevent looting. Even worse, several highly publicized bombings and attempted bombings of politicians and business leaders, including an explosion on Wall Street in September 1920 that killed 38 people, fueled the public's general sense of pandemonium. In all these cases, Americans blamed these incidents on communist and socialist aliens.

In January 1920, the General Intelligence Division of the Bureau of Investigation (renamed the Federal Bureau of Investigation in 1935), operating under orders from Attorney General A. Mitchell Palmer, launched what became known as "Palmer Raids." Federal agents, in cooperation with local police officers, raided private homes, newspaper offices, and meeting halls in 33 cities across the nation, without search warrants, and arrested more than 4,000 alleged radicals on the suspicion that they threatened national security. Many of those arrested were held in custody without access to counsel for weeks and even months, and while most were eventually released without ever being charged with a crime, almost 600 aliens were deported. Although the Palmer Raids drew criticism from those Americans who recognized that these tactics violated basic civil liberties and even the Constitution itself, many groups and organizations, including the newly formed American Legion (founded in 1919), supported any government action, however drastic, that combated the perceived threat of communism in the United States.

Immigration Patterns

Between 1890 and 1914, more than 17 million immigrants came to the United States, many of them from Russia, Italy, Austria-Hungary, Poland, and Germany.[1] But this so-called "New Immigration" spawned intense opposition among groups and organizations that sought to restrict the flood of foreign peoples to the nation's shores. The outbreak of World War I severely reduced the number of immigrants arriving from Europe. After the war ended, immigration levels returned to prewar levels, but new concerns about continued strike waves and radical aliens, coupled with anti-foreign resentment and demands for "One Hundred Percent Americanism," prompted the federal government to clamp down drastically on immigration. In 1921, Congress passed the Quota Act, which capped the total number of immigrants allowed to enter the United States at 385,000 per year. Three years later, the passage of the National Origins Act further reduced the number of newcomers arriving on American shores. Under this act, Congress imposed an annual immigration ceiling of 165,000—less than 20 percent of prewar immigration—and gave preference to applicants from Northern European, chiefly Protestant countries. Asian immigration was entirely prohibited. In 1929, Congress further restricted annual immigration to only 150,000 people. Millions of Americans agreed with President Coolidge's 1924 declaration that "America must be kept American" and supported legislation that made it more difficult for the foreign-born to take up residence in the United States.[2]

Sacco and Vanzetti

The nation's intense hostility toward immigrants also played a significant role in the notorious case of Nicola Sacco and Bartolomeo Vanzetti, two Italian-born workingmen who were arrested in 1920 for the robbery and murder of a shoe company paymaster and payroll guard in South

Braintree, Massachusetts. Their trial, which began in May 1921, sparked a nationwide debate about patriotism, civil rights, and anti-immigrant hysteria and soon became an international *cause cèlebré*. Neither defendant had a prior criminal record, but both were members of anarchist organizations. Despite the prosecution's flimsy evidence connecting the men with the crimes, as well as numerous examples of judicial prejudice, legal misconduct, and defense ineptitude, a jury convicted Sacco and Vanzetti in July 1921. In 1927, after a series of failed judicial appeals, Judge Webster Thayer, the presiding judge in the case, sentenced the two men to death. Their execution, on August 23, 1927, provoked rallies and riots in the United States, Europe, Asia, and South America by sympathetic protesters who believed that Sacco and Vanzetti had not been afforded a fair trial due to their immigrant status, poverty, and unpopular political beliefs.

RACE RELATIONS

Between 1915 and 1918, approximately a half million African Americans left the South for northern urban-industrial centers like Harlem, Chicago, St. Louis, and Detroit as part of the Great Migration. At least another 700,000 black southerners followed during the 1920s.[3] Most of these migrants moved north to find higher-paying jobs and to carve out better lives for themselves and their families. They also sought to escape segregation, sharecropping, and racial violence common in the South. The flood of African-American newcomers heightened competition with white workers for jobs, housing, and public facilities, and set off an unprecedented surge of race riots in northern and midwestern cities. During the so-called Red Summer of 1919, rioters in at least 25 separate violent outbreaks killed 400 people and injured countless others. Unlike many earlier incidents, African Americans involved in these postwar riots often armed themselves and fired back at rampaging white mobs in order to protect their families and their neighborhoods, making these clashes especially bloody. In Chicago, in the deadliest clash of 1919, 15 white residents and 23 black residents died during five days of rioting. More than 500 additional residents were injured and at least 1,000 families were left homeless as a result of arson and widespread property destruction.

For the most part, southern black migrants were disappointed by what they found in the North. Not only were well-paying jobs scarce for black workers in northern and midwestern cities, but racist practices also forced these new arrivals to suffer the indignities of segregated schools, theaters, housing, and other facilities. Although the 1920s saw a tremendous flowering of African-American arts, particularly in Harlem and other northern cities, the decade overall was one of tense, turbulent, and sometimes violent relations between black and white Americans. In 1921, for example, two days of rioting engulfed Tulsa, Oklahoma, during which white mobs killed at least 85 African Americans and torched much of the city's flourishing black business district. And in 1923, a sustained attack by a mob of white racists wiped out the small, predominantly black community of Rosewood, Florida. White mobs also perpetrated other forms of racial violence against African Americans. Between 1918 and 1922, according to records kept by Tuskegee Institute, mobs lynched almost 300 African Americans, more than 90 percent of them in the South, for a wide range of real and alleged crimes, including murder and sexual assault. But after this surge, the number of lynchings dropped off throughout the rest of the 1920s to an average of around 17 per year.[4] But as the frequency of lynchings declined, racist mobs employed increasingly brutal methods to execute African Americans, including setting their victims on fire, torturing and dismembering them, and sexually mutilating their corpses.

The Revival of the Ku Klux Klan

The resurgence of the Ku Klux Klan during the 1920s aggravated already strained race relations in the United States. The original Klan, which emerged shortly after the end of the Civil War, was a racist organization dedicated to terrorizing recently emancipated African Americans and their white Republican allies. This organization disbanded after 1870, but in 1915, an Atlanta evangelist and businessman named William J. Simmons revived the Klan in a cross-burning ceremony on Stone Mountain, Georgia. This resurrected Klan preached that white supremacy was under assault and that the increasing diversification of American culture was serving to "mongrelize" and therefore undermine native-born, white Protestant dominance. The Klan therefore targeted not just African Americans but also immigrants, communists, union leaders, Catholics, and Jews. They also pledged their devotion to protecting the American family, and meted out vigilante justice to bootleggers, wife-beaters, adulterers, and other perceived threats to their communities. By 1924, at the height of its power, the Klan boasted 2 million members nationwide, many of whom were small urban businessmen and recent rural migrants. The Klan dominated the political scene in Oklahoma, Texas, Colorado, and particularly Indiana, where an estimated 10 percent of the entire population belonged to the organization. Every one of Indiana's 92 counties contained a Klan chapter, and Governor Ed Jackson was himself a Klansman. But in 1925, David C. Stephenson, the Grand Dragon of Indiana, was arrested and convicted of the rape and murder of a 28-year-old state welfare worker named Madge Oberholtzer. The

Ku Klux Klan parade in Washington, D.C., in front of the U.S. Capitol, 1926.
Courtesy of the Library of Congress.

conviction of such a high-ranking Klan officer decimated popular support for the organization, and Klan membership in Indiana plummeted from 350,000 to 15,000 within a year.[5] In fact, by 1926, the Ku Klux Klan was in serious decline nationwide. Many Klansmen elected to office in 1924 had not proven particularly effective, and the general prosperity of the nation made it difficult to continue to scapegoat African Americans, Jews, Catholics, and immigrants. Furthermore, strict immigration quotas had been passed—a major victory for white supremacists. Nevertheless, actual or threatened violence by Klansmen continued to influence American race relations throughout the rest of the 1920s.

Marcus Garvey and Black Nationalism

During the 1920s, hundreds of thousands of African Americans joined black nationalist organizations that celebrated race pride and racial self-determination. The most powerful of these groups was the Universal Negro Improvement Association (UNIA), founded in 1914 by Marcus Garvey, a charismatic Jamaican printer. In 1916, Garvey immigrated to the United States and set up his UNIA headquarters in Harlem, where he preached the virtues of racial separatism and encouraged black Americans to withdraw from racist white society and to establish their own businesses and institutions. He promoted the UNIA by publishing a black-oriented newspaper, *Negro World,* and founding the Black Star shipping line to assist African Americans in emigrating to Africa. By the early 1920s, the UNIA claimed more than 1 million members worldwide. In 1922, when the Black Star line foundered, thousands of investors lost their money, and charges of corruption and the mishandling of funds tarnished the organization's reputation. Garvey was arrested for mail fraud in 1923, convicted and imprisoned two years later, and finally deported to Jamaica in 1927. The UNIA subsequently collapsed, but Garvey's message of black pride and separatism inspired hundreds of thousands of working-class African Americans to strive for fiscal and social independence from white society.

The New Negro

Although the phrase "New Negro" dates to the late nineteenth century, it was not until the 1920s that this label gained currency as a description for middle-class African Americans who advocated a new sense of militancy and racial pride. Indeed, Alain Locke, an African-American philosopher, critic, and editor, titled his Harlem Renaissance literary anthology *The New Negro* (1925) in order to signal these powerful currents of black artistic consciousness, renewed civil rights advocacy, and racial solidarity. The National Association for the Advancement of Colored People (NAACP) and other organizations waged court battles in an attempt to secure African Americans' civil and political rights. Black writers, musicians, and artists, especially those who resided in Harlem, the so-called "Mecca of the New Negro," used their work to celebrate African-American culture and challenge damaging racist stereotypes. Above all, "New Negroes" attempted to assert their own agency and participate fully in American culture, while resisting white America's attempts to cast them as a "problem" that somehow needed to be solved. Many critics, in hindsight, see the New Negro movement as overly optimistic and even naive, but at the time this impulse toward self-expression, self-assertiveness, and self-determination was a driving force among some middle-class African Americans.

NATIONAL PROHIBITION

On January 16, 1920, the Eighteenth Amendment to the U.S. Constitution went into effect. The amendment, passed in 1919 and also known as National Prohibition, read, in part, "the manufacture, sale, or transportation of intoxicating liquors within, the importation thereof into, or the exportation thereof from the United States . . . for beverage purposes is hereby prohibited." In 1919, Congress had also enacted what became known as the Volstead Act, which defined "intoxicating liquor" as any beverage containing a minimum of one-half of 1 percent alcohol, and outlined specific provisions for enforcing the amendment. For a first offense, violators could be jailed for six months and fined up to $1,000. Second-time offenders could be jailed for five years and fined $10,000. So-called "padlock laws" allowed enforcement agents to close down any illegal drinking establishment for one year, and the government could seize and sell any automobile or other vehicle used to transport liquor illegally. However, the Prohibition Bureau, a division of the Treasury Department created by the federal government to enforce its anti-alcohol laws, remained seriously underfunded and understaffed throughout the 1920s, and most cities and states refused to appropriate enough money to hire additional officers to enforce these laws. In fact, 30 states appropriated no money at all to support the Volstead Act, choosing instead to leave the entire responsibility of law enforcement in the hands of the federal government. Even so, many Americans stopped or at least curtailed their drinking, due to pro-temperance sympathy, respect for the Constitution, fear of prosecution, or a lack of funds to purchase expensive black-market liquor.

Drinking During Prohibition

Although beer, wine, and spirits became more difficult to obtain during National Prohibition, and many people did drink less, thirsty Americans could still usually secure whatever kind of liquor they desired. Almost overnight, illicit bars called speakeasies sprang up in cities and towns across America, and moonshiners (producers of homemade distilled spirits), rumrunners (alcohol smugglers), and bootleggers (alcohol distributors) quickly found a lucrative market for illegal liquor. Because National Prohibition reduced the ready availability of alcoholic beverages, the cost of liquor skyrocketed during the 1920s. Drinks that once cost a nickel before Prohibition could cost 50 cents or more after the passage of the new laws.

Although the price of alcoholic beverages rose during Prohibition, the quality of illegal booze declined. Bootleggers frequently adulterated genuine scotch, rye, and gin by diluting it with water and adding coloring, flavoring, and more alcohol. As a result, cocktails became popular during the 1920s, as drinkers used ginger ale, tonic water, or fruit juices to mask the unpleasant taste of low-grade liquor. Cocktail parties also became fashionable during Prohibition, since hosts could serve alcohol in their homes without much fear of being raided by Prohibition agents. But not everyone could afford the bootlegged liquor used to make cocktails. For example, farmers and working-class men often drank homemade beer, wine, or moonshine, and some desperate people actually resorted to swilling nasty concoctions of Sterno, aftershave lotion, hair tonics, over-the-counter medicines, and other inexpensive, alcohol-based household products. In fact, adulterated alcohol poisoned, blinded, and sometimes even killed tens of thousands of people during the 1920s—mostly poor and working-class drinkers who could not afford to buy their liquor from reliable bootleggers.

Prohibition drove much drinking into private homes, yet Americans could still purchase illegal liquor at a number of underground commercial establishments. As the black-market liquor economy sprang to life, the urban saloon evolved into the popular "speakeasy" that hid in plain sight among legitimate businesses in practically every city and town. According to one study, New York City alone contained more than 30,000 speakeasies by 1927.[6] Some were located in elegant upscale surroundings and catered to the fashionable society set. For example, the 21 Club operated in a posh Manhattan townhouse and sold authentic—and expensive—smuggled Canadian liquor. Most speakeasies, however, were modest establishments that operated behind locked doors in apartments, out-of-the-way commercial properties, or the back rooms and basements of legal businesses. Growing numbers of women patronized speakeasies as illicit public drinking became popular among the younger crowds of Americans. Prior to 1920, most women who entered working-class saloons were prostitutes, but after the enactment of the Eighteenth Amendment, it became acceptable and even fashionable for respectable middle-class women to drink in speakeasies, as long as a male companion accompanied them.

Prohibition and Popular Culture

National Prohibition influenced virtually every aspect of American culture during the 1920s, including slang, pop songs, and movies. Hundreds of new words entered the American language to describe drinking, drinkers, and various forms of alcohol. Colorful terms such as *happy sally*, *yack yack bourbon*, *jackass brandy*, and *cherry dynamite*, for example, referred to various kinds of moonshine, and terms such as *shellacked*, *fried*, *potted*, and *crocked* entered the vocabulary to describe the condition of being drunk. Prohibition inspired dozens of popular songs, many of which parodied already familiar tunes by adding new lyrics. Among the most memorable titles were "What'll We Do on a Saturday Night (When the Town Goes Dry)" (1919), "If I Meet the Guy Who Made This Country Dry" (1920), and "It's the Smart Little Feller Who Stocked Up His Cellar (That's Getting the Beautiful Girls)" (1920). Hollywood motion pictures also displayed images of glamorous young men and women flouting the drinking laws by patronizing a speakeasy or enjoying a cocktail party, and these scenes effectively taught moviegoers the etiquette of illegal drinking. Until the late 1920s, when the motion picture industry began to self-censor movies with questionable moral content, images of wild speakeasy revelry and blatant disregard for the Prohibition laws commonly appeared on the silver screen.

Prohibition and Crime

Prohibition laws led to a dramatic rise in the scope and scale of organized crime. Of course, organized crime was nothing new during the 1920s. But the tens of millions of dollars to be made in the black-market liquor economy motivated powerful gangsters, including George Remus in Cincinnati, Al "Scarface" Capone in Chicago, and Salvatore "Lucky" Luciano in New York, to exploit bootlegging as a new and lucrative business. George Remus—allegedly the inspiration for F. Scott Fitzgerald's character Jay Gatsby in the novel *The Great Gatsby* (1925)—made so much money from bootlegging that he would leave $100 bills under his guests' plates at dinner parties and once even gave brand-new 1923 Pontiac automobiles to all 50 of the female guests who attended one of his lavish social gatherings. In 1928 alone, the famous mobster Al Capone made an estimated $105 million—reportedly the highest income in the

Woman putting flask in her boot, Washington, D.C., 1922. Courtesy of the Library of Congress.

United States—from his bootlegging, gambling, and prostitution rackets. Gangland bootleggers occasionally paid for their crimes through jail time and fines, but they lived to a great extent beyond the reach of the law. Mob bosses would simply "put the fix" on corrupt police, federal agents, and even judges, paying them in exchange for protection from interference and prosecution. Gang-related violence repeatedly made headlines during the decade, and Americans were especially shocked by the 1929 "St. Valentine's Day Massacre," in which Capone's henchmen, disguised as police officers, mowed down six members of rival George "Bugs" Moran's gang and an innocent bystander in a blaze of shotgun and machine-gun fire at a Chicago garage.

The Repeal of Prohibition

By the early 1930s, widespread disregard for the law, combined with the added social and economic pressures of the Great Depression, made the futility of the Prohibition laws evident to all but the most ardent temperance supporters. On December 5, 1933, President Franklin D. Roosevelt signed into law the Twenty-First Amendment to the Constitution, repealing the Eighteenth Amendment (the only constitutional amendment ever repealed). Thus, the so-called "Noble Experiment" of National Prohibition came to an end after more than 13 years, but not without effecting long-lasting change on American culture.

WOMEN'S ROLES

Common images of audacious, short-skirted, bob-haired flappers make it easy to imagine that women of the 1920s invented for themselves identities that were entirely divorced from those of previous generations. This, however, was only partially true. While many women, especially young women, did indeed break from tradition when it came to hairstyles, clothing, and social behaviors, most still adhered closely to traditional gender roles. Young, unmarried women might flirt, "pet," and "play the field" much more than their mothers and grandmothers had, but the overwhelming majority still dreamed ultimately of marrying, settling down, and raising children. While women entered colleges and universities in unprecedented numbers throughout the decade, relatively few planned to pursue careers outside the home, at least not after they were married. In essence, the youthful, flamboyant flapper existed only temporarily, until social pressure placed her squarely in the familiar roles of wife, mother, and homemaker.

Women at Home

The structure of the middle-class American family did change somewhat during the 1920s, though the standard, two-parent nuclear family still remained the norm. The birthrate of middle-class families continued to decline—a trend that began during the early nineteenth century—as birth control became more widely available and more frequently practiced. The passage of more liberal laws made it easier to get a divorce, which in turn prompted a rise in the divorce rate (though it still seems very low compared to today). In 1900, about 8 percent of marriages ended in divorce, but by 1928, that number had more than doubled, to 16.6 percent.[7] Increasing numbers of married women took jobs outside the home, usually for reasons of economic necessity, and by 1930, more than 3 million married women were in the workforce. Still, the great majority of families followed traditional sex roles: the husbands were the principal breadwinners, while the wives had primary responsibility for cooking, cleaning, and taking care of the children.

During the 1920s, refrigerators, electric appliances, indoor bathrooms, and hot and cold running water became increasingly common household features, especially in urban areas, and transformed the lives of middle-class homemakers. In previous decades, families with sufficient means frequently relied on hired domestic help, and even middle-class Americans often employed at least a part-time maid or cook, but advances in such technologies as electric washing machines, vacuum cleaners, and refrigerators, coupled with the dwindling supply of domestic servants, made it customary for middle-class women to do their own housework. These so-called labor-saving devices, however, did little to lessen the overall time homemakers spent keeping house and in some cases, they may have actually created more work for women, as washing machines and vacuum cleaners, for example, helped to raise common standards of cleanliness. And technological changes came far more slowly to homes in rural America. By 1930, only 10 percent of the nation's farms were wired for electricity, and only 33 percent had running water.[8] Widespread electrification would not reach these country families until the 1930s and 1940s.

Women at Work

During World War I, with more than 3.6 million men engaged in military service, American business and industry actively recruited women to work in factories, office buildings, and munitions plants. The total percentage of wage-earning women increased only slightly, but many women did enter what had previously been male-only industries such as construction, railroads, and mining. Wartime propaganda celebrated these female employees as self-sacrificing patriots who were doing their part for the common good, but after the war ended, critics charged that working women neglected their husbands and children and took jobs that more properly belonged to men. As a result, even many single women lost their jobs to returning veterans. Unions did little to protect women workers, largely because they, too, believed it inappropriate for women to compete with men for jobs. In fact, relatively few women directly competed against men in the workforce. The great majority of wage-earning women worked as domestic servants, secretaries, telephone operators, typists, hairdressers, or department store clerks, or in other occupations that men seldom entered. College-educated women also tended to enter the "nurturing," female-dominated professions of teaching, nursing, or social work. Overall, few women worked for their own gratification; rather, their income, though usually paltry, was needed to help support their families. Nevertheless, many employers believed that working women—especially married women—took jobs only to acquire a little extra pocket money. This unfair and untrue bias justified a lower wage scale for women. During the 1920s, white women, on average, earned about half of what men earned for similar work, and black women earned about half of what white women did. Barriers for advancement remained high, and many women labored in mills and factories for years with little hope of a raise or a promotion. A comparatively small number of women became successful doctors, professors, lawyers, scientists, and business leaders in their communities, but lucrative jobs in management and administration eluded most women during the 1920s, regardless of their talent, education, or intelligence.

Women and Politics

In 1920, the Nineteenth Amendment to the Constitution was ratified, guaranteeing women the right to vote. Many political observers predicted that women would henceforth vote in a cohesive bloc and thus initiate dramatic reforms in American government and society. This, however, quickly proved not to be the case. After the passage of the suffrage amendment, the women's movement, whose diverse factions had united behind this common cause, once again splintered into dozens of political camps. One major divisive issue was the proposed Equal Rights Amendment (ERA) to the Constitution, introduced in Congress in 1923, which read simply, "Men and woman shall have equal rights throughout the United States and every place subject to its jurisdiction."[9] Members of the National Women's Party (NWP) and other feminist groups believed that the ERA logically extended the political rights granted to women by the Nineteenth Amendment. Opponents of the proposal, however, feared that the amendment would endanger or prohibit legislation specially designed to protect and assist women, such as the Sheppard-Towner Act (1921), which distributed federal matching grants to the states for prenatal and child health clinics, midwife training, and visiting nurses for pregnant women and new mothers. Although the ERA was reintroduced in Congress in 1924, 1925, and 1929, it never made it out of committee.

RELIGION AND FUNDAMENTALISM

By the 1920s, modern influences had infiltrated virtually every aspect of American society and culture, and religion was no exception. Modern religion, promoted by the Reverend Harry Emerson Fosdick and other liberal Protestant clergy, rejected literal interpretations of the Bible and embraced the notion that Christianity could co-exist with science. These ministers sought to make religion more relevant, even as new diversions tempted many members of their congregations to skip church in order to go to the movies, play golf, or take a Sunday drive. These liberal clergy emphasized the moral and ethical teachings of the "historical Jesus" and encouraged church members to seek the counsel of their ministers on both spiritual and personal matters. They also de-emphasized the supernatural and miracle-working aspects of Christianity and concentrated instead on dispensing practical advice about living as a Christian in an increasingly secular, materialistic world.

The rise of modern religion triggered a strong backlash among those Protestant Christians who clung to more traditional religious views. Conservative church leaders preached passionately about the dangers of modernity and warned their followers not to stray from biblical teachings. Their reaction became known as Fundamentalism, named after a series of pamphlets called *The Fundamentals* (1909–1914), which insisted on the literal truth of the Bible and Jesus Christ's critical role in saving humanity. Fundamentalism spawned a related movement called Pentecostalism, which appealed primarily to poor and working-class Americans, especially those in the Midwest and South. Pentecostals believed in faith healers and speaking in tongues, which, to them, signified the presence of the Holy Spirit. Fundamentalists and Pentecostals both believed that the modern world had become morally corrupt and that its emphasis on money making, consumerism, leisure, and science had seduced weak-willed Christians. Thus, leaders in these churches tended to preach "old-time religion" that stressed conservative morality and the truth of biblical stories.

The Fundamentalist movement produced several famous ministers who, ironically, spread the gospel using modern show business techniques. During the 1910s and 1920s, Billy Sunday, a former professional baseball player turned evangelist, toured the country with his vaudeville-like revivals, converting sinners and denouncing the evils of the modern world (including the teaching of evolution). Aimee Semple McPherson, a dynamic Pentecostal preacher and bona fide celebrity, proved beyond a doubt that Fundamentalist religion could seamlessly incorporate many elements of modern life. In 1923, McPherson established the 5,300-seat Angelus Temple in Los Angeles, dedicated to a religion she called the Foursquare Gospel, which promoted the ideas of divine healing, regeneration, baptism in the Holy Spirit, and the second coming of Jesus Christ. Rather than rehash old-style evangelizing, McPherson embraced Hollywood culture and became the star of her own show. Her services incorporated elaborate stage sets, jazz music, animals, and actors playing various parts. Beginning in 1924, she even broadcast her sermons and religious programs over her church-owned radio station, KFSG, all the while encouraging her tens of thousands of at-home listeners to kneel and place their hands on the radio as she preached. Her popularity was such that she managed to survive a highly publicized scandal in 1926. McPherson claimed that she was kidnapped from a California beach, drugged, and held against her will in Mexico for several weeks until she could escape. Journalists' dogged attempts to prove that she had actually slipped away for a tryst with a married man could not convince her devoted followers that McPherson was anything other than a selfless servant of the Lord.

Evolutionary Science and the Scopes Trial

Fundamentalists stressed the literal truth of the Bible as God's divinely ordained word, and so, of course, evolutionary teachings, which clearly contradicted the story of Genesis, became a particular target of wrath and condemnation. Between 1921 and 1922, legislatures in 20 states introduced bills banning the teaching of evolution in public schools. When Tennessee passed such a law in 1925, the American Civil Liberties Union (ACLU) offered to provide legal representation for any teacher willing to challenge this law in court. John T. Scopes, a high school biology teacher in Dayton, Tennessee, accepted the offer. When he explained Darwin's theory of evolution to his students, he was promptly arrested, thus sparking one of the most famous and sensational trials of the decade. William Jennings Bryan, former secretary of state, three-time presidential candidate, and one of the leaders of the Fundamentalist movement, argued for the prosecution. Clarence Darrow, a famous liberal trial lawyer and professed agnostic, assisted with Scopes' defense. The trial, held in July 1925, attracted thousands of spectators and reporters to the small town of Dayton. Curious onlookers crowded into the courthouse and participated in the festival-like atmosphere outside,

Defense attorney Clarence Darrow (center, wearing suspenders) during the Scopes trial, Dayton, Tennessee, 1925. Courtesy of the Library of Congress.

where stores capitalized on the media frenzy by selling souvenir pins that said "Your Old Man's a Monkey." Throughout the 12-day trial, Americans were riveted to the case, which had essentially devolved into the question of whether Darwin or Genesis was "right." Camera crews sent daily newsreel footage of the trial to movie theaters across the country. Hundreds of thousands of listeners tuned in to the proceedings from home, carried on WGN, Chicago, as this was the first trial ever broadcast live on radio. Darrow, who was forbidden by the judge from introducing any expert scientific testimony, called Bryan, a self-proclaimed expert on the Bible, as his only witness. Darrow proceeded to humiliate Bryan, who testified to the literal accuracy of biblical stories (including the tale of Jonah's being swallowed by a big fish and Joshua's making the sun stand still) and exhibited his vast ignorance of science. Sophisticated Americans thought Bryan ridiculous, and reporters such as H. L. Mencken, writing for the *Baltimore Sun*, lampooned Bryan and what they saw as the idiocy and backwardness of Fundamentalists in particular and southerners in general. In the end, a jury found Scopes guilty of breaking the law and fined him $100, but the Tennessee Supreme Court later overturned the case on a technicality. Nevertheless, anti-evolution laws prohibiting the teaching of Darwinism remained on the books, and evolution-free biology textbooks continued to dominate classrooms in high schools across much of the South.

SCIENTIFIC AND TECHNOLOGICAL ADVANCES

Part of what made ordinary life during the 1920s so different from that of previous decades was the rapid development of new technologies. While these modern advances made many conservatives and Fundamentalists uncomfortable, many middle-class Americans embraced new gadgets and inventions with few reservations. By 1928, approximately 17 million homes were wired for electricity, and these homes contained approximately 15.3 million electric irons, 6.8 million vacuum cleaners, 5 million washing machines, 4.5 million toasters, and 755,000 electric refrigerators. There were about 27 million homes in the United States at the time, so fully one-third of American families were not actively participating in this stampede toward electrification and modern appliances.[10] Nevertheless, middle-class consumers had caught the fever for new and better gadgets that they believed could improve the quality of their lives.

Long-distance communication technology also advanced during the 1920s. Telephones had long been in place in many American households, but ownership increased from 14.3 million in 1922 to 20.3 million in 1930, and in 1926, phones were first manufactured not as two separate pieces connected by a cord, but with the transmitter and receiver in a single handset.[11] Even experimental television made headlines. The first demonstration of long-range television transmission, from a signal in Washington, D.C., to a receiver in New York City, took place in April 1927. The image projected was the face of Secretary of Commerce Herbert Hoover. Two years later, the NBC radio network began broadcasting a regular television schedule, but a low-resolution signal and few receivers to capture it made this effort commercially unsuccessful. Still, these early television experiments paved the way for later breakthroughs in what has certainly become one of the most influential technological developments of all time.

MEDICAL ADVANCES

During the 1920s, a series of medical breakthroughs improved the state of medicine, saved countless lives, and opened the door to further refinement of diagnoses and treatments. Doctors first used insulin to treat diabetes in 1922, British scientist Alexander Fleming discovered penicillin in 1928, and advances in the treatment of scarlet fever and measles helped bring these dangerous diseases under control. In 1928, Dr. George

Papanicolaou, a Greek immigrant, published news of his medical breakthrough, the "Pap smear," which could reliably detect cervical cancer in women. Health care improved due to newly invented medical equipment, including the electrocardiograph in 1924, the "iron lung" respirator in 1928, and the electroencephalograph in 1929. Despite these advances, medical care in the United States during the 1920s must be considered spotty at best. Relatively few doctors lived in the rural South and Midwest, and residents of those regions were most likely to suffer from hookworm, pellagra, rickets, and other diseases caused by nutritional deficiencies. Americans living in urban centers or near medical schools enjoyed better access to advanced health care, but doctors in the 1920s still relied far more on bedside comforting and commonsense remedies than they did on pharmacological cures. Indeed, antibiotics had not come into common use, and much of modern medicine had yet to be invented. Still, progress was made, and by the end of the 1920s, increased understanding of nutrition and preventive health care had considerably lessened infant mortality rates and increased life expectancy.

NATIONAL NEWS STORIES

The phenomenal growth of mass-circulation magazines and newspapers during the 1920s prompted Americans to follow national news stories with insatiable curiosity and interest. Relentless reportage about sensational or newsworthy events united people from disparate parts of the country in their fascination, horror, or pity. For example, when spelunker Floyd Collins became trapped in Sand Cave (near Cave City, Kentucky) in 1925, a media circus erupted outside the entrance to the cave, as more than 150 reporters descended upon the area. For two weeks, radio broadcasts and front-page newspaper articles chronicled the heroic but futile attempts made by Louisville firefighters and local volunteers to rescue him. Some 15 days after he had become trapped, Collins died, but that did not mark the end of national attention. Later that year, hillbilly singing star Vernon Dalhart recorded "The Death of Floyd Collins," and picture postcards of the tragic scene, including at least one that pictured Collins' corpse being removed from the cave, appeared in mailboxes from coast to coast. Mass media had tapped into the nation's fascination with such sensational news, and literally dozens of other noteworthy events riveted Americans' attention during the 1920s.

Although several sensational court cases have garnered the clichéd label "the Trial of the Century" (including, of course, the 1995 O. J. Simpson trial), the 1920s saw more than its share of dramatic and highly publicized trials. The first of the decade to be so dubbed was the murder trial of Leopold and Loeb, which later inspired Alfred Hitchcock's 1948 film *Rope*. Eighteen-year-old Richard Loeb and 19-year-old Nathan Leopold, the privileged sons of two wealthy and prominent Chicago families, conspired to commit what they believed to be the "perfect murder." Their plan resulted in the kidnapping and brutal bludgeoning death of 14-year-old Bobby Franks in May 1924. A pair of Leopold's eyeglasses, inadvertently left near Franks' body, eventually led police to the two young men. Leopold and Loeb pleaded guilty to murder, and Clarence Darrow, the famous defense lawyer, argued passionately and, in the end, successfully to keep his clients from receiving the death penalty. Throughout the course of the month-long hearing, Americans closely followed newspaper and radio coverage of the case, simultaneously repelled and mesmerized by this motiveless "thrill killing."

Tabloid newspapers, which enjoyed higher circulations than most serious papers, cashed in on Americans' appetite for crime and scandal by reporting, in lurid and titillating detail, a series of shocking sex scandals and murder trials. Tabloids featured small pages, large type, and plenty of photographs, and they pandered to a mass audience for whom no story was too sordid or tawdry. Readers followed the breaking developments of trials in the pages of the tabloids as if they were following the convoluted plot twists of a Hollywood film. For example, when silent film comedian Roscoe "Fatty" Arbuckle was arrested and charged with the rape and murder of actress Virginia Rappe in 1921, he was effectively tried and convicted in William Randolph Hearst's chains of newspapers. In April 1922, after two trials that resulted in hung juries, Arbuckle was acquitted of all charges in a third trial, but the negative publicity irreparably damaged his film career. Other scandalous murder trials also fascinated the public. In 1926, Mrs. Albert Hall was tried for the murder of her clergyman husband, the Reverend Edward Wheeler Hall, and his supposed lover, Mrs. Eleanor Mills, a married member of his church choir. The trial ended in acquittal, but the intense tabloid coverage thrilled voyeuristic readers. The following year, a Queens, New York homemaker named Ruth Snyder and her lover, a salesman named Judd Gray, murdered her husband, Albert Snyder. Again, a frenzy of newspaper reportage kept readers glued to the trial. Both Snyder and Gray were convicted and executed in 1928, with Snyder garnering the dubious distinction of being the first woman ever electrocuted in the state of New York. Regardless of how grisly or tragic a story might be, Americans were hooked on sensational news stories.

THE STOCK MARKET CRASH AND THE END OF THE JAZZ AGE

When Herbert Hoover was elected president of the United States in 1928, neither he nor anyone else suspected that in less than a year the prosperity of America's Jazz Age would abruptly end, only to be replaced by staggering rates of unemployment, homelessness, and poverty. In fact, in his inaugural speech in 1929, Hoover commented, "I have no fears for the future of our country. It is bright with hope."[12] Indeed, the country did appear to have a bright future. Part of this optimism came from the astounding rise in the stock market. Stocks had been trading well above their market value, and investors had been purchasing these inflated stocks "on margin," which meant that the buyer merely had to provide a minimal downpayment—sometimes as little as 10 percent—and could then borrow the rest of the money at high interest rates. The loan, in theory, would be paid back out of the profits from the stock, whose value, people naively believed, would never stop rising. Indeed, the market value of all stocks, which stood at about $27 billion in 1925, had climbed to a remarkable $87 billion by 1929. The stock market seemed like the perfect place to make easy money, and so even middle-class Americans began to speculate on Wall Street. But on October 24, 1929—"Black Thursday"—the stock market collapsed. Orders to sell poured into the New York Stock Exchange, and stock prices plummeted. Panicked brokers began calling in their customers' debts, which led to more orders to sell off stocks. Some stocks, which found no buyers at any price, became worthless. As bad as this was, the worst was yet to come. Five days later, on October 29, so-called "Black Tuesday," a record 16 million shares of stock traded hands. By November, $30 billion in stock values had vanished. Companies were wiped out, banks were drained, and investors saw their life savings disappear.

In hindsight, economists and historians recognize the many factors that caused this devastating stock market crash. The economy appeared healthy, but in fact industrial production far outpaced consumer demand, and tremendous amounts of inventory were accumulating in warehouses. Overseas markets for American-made products had dwindled as a result of a severe depression in postwar Europe, and many American businesses were buried in debt. While the rich undoubtedly got richer throughout much of the 1920s, middle-class and especially working-class Americans saw their paychecks grow at a much slower rate. And while large segments of the population, primarily farmers, textile workers, and coal miners, lacked sufficient income to meet their basic needs, 60 percent of the nation's wealth lay in the hands of just 2 percent of the American people. The stock market crash did not directly cause the Great Depression, but it did accelerate the collapse of an already unstable economy and the onset of the worst economic crisis in American history. "Black Tuesday" marked the end of the prosperous and flamboyant Jazz Age and the beginning of a new era in American history, the Great Depression.

"History of 1929" cartoon by Daniel Fitzpatrick, *St. Louis Post-Dispatch*, December 31, 1929. Courtesy of the State Historical Society of Missouri, Columbia.

CONCLUSION

The 1920s represented, in many ways, an era of surprising contradictions and inconsistencies. A newly urbanized population clamored for the modern technologies of automobiles, refrigerators, radios, and electric appliances yet at the same time longed for the simpler lifestyles of rural America. Most Americans' standards of living rose, but so, too, did the number of violent, repressive clashes during the decade. Americans reveled in newfound freedoms afforded them by the automobile, suffrage, and consumer culture, yet simultaneously they sought to repress other freedoms through Prohibition legislation, Klan night riding, and religious Fundamentalism. The liberated "flapper" was lauded in music, movies, and advertising, but after a certain point she was nonetheless expected to settle down and adopt the lifestyle of a traditional married woman. All in all, the 1920s signified a profound shift in the behaviors, attitudes, and lifestyles of ordinary Americans, who found the modern world exciting but also extraordinarily complicated.

2
World of Youth

While it seems that elders have always complained about the foolish behaviors of the younger generation, historians mark the period of the 1920s as the first decade in which Americans experienced a sharply defined "generation gap." Prior to 1900, social and cultural change had been slow to come to the farms, villages, and sometimes even the cities of the United States, and generations of Americans had led lives that closely resembled those of their parents and even grandparents. With the emergence of a nationwide popular culture in the early twentieth century, however, middle-class youth enjoyed opportunities and experiences unknown to previous generations. During the 1920s, motion pictures, radio programs, modern advertisements, and mass-circulation magazines and newspapers encouraged young people to fashion identities for themselves modeled less on their elders than on Hollywood starlets and professional athletes who embodied popular ideals of glamour, rebellion, and self-indulgence. As younger Americans began to determine for themselves what was fashionable and appealing during the Jazz Age, they soon became the focus of a national popular culture increasingly enamored with the concept of youth itself.

Common stereotypes of youth culture during the Roaring Twenties invariably include the glamorous figure of the "flapper" and her beau, the dashing young "sheik." The carefree flapper has come to symbolize the flamboyant, reckless spirit of Jazz Age America, but the term itself predates the 1920s by at least a century. According to H. L. Mencken, *flapper*, in early nineteenth-century England, denoted "a very immoral young girl in her early teens"; by the early twentieth century the term had migrated to the United States, where it came to be used, in

Mencken's words, as "one of a long series of jocular terms for a young and somewhat foolish girl, full of wild surmises and inclined to revolt against the precepts and admonitions of her elders."[1] Perhaps more than any other icon, the flapper epitomizes those fast-changing fashions and cultural trends that many people today commonly associate with the 1920s—a young woman with bobbed hair, wearing a straight, slim dress and a long, beaded necklace, drinking gin, and dancing the Charleston to the wild syncopations of a jazz band. Flappers, according to the stereotype, were daring and uninhibited trendsetters who wore their stockings rolled down and their hemlines just below the knee and let their unlaced galoshes flap around their ankles. They smoked cigarettes, wore fur-trimmed jackets and stylish cloche hats, gallivanted around town in Ford roadsters, and enjoyed attending "petting parties." They embraced all sorts of popular fads and crazes and by doing so promoted such newfangled diversions as mahjong, crossword puzzles, dance marathons, and miniature golf.

The flapper's equally stereotypical male counterpart was a young man with slicked-back hair parted down the middle, in the style of the fashionable "sheik"—a term popularized by matinee idol Rudolph Valentino's 1921 movie of the same title. On a regular day, a well-dressed sheik might have worn knickers, argyle socks, a sweater vest, and a peaked cap or perhaps "Oxford bags"—huge baggy pants not unlike those favored by many of today's teenagers. Stepping out to a cocktail party or nightclub required a more formal outfit, consisting perhaps of a double-breasted suit, a bow tie, a bowler hat, and a raccoon coat. A sheik who attended college would have cheered for the varsity football squad and perhaps rushed a popular fraternity. He attended movies regularly, often with a date, to see the slapstick antics of Buster Keaton or the titillating melodramas of Clara Bow. The sheik, according to common stereotypes, listened to the sweet jazz music of Paul Whiteman's Orchestra and enthusiastically danced the fox-trot at co-ed parties, where bootleg liquor was plentiful. He was accustomed to his women friends drinking, smoking, and petting at parties, and the ethics of his parents' generation seemed to him stodgy and infinitely old-fashioned.

Of course, very few people, no matter how fashionable, actually conformed wholly to these hackneyed stereotypes so often associated with the Jazz Age. However, millions aspired to imitate the quintessential flapper and sheik, largely as a result of the powerful and pervasive influence of the mass media. Hollywood films, Tin Pan Alley songs, fashion magazines, advertisements, and pulp fiction all disseminated attractive, idealized images of the rebellious flapper and sheik that many young Americans found irresistible. Of course, not everyone wanted to follow the crowd, and at least some people complained bitterly that these stereotypes did not accurately represent their own manners and morals.

Nevertheless, as the younger generation as a whole became a primary focus of American popular culture, these clichéd images of wild, "flaming youth" proved to mask a youth culture that was actually very complex.

EDUCATION

Naturally, not all facets of youth culture revolved around socializing, dancing, and other leisure activities that the flapper figure embodied. Education ranked as one of the highest priorities for middle-class American families, and public school enrollment rose across the nation due not only to parental pressures but also to the compulsory school attendance laws that existed in all 48 states by 1918. Although they varied from state to state, most laws required children between the ages of seven and 14 to attend school. In 1920, the average daily attendance at American public schools was slightly more than 16 million students; by 1930 that figure topped 21 million.[2] Public schools in all of the 11 former Confederate states and in some border states like Kentucky and Missouri were segregated, and African-American children attended all-black schools that generally received only one-third to one-half of the fiscal appropriations of white schools. During the 1920s, American students generally stayed in school longer than they had in prior decades, largely because of the widespread demands of business and industry for a well-educated workforce. In fact, one of the greatest changes in education during the decade was the dramatic increase in the number of students who enrolled in high school rather than ending their education at the end of the eighth grade (or before). In 1920, 2.2 million students were enrolled in the nation's high schools, but by 1930, that figure doubled to almost 4.5 million.[3]

American primary and secondary schools performed a number of functions during the 1920s, only some of which could strictly be considered academic. Beyond basic instruction in reading, writing, and arithmetic, schools also taught principles of order, civic responsibility, morality, and "American" values and standards of behavior. Public school prayers and religious songs invoked a Protestant God, and textbooks emphasized the many virtues of the American system of government. In fact, a Wisconsin law passed in 1921 explicitly forbade the use of any school text that "defames our nation's founders . . . or which contains propaganda favorable to any foreign government."[4] Many public school pupils during the 1920s were the children of immigrants, and Progressive reformers saw public education as the ideal vehicle for "Americanizing" these children. Indeed, countless immigrant children had their names anglicized in public schools; for example, Josef became

Joe, and Jerzy became Jerry. Some of these changes arose in response to the anti-German hysteria triggered by World War I, and many German-American families felt pressured to anglicize their surnames to demonstrate their American patriotism and avoid harassment. Many immigrant children, especially those in large metropolitan areas such as New York City and Chicago, did not speak English when they first enrolled in public school, and few teachers were equipped to handle the educational needs of these non-native populations. Classes were conducted in English, and children either caught on to the language through their own efforts or left school altogether.

During the late 1920s, some educators began to design programs that better suited the special needs of immigrant children and other discrete groups of students, including gifted children and slow learners. Developing more specialized education programs required the categorization of students according to different levels of ability or experience. This demand paved the way for widespread educational testing, which became common practice during the 1920s. Some tests claimed to be able to measure intelligence and thus could "track" students into classes specifically designed for gifted, bright, average, slow, and special learners. Such tests were essentially unheard of at the turn of the century, but by 1924 at least 76 different mental tests were in use. Millions of children were subjected to these tests, which in fact measured not innate intelligence but specific knowledge. As criticism of standardized testing mounted, however, these so-called "intelligence tests" gave way in the late 1920s to "achievement tests," which claimed to evaluate how well students learned particular skills and knowledge sets. By the early 1930s, educators had at their disposal nearly 1,300 different achievement tests with which to assess students' educational skills and development, and American schoolchildren today live with the legacy of these first efforts at standardized educational testing.

Just as high school enrollment increased during the 1920s, so too did enrollment at American colleges and universities. Throughout much of the nineteenth century, college attendance ranked as a luxury enjoyed largely by the sons (and occasionally the daughters) of wealthy American families, but beginning in the 1890s, considerable numbers of young middle-class men and women attended colleges and universities across the nation. During the early decades of the twentieth century, a college education came to be perceived as a necessary step for middle-class sons and daughters on their way to their chosen profession. By 1920, college attendance became more widespread than ever before, and the middle class supplied the greatest proportion of post-secondary students. Nationally, college and university enrollment nearly doubled from approximately 600,000 in 1920 to almost 1.2 million students in 1930.[5] In 1900, 85,000 women attended college, but by 1920, that figure jumped to

283,000. A decade later, it reached 481,000—approximately 40 percent of the total number of college students nationally.[6] New undergraduate degree programs in sociology, political science, business, advertising, and physical education, among others, augmented the traditional academic disciplines of history, literature, mathematics, and classics. Enrollment in graduate programs also increased dramatically. In 1920, American colleges and universities awarded only 532 Ph.D. degrees, but in 1930, that figure almost quadrupled to 2,024 doctorates.[7] Despite these high enrollment figures, a college degree remained a comparatively rare accomplishment. By 1928, approximately 12 percent of college-aged Americans between the ages of 18 and 21 were enrolled in institutions of higher education. The figure for women was even lower; in fact, the number of women attending college in 1930 represented only about 10 percent of the total female population between those ages.

For those fortunate enough to attend, college offered students an enormous amount of freedom and leisure time. Although they spent much of their week sitting in lecture halls and studying in libraries, students still found plenty of hours in the evenings and on weekends to attend football games, rush fraternities or sororities, go to dances, and otherwise socialize with friends. At large universities, a well-established system of fraternities and sororities sponsored various extracurricular events, and the increased popularity of Greek organizations during the 1920s led to a dramatic rise in both the number of chapters and the construction of houses on campuses across the country. By 1930, approximately 35 percent of all college students were members of fraternities or sororities, and, after freshman pledges underwent the humiliating and sometimes brutal experience of hazing, affiliation with these organizations conferred a prestigious and enviable campus identity.

Throughout the 1920s, college sports captured the attention of millions of Americans across the nation, and college students in particular found themselves drawn to the excitement and competition of amateur athletics. Football was, by far, the most popular collegiate sport, and students flocked to pre-game pep rallies to cheer on their team and to show their school spirit. Besides watching the thrilling action on the gridiron, football games allowed students welcome opportunities to socialize, flirt, and even drink, all the while rooting for their alma mater. However, college football games—especially contests involving such powerhouses as Harvard, Princeton, Notre Dame, Iowa, and Michigan—were far more than mere social events for college students. The University of Illinois' All-American halfback Harold "Red" Grange, Notre Dame's famed "Four Horsemen," and other nationally known gridiron stars drew hundreds of thousands of spectators to games each weekend. During the 1920s, gate receipts at college football games actually exceeded those at profes-

University of North Carolina vs. University of Virginia football game, Chapel Hill, North Carolina, 1929. Courtesy of the North Carolina Collection, University of North Carolina at Chapel Hill.

sional baseball games, and the millions of dollars generated by football programs helped to fund less profitable college sports, such as baseball, swimming, and gymnastics.

Collegiate culture exerted a tremendous influence on American popular culture during the Jazz Age. Image-conscious high-schoolers, for example, slavishly imitated whatever new fads and fashions sprang from the nation's colleges and universities. The social aspects of college life figured prominently in the magazines, motion pictures, popular songs, and pulp novels of the Jazz Age, and many Americans considered anything "collegiate"—from a style of hat to a slang expression—"smart" and fashionable. The popular mass-circulation magazine *College Humor* focused exclusively on the leisure activities of university students, and catchy hit songs such as "Collegiate" (1925) and "I Love the College Girls" (1926), both performed most famously by Fred Waring and His Pennsylvanians, were heard on radios and phonographs across the country. Silent films, including *The Plastic Age* (1925), *Brown of Harvard* (1925) (John Wayne's first film—he was an extra), *The Freshman* (1925), and *College* (1927), to name only a handful, demonstrated the fun and frivolity of campus life to millions of American moviegoers. Even those Americans who had never been—nor would ever go—to college tended to agree that university students reigned as the chief arbiters of fashion and taste during the Roaring Twenties.

WORK

Child labor divided sharply along class lines. Generally, the children of working-class and immigrant families took jobs because their contribution to the household income was required to make ends meet. Middle-class children, on the other hand, might occasionally hold a part-time job delivering packages, caddying at golf courses, jerking sodas, scooping ice cream, or doing other light work, in order to pick up a bit of extra spending money. The rising salaries of most middle-class families enabled their teenaged children the freedom to attend school full-time, if they so chose, and to engage in sports, clubs, and other extracurricular and leisure activities.

As a result of a series of compulsory education laws and child labor laws, the total number of child laborers declined in the United States during the 1920s. According to the 1920 U.S. Census, fewer children between the ages of 10 and 15 were classified as "gainfully employed" than had been during previous decades. While more than 18 percent of children fell into this category in 1910, that figure dropped to less than 9 percent in 1920 and to only 5 percent in 1930. These decreasing numbers reflected an overall shift away from the hiring of child laborers in coal mining, textile manufacturing, and other industries that historically have ranked among the greatest employers of children. This trend, however, reveals only the broad contours of national developments, since rates of child employment remained high in Mississippi, South Carolina, Alabama, Georgia, and Arkansas—all southern states plagued by agricultural dependence and rural poverty. Rates of child labor were the lowest in Ohio, California, Michigan, and Maine. In Mississippi, the state with the highest level of child employment in 1930, nearly 25 percent of all children between the ages of 10 and 15 were gainfully employed. In contrast, only 1 percent of children in Ohio claimed to work.[8]

These data belie the fact most child labor was difficult to document and regulate, and the census almost certainly underestimated the total number of working youth across the nation. Rural children, for example, cut hay, picked fruit, chopped cotton, harvested grain, and milked cows, often for their own families (especially sharecropping families) but sometimes as low-wage employees for others. Thousands of migrant families, many of them Mexican immigrants, followed the harvests of various crops across the West Coast and Great Plains. Children as young as 5 and 6 worked alongside their parents and siblings, laboring at backbreaking tasks for just pennies an hour. Migrant children seldom attended school with any regularity, since the livelihood and sometimes

Newsboy selling the Washington *News*, 1921. Courtesy of the Library of Congress.

the very survival of their families depended heavily on the small amounts of money these children earned picking fruit, berries, beets, onions, tobacco, hops, or cotton.

Rural children weren't the only ones who worked instead of going to school during the 1920s. Many urban boys and girls from working-class families were hired as maids, messengers, and errand boys. Untold thousands worked on the streets of the nation's cities, peddling fruit and candy, selling newspapers, shining shoes, and doing odd jobs. Others, especially the sons and daughters of Eastern and Southern European immigrants, engaged in home trades, or piecework, assembling ready-to-wear clothing, artificial flowers, costume jewelry, and other inexpensive goods that could not be made by machine. These low-paying, exploitative jobs, conducted in private homes in both urban and rural settings, were virtually impossible to regulate and were seldom counted by census-takers.

ORGANIZED RECREATION

During the 1920s, millions of American youth participated in the Boy Scouts and Cub Scouts, the Girl Scouts and Brownies, the Camp Fire

Boy Scout Troop, Waynesville, North Carolina, circa 1920. Courtesy of the North Carolina Collection, University of North Carolina at Chapel Hill.

Girls, and other organizations designed to educate and supervise young people during the hours when they were not attending school. Beginning in the 1890s, educators and social workers came to believe that children, especially boys, needed extensive supervision in order to encourage their educational and moral development. Participation in extracurricular organizations, educators and social workers argued, promoted the ideals of upstanding manhood and womanhood, while at the same time it extended childhood and kept adolescents out of street gangs and away from criminal activity and other destructive pursuits. The Young Men's Christian Association (YMCA), the oldest youth organization in America, was founded in the United States in 1851, and by the 1870s, it had developed junior departments for boys under the age of 18 that sponsored hobby clubs, summer camps, religious programs, and sports teams. The Boy Scouts of America, founded in 1910, accepted members between the ages of 12 and 18 who enjoyed such activities as hiking, camping, woodcraft, and civil service. Younger boys joined the Wolf Cubs, the Boy Pioneers, and the Boy Rangers, all of which promoted similar civic and outdoor activities. The Boy Scouts sponsored unofficial Junior Troops and Cadet Corps during the 1920s, and, in 1929, the Cub Scouts began to accept boys as young as 9 years old, most of them drawn, as in most of these scouting clubs, from white-collar professional families.

Educators and social workers also sought to mold the character of middle-class American girls. The Girl Scouts of America, the Camp Fire Girls, and the Young Women's Christian Association (YWCA) prepared girls for their future roles as nurturing wives, mothers, homemakers, and responsible citizens. The Girl Scouts, established in the United States in 1912, combined outdoor activities and sports with community service initiatives, and by the end of the 1920s, the organization claimed more than 200,000 members. In 1910, Dr. Luther Gulick and his wife, Charlotte Gulick, founded the Camp Fire Girls of America—the first nonsectarian organization for girls in the United States. The club leaders taught girls domestic science skills such as housework, cooking, shopping, and nursing. But they also encouraged the girls' creative talents in art, music, and needlework. *American Girl* (the official magazine of the Girl Scouts) and *Everygirls* (the official magazine of the Camp Fire Girls) likewise endorsed less traditionally feminine pursuits, such as athletics, camping, and woodworking, but these magazines carefully steered away from articles that encouraged girls to aspire to careers outside the home. These girls' clubs boasted large memberships during the 1920s and, like the Boy Scouts and the YMCA, drew most of their members from white middle-class families.

While American cities offered more opportunities for organized childhood clubs and athletic teams, the nation's rural children also enjoyed extracurricular options of their own. For example, the white sons and daughters of successful farmers combined recreation with agricultural education through their membership in 4-H clubs (4-H, founded in 1902, stands for "Head, Heart, Hands, and Health"). By 1929, 750,000 4-H members attended weekly or monthly meetings to learn more about scientific agriculture and went to county and state fairs to exhibit their livestock and crops. These organizations, however, usually excluded African-American children, and few children of poor white farm families had either the money or the leisure time necessary to join a local 4-H chapter.

YOUTH CULTURE

During the 1920s, the commercial entertainment industry focused largely on the interests and activities of the nation's youth, and their penchant for socializing and celebrating made them frequent subjects of Hollywood films, Tin Pan Alley songs, Madison Avenue advertisements, and magazine articles. Cartoons of young women sipping from flasks, sitting on boys' laps, smoking cigarettes, and dancing provocatively, such as those famously drawn by John Held Jr., appeared weekly in *Collier's*, *Life*, *Judge*, *The New Yorker*, and other major magazines. Conservative critics vehemently criticized flappers, reproaching their careless morality, their bold sexuality, and their defiance of traditional behaviors. Parents wrung their hands as their brazen daughters with painted faces and powdered knees left the house on dates. Writer F. Scott Fitzgerald alleged in his 1920 novel *This Side of Paradise* that "none of the Victorian mothers—and most of the mothers were Victorian—had any idea how casually their daughters were accustomed to be kissed," but given the behavior of many young flappers, surely some mothers must have at least suspected.[9]

During the 1920s, the emergence of a distinctive youth culture greatly alarmed many conservative or religiously devout Americans. Historian Paula Fass writes that, after World War I, many adults perceived that youth culture had appeared "suddenly, dramatically, even menacingly on the social scene."[10] Parents and grandparents grumbled about what they considered the foolishness and decadence of the younger generation in dozens of scathing articles and editorials. Young people, they lamented, were contributing to the breakdown of the nation's traditional social and moral order. But many young people, in turn, resented being perpetually cast as scapegoats for the perceived social problems of modern America. One exasperated young man, writing in defense of his generation in *The Atlantic Monthly* in 1920, complained that "hardly a week goes by that I do not read some indignant treatise depicting our extravagance, the corruption of our manners, the futility of our existence, poured out in stiff, scared, shocked sentences before a sympathetic and horrified audience of fathers, mothers, and maiden aunts—but particularly maiden aunts."[11] These conflicts between teens and twentysomethings, on the one hand, and their parents and grandparents, on the other, initiated an ongoing inter-generational struggle over appropriate standards of behavior and fashion that has only seemed to intensify since the 1920s.

The generation gap originated during the 1920s largely as a result of many young people's rejection of the social roles and mores that had dominated American life since at least the 1890s. Some historians attribute the emergence of the generation gap to the horrific slaughter of World War I, the first war of the Machine Age, which made traditional value systems appear irrelevant if not patently ridiculous to many younger Americans. Others locate its origins in the nation's rapid modernization and industrialization, which dramatically altered social, racial, and gender roles. During the 1920s, younger Americans enjoyed a wide range of new amusements and technologies, including automobiles, movies, and radio, which made their social world far more expansive than the one their parents had known at their age. Undoubtedly, the generation gap sprang from multiple and complex sources, but one of its major consequences was that millions of young Americans came to consider the prewar past and its conventions to be "pretentious" and "phony." As a result, they began consciously to forge their own set of behavioral and moral codes. In the process, these youth pioneered a brash new Jazz Age culture, complete with fast-changing fads in fashion, music, dancing, and slang that, although scandalous to many older Americans, delighted both the young and the young-at-heart.

Although they were widely criticized, young Americans simultaneously found themselves the focus of an intense cultural obsession. As immoral and disrespectful as they might have appeared to some of their elders, the younger generation came to be celebrated, even glorified, as glamorous trendsetters whose creativity and energy fueled the latest fashions. Almost overnight, motion pictures transformed youthfulness into a valuable and fascinating commodity. Dozens of Hollywood films—including such titles as *Blind Youth, Heart of Youth, The Soul of Youth* (all 1920); *The Price of Youth, Reckless Youth, Youth Must Have Love* (1922); *Daring Youth, Flaming Youth, Madness of Youth* (1923); *Sporting Youth, Wine of Youth, Youth for Sale* (1924); *Pampered Youth, Passionate Youth* (1925); and *Fascinating Youth* and *Thrilling Youth* (1926)—titillated and entranced moviegoers in the first half of the 1920s.[12]

America's consumer culture touted youthfulness as a commercial product that one could actually purchase. Madison Avenue advertising agencies bombarded consumers with messages proclaiming how miraculous new products could help them to retain and preserve their youthful appearance. Cosmetics and other beauty product advertisements constantly reminded women that happiness depended on a firm, clear complexion. As a 1928 magazine ad for Marie Barlow Facial Preparations announced, "men demand youth in women's faces." A later ad for the same product urged women to "preserve the radiant twenties, banish the fading thirties, prolong the fascinating forties" by using its beauty products. Thus, at the same moment that young people were being reproached for their unconventional standards and inappropriate conduct, they were also being idolized by adults twice and three times their age, who doggedly imitated their clothing fashions, hairstyles, slang phrases, and dance steps in an effort to recapture the elusive qualities of youth. Younger Americans were at once the nation's cultural trendsetters and its social scapegoats for a single reason—they were seen as the embodiment of all that was new, radical, and "modern."

Regardless of how members of the older generation felt about young people, they had no choice but to deal with them, for the cultural revolution they spearheaded was far too widespread and powerful to be ignored. A 1925 advertisement published in *The Saturday Evening Post*, addressing the older generation, recognized the tremendous influence that youth exerted on America's consumer-driven popular culture: "You may regard the new generation as amusing or pathetic; as a bit tragic, or rather splendid. You may consider their manners crude, their ideals vague, their clothes absurd. Their cynical, humorous discussions of social conditions may stir you to admiration or fill you with helpless rage. But it is useless to deny that these youngsters have a definite bearing on the thought, literature, and customs of our day."[13]

LEISURE ACTIVITIES

When the Eighteenth Amendment outlawed the manufacture, transportation, and sale of alcoholic beverages in 1920, few of its proponents ever imagined the profound influence this legislation would have on American popular culture. While studies about the effects of National Prohibition on national drinking patterns differ, it seems clear that many young people actually drank more during the so-called "Dry Decade" than they had previously. Indeed, young people themselves credited Prohibition laws with encouraging them to drink more than they perhaps might have otherwise. As a 1926 editorial published in the *Wisconsin Daily Cardinal*, the University of Wisconsin's student newspaper, asserted, "Without doubt, prohibition has been an incentive for young folks to learn to drink." Paula Fass agrees, arguing, "Prohibition got in youth's way because it was . . . an anachronism that made the young law-breakers in spite of themselves."[14] Thirsty young Americans did their share to keep the nation's black-market liquor economy booming by purchasing pints of bootleg gin and whiskey and by patronizing speakeasies and nightclubs. Drinking was seen as daring behavior that flouted both the law of the land and parental disapproval—factors that made alcohol all the more alluring and enticing to the young.

Like drinking illicit alcohol, smoking cigarettes served as another symbol of youthful rebellion during the Jazz Age, especially for young women. Prior to 1920, women who smoked publicly were usually believed to be prostitutes, bohemians, or avant-garde intellectuals. But after World War I, even respectable middle-class women began puffing on cigarettes as a public display of both their equality with men and their emancipation from Victorian codes of behavior. Indeed, cigarettes in the hands of women were sometimes called "liberty torches," but many conservative Americans still considered women smokers indecent, if not immoral. "Nice girls" did not smoke, went this logic, but tens of thousands of daring young women in the 1920s scoffed at this alleged connection between smoking and morality and challenged old-fashioned views of femininity and propriety by lighting up not just in the privacy of their own homes but in restaurants, cafés, movie theaters, or wherever the urge struck them.

During the 1920s, Hollywood motion pictures became a significant component of social life, and people of all ages, especially those in their teens and twenties, flocked to the grand movie palaces of urban business districts and the cheaper theaters of working-class neighborhoods. By 1930, according to some reports, Americans purchased an estimated 100 million movie tickets a week.[15] Going to the movies was a popular leisure activity for couples on a date as well as for larger groups of young people. Charlie Chaplin comedies, Mary Pickford melodramas, and Rudolph Valentino romances instructed viewers about current fashions in clothing, dancing, and, most important of all, personal conduct. Although the films of the 1920s seem, to twenty-first-century viewers, almost comically tame, many parents and educators at the time were deeply disturbed by the overt sexuality of motion pictures and blamed them for causing the "early sophistication" of young people and the relaxation of certain social taboos. Indeed, the cinema not only educated young people about courtship, love, and sex but also profoundly influenced their behavior, much to the alarm of many conservative adults. As one 16-year-old Indiana girl confessed, "I know love pictures have made me more receptive to love-making because I always thought it rather silly until these pictures where there is always so much love and everything turns out all right in the end." She added, "I kiss and pet much more than I would otherwise." But at least a few parents admitted that they were relieved that their children could learn about sex at the movies instead of at home.[16]

Popular music also occupied an important position in the cultural world of millions of young, middle-class Americans. Music classes enjoyed a prominent place in educational curricula, and children and young adults from diverse economic backgrounds often learned to sing and play an instrument, either at school, in private lessons, or through correspondences courses. Victrolas and radios expanded the already significant role that music played in the daily lives of American youth, and many spent whatever pocket money they had on the latest recordings of jazz and pop songs. Trendy young people sang and danced to such hit songs as "Ain't We Got Fun" (1921), "Yes! We Have No Bananas" (1923), "My Blue Heaven" (1927), and whatever other numbers appealed to them at the moment. Increasingly, though, as a result of the rapid expansion of the commercial entertainment industry during the 1920s, young people listened to music more often than they performed it themselves. Dancing ranked as one of the most important social activities of American youth, and although the older generation loudly criticized the close, sexually suggestive dances enjoyed by the young, little could prevent high school- and college-age youth from dancing the shimmy, the Charleston, the Black Bottom, and even the exotic tango at every opportunity. Knowing the words to the latest hit songs and the steps to the most recent dance crazes provided, for many young people, an index by which to gauge the cultural sophistication and stylishness of one's peers.

Wearing the most up-to-date clothing also served as a benchmark by which American youth evaluated one another. Pressure to keep up with the current styles prompted many young women to spend significant amounts of their allowance or paycheck on dresses, hosiery, hats, shoes, and other fashion accessories in an effort to avoid appearing out-of-date or "frumpy." Even school-age children pressured their parents to finance their fashionable wardrobes, for popularity seemed to depend largely on one's ability to wear the right outfit. For example, one teenage Indiana boy candidly informed his mother that, when his younger sister entered high school, she had to wear silk stockings or else "none of the boys will like her or have anything to do with her."[17] But keeping up with the rapidly changing fashions of the 1920s proved time-consuming and expensive. Although young men did not face quite the same pressures as young women did, a well-dressed sheik did need to acquire some relatively high-priced wardrobe items, especially during the mid-1920s, when raccoon coats were all the rage.

While reading may not have preoccupied them in quite the same way that movies, music, and clothing did, young people did purchase significant numbers of books and magazines during the 1920s. Pulp fiction magazines were a particular favorite among young Americans, and these magazines, often printed on cheap paper and featuring colorful covers with lurid story titles, could be purchased for 25 cents or less at chain drugstores or newsstands. Girls enjoyed reading romance magazines, such as *Love Story Magazine* and *Heart Throbs*. Articles with titillating titles such as "Indolent Kisses," "The Primitive Lover," "How to Keep the Thrill in Marriage," and "What I Told My Daughter the Night Before Her Marriage" taught girls more about sex and romance than they might otherwise have learned from their mothers.[18] While teenage boys and young men also picked up magazines full of sex-filled tales, such as *Snappy Stories* and *Saucy Stories*, their reading tastes tended to favor adventure stories, crime fiction, and science-fiction tales. Young people read serious fiction as well, but often gravitated toward portrayals of their own age group. F. Scott Fitzgerald's novels and short stories depicting Jazz Age debauchery were popular, as were other best-selling novels about the younger generation, including Percy Marks' *The Plastic Age* (1922) and Warner Fabian's *Flaming Youth* (1923).

During the 1920s, language itself proved to be a significant indicator of a person's membership in America's trendy youth culture, distinguishing insiders from outsiders. Slang terms, ubiquitous for a few weeks and apparently gone the next, not only attested to the fleeting popularity of many Jazz Age fads but also measured how attuned people were to the latest linguistic turns-of-phrase. Hollywood motion pictures, even silent ones, played an important role in circulating and popularizing new expressions. Rudolph Valentino's 1921 box-office smash *The*

Sheik, for instance, led to the coinage of the terms *sheik* and *sheba* to describe attractive, eligible young men and women, while Clara Bow's famous 1927 film *It* made the title word a much-used euphemism for "sex appeal." Plenty of slang terms evolved to make fun of various types: a *dumb Dora* was "a stupid woman," an *Ethel* was "an effeminate man," and *milquetoast* described "a timid person" (named after Caspar Milquetoast, a 1924 comic-strip character created by *New York Herald Tribune* illustrator H. T. Webster). Something wonderful might have been described as *the bee's knees, the cat's pajamas, the elephant's eyebrows, the eel's hips, the butterfly's boots,* or *the gnat's whistle.* To *know your onions* meant to understand what was going on. To *mind your own potatoes* meant to mind your own business. An aggressive female flirt was a *vamp*, an attractive woman might be called a *tomato*, a ladies' man might be a *cake-eater*, and a fashionably dressed man was called *Joe Brooks.* Literally scores of slang words entered the American language as a result of National Prohibition. Various alcoholic drinks were known as *white mule, coffin varnish, horse liniment, monkey rum, panther sweat, rot gut,* or *tarantula juice.* Speakeasies were sometimes called *blind tigers* or *blind pigs,* and a drunk person might be described as *oiled, fried, tight, wet, blotto, corked, stewed, tanked,* or *lit up like a Christmas tree.* Ultimately, words circulated in and out of fashion as quickly as popular songs and dances during the 1920s, and keeping pace with popular slang meant keeping pace with youth culture.

COURTSHIP AND SEX

Youth culture of the 1920s seemed full of rebellion and frivolity, yet young people still adhered diligently to unwritten codes that dictated exactly how they should behave within their peer groups. In other words, the Roaring Twenties were not a free-for-all during which all social conventions were ignored. While movies, songs, and magazines often portrayed young people as licentious and sex-crazy (and studies do reveal that more unmarried people experimented with sex than they had in previous generations), far fewer sheiks and flappers engaged in casual premarital intercourse than the older generation suspected.

Courtship rituals, however, did change dramatically during the 1920s. After World War I, dating replaced older courtship traditions in which suitors called on young women in their homes and visited with them under the watchful eyes of chaperones. Young adults from "respectable" homes generally did not spend unsupervised time together until their families approved of the match and the couple was close to marriage. During the 1920s, however, the practice of adult chaperones and parlor engagements faded rapidly, in part because many young couples took to the road in their automobiles, thus escaping parental supervision for an evening. In Emily Post's 1922 edition of *Etiquette in Society, in Business, in Politics and at Home,* one chapter on courtship was titled "The Chaperon and Other Conventions." In the 1927 revision, however, the same chapter, now retitled "The Vanishing Chaperon and Other New Conventions," emphasized that a girl with proper ethics and strength of character needed no chaperone to tell her how to conduct herself. (In 1937, this chapter was again retitled "The Vanished Chaperon and Other Lost Conventions.")[19]

The 1920s also saw the blossoming of modern dating, albeit with certain restrictions and expectations. Dating nearly always involved a boy's inviting a girl to spend an afternoon or evening with him, perhaps at a party, a movie, a meal, a dance, or some other amusement. The boy was expected to pay for all expenses, and in return the girl provided lively companionship and, commonly, physical affection known as "petting," which consisted of kissing, hugging, and caressing of varying intensity. Only a couple of decades earlier, casual behavior of this nature would have branded a young woman as disreputable and impure. During the 1920s, however, many young people engaged in petting as a safe way to experiment with sexual intimacy before marriage.

Dating during the 1920s generally required significant outlays of cash in order for a young man to be able to take his date to restaurants, movie theaters, and dance halls, and not everyone could afford to participate fully in these modern dating rituals. Working-class men who could rarely afford dates often had to content themselves with calling upon a girl at her home or visiting with her while at work or after church. Rural youth also had fewer opportunities for dates but would find ways to spend time together at picnics, fairs, church suppers, or the girl's home. Access to an automobile made it much easier to spend private time together, but not every family had a car, and those families that did often restricted their children's use of it.

On college campuses, where young people spent a great deal of unsupervised time in mixed company, a social phenomenon emerged known as "petting parties," at which young men and women paired off to "fool around." While petting was socially accepted, however, sexual intercourse generally was not. In fact, many popular young women aspired to attract a number of different suitors to compete for her time and attention, and while she might pet with all of them, she would likely not have sex with any of them. Casual premarital sex could destroy a young woman's reputation, and promiscuous girls were labeled "fast" or "cheap" by their social set. While the rate of premarital sexual activity did apparently increase slightly during the 1920s, most of the time it was among couples who were already engaged to be married. Studies indicate that college students of the 1920s were aware of condoms, dia-

University of Missouri homecoming celebration, Columbia, Missouri, 1921. Courtesy of the State Historical Society of Missouri, Columbia.

phragms, and other contraceptive devices, due no doubt in part to the widely publicized efforts of reformer Margaret Sanger and the American Birth Control League (founded in 1921) to bring safe, effective, and legal birth control to the American public. Nevertheless, most of the students surveyed considered contraception a practice reserved primarily for married couples.

Contrary to their portrayals as debauched, immoral pleasure seekers, young people of the 1920s, while not necessarily law-abiding, were actually quite a bit more innocent than their elders believed them to be. Although the young collectively indulged in behaviors that their parents considered radical and rebellious, little evidence exists to suggest that they succumbed to higher rates of alcoholism or premarital pregnancy than their elders had at their age. That is, much of the wild behavior of the Jazz Age's "flaming youth" was an illusion created for the benefit of their peers and their exasperated elders. For example, many anecdotal sources suggest that young, popular women reveled in playing the part of a "speed," but that did not necessarily mean that they "went the distance" with any of the boys they kissed and petted. Likewise, visible drunkenness was considered quite funny and "smart" among some crowds, so naturally some partyers exaggerated their level of intoxication. For many, then, participating in the trendy behaviors of American youth culture was, in other words, an example of braggadocio, of appearing to live on the cutting edge of social fashions while privately maintaining personal values that were far more traditional.

CONCLUSION

Overall, the Jazz Age marked a radical change in the lives of millions of American children and adolescents. Fewer children and teens held down full-time jobs, and more of them attended school regularly than in previous decades. College and university enrollment soared, and movies, songs, and magazines celebrated college youth as the epitome of fun-loving revelry and fashion. Many young, middle-class Americans rebelled against what they saw as outdated Victorian standards of morality by embracing all of those behaviors their elders found most disturbing—drinking, smoking, dancing, joy-riding, and petting, yet not all of the nation's youth could afford to engage in such frivolity. Poverty, Jim Crow segregation, and lack of educational and economic opportunities circumscribed the lives of hundreds of thousands of African-American, immigrant, and working-class children and adolescents. They inhabited a Jazz Age world far different from that of their middle-class peers—a world that was not a carefree, untroubled playground, but a difficult and sometimes dangerous place to live and work.

Part II

Popular Culture of the 1920s

3

Advertising

Advertisements cannot be interpreted as a simple mirror of American life, and those from the 1920s admittedly offer us a distorted understanding of people's daily activities during this era of unprecedented consumerism. Advertisements reflect certain ideals in fashion and popular taste, but an ad picturing a beautiful woman in a fashionable dress testifying to the benefits of the latest linoleum flooring provides little information about what average Americans actually had on their kitchen floors. Nevertheless, such ads do reveal what kinds of products were available during the 1920s and what sorts of strategies advertisers used to convince American consumers to hand over their hard-earned dollars.

During the 1920s, an army of sophisticated professional salespeople, graphic designers, and copywriters bombarded Americans with attractive, persuasive advertising campaigns. Advertising agencies, such as the firms Lord and Thomas and the J. Walter Thompson Company, employed a host of strategies to promote their clients' products in a variety of venues, including newspapers, magazines, billboards, and radio. Modern advertising sought to convince consumers that the key to increased status, health, happiness, wealth, and beauty was to be found in the mass-produced goods available in the nation's department stores, chain stores, and mail-order catalogs. In prior decades, Americans had tended to define themselves at least in part based on factors such as race, ethnicity, region, occupation, religion, and politics. During the 1920s, however, Americans increasingly came to define themselves through the houses, cars, clothes, and other goods and services they purchased.

MASS CONSUMERISM

During World War I, the U.S. government had encouraged Americans to conserve food and fuel and to sacrifice for the good of the war effort by consuming only the basic necessities. But during the 1920s, the increasing prosperity and the simultaneous growth of the American middle class led to soaring levels of consumerism. Between 1922 and 1927, the average per capita income rose by 30 percent, and although a serious depression continued to plague agriculture, most aspects of the American economy seemed to be healthy and growing in the years preceding the stock market crash of October 1929. As Americans earned more disposable income and new products came on the market, companies tempted consumers with a wider variety of goods at comparatively low prices. Not surprisingly, competition increased dramatically among rival automobile manufacturers, food producers, and department stores.

American consumerism also exploded in part due to the increasing popularity of affordable installment plans. Prior to 1920, going into debt to buy something was considered not only imprudent but also unseemly. Buying a home, of course, often required a mortgage, and other large purchases such as automobiles sometimes involved financing over time, but it wasn't until the 1920s that ordinary middle-class consumers began buying large numbers of more expensive items on the installment plan. In fact, between 1920 and 1929, installment purchases quintupled and in 1929 accounted for 90 percent of all vacuum cleaner, radio, and refrigerator sales, 70 percent of furniture sales, and 60 percent of auto sales.[1] Gradually, the stigma associated with buying on credit disappeared. Advertisers contributed to the erosion of the old ethos of saving one's money and avoiding debt by emphasizing the ease with which consumers could pay merely $5 a week for a lovely fur coat or $20 a month for a suite of living room furniture, all the while enjoying the merchandise instead of "wasting time" saving up for it.

THE MODERN ADVERTISING INDUSTRY

Most Americans not only had more money jingling in their pockets during the 1920s than they had in previous decades, but they also increasingly equated personal success with material goods. Modern advertising fueled this new attitude. Billboards, newspapers, magazines, and radio commercials all touted the virtues of their various advertisers' products, and companies poured enormous sums of money into advertising. Collectively, American companies spent around $700 million on advertising in 1914, but by 1929 that figure ballooned to nearly $3 billion.[2] This cycle of advertising and consumption accelerated dramatically throughout the 1920s as new consumer products came on the market and ad agencies devised new campaigns to promote them. At bottom, advertisers attempted to convince consumers that choosing a particular company's brand-name product instead of one sold by a competitor would most assuredly enhance their health, safety, beauty, even the quality of their lives. Companies gladly spent a fortune on advertising because they quickly found that advertising paid. For example, thanks to an extensive and successful advertising campaign, the American Tobacco Company, the manufacturers of Lucky Strike cigarettes, saw its earnings swell from $12 million in 1926 to $40 million in 1930.[3]

Modern advertising, which had been evolving since the turn of the twentieth century, flourished during the 1920s. The modern advertising agency consisted of teams of professional salesmen, graphic designers, and copywriters who created sophisticated advertising campaigns and then placed them in appropriate venues. Unlike advertisements of the late nineteenth century, which sought primarily to inform consumers of a particular product's features and availability, many modern ads created associations between a product and such desirable traits as youthfulness, attractiveness, intelligence, and popularity. As a result, these modern ads helped to create a need rather than merely to fulfill an existing one and thus actually encouraged Americans to buy newly developed or "improved" items that they had never before considered necessary. To keep pace with high production levels and create an expanding market, it became essential for companies constantly to boost consumer demand. So, in order to ensure a steady stream of customers, companies developed persuasive advertising campaigns that taught consumers regularly to purchase brand-name, often non-essential products.

The change to aggressive, hard-sell advertising did not happen overnight, and as late as the early 1920s, some print advertisements still functioned largely as informative declarations of a particular product's merits. These advertisements sought to create a subtle but positive impression on consumers. For example, a 1919 advertisement for Eaton's Highland Linen writing paper lauds its crisp texture, lovely color, and "dainty attractiveness" and then gently assures consumers that they can purchase this tasteful notepaper with confidence. This advertisement contains no hard-sell attitude or disparaging words directed at its competitors, nor does it link the consumer's character with the purchase of this particular brand of stationery.[4]

As the 1920s progressed, however, clever copywriters developed advertisements that appealed more overtly to consumers' psychological needs and fears. Increasingly, ads featured people enjoying a product, rather than merely showing the product itself. The language of advertisements became much more personal and intimate, inviting consumers to participate vicariously in a product-related fantasy. In 1923, just four years after its gentle, impressionistic advertisement appeared, Eaton's Highland Linen writing paper released a more "modern" ad that featured an image of two well-dressed women whispering as a third woman walks away. The startling caption directly questions the audience: "Would you criticize a Friend behind her back?" The text of the advertisement equated a woman's inferior writing paper with her overall lack of taste and careless disregard for others. Purchasing Eaton's Highland Linen paper, the ad reassured consumers, would prevent such "embarrassing situations" from ever occurring.[5] Advertisements such as this one essentially encouraged American consumers to judge themselves and each other based not on strength of character but rather on the brand-name products they purchased.

During the 1920s, the admen who designed such advertising campaigns were, in fact, mostly men, but about 10 percent of advertising professionals were women. Although few women occupied powerful executive positions, large numbers of them worked as assistants or as copywriters. Nevertheless, a handful of women did attain unusual heights, including Helen Woodward, a copywriter and executive who admitted, in 1926, that "to be a really good copywriter requires a passion for converting the other fellow, even if it is to something you don't believe in yourself."[6] Many of the men who joined advertising firms were college graduates, and some had even earned degrees from the new business schools or advertising programs that flourished in the 1920s. For example, between 1920 and 1930, enrollment tripled in Harvard Business School's marketing, advertising, retailing, finance, management, and consumer psychology programs. Many of these university-trained advertisers gravitated toward the emerging field of market research and learned how to track consumer reactions to particular products and advertisements using statistics, surveys, and other systematic analytical methods.

Even as sophisticated and convincing advertising campaigns enchanted American consumers, some criticized the advertising industry as wasteful, misleading, and in some cases actually sinister. A 1925 article in *The New Republic* bemoaned the fact that for every dollar spent on advertising in the United States, only 70 cents was spent on education. Yet the writer went on to acknowledge that there was something hypnotic and attractive about the illusions that advertisements created—a dream world of "smiling faces, shining teeth, school girl complexions, cornless feet, perfect fitting union suits, distinguished collars, wrinkleless pants, odorless breaths, regularized bowels, happy homes in New Jersey (15 minutes from Hoboken), charging motors, punctureless tires, perfect busts, shimmering shanks, self-washing dishes—backs behind which the moon was meant to rise."[7] Advertisements promised they could provide a beautiful world full of creature comforts and gleaming new products, and American consumers desperately wanted to live in this world.

THE GOSPEL OF ADVERTISING

One of the most significant advertising-related publications of the 1920s was Bruce Barton's *The Man Nobody Knows: A Discovery of the Real Jesus* (1925), which remained on the non-fiction best-seller list for two years. Barton, a career salesman and copywriter who hawked everything from newspapers to shirt collars to safety razors, believed that the modern business ethos originated in the Christian gospel. His book, in fact, was a breezy philosophical argument about the close relationship between salesmanship and Christianity. Specifically, Barton claimed that Jesus Christ was the greatest salesman in the history of the world, and that he established Christianity in much the same way that a modern businessman launches a successful company. Barton cited Jesus' ability to pick effective colleagues (his 12 disciples), his simple but powerful use of language (the parables), and his commitment to lifelong service as indicators that Jesus was the forerunner of the modern salesman and corporate executive. *The Man Nobody Knows* seems to have appealed to readers largely because they found comfort in this connection, however tenuous, between Jesus and the rampant corporate capitalism and mass consumerism that engulfed American life during the 1920s. If Jesus was a salesman, went this logic, then modern advertising, marketing, and consumerism could be considered a form of Christian devotion.

Another important figure in the developing field of modern advertising was Dale Carnegie, a distinguished business management consultant. During the 1920s, Carnegie toured the nation, giving lectures to businesspeople about how best to present oneself, manage groups of people, and manipulate them into doing whatever one desired. He emphasized that one's personality was the key to success and told his followers to "believe that you will succeed, and you will."[8] Carnegie understood the importance of making a positive impression, as well as how crafting a particular impression can lead to success and profit. Many of the techniques that Carnegie advocated became pillars of the modern advertising industry and formed the basis of his perennial best-selling book, *How to Win Friends and Influence People*, published in 1936.

ADVERTISING STRATEGIES

By the 1920s, advertisers and retailers were perfectly aware that while men were ordinarily the primary wage earners in their families, women did most of the actual purchasing. As a result, a considerable percentage of advertising in the 1920s targeted female consumers. Print advertisements by the hundreds appeared in the mass-circulation women's magazines of the day, such as *Ladies' Home Journal* and *Good Housekeeping*, touting everything from food products, clothing, and electric kitchen appliances to cosmetics, anti-aging creams, and weight-loss regimens. Many advertisers appealed to women by suggesting that buying a certain product would make them better wives and mothers. Some print ads blatantly correlated the intensity of a mother's love with the purchase of a particular brand of soup or toothpaste or detergent, suggesting in no uncertain terms that choosing a rival product would jeopardize the health or safety of one's children. Other companies tempted homemakers with promises that buying their products would streamline meal preparation and lighten their domestic workload. Refrigerator manufacturers, for example, spent approximately $20 million a year on advertising by 1931 in an effort to bring new electric refrigerators into every American home. One advertisement for a General Electric refrigerator included a testimonial from a housewife who claimed earnestly that "the thing that appeals to me most is the way it has cut my housekeeping job. I only market twice a week now, because I have plenty of space and just the right temperature to keep all sorts of foods in perfect condition. . . . Cooking has become easier, too. Desserts which used to be the most difficult part of the dinner to prepare, now are beautifully simple—and ever so much more attractive."[9]

One of the most successful and ubiquitous advertising techniques during the 1920s was the relentless appeal to modernity. Modernity equaled progress, and when it came to the latest automobile model, washing machine, or hat, whatever was new was often seen as automatically desirable. The Campbell Soup Company, for example, exhorted homemakers to try its lines of condensed soups because opening a can was not only fast and easy but also the "modern way of 'making' soup." Other advertisements warned consumers that appearing old-fashioned or outdated could actually result in some personal tragedy—anything from losing a suitor to losing a job to losing one's self-respect. An advertisement paid for by the Association of Laundry Owners, captioned with the question, "Just what is it to be A Good Wife in this Modern Age?" urged women to send their clothes out to be cleaned rather than do it themselves. Doing so created the leisure time women supposedly needed to be "a truly good wife—a worthy companion of the twentieth century husband." Johnson's Baby Powder proudly (if cryptically) announced, "You modern mothers have set your babies free!" by using its particular brand of talcum powder. And Sealex Linoleums, which associated fashionable clothing with fashionable home decor, pictured a slim young woman in an attractive dress standing on a colorful linoleum floor. Next to the picture, a caption read: "Floors that match Smart, Modern Clothes."[10] Evidently, one's home, as well as one's clothes, needed to be fashionable and coordinated before one could be considered thoroughly modern.

THE SATURDAY EVENING POST 143

Do wives think differently today?

Changing habits prove they do

DOESN'T it seem only yesterday that wives were so busy with household cares that they found but little time for anything else?

How different is the new order that has been ushered in. Today, your wife finds opportunity to vary her interests . . . to be a companion to your children . . . to study closer your welfare. She has won a new freedom and happiness in her daily life.

What has brought about this change? Your wife will tell you . . . thinking differently . . . thinking of housekeeping in much the same terms as you think of your business problems . . . discarding time-worn ideas and old-fashioned methods in favor of a new-day efficiency in home management.

Whenever wives meet, these modern methods of homekeeping are discussed. Particularly, do they speak of how one important problem—that of food buying—has been simplified.

No longer do you find these women visiting store after store in search of goodness and value in foodstuffs. They confine their purchases to the one store which experience has taught them provides both the good foods and the good values they seek.

Daily they go to the A & P, knowing that a few minutes spent selecting foods solves what was formerly a vexing problem. For A & P's shelves are filled with the finest foods that a great world-wide buying organization can secure . . . nationally advertised brands . . . the choicest imported luxuries . . . foods locally famous. And women have learned that substantial savings go hand in hand with this quality.

This changing habit in food buying—the result of wives thinking differently today—is nation-wide in scope. Like guideposts along the highways, A & P stores everywhere point the way to good foods and good values.

At the A & P she is sure to find the popular, nationally advertised brands of groceries.

THE GREAT ATLANTIC & PACIFIC TEA COMPANY

Advertisement for A&P Grocery Stores, *The Saturday Evening Post*, July 14, 1928.

Advertisers also exploited a different aspect of modernity—the intense anxiety that some Americans experienced in response to a faster-paced lifestyle, mass consumerism, intrusive technologies, and the erosion of long-standing traditional values. Although "progress" was largely heralded as positive and healthy, certain aspects of modern life did seem overwhelming to ordinary Americans, regardless of how much they enjoyed wearing the latest style of dress or cooking with the newest electric stove. "Anti-modern" advertisements for products that were intended to reduce stress and tension filled magazines and newspapers. For example, one Post Bran Flakes advertisement featured a picture of a harried businessman rushing to work. This cereal, the ad suggested, promoted good health and regularity despite living a modern life characterized by the daily hassle of "[g]etting up by the alarm clock; racing through our meals; hurrying from this appointment to that as though our lives depended on it."[11]

Advertisers also helped to fuel the 1920s trend of worshiping youthfulness in all its forms. Fashions, particularly women's fashions, emphasized a slim, youthful figure, and the cosmetics industry boomed as millions of American women proved willing to try all sorts of products that promised to restore the eyes, hair, and skin of their younger years. The advertising industry capitalized on this trend by generating ads that appealed to consumers' desires to prevent and even reverse the aging process. For example, one 1928 advertisement for Lysol disinfectant, which appeared in *Ladies' Home Journal*, pictured two fashionable young women, clad in smart cloche hats and fur-trimmed coats, glancing back at a couple who has just walked past them. One woman comments cattily to the other, "She looks old enough to be his mother," and the advertisement's copy goes on to explain how this unfortunate woman, who is actually five years younger than her husband, has succumbed to the ravages of age by not relying on Lysol for her feminine hygiene needs. The ad sadly notes that "in this enlightened age, so often a woman has only herself to blame if she fails to stay young with her husband and with her woman friends." Likewise, an ad campaign for Palmolive soap exploited the notion that women of all ages sought to "keep that schoolgirl complexion" and that Palmolive soap provided the foundation of "modern beauty culture."[12]

Using another pervasive and effective strategy, advertisers of the 1920s also traded on consumers' deepest insecurities. Listerine mouthwash ads emblazoned with the questions, "Are you sure about yourself?" and "What secret is your mirror holding back?" caused readers to consider seriously the relative sweetness of their own breath.[13] Heartrending stories of the lonely spinster who was denied a chance at marital bliss or the lovely girl who lacked a suitor all concluded that chronic halitosis could be a primary source of women's misery. These overt suggestions that sour breath led inevitably to loneliness and unhappiness motivated many shoppers to purchase bottles of Listerine. Deodorant advertisements, such as ones for Odor-o-no, pointed out that unpleasant underarm odor might also be a serious impediment to romance. These convincing advertisements prompted consumers to purchase the product despite its harshness and inconvenience—the red paste actually ate into fabric and often irritated the skin, and users had to hold their arms up in the air for 10 minutes after applying Odor-o-no so it could dry. Scott Tissue launched a particularly striking fear-mongering campaign in 1928, which portrayed a doctor and a nurse in surgical masks looking down on an unseen patient, presumably on an operating table. The large print reads, "[A]nd the trouble began with harsh toilet tissue." The ad goes on to explain how "rectal trouble" is often caused and always exacerbated by inferior toilet tissue and that women should trust their family's health and safety only to Scott's brand of tissue.[14]

While such advertisements played on consumers' concerns about poor hygiene issues such as bad breath or body odor, others focused on more abstract anxieties about being humiliated in public or being harshly judged by others. Book companies selling collections of literary masterpieces, for example, suggested that without the knowledge included in these volumes, readers would surely bore their guests at parties and ultimately be ostracized from their social set. An ad for the Cleanliness Institute of New York showed a worried mother looking out the window at a group of children playing outside. The caption reads, "What do the neighbors think of *her* children?" and implies that grubby children are a reflection of their parents and that "people have a way of associating unclean clothes and faces with other questionable characteristics." Another advertisement, this one for Wonder Bread, insinuated that people were secretly whispering about one woman's husband, who "always ate in town. Tasteless 'bargain bread' was to blame," claimed the ad, but as soon as the wife bought a loaf of Wonder Bread, her husband's desire to head downtown for supper vanished (as did, one supposes, the malicious gossip).[15]

While many of these campaigns expressly targeted women, others exploited men's insecurities. An advertisement for Gillette razor blades showed a picture of a dismayed-looking man, surrounded by disembodied, accusing eyes, along with the caption, "I was never so embarrassed in my life." The copy explained how this man, who had skipped his morning shave, "would rather take a beating" than risk losing the respect of his peers by appearing in public with stubble on his face. Williams Luxury Shaving Cream announced in one of its ads the alarming news that "Critical Eyes are sizing you up right now," so "keep your face fresh, firm, fit" by shaving with its brand-name product. Another male-oriented advertisement, this one for the Equitable Life Assurance Society

124 THE SATURDAY EVENING POST August 18, 1928

DON'T FOOL YOURSELF

Since halitosis never announces itself to the victim, you simply cannot know when you have it.

Halitosis makes you unpopular

It is inexcusable . . . . . . can be instantly remedied.

NO matter how charming you may be or how fond of you your friends are, you cannot expect them to put up with halitosis (unpleasant breath) forever. They may be nice to you—but it is an effort.

Don't fool yourself that you never have halitosis as do so many self-assured people who constantly offend this way.

Read the facts in the lower right-hand corner and you will see that your chance of escape is slight. Nor should you count on being able to detect this ailment in yourself. Halitosis doesn't announce itself. You are seldom aware you have it.

Recognizing these truths, nice people end any chance of offending by systematically rinsing the mouth with Listerine. Every morning. Every night. And between times when necessary, especially before meeting others.

Keep a bottle handy in home and office for this purpose.

Listerine ends halitosis instantly. Being antiseptic, it strikes at its commonest cause—fermentation in the oral cavity. Then, being a powerful deodorant, it destroys the odors themselves.

If you have any doubt of Listerine's powerful deodorant properties, make this test: Rub a slice of onion on your hand. Then apply Listerine clear. Immediately, every trace of onion odor is gone. Even the strong odor of fish yields to it. Lambert Pharmacal Company, St. Louis, Mo., U. S. A.

The new baby—
LISTERINE SHAVING CREAM
—you've got a treat ahead of you.
TRY IT

READ THE FACTS
1/3 had halitosis

68 hairdressers state that about every third woman, many of them from the wealthy classes, is halitoxic. Who should know better than they?

LISTERINE
The safe antiseptic

Advertisement for Listerine, *The Saturday Evening Post*, August 18, 1928.

of the United States, addressed many Americans' fears of being submerged in a homogeneous mass society. It pictures a man standing far above an enormous throng of similarly dressed men, while the reassuring caption below reads, "You're NOT just one of a crowd."[16]

Despite anxieties about being overwhelmed by the powerful forces of modern life, not all Americans needed to be told that they were unique individuals. Indeed, some successful advertising campaigns took the opposite approach and appealed to consumers based on their perceived need to hop on the proverbial bandwagon. The Campbell Soup Company, for example, launched a series of ads during the 1920s for canned pork-and-beans that claimed, "America overwhelmingly prefers these pork-and-beans." The advertising copy goes on to explain that "Years ago tastes for beans varied in different parts of the country. Certain sections were justly proud of the way they cooked and served them. But today there's no doubt whatever about the pork-and-beans the whole country prefers."[17] Rather than see the homogenization of national cuisine as a disadvantage, advertisers urged consumers to take comfort in the fact that millions of Americans could not be wrong, and so choosing what the masses chose was a wise decision.

By the 1920s, advertisements employed every psychological strategy imaginable to appeal to consumers' dreams, fears, aspirations, and identities. Some ads traded on "snob appeal," intimating that only consumers of wealth, culture, and class would be interested in, or even deserved to own, such a tasteful product. Images of elegant people in stylish clothes, admiring a new refrigerator or zipping about town in a new roadster, conveyed a certain level of upper-class respectability and sophistication. Other advertisements offered scientific information and medical advice or even warned about the hazards of unsanitary conditions. For example, one Hoover vacuum ad carried the alarming caption: "Dirty Rugs Are Dangerous—How Do You Clean Yours?"[18] Other advertisements appealed to American consumers' desires to improve their minds and to embrace modern lifestyles. In short, sophisticated, if not subtle, psychological approaches fueled much of the print advertising of the 1920s.

SPOKESPERSONS

Although celebrity endorsements of consumer products were not new in the 1920s, they carried considerable weight in a nation highly attuned to the behaviors of its favorite movie stars and sports idols. When Hollywood sex symbol Clara Bow lent her name to a line of hats, for example, or football hero Red Grange's image appeared on a candy bar, American consumers paid attention—and bought. Lucky Strikes cigarettes launched a highly effective celebrity endorsement campaign in the late 1920s that combined Americans' fears of being overweight with their desires to emulate their beloved stars. The American Tobacco Company, the cigarette's manufacturer, hired famous actors, singers, athletes, and even military heroes, sometimes for thousands of dollars, to recommend that consumers watch their figures and "Reach for a Lucky instead of a sweet." As smoking became increasingly popular among women, advertisements carried testimonials from famous women such as aviator Amelia Earhart and actress Constance Talmadge. Lucky Strikes touted its cigarettes as "[t]he modern way to diet! Light a Lucky when fattening sweets tempt you. . . . The delicately toasted flavor of Luckies is more than a substitute for fattening sweets—it satisfies the appetite without harming the digestion."[19]

Advertisers soon realized that while consumers found celebrity endorsements appealing, spokespersons need not be famous. In fact, they need not even be real. A popular advertising gimmick of the 1920s was to invent an imaginary figure, usually a woman, to function as a spokesperson for a particular product or company. In 1921, the advertising department of the Washburn-Crosby Company created a fictional model homemaker and nutrition expert named Betty Crocker for use in an advertising campaign promoting its Gold Medal flour. She was so named by combining a popular woman's name, "Betty," with the surname of the retired company director, William G. Crocker. Originally, the company used Betty Crocker's name to sign letters written in response to the thousands of requests it received each year from homemakers seeking baking advice. Her signature, company executives believed, offered a more personal and authoritative touch to these letters, and a secretary who had won a handwriting contest among the company's female employees supplied Betty Crocker's signature. The Washburn-Crosby Company soon began to publish cookbooks under her name and established the Betty Crocker Kitchens, in which a team of home economists tested and created recipes that called for the use of the company's Gold Medal flour. By the late 1920s, many fictitious spokespersons were endorsing brand-name products. The Postum Company invented Carrie Blanchard, who received thousands of letters from fans. And Libby Foods created Mary Hale Martin, whose name was signed to advice columns in Libby's advertisements as well as to "personal replies" sent in response to consumers' letters.

ADVERTISING AND RACE

Unfortunately, not all company spokespeople were as culturally inoffensive as Betty Crocker. Since the late nineteenth century, advertisers had tapped into familiar Old South racial stereotypes to sell their products. Images of happy, docile African-American servants eager to serve their masters (i.e., the consumers) proliferated on brand-name packaging of the 1890s and endured well into the 1920s and beyond. Among the best known of these fictional spokespersons were Aunt Jemima, a "mammy" figure who advertised self-rising pancake flour for the Davis Milling Company (later acquired by the Quaker Oats Company), and Rastus, the black chef featured on Nabisco's Cream of Wheat box. Interestingly, both of these figures still appear on packaging today; although Aunt Jemima has lost her headkerchief in the process of being "updated," the image of Rastus remains virtually unchanged. Other popular racial stereotypes employed in advertising during the 1920s were the Gold Dust Twins—two little black children ("pickaninnies") who appeared on Gold Dust soap powder labels. With the servile slogan "Let the Gold Dust Twins Do Your Work," these twins became synonymous with the product they represented, and they came to life between 1923 and 1926, when white actors impersonating the twins starred in *The Gold Dust Twins,* a musical-variety program broadcast on WEAF, New York.

During the 1920s, Aunt Jemima and Rastus were particularly visible brand-name characters designed to appeal to white consumers who found comfort in old-timey images of happy, non-threatening black domestics who "knew their place" and served their white employers with a smile. A brief, fictionalized biography of Aunt Jemima, which appeared in a 1920 *Saturday Evening Post* advertisement, actually described a supposed 1864 encounter she had with a Confederate general, during which she prepared him a heaping plate of her delicious pancakes. Cream of Wheat ads featured Rastus dressed in white chef's apparel, grinning delightedly as he served white children steaming bowls of cereal. Despite efforts by African-American leaders to combat these insidious slave-oriented stereotypes, advertisers continued to rely on Aunt Jemima and Rastus to sell brand-name products to American consumers.

PUBLICITY STUNTS

Traditional advertising strategies convinced millions of American consumers to purchase particular brand-name products, but some companies also relied upon attention grabbing and often bizarre publicity stunts to sell their goods. One popular publicity stunt was the look-alike contest, which attracted crowds of people who dressed up like Jackie Coogan, the child star, or Charlie Chaplin, the "Little Tramp," often in exchange for complimentary movie tickets. In 1927 Douglas Fairbanks and Mary Pickford participated in a famous publicity stunt when they became the first movie stars to plant their footprints in the wet cement on the sidewalk in front of Grauman's Chinese Theater in Hollywood.

Charlie Chaplin look-alike contest to promote the film *The Idle Class* at the Liberty Theater, Bellingham, Washington, 1921. Courtesy of the J. W. Sandison Collection, Whatcom Museum of History and Art, Bellingham, Washington.

Over the years, dozens of other celebrities have been invited to add their handprints or footprints to the "Walk of Fame" lining the sidewalk on Hollywood Boulevard, and this tradition lives on to this day.

Even before Charles Lindbergh's historic transatlantic flight in 1927, aviation-related events attracted extensive media coverage. Ballyhoo men hired pilots to fly airplanes towing promotional banners, and clever businesspeople tried to find new ways to capitalize on the advertising potential offered by the airplane. In 1923, for example, Otto Schnering, the owner of the Curtiss Candy Company, hired a pilot to drop thousands of his new Baby Ruth candy bars, each attached to a tiny parachute, over the city of Pittsburgh, Pennsylvania. This promotional gimmick proved so successful that he later expanded his candy bar drops to metropolitan areas in 40 other states.

In 1924, Procter and Gamble launched the first Ivory soap carving competition, which became a tremendously successful and long-running advertising stunt. Thousands of people carved statues out of blocks of soap, and the winning sculptures toured the nation in a traveling exhibit, attracting even more attention for Ivory soap. Also in 1924, Macy's department store sponsored its first Thanksgiving Day parade. Originally called a Christmas parade, though held around Thanksgiving, the procession included floats and displays of all the latest toys, which, of course, were for sale in Macy's toy department. In 1927, the parade began to feature the familiar enormous helium balloons, with the first ones shaped like Felix the Cat and the Toy Soldier.

Another popular publicity stunt during the 1920s was flagpole sitting, and Alvin "Shipwreck" Kelly, a professional Hollywood stuntman, reigned as the undisputed king of flagpole sitters. In 1929, he perched atop a pole in Baltimore for 23 days and seven hours. The following year, he broke his own record by spending 49 days aloft above the Atlantic City, New Jersey, boardwalk. More often, though, he would balance on a flagpole as a paid publicity stunt for movie theaters, car dealerships, and other businesses. The large crowds that such an event attracted were full of potential customers, reasoned the business owners who hired Kelly, and the media coverage also drew attention to the sponsoring store or theater. Adventuresome teens and college students also participated in the craze, usually not to advertise a particular business but instead for the personal celebrity it briefly bestowed upon them.

ADVERTISING VENUES

Much of what made advertising so profitable in the 1920s was the industry's expansion in a range of influential venues. Magazines and newspapers provided the major print advertising outlets, just as they had in the 1890s, and the rapidly increasing circulations of the larger national publications provided retailers with the chance to advertise their brand-name products literally coast-to-coast. As the new medium of radio became more popular, companies broadcast their commercial messages over the nation's airwaves, but advertisers didn't stop there. Eye-catching billboards along roads and highways gave motorists the chance to learn about everything from the newest typewriter to the tastiest breakfast cereal. In 1925, the Burma-Vita Company launched its famous billboard advertising campaign for Burma-Shave shaving cream. The company's first billboards were erected in Minnesota, but soon Burma-Shave signs were dotting the roadways across the nation. Streetcar ads catered to the industrial laborers who rode the cars back and forth to work. Neon signs, first introduced in 1923, provided a modern, high-tech look that made it easier to advertise products at night. Department stores improved their window displays by hiring, for the first time, professional window dressers to present merchandise in appealing and creative ways. Comic strip characters hawked dolls and toys in the pages of the "funny papers," presaging the consumer tie-ins we see today between animated cartoons and children's toys. Small-scale advertising also continued apace, as hired boys walked the streets of cities and towns wearing sandwich boards to promote a restaurant's lunch special or a department store's big sale. Giant corporations sponsored early "commercials" that ran in motion picture theaters before feature presentations. Even architecture itself became a form of advertising, as roadside restaurants developed unique architectural designs to catch the attention of passing motorists. A coffee shop in the shape of an enormous coffee pot or an ice cream stand built to resemble a giant milk bottle was sure to attract customers. Overall, advertising in the 1920s was distinctive not just for its sophisticated approaches to salesmanship but also for its creative ventures into diverse advertising venues.

Print Advertisements

The most popular and powerful national print advertising venue during the 1920s was the mass-circulation magazines, which, by the end of the decade, collectively sold more than 200 million copies a year. Magazine publishers quickly realized that profits lay not in subscription charges or newsstand revenues but in the sale of valuable advertising space. *The Saturday Evening Post*, *Ladies' Home Journal*, *Collier's Weekly*, *Life*, *Vanity Fair*, and *Scribner's* all sold for about one-fourth to one-fifth the actual cost of printing them, yet their publishers raked in enormous profits from the automobile, cigarette, cosmetics, clothing, and food manufacturers that purchased full-page ads in each issue. In 1917, for example, *The Saturday Evening Post*'s circulation was just under 1.9 million and generated advertising revenues of about $16 million. By 1928, circulation had risen by about 50 percent (to about 2.8 million), but advertising revenues had increased 300 percent (to more than $48 million).[20] Women's magazines alone, including popular publications such as *Ladies' Home Journal, Good Housekeeping,* and *McCall's,* earned more than $75 million in advertising revenues in 1928.

As advertisers strove to distinguish their clients' brand-name products from those of their competitors, print advertisements in magazines became more eye-catching and colorful. Few photographic images appeared in advertisements in the early 1920s, but by the end of the decade, the reliance on photography, including art photography, increased dramatically. As late as 1924, more than three-quarters of the advertisements in most popular magazines were still printed solely in black-and-white. However, during the mid-1920s, the production of color advertisements rose significantly. The Coca-Cola Company, for example, ran four-color magazine ads and billboard posters, employing slogans such as "Enjoy Thirst," "Refreshment Time," "It Had to be Good to Get Where It Is," and "The Best-Served Drink in the World." In 1929, Coca-Cola's advertising department created its legendary slogan, "The Pause That Refreshes," which first appeared in a series of advertisements in *The Saturday Evening Post.*

Daily newspapers represented another important advertising venue, but newspaper ads tended to be smaller and less elaborate than magazine ads. Nevertheless, newspapers did aid advertisers and retailers by promoting local businesses and sales. Grocery stores were one of the primary industries to capitalize on daily newspaper advertisements. In the early 1920s, the Kroger grocery store chain began printing its weekly food prices and special sales in newspapers; by the end of the decade, this practice became widespread in the grocery industry. In fact, by 1929 the manufacturers of drugs, toiletries, food, and beverages spent more money on newspaper ads than did any other industry.

Radio Advertisements

At the beginning of the 1920s, the radio industry was still in its infancy. Radio hobbyists listened to crystal sets with earphones, and few if any Americans had any inkling that this new medium would not only become a powerful force in our nation's popular culture but also generate, within a very few years, millions of dollars in annual advertising revenue. As broadcast signals reached farther and farther, and radio's popularity soared, public opinion at first maintained that the airwaves were a public trust that should be kept free from commercial sponsorship. This, however, was not to remain the case for long. In 1922, a real-estate corporation became the first paid radio sponsor on WEAF, New York, signaling the advent of commercial radio advertising.

Initially, the commercial radio industry remained wary of alienating listeners who might find on-air advertisements intrusive and annoying. Print advertisers, who considered radio advertising unwelcome competition, also warned against cluttering the airwaves with unwanted commercial messages. Critics of radio advertising argued that listeners would directly support their favorite stations, and thus the stations themselves would need no advertising revenue. However, radio listeners resisted any plan that would force them to pay for a service currently provided free of charge. So, even though many early radio listeners no doubt found advertisements bothersome, there was little recourse for the general public. Commercial sponsorship had arrived, and it was here to stay.

Still, the radio broadcasting industry proceeded cautiously and for several years prohibited blatant "commercials" that directly offered or described merchandise. Rather, radio program sponsorship attempted merely to boost the name recognition of participating companies and their products. One common advertising practice was for companies to hire a band, orchestra, or other musical act to perform on a program named after the sponsor and then hope that listeners who enjoyed the show would also purchase the company's products. In 1923, for example, the New York chain of Happiness Candy Stores hired two popular recording and vaudeville stars, Billy Jones and Ernest Hare, to team up on radio as the Happiness Boys. Jones and Hare sang songs and told stories during their half-hour music-and-comedy program called *The Happiness Boys* and in doing so promoted Happiness candy. Beginning in 1923, the A&P chain of grocery stores sponsored a program called *The A&P Gypsies*, which featured a band that played distinctive and recognizable exotic music, first for New York listeners and then, after 1927, for nationwide audiences on the NBC network. By the mid-1920s, the Ipana Toothpaste Company was sponsoring *The Ipana Troubadours*, the B. F Goodrich Company was financing *The Goodrich Silvertown Orchestra*, and the Cliquot Club Ginger Ale Company was promoting *The Cliquot Club Eskimos*. The Eskimos soon evolved into a full-fledged dance orchestra and, as early as 1926, developed what is considered to be the first radio show theme song: "The Cliquot Foxtrot March."

Advertisers did not limit themselves to musical programs, however. As early as 1923, the National Carbon Company, the manufacturer of Eveready Batteries, struck upon an innovative strategy when it began to sponsor the first major radio variety show, *The Eveready Hour*. This hour-long program, which aired on WEAF in New York and featured a mixture of music, news, drama, and comedy, proved an immediate hit with radio audiences. In 1926, the NBC network picked up the show for

Billy Jones and Ernest Hare, better known as the Happiness Boys, at the microphone, 1923. Courtesy of the Library of Congress.

broadcast on more than 30 stations across the country. Top celebrities such as Will Rogers and D. W. Griffith made guest appearances, and regular cast members toured the nation to promote Eveready products. Between 1927 and 1928, Eveready spent $400,000 on the program, but its battery sales skyrocketed.

Radio advertisers quickly realized that women not only controlled the purse strings in most American homes but also made up the largest segment of the listening audience. Thus, radio advertisers soon devised strategies to appeal specifically to female consumers. Daytime radio programming catered to homemakers who listened to the radio while they cooked, cleaned, or washed. The first women's radio programs, sponsored by companies that produced items commonly purchased by homemakers, were largely instructional in nature. Daytime programs about cooking and sewing offered suggestions about incorporating a particular brand of food into one's menu planning or about using a particular company's clothing patterns to sew the latest fashionable dress. These programs frequently touted the reliable advice of their "experts," who taught ordinary women how better to shop, keep house, entertain company, and generally care for their families.

By the late 1920s, women listeners regularly tuned in to hear their favorite experts give advice about homemaking. A woman impersonating the fictional Betty Crocker had her own radio cooking show on the NBC network, during which she lauded the foodstuffs produced by her "inventor," the Washburn-Crosby Company (later General Mills). "Aunt Sammy," another fictional radio figure, offered opinions on everything from how to clean linoleum to how to cook a meatloaf. Her popular program, *The Housekeeper's Half-Hour* (later titled simply *Aunt Sammy*), was sponsored by the U.S. Department of Agriculture. Rather than promote particular brand-name products, Aunt Sammy passed along helpful hints and general information about scientific nutrition, cooking, and housekeeping. Ida Bailey Allen, a real dietician and cooking instructor, also attracted a wide audience of American housewives with *The National Radio Home-Makers' Club* program, during which she dispensed wisdom on nutrition, menus, and beauty. Unlike most other 1920s radio programs, which were supported by a single commercial sponsor, Allen's show was underwritten by several smaller companies, each of which funded only a portion of her entire program—one of radio's first examples of the "spot advertisements" that dominate commercial broadcasting today.

Not surprisingly, though, many listeners during the 1920s did in fact consider radio advertising a profound annoyance. Readers could merely turn the page to skip an unwelcome or irrelevant magazine advertisement, but radio listeners could seldom avoid hearing commercials. An illuminating 1920s cartoon that appeared in the pages of the *New York Herald Tribune* depicted a well-dressed lady in a radio store, trying to choose between a big radio and a much smaller set. In a comment that spoke volumes about radio listeners' aversion to on-air advertising, she asked the attentive salesman, "Would I get shorter commercials from that little one?"[21]

ADVERTISING SWINDLES

Despite the general success of modern advertising techniques, the advertising industry itself attracted a great deal of controversy. Advertisers struggled to achieve respectability among other professionals, who often derided admen as mere hucksters and charlatans. This kind of low public opinion led, in 1911, to the founding of the Associated Advertising Clubs of America, which launched the "Truth-in-Advertising" movement. The movement marked the industry's first attempt to regulate itself, to minimize occurrences of consumer fraud, and to enhance its credibility with the American public. Advertisers felt compelled to assuage public fears that their industry would stop at nothing to sell products and that promotional claims were often purposefully misleading and not necessarily rooted in fact or science. The movement's immediate targets consisted of loan sharks, real-estate speculators, and other confidence men who knowingly swindled their customers. Perhaps not surprisingly, well-established corporations—regardless of how far their advertisements strayed from the truth—were seldom prosecuted.

Despite the good intentions of the Associated Advertising Clubs of America, advertising swindles bilked tens of thousands of Americans out of their life savings during the 1920s. One of the most notorious swindlers was the Italian immigrant Carlo "Charles" Ponzi, who launched his most famous fraudulent business scheme in Boston in December 1919. Ponzi claimed that he and his associates could make enormous sums of money for investors by taking advantage of favorable international monetary exchange rates. He promised his "clients" that he would return their capital investment, plus 50 percent, in fewer than 90 days; this get-rich-quick scheme suckered approximately 40,000 people into handing over anywhere from $10.00 to $50,000. He did manage to fulfill his promise to the first wave of investors, but, like all pyramid schemes, his investment business required increasing numbers of new investors to provide the money to pay off previous investors. Within a few months, Ponzi's whole scheme collapsed, and in August 1920, he was arrested for using the mails to defraud. Investigations revealed that more than $13 million of the $15 million he had collected had mysteriously disappeared. Soon Ponzi's name became synonymous with any pyramid scheme.

Ponzi was not the only unscrupulous salesman to take advantage of unsuspecting investors during the 1920s. Another costly investment debacle was the Florida land boom (and bust), which was actually just another Ponzi scheme. During the early 1920s, real-estate speculators purchased large tracts of land in Florida and built grand hotels and vacation homes in the hopes of luring middle-class American families (and their dollars) to the Sunshine State. Advertisers glamorized the image of life in Florida, and their ads enticed investors with stories of how easy it was to make money speculating in real estate. For the lucky ones, their investments paid off. Land bought in 1920 or 1921 could be sold to another investor in 1924 or 1925 at enormous profit—sometimes 100 times more than its original purchase price. In 1925, the *Miami Daily News* published a 504-page issue that consisted almost entirely of real-estate advertisements. Readers from across the nation, most of whom never had and never would set foot in Florida, sought out realtors who were all too happy to accept their downpayments by mail. Of course, this land boom could not last forever. By the mid-1920s, Florida land prices were so inflated that speculators could no longer sell their real estate at a profit, and buyers all but disappeared. To make matters worse, a devastating hurricane hit the Florida coast in 1926, destroying over 13,000 homes and killing nearly 400 people. The glamour of the Sunshine State faded in the minds of most Americans, and the Florida land boom came to an inglorious and unprofitable end.

CONCLUSION

The 1920s marked the era in which modern advertising came of age as a powerful and influential force in daily American life. By examining advertisements from this decade, we can learn a great deal about the aggressive advertising strategies that agencies used to sell products, as well as the enormous pressures these ads exerted on customers. However, magazine ads and radio commercials cannot tell us what items Americans actually purchased or what values Americans actually espoused. We cannot estimate, with any degree of certainty, how many women dressed in colors that matched their linoleum or really had their lives ruined by halitosis or inferior writing paper. We can understand, however, that mass consumer culture had taken an unprecedented hold on American life during the 1920s and that since then, this legacy of brand-name loyalty, buying on credit, and conspicuous consumption has remained an integral facet of daily life.

4

Architecture and Design

American architectural styles of the 1920s encompassed both traditionalism and modernism. On the one hand, old-fashioned designs still appealed to those architects and consumers who appreciated, for example, the classic beauty of colonial homes and Gothic office buildings. On the other hand, new architectural trends dramatically shaped many of the homes and commercial buildings constructed during the 1920s. Not every building, however, was either modern or old-fashioned. Certain examples of architecture from the decade artfully blended modern purposes with classical styles, such as the luxurious movie houses built to resemble ancient palaces, or White Castle hamburger restaurants housed in medieval-looking buildings. Thus, the architecture of the Jazz Age can best be described as a celebration of both the old and the new.

ARCHITECTURAL STYLES

Art Deco

During the 1920s and early 1930s, an eclectic design style emerged that later became known as Art Deco, a name derived from the 1925 Exposition Internationale des Arts Décoratifs et Industriels Modernes, held in Paris. The purpose of the exposition was to forge a relationship between art and industry, and although American architects did not directly participate in the event, its influence reverberated in the United States for decades to come. The exposition featured exhibits that combined industrial technology with earlier design styles, and the result was a stylized look that juxtaposed angular, geometric forms with designs found in nature, such as sunbursts, flowers, and stars. France remained the center of Art Deco innovation until the late 1920s, but American architects and designers soon began borrowing Art Deco themes to design everything from movie theaters and hotels to furniture and clothing. Bevis Hillier, a British art critic and historian, coined the term *Art Deco* in 1968. Prior to that, this style was often called Modernistic or Style Moderne.

Art Deco has evolved into a slippery, hard-to-define label that usually refers to a hodgepodge of elegant, sophisticated styles from the 1920s and 1930s, and it can describe any dramatic combination of modern technological styles and ancient artistic influences. Art Deco designs are often characterized by simplicity, dramatic geometry, and vibrant colors, and sometimes incorporate exotic patterns and iconography culled from Mayan and Aztec cultures, as well as from West Africa, India, and the Far East, and ancient Egypt, Greece, and Rome. The golden, jeweled treasures discovered when English archaeologist Howard Carter unearthed King Tutankhamen's tomb in 1922, for example, proved to be an important source of inspiration for Art Deco design. Art Deco became a fashionable style of design for the tiniest earrings, the tallest skyscrapers, and everything in between.

Some of the most enduring examples of Art Deco style are found in the American architecture of the 1920s. Architecture historians often divide the Art Deco period into two major categories: decorated Art Deco, popular primarily between 1926 and 1936, and streamline Art Deco, popular throughout the 1930s. While streamline Art Deco buildings look very simple, with rounded corners, small windows, and wide, smooth expanses of metal or glass, decorated Art Deco buildings tend to be highly ornamented with abstract, geometrical, or floral designs inspired by the 1925 exposition. Windows, doors, and rooflines are particular sites of Art Deco ornamentation. New York City's elaborate Chrysler Building, constructed between 1928 and 1930, remains perhaps the most famous American example of decorated Art Deco architecture from the 1920s.

The International Style

The International Style of architecture originated in Europe, but its influence pervaded the United States during the 1920s and 1930s. Its leaders included Walter Gropius, Ludwig Mies van der Rohe, and Charles-Edouard Jenneret (who went by the name Le Corbusier). Among the early American proponents of the International Style were architects Raymond M. Hood, Albert Kahn, Richard J. Neutra, and George Howe. The term *International Style* derived from a 1932 book called *The International Style* by historian and critic Henry-Russell Hitchcock and architect Philip Johnson. The book, along with the 1932 International

Exhibition of Modern Architecture at New York's Museum of Modern Art, generated widespread publicity for this style. Indeed, the International Style rose to become the dominant American architectural style of the twentieth century.

Although the International Style was not officially named until 1932, it exerted considerable influence on American architecture, particularly office buildings and skyscrapers, during the 1920s. Typically, International Style buildings emphasized an unornamented, simple functionality. They tended to be geometric and streamlined, with flat roofs and smooth facades, and were constructed primarily of inexpensive, mass-produced modern materials such as concrete, steel, and glass. Many International Style buildings resemble enormous boxes, which is essentially what they are. Even today, the skylines of American cities are cluttered with streamlined International Style banks and office buildings that lack any sort of superfluous decoration. Although some critics considered the look of International Style buildings boring and unimaginative, many architects saw beauty in the clean, crisp lines and sharp angles of these functional buildings. The Philadelphia Savings Fund Society Building, constructed between 1929 and 1932, represents one important example of 1920s International Style architecture in the United States.

SKYSCRAPERS

The advent of steel-framed structures in the late nineteenth century, combined with the invention of the modern gearless electric elevator, meant that buildings no longer had to be constructed like a pyramid in order to support their vertical thrust. The technology of steel skeletons and elevators ushered in a new era of towering urban structures, and no buildings represent more fully the dramatic changes and sweeping optimism of Jazz Age America than these majestic skyscrapers that reached toward the clouds in cities across the United States. By 1929, the nation counted 377 skyscrapers taller than 20 stories, and half of them (188) soared over the streets of New York City.[1] Flourishing corporations contracted ambitious, imaginative architects to design huge office buildings that reflected, in their eyes, the triumph of American business. Skyscrapers also served as magnificent symbols of a particular company's innovation and power. As a result, old buildings were razed and new landmarks were erected, including New York's Barclay-Vesey Building (1923–1927), the McGraw-Hill Building (1929–1930), the Chrysler Building (1928–1930), and the American Standard Building (1923–1924); Chicago's Tribune Tower (1922–1925); and San Francisco's Pacific Telephone and Telegraph Building (1924–1925). These colossal structures emerged from the ground as if to declare to the entire world the spectacular success of American business.

As new skyscrapers vied for the title of tallest building in various cities, Americans became increasingly attracted to the ever-rising skylines of the urban landscape. Indeed, much of the attraction of skyscrapers lay in their awe-inspiring appearance, for seldom did they garner immediate profits for their owners. Designing and building a skyscraper was tremendously expensive, and once constructed, the rents paid by the tower's tenants often barely covered the elevator and maintenance costs. Nevertheless, the psychological appeal of these massive towers proved irresistible, and dozens of skyscrapers were designed and planned during the boom years of the 1920s, although many were not actually built or completed until the 1930s.

An important turning point for American skyscraper design came in 1922, when the Chicago Tribune Company sponsored a design competition for the construction of a new office tower. The owner of the *Tribune*, Colonel Robert R. McCormick, offered a prize of $50,000 for the most beautiful and functional design, and the contest drew 281 entries from around the world. The winners were Americans John Mead Howells and Raymond M. Hood, who designed a huge Gothic tower topped by a tall, narrow spire. The architectural world, however, was far more enchanted by the second-place entry, submitted by the Finnish architect Eliel Saarinen (the father of architect Eero Saarinen, who later designed St. Louis' Gateway Arch). Eliel Saarinen envisioned a building that looked almost like a mountain—it was far less ornate than Howells and Hood's design—and instead of thrusting straight upward, its crown looked more like a gently tapering pyramid. Although the Howells-Hood design was chosen (and the building was completed in 1925), Saarinen's design exerted a more powerful influence on future American skyscraper design.

The Philadelphia Savings Fund Society Building (1929–1932), often considered the first truly modern American skyscraper, incorporated the sleek geometry of the European-influenced International Style. Designed by the American George Howe and the Swiss William Lescaze, the building combined modern style with urban practicality. It housed a number of small shops on the ground floor, with the banking floors rising above it and offices above that. The Philadelphia Savings Fund Society Building was only the second skyscraper in the nation to offer air-conditioning as a standard feature in its rental property and was one of the first constructed with a dropped ceiling of acoustical tile.

Stylistically, skyscrapers of the 1920s varied widely. Some skyscrapers featured crowns that resembled terraced pyramids, while others were flat-roofed, rectangular slabs. Architects who designed skyscrapers in New York City also had to contend with the city's 1916 zoning ordinance that, to prevent tall buildings from blocking too much sunlight from the streets below, required building walls progressively to set back from the building line as they rose from the base. When the setback building had

Building construction in St. Louis, Missouri. Courtesy of the State Historical Society of Missouri, Columbia.

been reduced to one-quarter of the size of the entire site, the building could continue to rise upward without getting any smaller. Architects responded to this ordinance by designing buildings that tapered toward the top, in a stair-step or ziggurat fashion, thus admitting plenty of sunlight to the surrounding city blocks. Although city laws imposed no actual limitations on the height of a skyscraper, the required setbacks effectively constrained building heights because, after a certain point, it was no longer economical to build tall, thin buildings with limited commercial space on the upper floors.

The most famous skyscraper designed during the 1920s was New York City's Empire State Building. Standing at the corner of Fifth Avenue and 34th Street, the Empire State Building, begun in 1930 and completed in 1931, incorporated striking Gothic styles and plenty of elaborate outside detailing, including a mast intended for mooring dirigibles (the mast was never used for this purpose, and in later years it served as a television antenna). In many respects, though, it is remarkable that the 1,250-foot, 102-story Empire State Building—at the time the tallest building in the world—was ever constructed at all. In October 1929, only one month after the plans for the project were approved, the Wall Street stock market crashed. As a result of the severely depressed economy, builders drastically compressed the construction schedule—the entire structure was completed in only 410 days and came in well below its estimated $50 million budget. Although the outside of the building boasts intricate Art Deco detailing, the inside of the skyscraper is comparatively simple. One exception, however, is the lobby, which is lined with 10,000 square feet of marble and contains a huge brass relief image of the building that is inscribed with the words "The Eighth Wonder of the World."

Clad in gleaming stainless steel, the 1,046-foot, 77-story Chrysler Building, the headquarters of the Chrysler Corporation, is another notable example of Art Deco architecture as well as an important New York City landmark. Designed by architect William Van Alen, the building briefly ranked as the world's tallest man-made structure. The Chrysler Building did not resemble the modern architectural style of the Philadelphia Savings Fund Society Building, but it was nevertheless thought extremely modern in its construction, decor, and operation. The building boasted an innovative heating system and 32 high-speed elevators, inlaid with dozens of exotic woods from around the world. No two elevators were alike. The ornamentation on the outside of the Chrysler Building reflected the new technology of the automobile, with enormous decorative car wheels, radiator caps, and steel eagle gargoyles—replicas of the 1929 Chrysler hood ornament. The spire on top emerged from shiny crescent-shaped steps designed to resemble a silver sunburst—a very popular Art Deco motif.

The crown of the Chrysler Building, New York City. Courtesy of the Library of Congress.

CHURCHES AND TEMPLES

The impressive new skyscrapers that soared above the nation's cities belonged not only to large corporations but to religious organizations as well. The 1920s saw the advent of a new trend in American church architecture: the skyscraper church. These high-rise houses of worship were designed so that the bottom few floors were devoted to the church itself, while the upper floors were reserved for offices and apartments. The revenue collected each month from renting the upper floors helped to finance the operation of the church below. One of the more impressive skyscraper churches was the Chicago Temple of the First Methodist Episcopal Church, completed in 1924. This 568-foot skyscraper cost $4 million and was, at its completion, both the tallest church in the world and the tallest building in Chicago. The lower five floors comprised the 2,000-seat church, along with a gymnasium and a number of classrooms and meeting rooms. Atop the church's spire sat an illuminated revolving cross that could be seen from four different states. The floors in between the church and the spire were rented to various companies that found it made good business sense to set up shop in this highly visible, widely advertised church building. Other skyscraper churches were erected in Detroit, San Francisco, Minneapolis, and several other major cities. The Northwest Methodist Temple in Minneapolis, for example, generated revenue from a hotel that occupied one entire wing and most of the building's 300-foot tower. These skyscraper churches combined traditional religious devotion with the new cult of American business prosperity.

Of course, not every church constructed during the 1920s was a skyscraper. In fact, church architects were, for the most part, particularly slow to adapt to architectural innovations, and the majority of churches constructed during the 1920s featured more traditional Gothic, Roman Classic, Baroque, or Georgian styles. For example, the Third Church of Christ, Scientist (1920–1923), on Park Avenue in New York City, resembled a Roman temple, and All Souls' Unitarian Church in Washington, D.C. (1923), was built in classic Georgian style. And some churches in the West and Southwest, such as St. Vincent de Paul Catholic Church in Los Angeles (1925), adopted architectural styles derived from Spanish traditions.

UNIVERSITY, GOVERNMENT, AND INDUSTRIAL ARCHITECTURE

The construction of college and university buildings soared in the United States during the 1920s, as enrollment in higher education increased. Between 1920 and 1930, the number of students enrolled in the nation's colleges and universities nearly doubled, from approximately 600,000 to almost 1.2 million students.[2] Clearly, more classroom buildings were needed to accommodate such a flood of undergraduates (and their accompanying tuition dollars). Wealthy industrialists and businessmen helped to meet this need by lavishing money on educational institutions to construct new buildings, dormitories, and libraries. Giving money to universities made fiscal sense to prosperous Americans, because the federal government considered universities to be non-profit institutions, and thus all donations were tax-deductible.

Although several major institutions of higher learning were actually founded during the 1920s, many existing colleges and universities also expanded their campuses during the decade. Much of this university construction incorporated older, more traditional styles rather than the new look of Art Deco or International Style architecture. For example, the Harkness Quadrangle at Yale University, designed by James Gamble Rogers in the Beaux-Arts Gothic style, added a dramatic focus to the campus when it was built in 1921. The Harvard Business School's design competition in 1925 led to a cluster of new red-brick Georgian buildings. In 1924, James B. Duke, the founder of the American Tobacco Company, established a $40 million endowment to create Duke University in Durham, North Carolina, on the site of what was formerly a small school called Trinity College. The Duke family spent $19 million rebuilding the old campus and adding 11 Georgian-style buildings, made of red brick and white marble, between 1925 and 1927. This campus housed the undergraduate college for women. And between 1927 and 1930, a brand-new campus, built in the Tudor Gothic style out of native North Carolina stone, was constructed one mile to the west of the original campus to house the undergraduate college for men and the professional schools.

Federal, state, and local governments also spent some of their tax revenues to construct impressive new monuments, courthouses, and office buildings. Architect Bertram Grosvenor Goodhue's innovative 1920 design for the Nebraska State Capitol included a 400-foot tower rising from a low, square base. Construction was completed in 1928 (eight years after Goodhue's death) at a cost of just under $10 million. Washington, D.C.'s famous Lincoln Memorial (1920–1922) was designed by architect Henry Bacon in the classic Greek architectural tradition and featured a sculpture of a seated President Lincoln by noted American sculptor Daniel Chester French. Constructed entirely of white marble, the monument is surrounded by 36 Doric columns that represent the 36 states that were members of the Union at the time of Lincoln's assassination. The 1920s also saw the federal government commission the construction of a new building for the Department of Commerce. In 1929, President Herbert Hoover, the former secretary of commerce during the Coolidge administration, himself laid the cornerstone for the building, which, when completed in 1932, was the largest office building in the world.

During the 1920s, the innovative design of new manufacturing plants simultaneously increased the productivity of these factories and affected the ways that millions of American workers performed their jobs. Automobile tycoon Henry Ford was only one of the American industrialists who sought to incorporate the most modern design elements into his factories. Industrial architect Albert Kahn designed the Ford Motor Company's enormous River Rouge plant (constructed between 1918 and 1926) on the outskirts of Detroit, Michigan, which dramatically improved upon previous designs of manufacturing plants. Unlike earlier automobile factories, which were dark, cramped, and inefficient, Kahn developed well-proportioned, bright, and efficient plants, which took into account how assembly lines functioned, at the 2,200-acre River Rouge complex. The entire complex was self-sufficient and contained everything necessary for the production of automobiles, including blast furnaces, steel mills, foundries, an engine plant, a glass factory, a tire plant, and its own power generators. Other automobile manufacturers, including General Motors, soon followed suit by constructing similarly modern plants.

RESTAURANTS

During the 1920s, restaurant architecture, especially the interiors of lunchrooms and cafeterias, reflected the modern styles of the Machine Age. While lunchrooms and cafeterias were often located in larger downtown buildings of varying architectural styles, the interiors of these restaurants typically featured simple, sanitary, and functional designs. Often walls and ceilings were painted gleaming white, in order to emphasize the cleanliness of the restaurant. Wooden floors were covered with easy-to-clean tile or linoleum. Counters, tabletops, and stools were made of porcelain enamel, which was impervious to grease and dirt. Refrigerators, stoves, sinks, dishwashers, and coffee urns were clad in sparkling stainless steel. The most up-to-date restaurants even installed air-conditioning systems. This emphasis on new, shiny, man-made materials made these modest restaurants some of the most modern-looking public places in the 1920s.

The White Castle hamburger chain, which was founded in Wichita, Kansas, in 1921, launched the multi-billion-dollar industry we now know as fast-food restaurants. Long before the golden arches of McDonald's or the orange roofs of Howard Johnson's restaurants made these restaurants instantly identifiable, White Castle became the first American restaurant chain to develop its own recognizable architectural style. The first White Castle buildings, freestanding structures modeled on the architecture of Chicago's famous Water Tower, were constructed of rusticated concrete blocks—a cheap and popular building material. The tops of the walls were built like the ramparts of a medieval castle, and one end of the building sported a corner turret. Throughout the 1920s, though, White Castle experimented with other building materials, including stucco and white enameled brick, before finally settling on durable, prefabricated porcelain-enameled steel panels. The restaurant chain's combination of distinctive medieval architecture and inexpensive, fast-food service proved tremendously popular with American diners. Most importantly, although these restaurants started out small—only 10 by 15 feet—they were easily identified by passers-by. By the end of the 1920s, other restaurant chains had adopted their own distinctive architectural styles.

MOVIE PALACES

Unlike the cookie-cutter standardization of restaurant chains, the grand movie palaces built during the 1920s each boasted a unique design. The large movie theaters found in the downtown business districts of the nation's major cities featured some of the most opulent and ornate architecture of the decade, and their luxurious interiors created among moviegoers the sensation that attending a film was a special experience. Enormous, elegant theaters offered not only admission to see a motion picture but also the intangible experience of immersing oneself briefly in a world of extraordinary wealth and comfort. The Roxy Theater (billed as America's "Cathedral of the Motion Picture"), built in 1927 near New York City's Times Square, seated nearly 6,000 patrons, and its immense lobby and foyers contained a dozen five-story green marble columns and an oval rug, woven to order, that weighed more than two tons. Movie palaces featured lavishly appointed smoking lounges, rest rooms, and powder rooms, and many were among the first public buildings to install air-conditioning systems. Babysitting facilities were included in the price of admission at many movie palaces, and some actually featured kennels in which to board patrons' pets during the film. The largest theaters, such as the Roxy and San Francisco's Fox Theater (built in 1929), even had adjoining hospitals to tend to patrons' medical emergencies. These magnificent palaces proved to be tremendously popular, and while not every new movie theater could approach the splendor of the Roxy or the Fox, even small theaters tried to furnish elegant surroundings and amenities that offered moviegoers a welcome escape from their more ordinary lives.

Theater architects and designers routinely mixed European styles to create a lavish display of wealth and elegance. Most palaces, particularly

Interior of the Earle Theater, Washington, D.C., circa 1920. Courtesy of the Library of Congress.

their exteriors and lobbies, were inspired by classical European architecture. In fact, many theater exteriors and interiors replicated Old World churches, monuments, and palaces. La Salle de Spectacle, the eighteenth-century opera house at Versailles, served as the model for the Ringling Theater, constructed in Baraboo, Wisconsin, in 1915. The theater lobby also featured a one-third-scale replica of the frieze decorating the choir gallery in the cathedral at Florence. The lobby of San Francisco's spectacular Fox Theater boasted throne chairs, statuary, and a pair of vases once owned by Russian czars. Its picture gallery was an exact replica of a Versailles chapel, and the curtain, which alone cost $8,900, was made out of gold kidskin, padded lamé, 2,500 glass reflectors, and silk rope fringe.

Foreign influences on American movie palaces extended beyond Europe, however, to include Egypt and the Far East. Grauman's Egyptian Theater (1922), built by Sid Grauman in Hollywood, featured a forecourt lined with massive Egyptian columns, hieroglyphics, and huge dog-headed Egyptian god statues. Employees dressed as robed Bedouins carrying spears paced the building's parapet all day long. Other movie palaces offered patrons a taste of exotic Orientalism. For example, Grauman's Chinese Theater, which opened a few blocks away in 1927, resembled a giant red pagoda and had images of huge silver dragons on the ceilings. The Fox theaters in Detroit and St. Louis were decorated in a Persian style, and their employees, dressed as Turkish warriors and armed with scimitars, stood by the throne chairs in the lobbies.

One of the most important and influential theater architects of the 1920s was the Scottish-born Thomas W. Lamb, who designed more than 300 movie houses (mostly for Loew's theater chain) during his career. Many of Lamb's elegant movie theaters contained elaborately decorated domed ceilings constructed to resemble nineteenth-century European opera houses. His Loew's State Theater, constructed in St. Louis in 1924, incorporated Corinthian columns, marble balustrades and staircases, and ornate fountains. Lamb outdid even himself in 1927, when he designed the incredibly lavish Loew's Midland Theater in Kansas City, Missouri. This 4,000-seat baroque and rococo temple contained more than 6 million square inches of silver and gold leaf, mahogany walls topped by plasterwork cherubs, and a dome hung with two elaborate crystal chandeliers. The interior work required the labor of 15 sculptors, and valuable antiques purchased from tycoon William K. Vanderbilt's demolished New York City townhouse provided the finishing touches.

In 1923, Austrian-born John Eberson created another style of movie palace when he designed the Houston Majestic, the nation's first "atmospheric" theater, in Houston, Texas. Atmospheric theaters could be built for just a fraction of what it cost to build a standard domed theater, because their ceilings consisted of a plain concrete surface that was painted midnight blue. By projecting images onto the ceiling with a device called the Brenograph magic lantern, these atmospheric theaters gave audiences the sensation of watching a film under a night sky filled with clouds, moon, stars, and even an occasional airplane. Other visual images could also be projected onto the ceiling, including the Northern Lights, angels, flying birds, butterflies, fire, lightning storms, rainbows, and volcanoes. The walls of the atmospherics were usually decorated to resemble open courtyards in various exotic locales. Chicago's Avalon Theater (1927), one of Eberson's most elaborate projects, combined Middle Eastern decor with projected ceiling images to suggest the feeling of being in a Persian mosque. Another one of Eberson's splendid theaters, Loew's Paradise (1929), built in the Bronx for $4 million, contained an auditorium that was designed to give moviegoers the impression they were sitting in an extravagant Venetian palace.

GAS STATIONS

As automobiles began to crowd America's roadways during the 1920s, gas stations inevitably sprang up across the nation. Prior to World War

I, most filling stations were little more than a shed with a gas pump out front. But beginning around 1917, larger gas stations began to appear, with multiple pumps and indoor offices. Since filling stations competed to sell products—gas and oil—that were virtually indistinguishable from station to station, owners soon realized that they had to attract consumers based on the distribution facility itself. During the early 1920s, most gas stations were built to resemble small, neat houses. These homey domestic structures blended in with the houses in surrounding residential neighborhoods and projected an image of friendliness and efficiency. Just as some of the nation's leading restaurant chains attempted to make their architecture synonymous with their identity during the 1920s, some oil companies hired architects to design a particular style of gas station that motorists could readily identify with their brand of gasoline. For example, the Pure Oil Company built filling stations that looked like charming English cottages, Socony-Vacuum capitalized on the popularity of colonial houses, and Wadham's Oil Company built its stations to look like Chinese pagodas. Other companies designed stations to look like suburban bungalows, Spanish haciendas, or mini–Tudor mansions.

During the mid-1920s, many filling stations began to expand their services to include not only gasoline fill-ups and oil changes but also engine repairs, tire changes, battery and headlight replacements, and other services. Filling station operators responded to motorists' needs by grafting service bays and storage rooms onto their existing structures. By the end of the 1920s, these full-fledged "service stations" demanded an architectural style different from that of the tidy little house. So, architects created the "box-style" station, which contained an office, bathroom, utility room, service area, and one or more garage bays configured in a rectangular layout. The gasoline pumps were usually located on islands a short distance away from the service area. These box stations remained the standard in gas station architecture until the 1930s, when those constructed in the Streamline Moderne style eclipsed them in popularity.

MIMETIC ARCHITECTURE

During the 1920s, motorists driving throughout the nation would occasionally encounter freestanding buildings designed to resemble enormous windmills, dogs, Indian heads, root beer barrels, pigs, castles, tepees, coffee pots, or any number of other fanciful designs. This architectural style, known as mimetic or programmatic architecture, was intended not just to amuse but, more importantly, to provide publicity for a business and to attract customers. Typically, the shape of the building in some way represented the business housed within. For example, a Dayton, Ohio, business that sold Liberty Bonds during World War I was built in the shape of an enormous cash register, and the Big Pump, a Maryville, Missouri, filling station, was constructed to look like, obviously, a big gas pump. Some dairies along America's highways were built to look like giant milk cans or oversized cows. Other architectural novelties, such as the famous Brown Derby restaurant in Hollywood, completed in 1926, resembled a gigantic hat, and the Toed-In Drive-Inn in Sacramento, California, was shaped like a giant toad. The architecture of Coon Chicken Inns, a small fried-chicken restaurant chain in Utah and Washington State, was even more outlandish. Its buildings featured an enormous, 10-foot-high sign on which was painted a grossly stereotypical face of a black waiter with a winking eye, huge lips, and a wide grin. At the chain's Salt Lake City restaurant, customers actually entered the building through the waiter's gaping mouth. While mimetic architecture existed prior to the 1920s, this style became exceedingly popular during the Jazz Age, when modern advertising techniques increasingly pressured Americans to consume like never before.

RESIDENTIAL ARCHITECTURE

During the 1920s, avant-garde European architectural styles made their way across the Atlantic to the United States, but the overwhelming majority of American homes built during the decade reflected more traditional, conservative architectural styles. In particular, middle-class Americans preferred homes that reminded them of a romantic English cottage, an eclectic Spanish villa, a rustic French farmhouse, or a stately colonial mansion. Homeowners gravitated toward these classic architectural styles, even as they filled their traditional-looking houses with all of the latest electric appliances and modern conveniences. Of course, a few American houses were built in the modern Art Deco or International Style, but these were far from the norm in standard home construction during the 1920s.

Most of the new suburban houses built during the 1920s did not feature particularly interesting architectural styles. Indeed, many subdivisions across the nation contained row upon row of what is known as the common bungalow-style house. *Bungalow* came to be used in the early decades of the twentieth century to describe a variety of house that had an efficient floor plan arranged around a central living room, a low sloping roof, wide eaves, and a prominent front porch supported by two or more columns. Porches were perhaps the most consistent feature of bungalow houses, and before air conditioners became household fixtures, porches provided comfortable spaces for people to cool off in hot weather and to visit with their neighbors. Two California architects, brothers Charles Sumner Greene and Henry Mather Greene, are often credited with launching the bungalow craze. From 1903 to 1922, they designed a number of different models of these simple, one- or one-and-a-half-story homes and then published their plans in national magazines, pattern books, and mail-order catalogs. These houses were also called "Craftsman bungalows," a term likely borrowed from the magazine *The Craftsman*, founded by Gustav Stickley, an American furniture maker, house designer, and leader of the Arts and Crafts movement during the early twentieth century.

During the 1920s, many new houses were built in either the American Four-Square or Prairie Box styles, both of which featured a simple box-shaped floor plan. These houses were taller than regular bungalows—usually two or two-and-a-half stories high—with four rooms on each floor that provided occupants with a roomy interior despite the small size of city or suburban lots. American Four-Square homes often featured a large dormer window on the front of the house, and, like the popular bungalow, a large front porch suitable for visiting with friends or relaxing in the shade. Inside, they resembled the bungalow with their open floor plans and built-in shelves and cabinets. Like bungalows, Four-Square houses were popularized by the sale of blueprints in pattern books, catalogs, and mail-order kits.

Colonial Revival houses were also common sights in the American suburbs of the 1920s, reflecting homeowners' abiding interest in their colonial past. Colonial Revival houses were usually shaped like rectangular two-story boxes, and they often incorporated elements of Federal or Georgian architecture from the late eighteenth and early nineteenth centuries. Tudor-style houses, based on architectural styles from sixteenth-century England, also became fashionable during the 1920s. These houses usually featured steeply pitched, front-facing gables, tall windows, and distinctive ornamental half-timbering. Tudor-style houses were traditionally clad with stucco or masonry, but in the 1920s, with the advent of new masonry veneering techniques, many of these homes were built to resemble the look of brick or stone without their considerable expense.

A more eclectic style of American home architecture was the Spanish Colonial Revival style (sometimes called Spanish Eclectic), which took its inspiration from the Spanish churches, forts, and houses of the American Southwest. Many homes in Florida, California, and the Southwest that were built in this style featured red tile roofs, arched windows, decorative railings, and stucco siding. This style of residential architecture gained popularity after the 1915–1916 Panama-California Exposition held in San Diego. The Spanish Baroque buildings architect Bertram Grosvenor Goodhue designed for the exposition received extensive press coverage. Soon, other fashionable architects sought inspiration in Span-

Sears, Roebuck and Co. advertisement for home building plans, 1928. Courtesy of the Library of Congress.

ish architectural traditions, and while most of these homes were concentrated in California and the southwestern United States, examples of Spanish Colonial Revival homes exist in many states across the nation. This style reached its zenith in the 1920s and early 1930s but fell rapidly out of favor during the 1940s.

INTERIOR DESIGN

More so than ever before, middle-class Americans during the 1920s consciously decorated their homes and offices to reflect their sense of personal style and taste. While Art Deco and the International Style exerted considerable influence on those individuals most attuned to architectural and stylistic trends, most Americans favored more traditional design styles. For design-conscious consumers of all tastes, general advice about interior decorating was easy to find. *House Beautiful*, *Arts & Decoration*, *Fruit, Garden and Home* (founded in 1922 and renamed *Better Homes & Gardens* in 1924), and other national magazines offered their massive readership suggestions about how to arrange furniture, acquire antiques (or reproductions), and generally make one's home more attractive. Even fashion magazines such as *Vogue* and *Harper's Bazaar* published the occasional article about interior design. Eager to capitalize on the newfound interest in home decorating, publishers released dozens of interior design guidebooks, including Ethel Davis Seal's famous *Furnishing the Little House* (1924), which established the premise that there are "certain well-defined principles of beauty" that any homeowner can understand and use.[3] For those who took the art of interior design even more seriously, one could attend any of the dozens of professional interior design schools that sprang up across the United States. Wealthy and fashionable homeowners often hired professional designers to provide them with interior decors that were elegant, tasteful, and harmonious.

Although few Americans completely furnished their homes with Art Deco objects, this style did creep into the living rooms, bedrooms, and kitchens of millions of ordinary Americans. Oriental-looking lacquered screens, stylized ceramic statues, geometrically patterned floor coverings, inlaid dressing tables, and goods constructed of man-made materials such as plastics, glass, and chrome all represented the new Art Deco look. Certain mass-produced items, such as sleek tubular furniture and objects made of colorful Bakelite plastic, also contributed to the elegant and sophisticated look of Art Deco interior design that became fashionable in middle-class American homes.

IMPORTANT AMERICAN ARCHITECTS

Albert Kahn

Albert Kahn reigned as the most influential and prolific industrial architect of the 1920s. He specialized in designing automobile factories and, despite his lack of a college education or professional training, designed more than 1,000 buildings throughout the course of his career, many of them for Ford, Chrysler, Packard, and other major automobile manufacturers. Born in Germany, Kahn and his family immigrated to Detroit in 1880, when he was 11 years old. He apprenticed with a Michigan architect, George D. Mason (a partner in the Detroit firm of Mason and Rice), and started his own architectural firm in 1895. In 1904, while designing his tenth Packard automobile factory, Kahn suggested using a new building technique—reinforced concrete. His innovative design proved so successful that it solidified Kahn's career in industrial plant design.

In 1918, Kahn began constructing the Ford Motor Company's enormous River Rouge plant, which, when completed in 1926, became the largest single manufacturing complex in the United States. As in his other projects, Kahn relied on simple geometric shapes and modern materials, such as steel roof trusses and glass walls, to create facilities that were as pragmatic and efficient as the assembly lines they housed. Although Kahn became particularly well known for his bright, well-proportioned factories, he also designed and built office buildings, banks, and even private homes, including Edsel Ford's estate in Grosse Pointe Shores, Michigan.

Raymond M. Hood

Raymond M. Hood ranks as one of the most renowned architects in the history of the Art Deco period. Born in Rhode Island, he attended Brown University, the Massachusetts Institute of Technology, and the premier architecture school in the world at the time, the École des Beaux-Arts in Paris. Hood's first major commission came when he (along with John Mead Howells) won the *Chicago Tribune* Company's architecture contest in 1922, and they subsequently received the contract to design the huge Gothic skyscraper. Hood's success led to other important commissions, including the auditorium and foyer of New York City's Radio City Music Hall, the RCA Building at Rockefeller Center, and the Daily News Building.

William Van Alen

William Van Alen is best remembered as the innovative designer of the distinctive Chrysler Building in New York City, arguably the greatest Art Deco skyscraper ever built. Van Alen studied in Brooklyn at the Pratt Institute and then, after spending several years working in various New York architectural firms, won the 1908 Lloyd Warren Fellowship, which allowed him to travel to Paris to study at the École des Beaux-Arts. Upon returning to New York in 1911, he earned a reputation for designing commercial structures that defied traditional conventions. Van Alen was one of the first architects to use stainless steel over a large exposed building surface, as exhibited on the Chrysler Building. Even today, the Chrysler Building's shiny tower remains one of the Manhattan skyline's most recognizable landmarks.

Paul Revere Williams

Paul Revere Williams, a Los Angeles native, was one of the foremost commercial and domestic architects of southern California and the first African-American architect to be admitted as a fellow in the American Institute of Architects. Williams graduated from the University of Southern California in 1919, became a licensed architect in 1921, and opened his own firm just a year later. His numerous commissions to design homes for Hollywood celebrities led to his nickname, "the Architect to the Stars." His clients included such motion picture and television stars as Lon Chaney, Bill "Bojangles" Robinson, Tyrone Power, and, in later decades, Frank Sinatra, Lucille Ball and Desi Arnaz, and Zsa Zsa Gabor. Over the course of his long and productive career, Williams designed close to 3,000 homes, commercial buildings, and government structures and became one of the most successful African-American architects of the twentieth century.

Frank Lloyd Wright

Frank Lloyd Wright, America's most famous twentieth-century architect, did not find the 1920s to be his most productive decade. Nevertheless, in 1922 he finished supervising the construction of the impressive Imperial Hotel in Tokyo, Japan, which was built on an innovative "floating foundation" designed to withstand earthquakes. Later that year, after returning to the United States, Wright began to experiment with architectural forms and structures based not on the traditional rectangles and squares but on circles, spirals, arcs, and angles. He also spent considerable time during the decade corresponding with leading European architectural thinkers, and his work and ideas were widely disseminated in architectural and design journals throughout the world. In 1928, Wright began writing his autobiography (first published in 1932 as *Frank Lloyd Wright: An Autobiography*), which explained his complex theories of architecture.

CONCLUSION

Architectural trends are not as short-lived as fashions in hats or hairstyles, and so many examples of groundbreaking architectural design (such as the Chrysler Building in New York City) still exist for us to examine and admire today. But unlike ephemeral fashion trends, which may last only weeks or months, architectural and design movements usually take years to filter down into popular culture. Even as ordinary Americans marveled at the impressive new skyscrapers and office buildings that began to dot urban landscapes, when it came to their own homes, most preferred more traditional styles of residential architecture and interior design. As a result, few middle-class families built or bought homes that reflected the most up-to-date architectural styles. Modern design styles, however, were incorporated into hundreds of different kinds of household objects, including furniture, lamps, clocks, and other accessories. As a result, many homes featured an eclectic array of old and new furnishings—an ornate, Chinese-inspired Art Deco screen might stand, for example, next to a colonial American antique chair. Overall, the architectural and design styles of the 1920s were not uniform but rather encompassed both traditional and modern tastes.

5

Fashion

Fashion, whether a particular shade of lipstick, style of hat, or model of automobile, suggests a fleeting appeal. By definition, fashion is new, smart, and up-to-date. The social pressures to be fashionable encourage people to buy, to discard, and then to buy again, according to the dictates of the moment. During the 1920s, the notion of keeping up with fashion trends and expressing oneself through material goods seized middle-class Americans as never before. Purchasing new clothes, new furniture, new appliances, new automobiles, new *anything* indicated one's level of prosperity, and the ability to consume represented an important social marker in the 1920s. Being considered old-fashioned, out-of-date, or—worse yet—unable to afford stylish new products was a fate many Americans went to great lengths to avoid during this decade of unprecedented consumerism.

More than anything else, fashionable clothes served as the principal marker of social respectability. As Emily Post put it, in her best-selling guide *Etiquette in Society, in Business, in Politics and at Home* (1922), "In the world of smart society—in America at any rate—clothes not only represent our ticket of admission, but our contribution to the effect of a party. What makes a brilliant party? Clothes. Good clothes. A frumpy party is nothing more nor less than a collection of badly dressed persons."[1] Although Post cautioned her readers to resist following the latest clothing trends to the extent that they overspent or purchased unflattering outfits, she underscored the importance of paying meticulous attention to one's clothing and appearance.

FASHION AND POPULAR CULTURE

Since the mid-nineteenth century, *Godey's Lady's Book*, *Harper's Bazaar*, and other national women's magazines had conveyed the latest clothing fashions to their readers, but prior to 1900, fashion trends changed relatively slowly. By the 1920s, the postwar explosion of magazines, newspapers, modern advertisements, radio commercials, and Hollywood motion pictures dramatically accelerated the pace of fashion developments. Tens of millions of Americans, both men and women, looked to national celebrities and glamour magazines as guides to what sorts of hairstyles and clothing were "in." Fashion shows and beauty contests—including the Miss America Pageant, founded by H. Conrad Eckholm in 1921 in Atlantic City, New Jersey—received widespread media coverage that relayed to audiences up-to-the-minute fashion trends. In 1927, Sears, Roebuck and Company advertised boots endorsed by Gloria Swanson and hats modeled by Clara Bow and Joan Crawford, correctly implying that women would pay good money to imitate their favorite Hollywood stars.

And pay they did. Clothing represented a primary investment for millions of young women of the 1920s, and the pressure to keep up with the latest fashions caused them to spend significant amounts of money on dresses, hosiery, hats, shoes, and other clothing accessories. Emily Post warned, in *Etiquette*, that women should not spend a disproportionate amount of their income or allowance on clothing. Nevertheless, pressure to conform to fashion trends and look attractive often led to overindulgence at department stores or dressmakers' shops. Many American consumers justified clothing expenditures as a necessary and prudent investment in one's future, reasoning, for example, that well-dressed women were more likely to attract a suitable husband than "frumps" would be. Older, more conservative Americans interpreted this dedication to fashion trends as merely another example of the recklessness and self-indulgence of the modern "flapper."

Despite the seeming extravagance of purchasing trendy clothing, the latest Jazz Age fashions were actually more affordable and accessible to ordinary Americans than they had ever been before. During the 1920s, women's clothing fashions were largely dictated by French haute couture. *Haute couture*, which simply means "high sewing" or the best sewing, is the most elite, expensive sort of fashion, in which each garment is cut and fitted individually, every stitch is done by hand, and every bead, feather, or rhinestone is affixed one at a time. Of course, few Americans—or anyone, for that matter—could afford haute couture, but American clothing manufacturers and buyers regularly traveled to Paris to attend the glamorous fashion shows hosted by famous French design-

Four beauty contest winners, Washington Bathing Beach, Washington, D.C., 1922. Courtesy of the Library of Congress.

ers. Back in the United States, they then re-created the latest Parisian designs in inexpensive fabrics and sold them as ready-to-wear fashions. For an additional measure of authenticity, clothing retailers liberally sprinkled their advertisements with French phrases, since fashion-conscious shoppers devoured anything with a Parisian flair. Although the level of workmanship in no way compared to haute couture, most buyers of ready-made clothing were quite willing to sacrifice quality for quantity. For the first time, high fashion became accessible to even the working classes, as cheap factory-made clothing and inexpensive sewing patterns for up-to-date styles were widely available.

WOMEN'S FASHIONS

One of the primary changes in women's clothing during the 1920s stemmed from a dramatic shift in American standards of beauty and fashion. Prior to World War I, the so-called Gibson girl, with her hour-

A fashionable young woman posed beside a roadster, 1926. Courtesy of the Library of Congress.

glass figure, long, upswept hair, floor-length skirt, and high-collared blouse, represented the model of American beauty and femininity. In contrast, the most desirable female figure during the 1920s was the slender, tubular shape of adolescence. Not surprisingly, this flat-chested, slim-hipped body type, nicknamed the "garçonne" after the French term for "young boy," did not come naturally to most women. Aggressive dieting and binding the breasts became the norm for many women who wore the slim, long-waisted dresses so fashionable during the decade. Because these styles looked attractive on only the slenderest bodies, millions of women went on severe diets in order to accommodate the current fashions.

It wasn't enough, however, merely to be thin—one had to be *young* to be fashionable. The worship of youth colored every aspect of 1920s fashion, but it was not necessarily innocent, romantic youth that women emulated, but instead a more worldly, sexually charged adolescence. Shorter skirts and longer waists were reminiscent of little-girl fashions, but bare legs, bold, short haircuts, and scarlet lipstick suggested a youthfulness that was also openly sexual. With the addition of a stylish heel to the child's Mary Jane shoe, women juxtaposed juvenile fashions with the rolled-stocking, bared-knee sexuality of the modern woman. Her short hair, brief outfits, and brazen use of cosmetics scandalized many older Americans, particularly conservative politicians and clergymen. Women's adherence to these new fashions, they argued, was not only unladylike but also immoral. Still, women of all ages embraced the new fashions as just another aspect of modern life.

During the 1920s, women's clothing caused countless scandals, but it also freed modern women from the discomfort of corsets, pointed shoes, and impossibly large hats. Many happily accepted this modern, simple style of dress, which involved fewer decorations and far less actual material than the fashions of previous generations. Men's fashion offered women a model for jackets tailored like blazers, blouses resembling men's shirts, and even, for the more daring, pants copied from men's trousers. Overall, women's fashion was simpler than it had been in the past, and in practical terms this meant women could drastically reduce the time they spent washing, ironing, and mending elaborate dresses, hats, and undergarments.

RETAIL CLOTHING

Ready-made clothing was an important innovation in American fashion. In most American homes during the mid-nineteenth century, clothing had been made by hand, at home, often out of either homespun fabric or simple, store-bought goods. By 1890, however, the booming industry of ready-to-wear clothing offered consumers the option of buying clothing right off the rack, available in a variety of sizes and colors. By the 1920s, most Americans wore wardrobes consisting largely of ready-made clothing, although the wealthiest urban dwellers still bought couture fashions and the poorest rural dwellers still wore homemade clothing. Of course, many middle-class women continued sewing at least some of their own and their family's clothing during the 1920s, and widely available pattern books and magazines made it easy for them to create the latest fashions at home.

During the 1920s, department stores such as Gimbels, Marshall Field's, Wannamaker's, and Macy's offered shoppers a wide variety of merchandise arranged in attractive combinations. In fact, these department stores commonly used mannequins to display clothing that had already been assembled into eye-catching outfits. Evening dresses, for example, were tied in with matching shoes and handbags to tempt shoppers into purchasing an entire ensemble. Similarly, whole departments were grouped together in order to encourage multiple purchases. Handbag and hosiery sections adjoined shoe departments, and children's clothing departments bordered children's toy sections. Carefully designed displays ensured that department store customers would not only remain aware of the latest fashion trends in clothing but would also covet, and perhaps purchase, entire outfits rather than single items.

Mail-order catalogs also encouraged the mass consumption of ready-to-wear clothing, especially among the nation's millions of rural families. Since the Montgomery Ward Company issued the first mail-order catalog in 1872, American shoppers had gradually become accustomed to purchasing goods through the mail. With the rise of ready-made clothing and the advent of free rural mail delivery, consumers who lived far from urban centers could stay abreast of current fashions by ordering these modestly priced fashions, purchasing a sewing pattern, or copying the styles from scratch. America's most widely distributed mail-order catalog was published by Sears, Roebuck and Company, which claimed to be "the World's Largest Store." Sears produced its first catalog in 1896 and, by the 1920s, its biannual publication represented an important aspect of consumer culture. The Sears Winter/Fall catalog of 1927 featured 11 whole pages of nothing but women's hats, and about five dozen sewing patterns, costing around 20 cents apiece, for everything from infant clothes to women's party dresses.[2] The fashions available through Sears did not necessarily reflect cutting-edge haute couture, but they served perfectly well to keep families of moderate means stylishly clothed.

WOMEN'S DRESSES

During the 1920s, lavish evening gowns became an obvious symbol of the wearer's wealth and social standing. Made of luxurious fabrics such as velvet, satin, crepe de chine, or silver and gold lamé, evening dresses shone with metallic embroidery, sparkled with beads, glittered with rhinestones, even fluttered with fringe. Formal evening gowns would have been appropriate attire for balls, the opera, the theater, elegant dinner parties, and upscale restaurants. Gowns were designed in the basic shape of a sleeveless tube, with either deep U- or V-shaped necklines or high-cut, wide, boat-style necklines. After about 1926, plunging necklines were cut not into the fronts but into the backs of gowns, and women sometimes draped long necklaces of beads or faux pearls down their exposed backs. Early in the decade, waistlines fell to about hip-level, and hemlines rose to just below the calf. The low waistline became the standard for the remainder of the 1920s, but by around 1925, dress hemlines inched up to just below the knee—as short as they would get during the Jazz Age.

During the day, stylish women wore afternoon dresses to luncheons, teas, matinees, and daytime dances. Sometimes called "tea-gowns," these dresses featured long flowing sleeves in the early years of the 1920s. By 1925, though, the afternoon frock had become much more streamlined and slender, with a knee-length skirt and short or fitted sleeves. Afternoon dresses came in a variety of bright colors and varied patterns. Often they were adorned with narrow belts, sashes, bows, or artificial flowers at the dropped waist. In 1926, a stylish addition to afternoon dresses was the "gypsy girdle"—a wide sash fastened over the hips and accented with a clasp studded with rhinestones or other faux jewels. Also in 1926, French designer Gabrielle "Coco" Chanel introduced what remains a fashion staple in women's wardrobes: the simple but elegant "little black dress." During the late 1920s, French designer Madeleine Vionnet pioneered dress design using the "bias cut" (a term used to describe fabric cut on the diagonal) to soften the severe angular shapes of fashionable dresses. Bias-cut skirts, collars, and sleeves fell in delicate folds and clung gracefully to a woman's figure.

During the 1920s, women's suits contained many of the same features found in men's clothing styles. Women's suits were practical but elegant, usually made of wool, with straight, hip-length suit jackets worn over straight matching skirts, and typically came in the standard colors of navy, brown, tan, or black, possibly with white pinstripes. Jackets might be single- or double-breasted, or "edge-to-edge," which meant that the two front panels just barely came together and were fastened with a single metal link button (like a cufflink). Skirt silhouettes were very narrow, although they might include box or knife pleats. Coco Chanel introduced what has since become known as the classic Chanel suit: a boxy jacket trimmed with contrasting ribbon or braid, worn over a straight skirt. The jacket was lined in the same material as the matching blouse, and the jacket and skirt were made of soft jersey or tweed. The Chanel suit was appropriately accessorized with a matching scarf or some inexpensive costume jewelry. Women's suits were considered appropriate attire for work or for travel, but not typically for entertaining.

An even more casual element of a woman's wardrobe was the morning dress, also called the housedress. These informal frocks were usually made of cotton fabric in various striped, plaid, or checked patterns, and women wore them in the home while they did their domestic chores. Housedresses loosely followed the fashion of more formal dresses, and by 1925, they were shorter and slimmer than they had been before. Mail-order catalogs featured page after page of these housedresses, which indicated they were a popular and necessary component of a middle-class woman's wardrobe. The 1927 Sears catalog even featured an entire page of practical and inexpensive "apron frocks," some of which had wraparound fronts that could be reversed when they became soiled. Needless to say, these were not the kinds of dresses typically seen in upscale fashion magazines of the day.

WOMEN'S SPORTSWEAR

During the 1920s, women, particularly those of the middle and upper classes, increasingly engaged in outdoor sports such as tennis, golf, boating, and swimming. Designers largely appropriated men's fashions to create women's outdoor clothing, including serge or tweed knickers to wear while hiking and flared jodhpurs to wear while horseback riding. Women golfers wore pleated, knee-length skirts topped with patterned sweaters and flat, oxford-style, rubber-soled shoes. Tennis players sported flat, rubber-soled shoes, white hose, and short, slim dresses made of white rayon, cotton, or silk. Coco Chanel introduced loose, bell-bottomed trousers made of silk, cotton, or crepe de chine for women to wear while boating. Women soon began wearing these wide-legged pants, known as "beach pajamas," over their bathing suits at the beach.

For ordinary casual wear, women wore long soft blouses that were often banded or belted at the natural waist. Women also adopted the middy blouse, which resembled the top half of a sailor's uniform and was a traditional style for children's clothing. The vest-style blouse, patterned after a man's vest, had long or short sleeves and a notched collar. These blouses could be worn either outside or tucked into the waistband of a skirt or knickers. Another man's style, the lumberjack shirt, made of wool plaid and typically worn with knickers, also found its way into women's casual wardrobes. In cool weather, women (like men) donned colorful Fair Isle sweaters, popularized in 1922 by Edward, Prince of Wales, or coat sweaters, introduced by Coco Chanel, which were cardigan-style sweaters with a high shawl collar, pockets, and sometimes a belt.

WOMEN'S BATHING SUITS

Prior to World War I, "bathing costumes," as they were known, were modest garments made of itchy woolen fabric. For men, bathing costumes consisted of a sleeveless knit tunic worn over (or sometimes attached to) a pair of knit shorts that reached several inches down the thigh. Women's costumes usually consisted of a loose overblouse, a knee-length skirt, and stockings—an outfit barely less voluminous than streetwear. Although women's bathing costumes were certainly not conducive to actual swimming, this actually caused few problems, since recreational swimming was not a tremendously popular activity during the early years of the twentieth century. Still, trying to swim in these bathing costumes proved inordinately difficult. In 1908, Annette Kellerman, a champion swimmer and later a vaudeville and movie star, wore a sleek one-piece body stocking into the surf at Revere Beach near Boston and was promptly arrested for indecent exposure. Nevertheless, this risqué one-piece bathing suit, which came to be known as the controversial "Kellerman suit," marked the beginning of a dramatic change in women's swimwear from bulky, unathletic swimming dresses to form-fitting modern bathing suits.

The 1920s marked the founding of three major bathing suit manufacturers, eventually known as Jantzen, Cole, and Catalina, that succeeded in popularizing beach fashion and breaking down older prohibitions on suitable bathing garments. Danish immigrant Carl Jantzen, along with his partners John and Roy Zehntbauer, invented a machine that could knit a stretchy fabric that was ribbed on both sides. This fabric was much more elastic than ordinary jersey, the fabric most commonly used to make swimwear, and it clung to every curve of the body. In 1921, Jantzen began developing one-piece bathing suits that looked as if they were actually two pieces. These tubular maillot suits, sometimes called "California-style" suits, consisted of a scoop-necked, sleeveless top that was sewn at the waist to a pair of trunks. Often these unisex suits were embellished with bold, colorful stripes across the chest, hip, and thigh. Jantzen marketed these suits with matching swimming socks and caps topped with a pompon. But because swimming was still not a particularly popular recreational activity, Jantzen realized that the market for swimwear was relatively limited. To encourage Americans to swim and, therefore, to buy more swimsuits, Jantzen founded the Jantzen Swimming Association in 1926 and immediately launched a national campaign called "Learn to Swim," which offered free swimming lessons across the country, certificates of completion, local competitions, and endorsements from champion swimmers. By 1930, Jantzen was the world's largest producer of bathing suits, selling more than 1.5 million suits a year.

While Jantzen's Oregon-based company specialized in athletic-looking suits that were actually suitable for swimming, Fred Cole's rival company in Los Angeles focused on creating dramatic fashion suits that were designed primarily for glamorous sunbathing. In 1925, Cole began marketing the "Prohibition Suit," which had a low-cut neckline and tiny skirt that was shockingly revealing for the time. Catalina Swimwear, also based in California, offered America's bathing beauties a range of swimsuits that were sexier than Jantzen's but not nearly as daring as Cole's. Catalina's "Rib Stitch 5" suit, for example, introduced the nearly backless bathing suits that became immensely popular among women in the late 1920s. Catalina also served as the official swimsuit provider for the Miss America Pageant in Atlantic City.

Swimwear, like many other aspects of American popular culture during the Jazz Age, was also subject to a number of short-lived, usually ill-conceived fads. Some of the more imaginative novelty bathing suits introduced during the 1920s were made of badly chosen materials that ranged from rabbit fur to seaweed to wooden barrel staves. While never appropriate for actual swimming, these suits did generate a bit of extra notoriety and attention on America's beaches. Perhaps not surprisingly, the evolution of form-fitting swimwear also caused significant controversy during the 1920s, as directors of public beaches, resorts, and country clubs implemented strict dress codes for which violations were punishable by fines and, occasionally, even imprisonment. Regulations, along with the level of enforcement, varied from beach to beach. Typically, dress codes dictated that trunks (or bloomers) and skirts could rise no higher than so many inches above the knee, and sometimes female bathers were required to wear stockings, usually (but not always) rolled above the knee. Some public beaches and resorts actually hired "beach censors" to patrol the swimming area in order to maintain order among bathers and enforce dress codes. Chicago's Clarendon Beach even employed a woman as a "beach tailor" who enforced women's dress codes by stitching up loose armholes and sewing longer, more modest skirts onto too-short bathing suits. Men's swimwear was also regulated, but it seems that dress codes for men were enforced far less stringently than they were for women.

A "bathing beach policeman" measuring the distance between knee and bathing suit, Washington, D.C., 1922. Courtesy of the Library of Congress.

WOMEN'S UNDERGARMENTS

As was the case for virtually all women's clothing during the 1920s, women's underwear also became lighter and less constricting. Old-fashioned corsets had long been criticized by women's activists and even doctors, who claimed they were not only uncomfortable but also unhealthy. Nevertheless, corsets were marketed throughout the 1920s and were still regularly purchased, particularly by older women. Over time, though, less burdensome corsets and lightweight rubber girdles gradually supplanted traditional lace-up, boned corsets. By the end of the decade, many women dispensed with "foundation garments" altogether, instead opting for the brief new "step-ins" or "cami-knickers," which were light one-piece undergarments that amounted merely to a silk or rayon camisole stitched to a pair of thigh-length panties.

Most brassieres manufactured during the 1920s were intended to flatten rather than accentuate women's breasts. These cup-less brassieres, also called bandeaux, were made of cotton, silk, or rayon, and fitted snugly against the woman's body in order to smooth her silhouette under the straight, narrow dresses of the day. Some bras during the mid- to late-1920s, however, were deliberately designed to separate and lift women's breasts. In 1922, Ida Cohen Rosenthal developed the support bra and founded the Maiden Form Brassiere Company (later renamed Maidenform). These "uplift" brassieres often featured elastic inserts and were widely advertised as preventing the bust from sagging.

WOMEN'S SHOES AND HOSIERY

Because the shorter skirts of the 1920s exposed more of women's legs, American designers and consumers began to consider shoes and hosiery to be important fashion accessories. At the beginning of the decade, many shoes featured pointed toes and two-inch, curved "Louis" heels, broad one-and-three-quarter-inch "military" heels, or one-inch "walking" heels. Comfortable rubber soles and heels, introduced during World War I, also steadily gained in popularity throughout the 1920s. As the decade progressed, women's shoes with rounded toes and chunky, two-inch "Cuban" heels or, conversely, slender "spike" or "Spanish" heels became common. Dressy women's shoes often featured a strap across the top of the foot—either one strap, two straps, three straps, cross straps, or T-straps—often made of brocade, satin, or some other delicate material. The straps buttoned on one side of the shoe, and fashionable button covers made of enamel, rhinestones, silver, gold, or brass added a little extra flair to otherwise simple shoes. Not only were these strapped shoes fashionable, but they also prevented women from accidentally kicking them off during an exuberant performance of the Charleston or other high-stepping dance. A plain pump, nearly identical to those worn today, was also a popular footwear choice. In the early 1920s, most women's shoes were available in the conventional colors of brown, tan, black, white, or gray. As the decade wore on, however, women began to sport shoes in silver, gold, red, green, and other dramatic colors.

Women's hosiery also represented an important fashion consideration, largely as a result of rising skirt hemlines. Black cotton or lisle stockings vanished among the fashionable set and were replaced by beige or tan hose made of silk or, after 1923, rayon (then called "artificial silk"). Affordable cotton stockings were still available throughout the decade, but fashion dictated that women spend the extra money to sheath their newly exposed legs in luxurious silk. While a pair of plain silk stockings could be purchased for about a dollar, fancier silk hose could cost six dollars or more per pair. Women wore garter belts to keep their thigh-high stockings from sagging or falling down. Sometimes women rolled the tops of their stockings over garters worn just above the knee, but flapper fashion dictated that stockings be rolled down to expose delicately powdered knees. More conservative Americans considered bare knees the epitome of immoral dress, but as the 1920s progressed, stockingless knees became an increasingly common sight.

WOMEN'S HAIRSTYLES

Although popular conceptions of the Jazz Age suggest that every fashionable woman bobbed her hair during the 1920s, some women did keep their hair long. Long-haired women did not customarily wear their hair loose; rather, they pulled it back to the nape of the neck and wound it into a smooth chignon or knot. Another fashionable style at the beginning of the decade involved coiling long hair into two buns that rested one behind each ear. This hairstyle, known alternately as "earphones" or "cootie garages," fell out of favor by the mid-1920s. However, more enduring was the ubiquitous bob, cut short and straight at about chin-length, which dancing sensation Irene Castle introduced in the United States shortly before World War I. When other celebrities such as French fashion designer Coco Chanel and Hollywood film star Louise Brooks also adopted this short, blunt haircut, women across the United States followed suit. Many women actually had their hair cut by men's barbers, since some hairdressers, fearing that short, simple hairstyles would put them out of business, simply refused to shear off women's long tresses. The bob could be worn with or without bangs, and was often accompanied by side curls plastered to the cheek or by a single curl dramatically set in the middle of the forehead. Around 1923, the standard bob haircut began to evolve into different, even shorter styles. The shingle haircut, or "boyish bob," tapered to a point at the nape of the wearer's neck and often featured waves or short curls on the sides. The even more radical "Eton crop," which was trimmed above the wearer's ears and shaved in back, appeared in 1926. These streamlined haircuts were perfect for tucking underneath a stylish cloche hat so nothing but perhaps a side curl or two was visible. While young women in their late teens and twenties were the first to engage in the bobbed hair craze, by the end of the decade women of all ages were wearing the convenient and versatile bob.

"Marcel waves," as they became known, were a tremendously popular feature of the bobbed haircut. In 1872, Marcel Grateau, a French hairstylist, invented a method by which hair could be curled or waved with the use of a curling iron heated on a stove until it was nearly scorching hot. By the 1920s, more convenient electric curling irons and crimpers became available, making it even easier for women to "marcel" their hair into the deep horizontal waves that were then fashionable. The water wave comb was another implement designed to create wavy hair. Wet hair was set with a series of combs, often made of aluminum or celluloid, which gently pushed the hair into waves. A scarf or ribbon was then wrapped around the head to keep the combs in place until the hair dried into soft waves and the combs could be removed. Women also created "finger waves" by applying "finger waving lotion" to their damp hair, then combing and pinching their short tresses into waves with their fingers. Until the damp waves were completely dry, women protected their efforts with delicate nets made of real human hair. By the late 1920s, "permanent waves" were also available to women willing to undergo the strong chemical treatments. Although women went to great trouble creating curls and waves in their naturally straight hair, short hair was in general a real timesaver. Women with long hair might spend several hours a week brushing, washing, drying, braiding, and arranging their elaborate hairstyles, but marcelling a short bob took only a few minutes every day.

While white women worked hard to make their hair wavy or curly, many African-American women worked just as hard trying to make their hair straight. Black newspapers and magazines advertised dozens of special pomades, oils, soaps, shampoos, hot irons, and combs that were intended to help relax and straighten curly or kinky hair. Madame C. J. Walker, the nation's first black woman millionaire, developed a revolutionary system to soften and straighten black women's hair around the turn of the century, using a combination of special hair preparations and hot irons. In 1906, she founded the Madame C. J. Walker Manufacturing Company, and later she established a Harlem-based beautician school called the Walker College of Hair Culture, which claimed to teach its hairdressing students how to straighten kinky hair without using curling irons, and promoted a secret formula that supposedly accelerated hair growth. The Walker Manufacturing Company flourished during the 1920s under the leadership of Madame Walker's daughter, A'Lelia Walker, one of the richest and most extravagant residents of Harlem during the Jazz Age. Madame C. J. Walker realized not only that the African-American community represented a virtually untapped consumer market, but also that many black women were attracted to products that promised a more "Caucasian" appearance and, by association, the social acceptance unavailable to those with kinky hair and other so-called "African" features.

WOMEN'S COSMETICS

The cosmetics industry boomed during the 1920s, and thousands of beautician schools and beauty parlors sprang up that sold makeup and face creams, astringents, lotions, and other products guaranteed to preserve or restore the bloom of youth. Prior to World War I, an American woman who visibly wore makeup, or "paint," as it was often called, was immediately suspected of being immoral—a woman of "easy virtue." But during the 1920s, wearing cosmetics became not just fashionable but respectable. Inspired at least in part by the glamorous Hollywood movie stars who painted dark red lipstick on their mouths and applied heavy black mascara to their eyelashes, women of every age began to apply rouge, powder, lipstick, and eyeliner to their faces. They plucked their eyebrows into dramatic arches and then redrew them using eyebrow pencils. They accented their lashes with mascara and reddened their lips into the pouty, "bee-stung" look popularized by Clara Bow and Theda Bara. Sales of cosmetics soared from $17 million in 1914 to $141 million in 1925.[3] Both Elizabeth Arden and Helena Rubenstein managed successful cosmetics empires in the 1920s, marketing their makeup and skincare products to a nation of female consumers longing for the latest beauty-enhancing invention. Following the lead of Coco Chanel and other fashion mavens, American women of the mid-1920s also stopped protecting their skin from the sun and instead gloried in deep bronze suntans. A winter tan, in particular, became a prestigious status symbol, indicating that the possessor had both the money and the time to vacation in sunny locations such as California, Florida, or even Italy. Those without much disposable income often had to settle for self-tanning liquids and powders that claimed to achieve the effect of a natural suntan.

Not all women, however, desired a dark skin. Some African-American women spent a great deal of time and money attempting to lighten their skin so it more closely resembled a white complexion. Hundreds of bleaching lotions and other whitening potions were marketed in beauty shops, drugstores, newspapers, magazines, and mail-order catalogs. Advertisements for products with suggestive names such as "Black-No-More," "Fair-Plex Ointment," and "Cocotone Skin Whitener" promised (or at least implied) that, with repeated applications, African-American women would be rewarded with an attractive, pale skin tone. Not surprisingly, the very idea of skin whiteners sparked intense controversies in African-American communities. While many women, particularly light-complexioned African Americans, bought these ointments and believed the advertisers' false claims, others spurned these products and vehemently rejected the notion that lightening one's skin was either desirable or possible.

WOMEN'S HATS, HANDBAGS, AND JEWELRY

As they had in previous decades, hats remained a standard component of American women's wardrobes during the 1920s, and while hats were not worn in the home or with fancy evening gowns, they were required apparel for most social engagements. Earlier in the century, enormous, wide hats were the rage, often adorned with long, dramatic feathers and pinned to a woman's hair with dangerously sharp hatpins. In 1913, the Audubon Society succeeded in introducing a ban on importing the plumage of such rare birds as egrets and birds of paradise, whose feathers had customarily been used in millinery. The lack of dramatic plumage, coupled with the popular short haircuts of the 1920s, signaled the end of the oversized hat. Large, striking hats did endure for the first few years of the decade, but around 1923, when the cloche hat (*cloche* means "bell" in French) was imported to America from Paris, small, trim hats became de rigueur for stylish women. The cloche hat's deep crown and narrow brim fitted snugly over a woman's head and concealed her eyebrows and nearly all of her bobbed hair. Cloches were made of just about every material, including straw, felt, satin, velvet, rayon, and cotton, and could be worn at any time of the year. By 1928, some cloche hats had even been stripped of their small brim, making them look almost like a helmet. Cloches were often decorated with appliqué, ribbons, rhinestones, buckles, beads, small feathers, artificial flowers, or decorative clips, and most trimmings rested over the ear rather than on the front of the hat. Ornamental Art Deco hatpins, usually made of zinc, celluloid, or Bakelite, came into vogue late in the 1920s. Rather than attach the hat to a woman's hair, these pins, often adorned with faux jewels, were intended merely to decorate an otherwise plain hat.

Although cloches were by far the dominant style of women's hats during the 1920s, other styles also enjoyed a certain measure of popularity. The turban, which basically amounted to a length of material wrapped horizontally around the head, offered one fashionable alternative to the cloche. During the 1910s, dancer Irene Castle initiated the fashion of wearing decorative bandeaux—headbands that wrapped around the forehead and could be made of anything from ribbons to rhinestones. By the beginning of the 1920s, women were wearing these headpieces, also nicknamed "headache bands," as a standard part of their evening dress. Women also found soft tams and berets appealing, and when Greta Garbo wore a man's slouch hat in the popular film *A Woman of Affairs* (1928), she ignited another national craze among American women. *Garbo* soon became a synonym for this style of soft felt hat with a high crown and drooping brim. And women riding in open cars sometimes protected their hair by donning leather aviator helmets resembling those worn by World War I pilots.

The pared-down women's fashions of the 1920s left little room for pockets, and so a well-dressed woman needed to carry a handbag in which she could keep her compact, lipstick, and a few other necessities. While morning appointments generally called for a more casual handbag made of fabric or leather, afternoon and evening engagements required a dressier bag, often constructed of mesh or fancy beadwork. Some bags, called reticules, were pouch-style bags that closed with a drawstring and were made of fabric or, for eveningwear, crocheted out of strands of glass beads. The *pochette*, another popular style of handbag, was a simple, flat, rectangular bag that featured a clasp at the top and a short carrying strap. Metal mesh bags, introduced in the United States in the nineteenth century, also enjoyed tremendous popularity in the 1920s. They could be plated in gold or silver, or enameled in Art Deco patterns resembling flowers, birds, sunbursts, or Egyptian or Oriental motifs. The late 1920s saw a vogue in reptile-skin bags, including those made from the hides of lizards, alligators, and snakes. Stylish women who carried these bags sometimes wore matching pairs of gloves.

During the 1920s, Coco Chanel introduced inexpensive lines of what she called "illusion jewelry," better known as "costume jewelry," and soon the costume jewelry market exploded. Long strands of imitation pearls, faux gems, and opaque glass beads adorned the necks of both wealthy women and struggling shopgirls across the nation, for they were as affordable as they were attractive. A popular long necklace made of glass beads and ending in a beaded tassel, called a *sautoir*, became known as "flapper beads." Pendant earrings, frequently made of glass, often dangled below a woman's bobbed hair. Bangle bracelets, constructed of celluloid, Bakelite, chrome, or aluminum, were frequently worn several at a time, often on the upper arm left bare by a sleeveless evening dress. Trends that affected clothing often affected jewelry. The 1922 discovery of King Tutankhamen's tomb, for example, initiated a craze for Egyptian-style jewelry, and the popularity of African-American nightclub entertainer Josephine Baker sparked a rage for heavy African ivory bracelets. Of course, those women who could afford it still bought "real" jewelry, but fashion trends favored those necklaces made of inexpensive glass, wood, and even papier-mâché beads.

MEN'S FASHIONS

Just as women dieted away extra pounds in order to achieve the lean, boyish figure demanded by Jazz Age fashion, so too did men work to attain the ideal strong, slim body. One proponent of this new muscular male body was strongman Angelo Siciliano who, in 1922, won the title of "Most Perfectly Developed Man" and subsequently renamed himself Charles Atlas. Atlas, an Italian immigrant who had, as a youth, been bullied because of his scrawny physique, began a mail-order business that promoted his muscle-building "Dynamic Tension" exercises. By the end of the 1920s, advertisements for his bodybuilding regimen appeared regularly in the back of men's true crime and adventure magazines. When underweight weaklings or flabby idlers sent away for his program, they would receive instructions on strength-building exercises, explanations of how to adopt a low-fat diet, and lessons on the importance of cleanliness and thoroughly chewing one's food. More than just a strength-building system, the Atlas program advocated meticulous personal grooming, straight posture, and general good health. It also demonstrated how to achieve the kind of body that looked attractive in the latest clothing styles.

While American women turned to Parisian designers to set the latest fashions, American men turned to prestigious London designers on Bond Street and Saville Row. The most formal suit a man of the 1920s might own consisted of a black or midnight-blue worsted swallow-tailed coat ("tails"), trimmed with satin, and a pair of matching trousers, trimmed down the sides with wide braid or satin ribbon. These were worn with a white, waist-length linen or piqué vest over a starched white dress shirt. Dress shirts had buttonholes on both sides of the front opening, but no buttons. Men kept their shirts closed by threading removable buttons, called studs, between each set of corresponding buttonholes. A stiff, detachable collar attached to the shirt with collar buttons, and cufflinks fastened the French-style cuffs. A white bow tie, black silk top hat, white gloves, patent leather oxford shoes, spats, a white silk handkerchief, and a white flower boutonnière completed the outfit. Such a formal outfit, or "full dress," as it was known, would have been appropriate for only the most important occasions, such as balls, large formal dinners, evening weddings, and opera performances. Not surprisingly, only wealthier gentlemen could have afforded—or would have needed—such a suit.

A gentleman's semiformal suit, called a tuxedo, could be worn to nearly every evening engagement. Like a full-dress suit, a tuxedo was made of black or dark blue worsted material, but the tuxedo jacket had no tails and the tuxedo pants were trimmed, if at all, in very narrow braid or ribbon. The tuxedo vest could be black or white, but, unlike the obligatory full-dress white tie, tuxedos ties were always black. In fact, just as today, party invitations that indicated the affair was "black tie" meant that men were expected to wear tuxedos. Men usually completed their tuxedo outfit with all the same accessories as the full-dress suit,

Advertisement for Arrow Collars and Shirts. Courtesy of the Library of Congress.

except that instead of top hats they would wear dark, dome-shaped hats called bowlers. Tuxedos were appropriate attire at the theater, small dinner parties, entertaining in the home, and dining in a restaurant.

A standard, conservative business suit in the 1920s consisted of a jacket, trousers, and a vest and was sold in not just black but any number of shades of gray, tan, brown, blue, or green. Instead of a bowtie, one would wear an ascot or a "regular" four-in-hand, which was a long necktie tied in a slipknot with one end hanging in front of the other. At the beginning of the decade, men's business suits fitted relatively snugly, often with a jacket that tapered at the waist, but in later years the silhouette of business suits relaxed considerably and jackets became longer and roomier, with a less defined waist. Trousers had cuffs, front creases, and button or hook-and-eye flies throughout the 1920s (zippers were not widely used on trouser flies until the 1930s). Professional men wore business suits to work, obviously, but also to other daytime occasions, including theater matinees and church services.

During the early 1920s, most men's dress shirts had, instead of a collar, a narrow neckband with a buttonhole in both the front and back. Detachable collars, which came in a variety of styles, were designed with two buttons so they could attach easily to the shirts. Men could choose a collar that was stiff, semi-stiff, or soft, with flaps that were pointed, rounded, or wing-style (stiff points that folded down in front, like today's tuxedo shirt collars). Washable collars were made of fabric; others were made of celluloid and could be wiped clean with a damp cloth. By the middle of the 1920s, however, many men preferred shirts with attached collars—they were softer and much more comfortable than most of the rigid, detachable collars.

Like women, men of the 1920s usually wore hats whenever they left the house. Certain hats, such as top hats and bowlers, were reserved for formal occasions. More casual hats included the popular fedora, which was usually made of soft felt and featured a decorative ribbon around the base of the crown and a distinctive crease that ran from front to back across the top. The brim of a fedora usually curled up slightly, but young men often turned the front of the brim down, and flamboyant dandies wore their fedoras with one side turned up and one side turned down. Another common men's hat of the decade was the peaked cap, which was a flat hat with a short front brim, often made of plaid, tweed, or herringbone woolen material, corduroy, or solid-colored poplin.

MEN'S COLLEGIATE STYLES

As was the case for women's fashions, national celebrities exerted a profound influence on middle-class men's fashion during the 1920s. Like women, men embraced clothing styles that enhanced or increased their youthful appearance. Sports stars such as golfer Bobby Jones and tennis player Bill Tilden became fashion trendsetters whom their fans tried to emulate. Well-dressed young men might wear golfing knickers and a sweater or loose, white flannel trousers and V-necked sweater vests over a collared shirt, whether or not they actually played golf or tennis. Silent film star Rudolph Valentino introduced the image of the suave, sophisticated "sheik" to American men with the release of his 1921 movie *The Sheik*. Young men copied his look by shaving their beards and moustaches and parting their slicked-down hair in the middle or just off to one side. In 1927, after Charles Lindbergh completed his historic transatlantic flight, tens of thousands of men (and some women) bought leather aviation jackets and helmets to wear when riding in open automobiles. The attractive and charming Edward, Prince of Wales, provided perhaps the strongest celebrity influence over American men's fashion. Men across the nation imitated every aspect of his extensive, impeccable wardrobe, from his stylish tweed plus-fours (baggy knickers worn with knee socks) to his colorful Fair Isle knitted sweaters.

Another British influence on young men's fashion emerged around 1925, when the students at Oxford University in England began to wear extremely loose, baggy trousers that extended all the way down to the tops of their shoes. Supposedly, students wore these "Oxford bags" to cover their knickers, which were considered improper classroom attire. These wide-leg trousers—sometimes measuring as much as 30 inches around the knees—caught on among the fashionable younger set in America. Other, not-quite-so-baggy flannel trousers also became popular choices on college campuses, and by the end of the decade the slim-fitting pants that had been fashionable in the early 1920s were decidedly passé.

Collegiate men usually wore some style of sports jacket along with their loose-fitting pants. Some blazers featured a front pocket decorated with a badge or crest. Other jackets were designed in the Norfolk style, with a belt across the waist and box pleats down the sides. College freshmen were frequently required to wear a "dink"—a small felt cap in the school colors—for the first few weeks of classes. The dinks made it easy for upperclassmen to identify the new freshmen and thus contribute to their "hazing" experience. As for outerwear, the bulky, knee-length raccoon overcoat made a strong fashion statement among college men who could afford it during the 1920s, as did the belted trench coat, modeled after British soldiers' apparel in World War I, and the formal knee-length Chesterfield coat, with its distinctive black velvet collar.

MEN'S SHOES, UNDERGARMENTS, AND ACCESSORIES

While formal and semiformal wear required shiny patent-leather shoes, men's casual footwear during the 1920s encompassed a range of styles. The oxford shoe—a low-cut, low-heeled, laced shoe—largely replaced old-fashioned tall, lace-up boots. Sport oxfords were made with comfortable rubber soles and came mostly in the traditional colors of black, brown, tan, and white. Two-toned oxfords, made of white buckskin and black or brown leather, were also popular favorites. Rubber galoshes with buckles or snaps protected these relatively flimsy shoes in rainy or snowy weather. Men's socks were made of cotton, silk, wool, or rayon. Tall, ribbed socks worn with knickers often featured colorful plaid, striped, or Argyle patterns. Because men's dress socks lacked elasticity, men had to wear adjustable hose garters around their calves to keep their socks from falling down.

During the 1920s, men's undergarments often consisted of the one-piece "union suit," which was a combination of undershirt and underpants. For cold weather, woolen union suits had long sleeves and long pants and featured a convenient "drop seat." For summer, loose one-piece cotton undergarments had short pants and sleeveless tops and buttoned up the front or at the tops of the shoulder straps. These light cotton garments resembled the brief "step-in" underwear that many women wore. Separate undershirts and undershorts for men were also widely available.

Men's wallets were larger in the 1920s than they generally are today, primarily because American paper currency was larger. In 1929, American bills were reduced to their present size (6⅛ × 2⅝ inches), but before that, they measured 7$\frac{7}{16}$ × 3⅛ inches. These larger wallets usually folded into thirds, rather than today's common bifold, and were customarily made of leather, pigskin, or sometimes ostrich skin. Most men also carried some sort of timepiece, either a pocket watch on a chain or a convenient wristwatch—a style that was introduced in the 1920s and soon eclipsed the popularity of pocket watches. Despite National Prohibition, some men (and women) also carried pocket flasks—chrome-plated, monogrammed flasks were particularly trendy. Cigarette cases and lighters also found their way into many men's pockets and came in a variety of decorative styles. Personal jewelry for men was usually fairly minimal in the 1920s, except, of course, for wedding or signet rings and the studs and cufflinks required to fasten dress shirts.

CHILDREN'S FASHIONS

For children, as for adults, ready-to-wear clothing was widely available and quite popular during the 1920s. Infants, both boys and girls, often wore long dresses with matching bonnets. Slightly older babies might wear romper suits, which were one-piece garments that combined shirt and shorts. By the time they were toddlers, though, children tended to wear more gender-specific clothing. Little girls wore "bloomer dresses," which were short, loose dresses, often of checked or plaid material, coupled with matching panties that just peeked out below the bottom of the skirt. In the early 1920s, girls up to about the age of 14 commonly wore loose, feminine dresses that were frequently embellished with lace, ruffles, or artificial flowers and tied with a sash. Also popular were long skirts topped with sailor-style middy blouses made of wool flannel, jean cloth, or serge. These long-sleeved blouses featured a shawl collar, contrasting necktie, and sometimes even nautical insignia on the sleeves. Girls also wore thigh-length cardigan sweaters that buttoned up the front and, in some cases, belted around the middle. In cold weather, girls might wear a short wool coat, some of which came trimmed with squirrel, beaver, or rabbit fur around the neck and cuffs. By the end of the 1920s, young girls had adopted many aspects of flapper fashions—their loose dresses were short and long-waisted, their hats were simple versions of the adult cloche, and their hair was stylishly bobbed. Matching dresses, either big-and-little sister dresses or mother-and-daughter dresses, also became trendy late in the 1920s.

Boys younger than five years old usually wore shirts that buttoned to short matching pants. Often these little two-piece outfits looked like sailor suits, complete with nautical necktie. Catalogs from the late 1920s also included playsuits for young boys that were designed to look like police uniforms or Native American costumes (complete with a feather headdress). Boys between 5 and 10 years old frequently wore knicker suits consisting of short pants, a belted jacket, and sometimes a matching vest. Dark stockings and lace-up ankle boots completed the outfit. Late in the 1920s, beltless jackets that more closely resembled adult fashions gradually replaced belted jackets. Young boys usually wore flat, peaked caps made of wool or wool blend fabric, just as many of their fathers and older brothers did.

CONCLUSION

Clothing fashions, like many other elements of American popular culture, changed rapidly throughout the 1920s. Hemlines rose and then fell, bathing suits became lighter and briefer, and, in many instances, masculine designs influenced women's clothing. Throughout all of these fashion changes, motion pictures, fashion magazines, mail-order catalogs, department store displays, and sophisticated advertising campaigns encouraged consumers to believe that keeping up with the latest fashions was critical to their social success and happiness. Purchasing an authentic designer wardrobe required a substantial financial outlay well beyond the reach of most middle- and working-class Americans. Fortunately, though, the widespread availability of inexpensive, ready-to-wear clothing in department stores and mail-order catalogs made fashionable outfits more accessible to ordinary Americans than ever before.

6
Food and Drink

The 1920s saw the emergence of an American cuisine that was more homogeneous than ever before. Prior to World War I, no distinctive American cuisine existed, and diets varied widely according to people's ethnicity, class, income, and region. But during the 1920s, a more standardized diet developed, consisting largely of salads and light, simple meals that frequently included processed food products. The growing popularity of brand-name foods, the influence of scientific nutrition, and the mass marketing of new kitchen appliances, especially gas stoves and electric refrigerators, all contributed to the creation of a national cuisine. So, too, did the widespread use of cookbooks, the rise of mass-circulation women's magazines, and the introduction of radio cooking shows. Restaurant dining also became more common, and the number of commercial eating establishments dramatically increased throughout the United States. Furthermore, many immigrant families, eager to assimilate more fully into American society, incorporated American cooking styles and eating habits into their traditional Old World cuisine. All of these national forces and trends resulted in more and more Americans eating similar foods, prepared in similar ways, and thus sharing a popular food culture that we can recognize as identifiably modern.

DINING IN THE HOME

American Homemakers

As in previous decades, Americans continued to eat most of their meals at home during the 1920s, and cooking those family meals remained almost exclusively the responsibility of women. However, cooking occupied a far less important role in middle-class women's daily routines than it had for previous generations. The preparation of family meals during the 1890s was a time-consuming task, with dinner sometimes requiring the better part of an afternoon to prepare. The 1920s, however, witnessed a trend toward simpler meals that could be prepared comparatively quickly. Several factors accounted for this transformation in home cookery. First, servants, once common in middle- and upper-class homes during the late nineteenth century, began to leave domestic service to take jobs as department store clerks, secretaries, typists, and telephone operators. Thus, middle-class wives who found themselves doing their own grocery shopping and cooking gravitated toward easy-to-prepare dishes. Second, more than 3 million married women had entered the workforce by the end of the 1920s, and these women had less time to prepare elaborate meals for their husbands and children. As a result, they too relied on quick recipes and one-dish meals to feed their families.

Many homemakers streamlined their daily meal preparation by relying on the dozens of packaged, commercially processed foods that became available during the 1920s. Many of these products, such as quick-cooking rolled oats or dry pancake mixes, were designed to make meal preparation both faster and easier. For example, women often combined canned pineapple and other fruits with Jell-O gelatin (introduced in 1897) to make molded salads, or mixed gelatin with mayonnaise, carrots, peas, and celery to make quick and simple vegetable salads. Not surprisingly, sales of canned goods and other prepared foods soared during the 1920s, and condensed soups, bottled condiments, and canned fruits and vegetables played an increasingly prominent role in the meals placed on America's dining tables.

New kitchen technologies and the introduction of electricity into many middle-class American homes also changed the way women prepared daily meals for their families. Gas and, to a lesser degree, electric ranges replaced wood- and coal-burning stoves in many kitchens, and by 1930, approximately half of all American homes were equipped with gas stoves. Electric refrigerators also revolutionized cooking by replacing old-fashioned, unreliable iceboxes. Refrigerators built for home use had been in existence since 1913, but during the early 1920s, most of them were too expensive for average consumers. In 1923, the cheapest model on the market cost around $450, at a time when approximately 80 percent of American families lived on an annual income of less than $2,000. However, methods of mass production reduced the price of refrigerators significantly during the last half of the 1920s, and by 1929, Americans were buying more than 800,000 refrigerators a year.[1] With the advent of widespread electrification, electric pop-up toasters, pressure cookers, coffee

Interior of a model kitchen, Frederick Apartments, Columbia, Missouri, circa 1926. Courtesy of Sabra Tull Meyer.

percolators, waffle irons, and mixers also became common fixtures in middle-class kitchens. Despite the increased use of convenient, commercially prepared foods and new labor-saving electrical appliances, urban housewives still devoted an average of 19 hours per week to preparing meals and cleaning up after them during the 1920s, while rural housewives spent a slightly greater amount (almost 24 hours per week) on those same chores.

Giant Food Corporations and New Products

Since the 1890s, giant food corporations had dominated American food processing and manufacturing, which by 1920 was one of the largest industries in the United States. These corporations, including General Mills, Incorporated (formed in 1928), Standard Brands (1929), and General Foods Corporation (1929), spent millions of dollars researching and developing better methods of preserving and packaging food. Sugar and flour, once sold in bulk, now came packaged in bags, and milk, once marketed only in glass bottles, now also came in inexpensive cardboard cartons. As more efficient methods of manufacturing tin cans developed, canning became an increasingly economical way to preserve and package foods such as fruits, vegetables, ham, tuna, and even cheese. Another technological advancement, flash-freezing, was also used to preserve foods in the 1920s. In 1924, Clarence Birdseye developed a process for flash-freezing fish, and five years later he sold his patents to the Postum Cereal Company (soon to be reorganized as the General Foods Corporation). In 1930, the company sold the first commercially packaged frozen fruits and vegetables under the brand name Birds Eye Frosted Foods, marking the advent of the frozen food industry.

These processing and packaging innovations allowed corporations to market a cornucopia of mass-produced foods during the 1920s. Americans had been eating cold breakfast cereals since the late 1890s, but several new breakfast cereals appeared on the market during the 1920s, including Post 40% Bran Flakes (1922), Wheaties (1924), and Kellogg's Rice Krispies (1928). In 1928, the J. L. Kraft & Brothers Company developed a processed cheese food called Velveeta, which came wrapped in a tinfoil package inside a wooden box and did not require refrigeration. Florida orange and grapefruit growers began selling canned pasteurized juice in 1929. Tomato juice, introduced in the mid-1920s, became a popular breakfast drink by 1928. Oscar Mayer & Company began marketing packaged sliced bacon in 1924, and George A. Hormel & Company sold the nation's first canned hams in 1926. Potato chips had been commercially manufactured and sold in bulk since the 1890s, but it wasn't until the 1920s, with the development of the continuous fryer and the waxed paper bag, that sales of potato chips soared. Other new foods introduced during the 1920s included Wonder Bread (1921, but not sold sliced until 1930), Quick Quaker Oats (1921), Welch's Concord grape jelly (1923), Land O' Lakes butter (1924), Green Giant canned peas (1925), Peter Pan peanut butter (1928), and Niblets whole kernel corn (1929).

Meals

Despite a severe depression that gripped the farming industry throughout the 1920s, technological advancements in agriculture and transportation provided both a greater abundance and a wider assortment of foods for Americans' dinner tables than ever before. Gasoline-powered tractors and improved methods of scientific farming produced larger crop yields. Refrigerated railcars and over-the-road trucks distributed fresh meats, fruits, vegetables, dairy products, and grains to grocery stores and restaurants across the nation. As a result, homemakers were able to purchase oranges, grapefruits, bananas, lettuce, and broccoli (first commercially grown in the United States in 1923) even during the winter months. Even those families living in small towns and rural areas could regularly enjoy fresh fruits that were once too expensive to afford. One U.S. Department of Agriculture study, for example, reported that in 1923 midwestern farm families in four states consumed an average of more than 100 pounds of citrus fruits and bananas per year.[2] Overall, food prices dropped significantly during the 1920s, which allowed even families with modest incomes to eat a wide variety of foods.

During the 1920s, middle-class Americans began to eat relatively light, healthful meals. Earlier generations had eaten breakfasts consisting of large amounts of bread, potatoes, and meats such as steak, chops, sausage, and ham. But during the 1920s, home economists and nutritionists advised homemakers to serve their families breakfasts of citrus juice, dry cereal, eggs, and toast. Common lunches consisted of a sandwich, soup, or salad. Dinners, which changed the least of the three daily meals, typically included a simply prepared meat, potatoes, one or two vegetable side dishes, and dessert. Overall, Americans became more health conscious and as a result consumed smaller amounts of red meats, fats, and starches than they had during previous decades.

Popular main courses and side dishes found on American dinner tables during the 1920s included broiled steaks and chops, meatloaf, Swiss steak, spaghetti and meatballs, and side dishes of potatoes, vegetables, and salads. One-dish meals and casseroles streamlined food preparation. For example, a 1920s cookbook recipe for a one-dish shepherd's pie actually contained meat, potatoes, and vegetables, all served within a marshmallow crust—a sort of meal and dessert rolled into one. Salads also became fashionable during the 1920s. Several well-known salads were invented during the decade, including the Cobb salad, developed in 1926 by Robert Cobb at his Brown Derby Restaurant in Los Angeles, and the Green Goddess salad, created by Chef Philip Roemer in 1923 at the grand Palace Hotel Restaurant in San Francisco. The most famous green, leafy salad of the decade was the Caesar salad, named for its creator, Caesar Cardini, an Italian chef who ran a restaurant in Tijuana, Mexico. In 1924, Cardini concocted his special salad for a group of visiting Hollywood celebrities, and soon the Caesar salad emerged as a favorite dish back in the States. Since gas and electric ovens made baking easier, cakes became a common dessert during the 1920s, especially pineapple upside-down cake, devil's food cake, and chiffon cake (invented in 1927). Other dessert favorites included molded Jell-O salads, fruit salads, heavenly hash, pineapple fluff, and chocolate mousse.

Cookbooks and Radio Cooking Shows

Cookbooks and promotional recipe booklets helped to popularize modern ways of cooking and baking. Cookbooks, many of which were written by famous culinary experts such as Alice Bradley and Ida Bailey Allen, were exceedingly popular with homemakers because following recipes produced appetizing meals but demanded few cooking skills. One of the standard cookbooks of the 1920s was *The Boston Cooking-School Cook Book*, by Fannie Merritt Farmer. Originally published in 1896, this cookbook appeared in several revised editions and remained a best-seller throughout the 1920s. With the aid of cookbooks and recipes clipped from magazines and newspapers, more adventuresome homemakers dabbled in foreign cooking. Many of the leading American cookbooks contained a few Italian and Mexican recipes, but the number of cookbooks devoted exclusively to foreign cuisine, such as *Mexican Cookery for American Homes* (1923), also increased significantly after World War I. Nearly all of the cookbooks published during the 1920s were written for housewives, but a few targeted other members of the family, such as *Young People's Cook Book* (1925) or *The Stag Cookbook, Written for Men, by Men* (1922), which included, for instance, recipes for preparing fresh fish and wild game.

During the 1920s, nearly every major food corporation of the 1920s distributed booklets filled with recipes that listed their brand-name products as necessary ingredients. Kitchen appliance manufacturers and women's magazines also published these promotional cookbooks. *Good Housekeeping*, the women's periodical with the largest circulation during the decade, published *Good Housekeeping's Book of Menus, Recipes and Household Discoveries* (1924), which, its introduction noted, "is offered to housewives with the hope that it will suggest new dishes by which the daily menu may be varied."[3] The magazine also awarded its "Good

Housekeeping Seal of Approval," introduced in 1910, to foods that the Good Housekeeping Institute had tested and approved, and this endorsement essentially served to promote the products of many of the magazine's advertisers.

Homemakers also tuned in to radio cooking shows during the 1920s for helpful advice about meal planning and cooking. In 1921, the advertising department of the Washburn-Crosby Company created a fictional homemaker spokesperson named Betty Crocker to assist in the promotion of its Gold Medal flour. Three years later, the company began its sponsorship of the nation's first radio cooking show, *The Betty Crocker School of the Air*, which was later broadcast on the NBC network. Another pioneering radio homemaker program was *Aunt Sammy*, first broadcast in 1926. Sponsored by the U.S. Department of Agriculture, the program could be heard on 50 stations across the nation and proved so popular with female listeners that it led to the publication of a cookbook titled *Aunt Sammy's Radio Recipes* (1927). Between 1928 and 1935, cookbook author Ida Bailey Allen, known as "the nation's homemaker," hosted *The National Radio Home-Makers' Club* on the CBS network, on which she provided cooking lessons and recipes.

Scientific Nutrition

New ideas about food science and nutrition, disseminated through home economics courses, cookbooks, women's magazines, and radio homemaker shows, also helped to transform American cooking and eating habits during the 1920s. Since the 1890s and particularly during World War I, home economists and nutrition experts had attempted to instruct Americans about how to cook and eat more heathfully. Additionally, a series of breakthroughs in food science in the 1910s and 1920s, including the discovery of vitamins A, B_1, C, D, and E, made Americans more aware of the importance of proper nutrition. During the 1920s, food scientists continued their crusade to spread the gospel of scientific nutrition, and American homemakers eagerly embraced these new ideas. Fruits and vegetables, once considered unnecessary for a well-balanced diet, came to be understood as crucial to maintaining good health. Milk, once viewed as only a children's drink, became popular among adults. Many mothers attempted to feed their children a nutrionally balanced diet to ward off sickness and encourage healthy development. In 1928, the Fremont Canning Company introduced Gerber Baby Food, a line of commercially manufactured strained vegetables for infants, and soon launched a national advertising campaign, featuring the now-familiar Gerber's baby, to promote its products.

Advertisement for California Sunkist oranges, *The Saturday Evening Post*, November 29, 1924. Courtesy of the Library of Congress.

Dieting and Calorie Counting

Based upon the advice of medical doctors and nutrition experts, many health-conscious Americans began counting calories and dieting, or "reducing," as it was commonly known. By 1920, scientists and physicians clearly understood calories and the relationship between obesity and diseases such as diabetes. Dieting manuals, along with commercial diet programs, reducing creams, and other weight-loss products, flooded the market in the 1920s. Dieting was particularly popular among young women in their teens and twenties, and the nation's leading women's magazines and daily newspapers ran feature articles, regular advice columns, and weekly menu plans intended to provide female readers with helpful hints about how to eat healthfully, count calories, and shed unwanted pounds.

Dieting for beauty's sake also became common among women. By the early 1920s, the curvaceous, hourglass figure of the Gibson Girl, once considered the epitome of female beauty, had been supplanted by the rail-thin, waistless figure of the flapper. Across the nation, women went on diets in order to conform to the new slimmer ideals of beauty as depicted in Madison Avenue advertising and Hollywood motion pictures. New clothing styles also fueled the dieting craze. Many of the fashionable dresses of the 1920s sported hemlines that revealed much of the legs and sleeveless bodices that exposed the arms, and in order to appear attractive in such outfits, women redoubled their efforts to slim down.

Dozens of doctors and dieting gurus contributed to this craze by publishing weight-loss books and articles. The most famous proponent of scientific dieting was Dr. Lulu Hunt Peters, a Los Angeles physician, whose *Diet and Health, With Key to the Calories* (1918) remained a national best-seller throughout the 1920s. Peters advocated a weight-reduction program that combined calorie counting with the practice of slowly chewing everything—even milk and soup. Dr. William Howard Hay's "Medical Millennium Diet" advocated a combination of slow chewing, meal planning, and daily enemas to control one's weight. Also popular was the "Hollywood Eighteen Day Diet," a restrictive, 585-calorie program that recommended eating only "grapefruit, oranges, Melba Toast, green vegetables and hard-boiled eggs."[4] Another leading figure in the diet industry was Sylvia Ullbeck, a Hollywood masseuse and weight-loss guru whose strict regimen of massages and dieting, popularized in the advice column she wrote for the motion picture fan magazine *Photoplay*, helped film stars such as Norma Shearer, Mae Murray, and Gloria Swanson shed unwanted pounds. Ullbeck claimed to massage with such force that "fat comes through the pores like mashed potatoes through a colander."[5] Dozens of medical doctors cautioned that many of these popular diet fads were potentially dangerous, but few heeded their warnings.

GROCERY SHOPPING AND CHAIN GROCERY STORES

Chain grocery stores sparked a food merchandising revolution during the 1920s. Chain stores purchased in volume from wholesalers and, as a result, could offer their customers cheaper prices and a wider selection than most independent markets. The nation's leading grocery store chain during the 1920s was the Great Atlantic & Pacific Tea Company, better known as A&P, founded in 1859. By 1929, the A&P was operating a chain of more than 15,400 stores across the nation, with combined total sales of more than $1 billion. Other grocery store chains, such as American, Kroger, National, and Safeway, also prospered during the 1920s, and by 1928, some 860 rival chains crowded the highly competitive food retailing business. With their lower prices and wider selection of goods, these chains drove many independent stores out of business. But small grocers fought back in 1926 by forming the Independent Grocers Alliance (IGA), a national trade association that made it possible for independent grocery stores to obtain the same wholesale discounts as the large chains and thus adopt similar merchandising strategies.

Another innovation that changed the retail food industry was the advent of self-service grocery stores. Prior to World War I, most food items were located on shelves behind the counter, and store clerks would gather, bag, and often deliver groceries for customers. But in 1916, Clarence Saunders introduced a new self-service shopping format at his Piggly Wiggly grocery store in Memphis, Tennessee. Piggly Wiggly shoppers would select items from the rows of open shelves, place them in baskets, and carry them to the front of the store, where a clerk would ring up their total. By 1920, 515 Piggly Wiggly stores were operating in cities throughout the South and Midwest. The chain continued to expand throughout the 1920s, reaching a total of more than 2,600 stores by 1929. Self-service grocery stores employed fewer clerks, so they could pass their savings on to shoppers in the form of lower prices. Self-service stores also allowed shoppers to handle and inspect the products before purchasing them. During the 1920s, most of the nation's grocery stores gradually converted to the self-service format of food retailing that Piggly Wiggly pioneered.

Interior of a District Grocery Store, Washington, D.C., circa 1920. Courtesy of the Library of Congress.

DINING OUT

The Growth of Restaurants

During the 1920s, Americans dined out in restaurants and other eating establishments more often than earlier generations did, and the total number of restaurants in the United States tripled between 1919 and 1929.[6] The increased patronage of commuters who ate their lunches out helped to fuel the dramatic growth of diners, cafeterias, and other quick-service restaurants. Expanding numbers of married women in the workforce also contributed to the increasing popularity of various kinds of eating establishments. Not only did working women patronize restaurants at lunchtime, but they also found it more difficult to juggle work and household responsibilities such as preparing family meals. Thus, dining out became an attractive choice for many American families, because it was convenient, offered opportunities to socialize, and left no dirty dishes in the sink.

National Prohibition also transformed the American restaurant industry during the 1920s. After 1920, when it became illegal to serve alcohol, many of the nation's first-class restaurants, which had once profited from the sale of expensive wines and spirits, went out of business. On the other end of the culinary spectrum, Prohibition also eliminated saloons as a source of inexpensive lunches for factory workers. Prior to 1920, most working-class saloons had offered "free lunches"—light meals of sausages, hard-boiled eggs, crackers, and cheese. These lunches were not actually free but came with the purchase of a five-cent glass of beer. When the nation's saloons shut their doors in compliance with the Eighteenth Amendment, however, the free lunches that so many industrial workers had relied upon vanished. With their disappearance, quick-service restaurants, such as lunchrooms, diners, and cafeterias, expanded and flourished throughout the decade.

Quick-Service Restaurants

During the 1920s, the growing numbers of businessmen, assembly-line workers, department store clerks, and secretaries demanded fast, convenient lunches, and thus a whole range of quick-service restaurants, including automats, cafés, lunchrooms, diners, cafeterias, and sandwich shops, sprang up in American cities and towns. Automats, which had been operating in the United States since 1902, served perhaps the quickest meals. Automats featured rows of coin-operated vending machines that offered customers an assortment of both hot and cold prepared foods. For as little as a nickel, a patron could purchase a ham sandwich, a bowl of soup, a dish of ice cream, or a slice of pie.

During the 1920s, lunchrooms also attracted noontime crowds. Usually located on the ground floor of downtown urban office buildings, lunchrooms sported U-shaped counters at which customers could eat cheap meals of grilled sandwiches, chili, meatloaf, or salads. By 1920, larger cities usually contained dozens of lunchrooms competing for the lunch and dinner traffic. Although most lunchrooms remained independently owned, chain lunchrooms made dramatic inroads into the restaurant market during the 1910s and 1920s. By 1920, lunchroom chains such as Thompson's Lunchrooms and Baltimore Dairy Lunch were operating more than 100 outlets throughout much of the Midwest and East Coast.

Diners remained popular among factory workers, taxi drivers, and other working-class Americans during the 1920s. Diners differed from lunchrooms primarily in that they typically occupied freestanding, stainless steel structures that contained a grill, counter, stools, booths, and rest rooms. Diners usually remained open 24 hours a day, although they catered principally to a breakfast and lunch crowd. Customers could order such simple dishes as sandwiches, hamburgers, chili, bacon and eggs, waffles, or pancakes. By 1932, an estimated 4,000 diners were operating across the United States.

Lunch counter of the Rainbow Grill, Bordentown, New Jersey. Courtesy of the Library of Congress.

Cafeterias, another variety of quick-service restaurants, allowed customers to assemble their own meals from a wide selection of inexpensive entrees, side dishes, and desserts kept warm on steam tables. This self-service system reduced operating costs by virtually eliminating the need for a wait staff. Several major cafeteria chains were launched during the 1920s, including Bishop's Cafeteria, Laughner's Cafeteria, Morrison's Cafeteria, and S&W Cafeteria. In 1929, New York City alone boasted 786 cafeterias, but the greatest concentration of chain cafeterias was found in the Midwest and South, where regional cuisine dominated the menu. In North Carolina and Georgia, for example, cafeterias typically served fried chicken, biscuits and gravy, corn bread, collard greens, Jell-O salads, and sweet potato pie.

Tearooms

The number of affordably priced, mid-range restaurants also grew during the 1920s, and one of the most popular formats was the tearoom, many of which were located in urban downtown districts. Most tearooms were owned and operated by women, and although such establishments were acceptable dining venues for the entire family, they generally catered to a predominantly middle-class female clientele. Tearooms served simple, moderately priced lunches and afternoon tea in warm, charming surroundings. Tearooms hoping to attract male customers sometimes offered hearty fare such as chopped beefsteak or tongue sandwiches. One of the most famous of this style of restaurant was the Russian Tea Room in New York City, opened in 1926 by exiled members of the Russian Imperial Ballet who had fled the Bolshevik Revolution. Although thousands of tearooms continued to operate throughout the 1920s, they declined in popularity by the end of the decade, as restaurants that offered faster service and lower prices attracted more customers.

Ethnic Restaurants

Partially as a result of National Prohibition, Italian cuisine became popular with Americans during the 1920s. An estimated one-quarter of all the immigrants who entered the United States between 1890 and 1914 were from Italy, and some of them opened pizzerias and ristorantes in the Italian neighborhoods of major American cities. Chefs often adapted traditional southern Italian cuisine to suit American tastes by adding meatballs to spaghetti dishes and expanding their menus to include such traditional fare as broiled steaks and chops. During Prohibition, many Italian entrepreneurs continued illicitly to serve wine, which was central to Italian food culture. Thus, these restaurants became little more than speakeasies that attracted customers who wanted to drink. Americans who patronized these ristorantes for their liquor often developed a fondness for spaghetti and meatballs, fettuccini Alfredo, and other Italian dishes.

Chinese food was another popular ethnic cuisine in the 1920s, and Chinese cooks altered traditional Cantonese, Hunan, and Mandarin cuisine to make it more appealing to American diners. As a result, the menus of many Chinese restaurants contained dishes such as chop suey, chow mein, and stir-fried rice, all of which originated in the United States. Other Americanized dishes featured such non-traditional ingredients as batter-fried meats, pineapple chunks, and maraschino cherries. Some Chinese restaurants in New England even sold chow mein sandwiches on a bun, with a special meatless version served on Fridays to accommodate Roman Catholics. Other ethnic restaurants that flourished during the 1920s included southern barbecue joints and rib shacks, German beer gardens, Swedish smorgasbords, French bistros and cafés, and Jewish delicatessens. In California and the Southwest, Mexican and Tex-Mex cuisine was popular fare in restaurants such as the famous El Charro Café, which opened in Tucson, Arizona, in 1922. French cooking, on the other hand, declined in popularity during National Prohibition because it was difficult to obtain the fine wines often required to prepare and accompany authentic Parisian cuisine.

Roadside Restaurants and Food Stands

During the 1920s, a bustling roadside restaurant industry emerged in the United States. Prior to World War I, when automobiles were less common, travelers had few places to purchase a meal along the road. But between 1920 and 1930, the number of automobiles in the nation jumped from 8 million to 23 million.[7] As a result, tens of thousands of cafés, barbecue shacks, hotdog kennels, and ice cream stands sprang up alongside the nation's highways and roads. These eating establishments catered specifically to motorists, sightseers, traveling salesmen, and vacationers and often used flashing neon signs (introduced in 1923), gaudy billboards, and distinctive architecture to attract passing motorists. Roadside restaurants and stands offered motorists fare ranging from quick-service hamburgers, hot dogs, and soft drinks to sit-down meals of steaks, potatoes, and salads. They frequently operated near public beaches, amusement parks, national parks, and other local attractions, thus catering to heavy tourist traffic. For example, Howard Johnson opened a handful of ice cream stands near the crowded Boston seashore during the mid-1920s, and he later parlayed these stands into a nationally known franchise of restaurants and hotels. In 1922, Roy W. Allen and Frank Wright opened three walk-up root beer stands in Sacramento, California, under the name of A&W (which combined the first letter of the owners' surnames). Two years later, after acquiring Wright's share of the business, Allen began to sell franchises to individual entrepreneurs and went on to build A&W into one of the nation's first chains of franchise roadside restaurants, with 171 outlets across the nation by 1933.

One of the revolutionary innovations of the 1920s roadside restaurant industry was curbside service. In 1921, J. G. Kirby and Dr. Reuben W. Jackson opened what is widely considered the nation's first drive-in sandwich restaurant, called the Pig Stand, along a busy highway on the outskirts of Dallas, Texas. A staff of "tray boys" delivered barbecued pork sandwiches and Coca-Colas to customers waiting curbside in their automobiles. Kirby struck upon this service concept after recognizing, as he once remarked, that "People with cars are so lazy they don't want to get out of them to eat."[8] By 1930, the Pig Stand Company, Incorporated was operating some 60 franchise roadside eateries across California and the Southwest. A&W stands and other roadside restaurants soon adopted the drive-in service format for many of their outlets. The Pig Stand, however, was the first restaurant specifically designed to provide curb service to motorists and, as such, it stands as the forerunner to the full-blown drive-in restaurants that we know today.

White Castle and the Rise of Fast-Food Hamburger Chains

During the 1920s, several decades before the rise of McDonald's and Burger King, White Castle heralded the advent of fast-food hamburger chains. In 1921, Walter Anderson and Edgar Waldo "Billy" Ingram opened a hamburger restaurant in Wichita, Kansas, under the name of White Castle. Hamburgers had a nasty reputation of being made from low-grade or spoiled meat scraps, so Anderson and Ingram stressed in their advertisements that their hamburgers were made from specially selected cuts of ground chuck delivered fresh to their restaurants twice a day. They also reassured wary customers by placing the grill directly in front of them, so they could see the sanitary conditions under which their food was being prepared. The first White Castle restaurant served hamburger sandwiches, smothered with cooked onions, for a nickel apiece.

The White Castle System of Eating Houses, as the chain was called, expanded rapidly during the 1920s due in part to its innovative marketing strategies. Originally, the chain catered to a largely working-class clientele, but during the last half of the 1920s it attracted a wider range of customers by advertising its sandwiches as a convenient carryout food and by urging customers to "Buy 'em by the sack." By 1931, White Castle was operating 115 restaurants across the Midwest and East Coast, all of which featured the same floor plan and distinctive medieval architecture that served as a sort of advertising for the chain. A host of imitator hamburger chain restaurants sprang up around the nation in the wake of White Castle's enormous success, including White Tower (1926), Little Tavern (1927), White Tavern Shoppes (1929), Toddle House (1929), Krystal (1932), and White Hut (1935), all of which replicated the original concepts of mass-produced food and standardized service developed by White Castle. By the end of the 1920s, the hamburger had surpassed the hot dog as Americans' favorite fast food, and fast-food hamburger chains contributed significantly to the emergence of a standard American cuisine.

CANDY BARS AND ICE CREAM

During the 1920s, Americans ate more ice cream and candy bars than previous generations did, in part because technological advancements made these sugary treats more widely available but also, perhaps, to

A 1929 photo of the first White Castle restaurant, Wichita, Kansas. Courtesy of White Castle System, Inc.

compensate for the decline in alcohol consumption during National Prohibition. Other trends also boosted the popularity of chocolate and frozen treats during the Jazz Age. In 1895, Milton S. Hershey marketed the first American-made chocolate bars (the Hershey Milk Chocolate Bar and the Hershey Almond Bar), but chocolate candy bars, long considered primarily a woman's delicacy, did not become widely popular until around

World War I. Beginning in 1917, the Hershey Chocolate Company and other American candy manufacturers supplied the U.S. government with 20-pound blocks of chocolate for distribution to American soldiers. After the war, returning veterans who had grown fond of Hershey's chocolate helped spark a boom in chocolate and candy bar sales in the United States.

Chocolate and candy bar manufacturers reaped huge profits during the 1920s as technological innovations and rising consumption allowed their businesses to expand and new products to be introduced. In 1921, the industry's leading manufacturer, the Hershey Chocolate Company, manufactured more than 8 million pounds of chocolate, with total sales of more than $20 million. By the end of the decade, its yearly sales topped $41 million. The other giant chocolate manufacturer of the 1920s was Mars Candies, founded in 1922 by a former candy wholesaler named Frank Mars. In 1923, Mars introduced his first candy bar, the Milky Way, a malted milk-flavored nougat center coated in chocolate. The Milky Way proved an immediate success and racked up sales of almost $800,000 in its first year on the market. By 1929, Mars' Chicago plant was churning out 20 million candy bars a year. Other candy manufacturers also prospered during the decade. In 1920, the Curtiss Company introduced the Baby Ruth, named not for the New York Yankees slugger, as is often assumed, but for President Grover Cleveland's daughter Ruth. By 1925, the Baby Ruth was one of the nation's best-selling candy bars. The Curtiss Company's second candy bar, the crunchy peanut butter and chocolate Butterfinger, first marketed in 1926, also proved to be a hit.

An estimated 30,000 different candy bars, most of them locally produced, were available during the 1920s.[9] Most of them were made of chocolate with centers of caramel, marshmallow, peanuts, crisped rice, or other ingredients. Candy bars produced during the 1920s usually weighed around 1.25 ounces and sold for a nickel. But most of them quickly disappeared from the market, including (not surprisingly) the Vegetable Sandwich, which billed itself as "A Delicious Candy Made With Vegetables." Other candy bars attempted to cash in on the popularity of national celebrities, fads, or trendy expressions of the Jazz Age. A Chicago candy company marketed Red Grange bars, which came with trading cards of scenes from *One Minute to Play* (1926), a Hollywood film about college football starring the All-American halfback. Other companies manufactured candy bars called Bambino and Big Champ (both named for Babe Ruth), the Big Hearted "Al" bar (named for New York Governor Alfred E. Smith, the 1928 Democratic presidential candidate), the It bar (named for the sensational Hollywood silent film starring Clara

Bow, whose portrait appeared on the wrapper), the Pierce Arrow (named for the luxury automobile), and, after 1927, the Lindy bar and several other candy bars named for aviator Charles Lindbergh. Although these candy bars are now long forgotten, a number of candy bars introduced during the 1920s remain popular today, including Oh Henry! (1920), the Charleston Chew! (1922), Mounds (1922), Reese's Peanut Butter Cup (1923), Bit-O-Honey (1924), and Mr. Goodbar (1925), to name only a handful.

A host of other candies and sweet treats also flooded the market during the 1920s. Although Frank H. Fleer, owner of the Fleer Chewing Gum Company, had developed a bubble gum called Blibber Blubber Bubble Gum as early as 1906, the unperfected product never reached the market. In 1928, one of the accountants at Fleer's company, Walter E. Diemer, accidentally invented a pink colored gum that was so elastic that one could actually blow bubbles with it. Within months, the Fleer Company began selling the gum under the name of Dubble Bubble, and it became the nation's first commercially marketed bubble gum. Among other new candies introduced during the decade were Switzer's cherry licorice (1920), Jujyfruits (1920), fruit-flavored Life Savers (1920), Chuckles (1921), Dum Dum suckers (1924), Goobers (1925), Sugar Daddy (1925), Milk Duds (1926), Slo Poke suckers (1926), Mike & Ike (1928), Y & S Twizzlers licorice (1928), and Hot Tamales (1928).

With technological advancements and the widespread use of refrigeration, ice cream and a variety of other frozen treats also became popular during the 1920s. Ice cream cones, first introduced at the St. Louis World's Fair in 1904, enjoyed unprecedented sales during the 1920s, but ice cream also evolved into several new frozen novelty treats. In 1920, Harry Burt, a Youngstown, Ohio, ice cream parlor operator, developed a chocolate-coated ice cream bar on a wooden stick that he called the Good Humor Bar. He soon began selling them in nearby neighborhoods using a fleet of trucks, each driven by a Good Humor Man and mounted with bells to alert customers of its approach. Other innovative frozen treats followed. In 1921, a Des Moines, Iowa, ice cream plant superintendent named Russell Stover, in partnership with Christian Nelson, introduced a chocolate-covered ice cream square called the Eskimo Pie, which sold 1 million units during its first year on the market. In 1922, William Isaly created a thick, square slab of vanilla ice cream covered in Swiss chocolate, and his ice cream novelty became enormously successful under the trademark name of Klondike Bar. In 1924, Frank Epperson began selling a frozen lemonade bar on a stick to visitors at an Oakland, California, amusement park. Originally, he called his frozen treat Epsicles but soon changed the name to Popsicles, which quickly became a nationally popular brand-name product.

BEVERAGES

Beer, Wine, and Spirits During National Prohibition

In 1920, with the onset of National Prohibition, the U.S. government succeeded in making beer, wine, and spirits more difficult to obtain, but the so-called "Dry Decade" was not so dry, and tens of millions of Americans continued to drink alcohol in defiance of the liquor laws. The cost of alcohol soared during Prohibition, but anyone with enough money could still usually purchase whatever kind of liquor he or she desired. One could buy a pint of whiskey from a neighborhood bootlegger or persuade a doctor to write a prescription for medicinal alcohol, which could then be filled at a local drugstore. During the 1920s, *The New Yorker* even published the current bootleggers' prices and new cocktail recipes within the pages of its weekly magazine. Speakeasies (illegal saloons) sprang up across the nation and sold drinks by the glass. Some resourceful Americans, especially those of German and Italian ancestry, even turned to brewing their own beer, distilling their own spirits, or making their own wines in their cellars and garages. Prohibition drove many Americans to switch from drinking beer, which was sometimes almost impossible to purchase, to drinking more potent alcoholic beverages. In 1919, beer had accounted for 55 percent of all sales of alcoholic beverages in the United States, with spirits accounting for only 37 percent. By 1929, however, liquor and spirits accounted for 75 percent of the overall alcohol consumption in the nation, compared to only 15 percent for beer.[10] Cocktails became especially popular during the 1920s, as drinkers used soft drinks and sweet fruit juices to camouflage the foul taste of inferior whiskey or gin. Hard-core drunks with little money sometimes even resorted to drinking cheap, alcohol-based household products such as aftershave lotion, hair tonic, and cough syrup. Thousands of unfortunate drinkers purchased from unreliable bootleggers liquor that had been tainted with poisonous chemicals. This adulterated booze blinded, crippled, and occasionally even killed these unlucky souls, most of whom were poor or working-class men.

Coffee and Tea

Among non-alcoholic beverages, coffee and tea remained popular drinks throughout the 1920s. Among the leading brands of coffee during the decade were Maxwell House, Sanborn & Chase, Folger's, MJB, and Hill Brothers. The introduction of instant coffee (in 1910) and the marketing of electric coffee percolators for home use also contributed to a sustained increase in coffee sales. During the 1920s, Americans annually consumed around 12 pounds of coffee per capita (approximately 500 cups), up from an average of 10 pounds for the previous decade.[11] Decaffeinated coffee first appeared on the American market in 1910, and in 1927, the Postum Cereal Company introduced Sanka (a contraction of *sans caffeine*, or "without caffeine"). Postum Food Coffee, a naturally caffeine-free, grain-based coffee substitute first manufactured by C. W. Post in 1895, was another hot beverage that sold well during the 1920s. Americans also continued to drink tea, served both hot and cold, during the 1920s, and the popularity of tearooms and tea parties, hosted by women's clubs and organizations, helped to boost tea sales. The introduction of the individual teabag, first developed in 1904, simplified the home brewing of tea. Iced tea, first served at the St. Louis World's Fair in 1904, was also popular in the United States, especially in the South.

Soft Drinks

For many Americans, soft drinks became the non-alcoholic beverage of choice during the 1920s. Since its origins in the late nineteenth century, the soft drink industry had enjoyed steadily increasing sales, and during the 1920s, Coca-Cola and Pepsi-Cola became favorite thirst-quenchers among Americans of all ages. Between 1920 and 1929, annual sales of soft drinks jumped from 175 million cases of soda to almost 273 million cases, or an average of 53 bottles per person.[12] Soft drink consumption rose dramatically as a result of both National Prohibition and, more importantly, aggressive advertising campaigns and expanding merchandising venues. The Coca-Cola Company, one of the pioneers of modern advertising and the nation's leading soft-drink manufacturer, continued its extensive million-dollar promotional campaigns, running colorful magazine ads, billboard signs, and radio commercials. Additionally, the firm created a series of advertisements with memorable slogans, including "The Pause That Refreshes," which first appeared in a 1929 ad in *The Saturday Evening Post*.

Expanding merchandising outlets also helped to boost soft drink sales. Originally, drugstores and soda fountains were the principal retail outlets for soft drinks, but beginning in the 1890s, many companies bottled their beverages for sale in saloons and grocery stores. During the 1920s, most soft drinks came in standard six- or seven-ounce bottles, and usually sold for a nickel. By around 1927, bottled soda accounted for the majority of soft drink sales. Other retail merchandising innovations also fueled sales. In 1924, the Coca-Cola Company began selling its product in six-bottle cartons, and these take-home cartons gradually caught on throughout the soft drink industry. The following year saw the introduction of the Sodamat, one of the earliest coin-operated soft drink vending machines.

The Coca-Cola Company and the Pepsi-Cola Corporation dominated the national soft drink market during the 1920s, but dozens of smaller, regionally produced colas also competed in the expanding soda market, often under highly derivative names. Among them were Celery Cola, Vera-Cola, Afri-Kola, Koca-Nola, Gay-Ola, Roxa-Kola, and Chero-Cola. Grape-flavored sodas, such as NuGrape, Bluebird, Brandywine, and Nuicy, were also popular during the 1920s. So, too, were orange drinks such as Orange Crush, Whistle, Howdy, and Orange Kist. Many of the manufacturers of these soft drinks went out of business or merged with larger companies before World War II, but several of the brands that have remained popular since the 1920s are Dr. Pepper, A&W Root Beer, and Moxie (which actually outsold Coca-Cola in 1920). Ginger ale was another favorite soft drink of the Jazz Age. Two of the best-selling ginger ales of the era were Cliquot Club Dry Ginger Ale and Canada Dry Pale Dry Ginger Ale, which billed itself as "the Champagne of Ginger Ale" and sold for 35 cents a bottle—seven times what the average soft drink cost.

Several other soft drinks also appeared on the market during the 1920s. In 1928, for example, the Howdy Company introduced 7-Up, originally called Bib-Label Lithiated Lemon-Lime Soda because it contained lithium, a chemical widely prescribed to treat depression. Fizzier than other soft drinks, 7-Up was advertised as a cure for upset stomach, and it soon became the firm's best-selling product. Yoo-Hoo also appeared on the market during the 1920s, when Natale Olivieri, an Italian immigrant, perfected a process that enabled him to bottle a chocolate drink that would not spoil. In 1927, Edwin Perkins, who ran a mail-order fruit drink syrup business, invented Kool-Aid. Originally, Perkins shipped his syrups in glass bottles through the mail, but the bottles often broke or leaked during transit. Inspired by Jell-O gelatin packaging, Perkins created a powdered form of his fruit drink syrups and began marketing a line of six flavors (cherry, grape, orange, raspberry, lemon-lime, and strawberry) that cost 10 cents per one-ounce package, under the new name of Kool-Ade (soon spelled Kool-Aid).

CONCLUSION

Two of the most significant culinary revolutions of the 1920s were the standardization of American cuisine and the emergence of modern cooking and eating habits among middle-class Americans. These developments resulted from a series of complex and interrelated social and cultural trends, including the modernization of kitchens, the rising sales of national brand-name food products, and the growing influence of scientific nutrition. Giant food corporations, promotional cookbooks, and mass-circulation women's magazines contributed to the creation of a more homogeneous national diet. Additionally, chain restaurants played an important role in this developing trend, as hamburgers, grilled sandwiches, and other American fare became popular nationwide. As a result, many of the meals homemakers served to their families in the 1920s, as well as many of the dishes customers ordered in restaurants, are the same ones that today constitute our contemporary American diet.

The 1920s

7

Leisure Activities

The 1920s witnessed the spectacular growth of the nationwide commercial entertainment and recreation industries, as rising numbers of Americans began to enjoy increasing amounts of consumer goods and leisure time. For most members of the middle and working classes, workweeks shortened substantially from previous decades, from an average of 60 hours in the 1890s to an average of 45 hours in the 1920s.[1] Vacations for both white-collar and blue-collar workers became increasingly common. Wages and salaries also rose, sometimes by as much as 30 percent, even as the cost of living remained comparatively steady. All of these employment-related trends provided ordinary Americans with both more leisure time and more disposable income to spend on an ever-expanding variety of recreational activities. Between 1919 and 1929, the amount of money Americans spent on recreation and leisure activities nearly doubled to more than $4 billion a year—a figure not surpassed until after World War II.[2]

But the rapid expansion of commercialized leisure also made ordinary people more sedentary. Instead of playing baseball, for example, many people attended games to watch professional or semi-professional teams. Rather than playing an instrument or joining a band, they listened to phonograph records or the radio. The chief recreational activities for most residents in Muncie, Indiana, observed sociologists Robert S. Lynd and Helen Merrell Lynd in *Middletown: A Study in American Culture* (1929), were "largely passive," such as listening to the radio, attending a movie, playing cards, or riding in an automobile.[3] Despite the increased opportunities to pursue a wider variety of recreational activities, most people chose to entertain themselves primarily through activities that could usually be done sitting down—a trend of passive recreation that has continued to this day.

TOYS AND GAMES

Although children today seem drawn to the latest high-tech electronic toys and computer games, many of the old-fashioned toys and games that children still enjoy were also favorites during the 1920s. Since 1903, when the first five-cent, eight-crayon box of Crayolas was introduced, coloring with crayons has ranked high on the list of childhood pastimes. Marbles, jacks, jigsaw puzzles, checkers, dominoes, tiddlywinks, and other games that first became popular in the nineteenth century, or even earlier, continued to delight children during the 1920s. Pails and shovels at the beach, tree houses and forts in the woods, baby dolls and dollhouses, stuffed animals and rocking horses, and rubber balls and spinning tops provided children with outlets for their creativity and energy. Children skipped rope and played dress-up, make-believe, hide-and-seek, and tag, just as previous generations had done and later generations would do. But by the 1920s, comparatively few of the children's playthings and games found in toy boxes and under the Christmas tree were homemade, but instead were commercially manufactured products. During the 1920s, as the nation's industrial production and mass consumer culture expanded, commercial toy manufacturing significantly increased in the United States. Prior to 1900, most toys sold in the United States were actually imported from Europe, particularly from Germany. By the end of the 1920s, however, the United States had become the world's leading toy manufacturer, with 539 toy companies in operation and revenues exceeding $90 million a year.

During the 1920s, many American children pored through mail-order catalogs and visited department stores, hoping to purchase the latest toys and games. Many of these toys revealed sharp distinctions between the appropriate playtime activities of girls and boys. Drawing upon contemporary ideas about gender roles, manufacturers produced a variety of toys and games designed specifically for girls. Among the most popular of these playthings were, of course, dolls, doll buggies, and dollhouses with miniature furniture. Life-size baby dolls, such as "Flossie Flirt" or "Sunshine," boasted real hair and eyelashes, winking eyes, turning heads and posable limbs, and many of them could utter "Ma-Ma." Another favorite among girls were Raggedy Ann dolls, first manufactured in 1918, and Raggedy Andy dolls, introduced two years later. During the 1920s, toy companies also manufactured toy sewing machines, sewing baskets, vacuum cleaners, irons and ironing boards, stoves and ovens, and even ringer washtubs and laundry racks for girls. Concern about children's educational and moral development influenced the kinds of toys and games that were sold during the 1920s, and playing with dolls, sewing machines, and washtubs supposedly prepared girls for their future adult roles as wives, mothers, and homemakers.

Toy companies also manufactured a wide range of gender-specific playthings for boys, who were considered more mechanically minded than girls. Toy catalogs were filled with miniature tool sets, popguns, bows and arrows, train sets, and even fully operational miniature steam engines. Among the most popular playthings for American boys were construction toys, including Lincoln Logs, which were invented in 1916 by John Lloyd Wright, the son of famous architect Frank Lloyd Wright. These sets of notched hardwood logs allowed children to build miniature structures and were named in honor of President Abraham Lincoln, who was famous for having lived in a log cabin as a child. The Erector set, one of America's oldest continuously produced toys, was introduced at New York's American Toy Fair in 1913 by its inventor, A. C. Gilbert. This set consisted of small metal girders, pulleys, wheels, and other parts that children bolted together to construct an almost limitless number of configurations, including model skyscrapers, drawbridges, steam shovels, dump trucks, cranes, derricks, and Ferris wheels. Basic kits cost less than $1.00 but larger, more elaborate kits, complete with hundreds of interlocking parts and tiny electric motors, could cost up to $15.00. Tinkertoys, which were introduced at the 1914 American Toy Fair, also amused countless children who loved to build things. Their inventor, Charles Pajeau, designed special wooden spools with one hole in the middle and eight holes on the perimeter, into which thin wooden dowels could be inserted. This simple concept allowed children to build all sorts of three-dimensional structures. After sluggish initial sales, Tinkertoys gained enduring popularity, and by the 1920s children across the nation were constructing spool-and-dowel models out of these popular, inexpensive kits.

Among the most popular commercially manufactured children's toys of the 1920s were mechanical wind-up toys, many of which reflected the modern fads and fashions of Jazz Age America. For example, one mechanical toy advertised in the 1927 Sears, Roebuck and Company catalog was called the "Charleston Trio." "When [the] strong spring is wound up," the ad reads, "Charleston Charlie dances while the small negro [*sic*] fiddles and the animal nods his approval." Others, such as "Chicken Snatcher," reflected the virulent racism and racial stereotypes of the age. According to the toy's description, "the scared looking negro [*sic*] shuffles along with a chicken dangling in his hand and a dog hanging on the seat of his pants. Very funny action toy which will delight the kiddies."[4]

Children also found miniature toy versions of their favorite vehicles endlessly fascinating. Boys, in particular, coveted Lionel electric train sets, first introduced in 1901. By 1921, 1 million Lionel trains traversed tiny tracks in homes across the country. Children also adored toy vehicles that weren't electrified or motorized. Wooden, steel, or cast-iron models of cars, trucks, buses, taxicabs, fire engines, tractors, steam shovels, motorcycles, airplanes, zeppelins, and boats remained popular favorites throughout the decade. Charles Lindbergh's historic 1927 flight from New York to Paris boosted sales of toy airplanes, and dozens of new model planes appeared on the market, some of them with wind-up mechanisms that actually allowed the toy to remain aloft for a few seconds.

Children also enjoyed playing with transportation toys. Four-wheeled, metal-stamped wagons, such as those manufactured by the Liberty Coaster Manufacturing Company (later Radio Steel and Manufacturing, which built the quintessential Radio Flyer wagons), came in handy for boys and girls who liked to pull younger siblings, deliver newspapers, or, most of all, race down hilly streets. Two- and three-wheeled scooters appealed to children who desired a speedy way to travel, as did the Flexible Flyer and Flying Arrow brand snow sleds, but nothing could compare to the attraction of a shiny new bicycle. Since the cycling craze of the 1890s, bicycles had also appealed to adults as both a recreational and a practical form of transportation. Three-wheeled cycles called velocipedes and regular bicycles, complete with headlamp and bell, were the ultimate acquisition for many youngsters.

FADS AND CRAZES

During the 1920s, a series of outlandish fads and crazes captured the imagination of ordinary Americans as they had in no other previous generation. The growing influence of Hollywood motion pictures, commercial radio, modern advertising, and mass-circulation magazines and newspapers created a nationwide entertainment industry capable of generating great enthusiasm for a new dance step, endurance contest, or parlor game. Advertising agencies and publicists, meanwhile, often encouraged these fads and crazes as a way to promote a particular commercial product or national celebrity, and fads played an important role in marketing and selling merchandise. Fads, in turn, offered something to their participants. Fads were novel (at least initially) and entertaining, and they provided people a forum for public self-expression. As such, even the most ridiculous fads often attracted tens of thousands of adherents because they offered, paradoxically, a way for people to conform to the social behavior of others and, at the same time, a way to distinguish themselves from everyone else. Thus, an American who adopted the latest fad could be both a good conformist and a daring trendsetter. In an increasingly bureaucratic and mechanized modern age, fads and crazes offered people opportunities to reassert their humanity, talent, and uniqueness.

Fads and crazes also garnered public attention for those Americans who craved the glare of the spotlight. Some people sought to perform feats so bizarre that no one else had ever done them, while others attempted to do something more times than anyone else ever had. For example, an Indiana high school student made headlines by chewing 40 sticks of gum while singing "Home, Sweet Home" and, between stanzas, chugging a gallon of milk. A New Jersey youth, subsisting only on eggs and black coffee, won a $150 contest by staying awake for 155 hours, continuously listening to the radio. A Boston man choked down 75 raw eggs in 10 minutes. A Chicago man slurped 1,260 feet of spaghetti in three hours. A Minnesota man gulped 85 cups of coffee (or five gallons) in seven hours and 15 minutes. A Texas man won a $500 bet by spending 30 days rolling a peanut up Pikes Peak with his nose.[5] Journalists and critics often denigrated these media-hungry record breakers, but during the 1920s, millions of Americans, particularly college students, participated in such fads with an enthusiasm that bordered on mass mania.

The relatively tame crazes of mahjong and crossword puzzles also occupied Americans' leisure hours during the 1920s. The most popular parlor game in the United States during the first half of the decade was mahjong, a Chinese game of skill usually played by four people using a set of 144 decorated bone tiles. Introduced to the United States in 1922, mahjong originated in the Ningpo region of China sometime in the mid- to late-nineteenth century. It was marketed in the United States, however, as an ancient Chinese game dating to the age of Confucius. Parker Brothers and other American game companies began manufacturing sets, complete with simplified rule books based on the original Chinese parlor game. By 1923, an estimated 10 to 15 million Americans were playing the game regularly. Members of ladies' clubs often enhanced their experience by playing mahjong while drinking tea and wearing Chinese silk robes and embroidered slippers. Cheap mahjong sets cost as little as a couple of dollars, but deluxe sets, with beautifully handcrafted, inlaid tiles, could run as high as $500. Mahjong became so popular that some newspapers, such as the *Seattle Daily Times*, published daily columns devoted to the rules and strategies of the game. And in 1923, singing sensation Eddie Cantor immortalized the game in the song "Since Ma Is Playing Mah Jong."

A crossword puzzle craze also captivated the nation in the mid-1920s. Although crossword puzzles date at least to 1913 in the United States, they did not gain widespread popularity until 1924, when Richard L. Simon and Max L. Schuster launched their new publishing company by releasing *The Cross Word Puzzle Book*, the first such collection of the word puzzles. The book became a national best-seller, and, as a result, the sale of dictionaries and thesauruses also soared. One company even manufactured what it claimed was the world's smallest crossword puzzle dictionary, which strapped, like a watch, to the wrists of puzzle solvers. Enthusiasts competed in crossword puzzle tournaments across the nation, and University of Kentucky students could actually take a college course on crossword puzzles, which, as one approving dean noted, were "educational, scientific, instructive and mentally stimulative, as well as entertaining."[6] By 1926, the crossword puzzle craze had run its course, although these word games remain daily features of newspapers to this day.

A series of trendy dances also swept the nation during the 1920s, including the Charleston, the Black Bottom, the collegiate, the varsity drag, the raccoon, and the tango. A related fad was the dance marathon, which began in March 1923, when Alma Cummings established an international record of 27 hours of nonstop dancing at a contest held in New York City's Audubon Ballroom. Cummings' widely publicized feat sparked a craze of endurance dancing that attracted national attention. Soon, contestants in cities across the country were fox-trotting and waltzing for days in an effort to break the record. By the end of 1923, the record for nonstop dancing, set by a Youngstown, Ohio, couple, stood at 182 hours and 8 minutes. "Of all the crazy competitions ever invented," remarked the *New York World*, "the dancing marathon wins by a considerable margin of lunacy."[7]

Dance marathons became mass public spectacles, with emcees, orchestras, teams of doctors and nurses, thousands of spectators, and dozens of vendors, who peddled everything from hot dogs and soda to shoes and sore foot remedies. By 1924, these contests featured continuous dancing 24 hours a day, usually with 15-minute breaks each hour to allow contestants to rest, eat a snack, and use the rest room. Stamina, not gracefulness, was the key to these competitions, since the objective was to outlast all of the other couples on the floor. Dance marathons could drag on for weeks, as dancing couples, near exhaustion and suffering from aching, blistered feet, shuffled across the floor. Radio broadcasts and tabloid newspaper coverage elevated the excitement of these marathons and allowed Americans to follow the day-to-day drama unfolding on the dance floor. The most famous dance marathon of the decade occurred in 1928, when Hollywood press agent Milton Crandall staged "the Dance Derby of the Century" at New York's Madison Square Garden. More than 100 couples competed for the $5,000 first prize, but after a grueling first week, only 13 couples remained. Thousands of spectators paid the $2.20 admission price to watch the spectacle, but the Board of Health stopped the marathon after 428 hours, when one contestant collapsed and had to be hospitalized. Although dance marathons flourished in the 1920s, their popularity soared during the Great Depression, when unemployed Americans competed for badly needed cash prizes.

Other endurance contests also enthralled the nation. In 1928, for example, sports agent and promoter C. C. Pyle organized a 3,422-mile transcontinental footrace between Los Angeles and New York City that an inventive sportswriter billed as the "Bunion Derby." A field of nearly 200 runners competed for prizes totaling $48,500. A 19-year-old Oklahoman named Andrew Payne won the first-place prize of $25,000 with a time of 573 hours. Many endurance contests featured even zanier activities, however. Americans competed in rocking-chair derbies, milk-drinking marathons, egg-eating races, gum-chewing contests, marathon eating, and even "noun and verb rodeos" (nonstop talking contests). Even children got swept up in the mania, competing in rope-skipping contests, ball-bouncing marathons, roof-sitting feats, yo-yoing competitions, kite-flying contests, and long-distance bicycle races. The rage for endurance competitions prompted journalist Nunnally Johnson, writing in 1930 in *The Saturday Evening Post*, to wryly remark about the United States: "First in war, first in peace, first in tree sitting, gum chewing, peanut pushing, and bobbing up and down in the water."[8]

Perhaps the most outrageous endurance craze of the 1920s was flagpole sitting, which, as its name suggests, amounted to perching on top of a flagpole for days and sometimes weeks. By far the decade's most famous flagpole sitter was Alvin "Shipwreck" Kelly, a Hollywood stuntman who ignited this fad in 1924 when he spent 13 hours, 13 minutes atop a flagpole as part of a publicity stunt to attract crowds to a Hollywood theater. Within weeks, flagpole sitting became a national spectacle, as scores of fame-seekers across the country attempted to break Kelly's record. Kelly's celebrity increased as businessmen and promoters hired him, reportedly at a rate of $100 an hour, to stage flagpole sitting exhibitions at store openings, amusement parks, and county fairs throughout the United States. To ensure his comfort and safety, he perched on a small, cushioned seat, 13 inches in diameter, sometimes outfitted with stirrups for his feet that helped him to maintain his balance. While aloft, he took five-minute catnaps and even shaved and had his hair cut, but he refused to eat solid food (for obvious reasons). Instead, he drank broth and water hoisted up to him in buckets, and a discreetly concealed tube transported his bodily waste down the flagpole. In 1930, 20,000 spectators watched Kelly shatter his own record after he sat atop a flagpole on the Atlantic City boardwalk for 1,177 hours—or more than 49 days. Unlike many of the fads of the 1920s, the flagpole sitting craze was relatively long-lived, but it eventually faded from the national scene during the Great Depression.

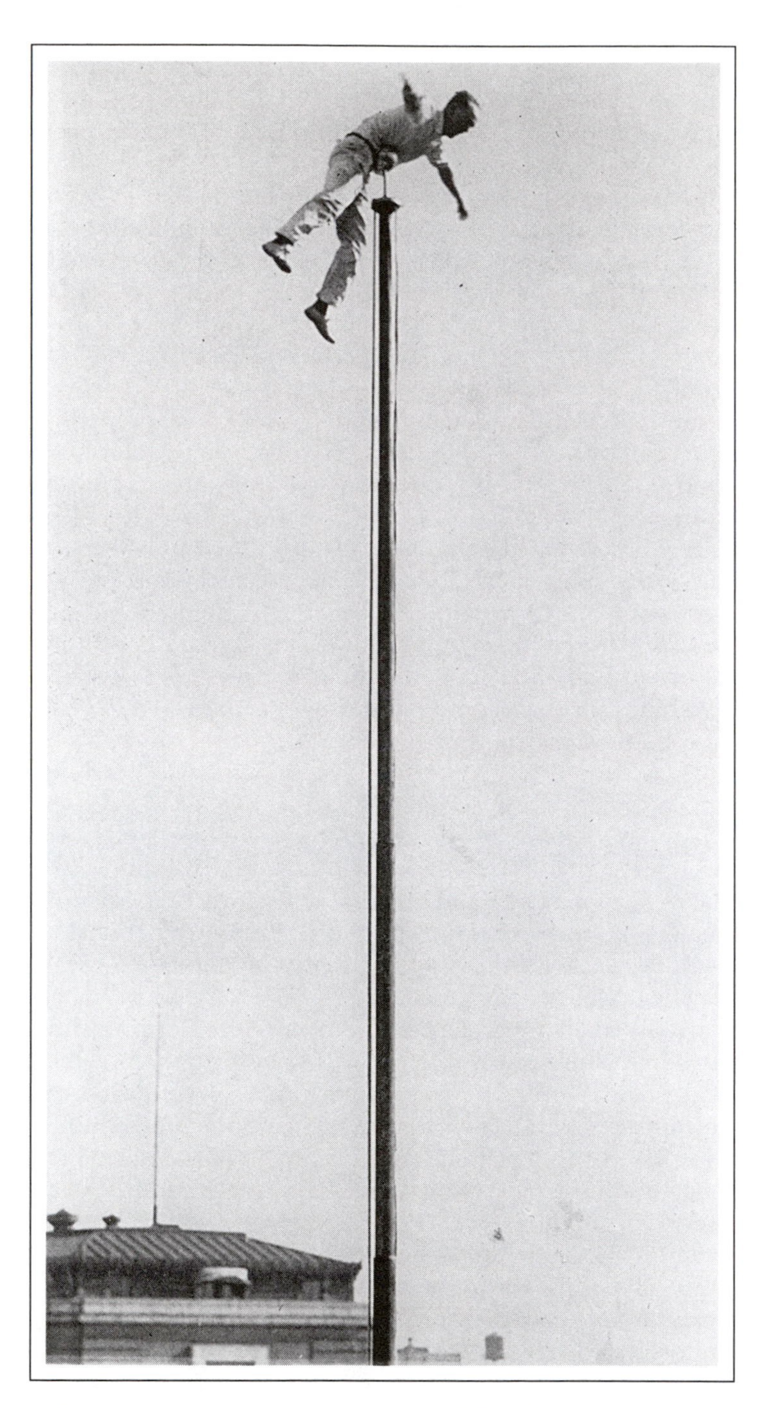

A "human fly" atop the Times-Herald Building, Washington, D.C., 1924. Courtesy of the Library of Congress.

Some crazes of the 1920s evolved out of new children's toys, such as the pogo stick. Patented in 1919 by George Hansburg, the pogo stick is basically a Y-shaped pole with two footpads and a spring that allows children—and adults—to bounce up and down and propel themselves short distances. Wooden pogo sticks had been manufactured in Germany before 1919, but they tended to warp in high humidity. Hansburg's stick, constructed out of a metal tube with an enclosed spring, proved to be a far more practical and durable model. Bouncing on pogo sticks became a national craze after Hansburg taught the chorus girls of *The Ziegfeld Follies* to use them, and they choreographed a show-stopping dance routine performed on pogo sticks. Also fueling the fad were publicity stunts such as endurance pogo-sticking contests, attempts at world records for most consecutive jumps, and even marriage ceremonies performed on pogo sticks.

The yo-yo also emerged as a popular fad during the late 1920s. The yo-yo probably originated in China, with the oldest surviving examples dating back to the fifth century B.C. in Greece. However, in Santa Barbara, California, in 1928, Pedro Flores, who remembered playing with a toy similar to a yo-yo as a child in the Philippines, founded the first American company to manufacture these spinning wooden disks. Flores named them "yo-yos" after the Filipino word for "spring." Flores looped a piece of string around the axle of the disk instead of tying it tight, an innovation that allowed the yo-yo to spin in place, or "sleep"—a mainstay of nearly every yo-yo trick. Flores charged between 50 cents and $1.50 for his first yo-yos, and soon they became a California craze. Flores further promoted what he called "the Wonder Toy" by sponsoring yo-yo spinning contests. Around 1930, Donald Duncan acquired Flores' company and obtained a trademark on the word *yo-yo*. He, too, began hosting highly publicized yo-yo competitions to boost sales of his Duncan yo-yo. Soon, children and adults across the country were "walking the dog," "rocking the baby," or spinning their yo-yos "around the world."

Miniature golf, also called "Tom Thumb golf" and "pygmy golf," became a national rage during the late 1920s. Most historical accounts credit Garnet Carter, the owner of a hotel and golf course on Lookout Mountain near Chattanooga, Tennessee, with developing the first American miniature golf course in 1927. Carter originally built his tiny course, which he called "Fairyland," to generate publicity for his resort, but his miniature links attracted so many golfers that he soon began charging his guests to play. By the end of the 1920s, an estimated 4 million people a day were putting on the nation's nearly 40,000 miniature golf courses—some of them indoor—complete with tiny windmills, clown faces, and medieval castles. Miniature golf became so popular that Hollywood stu-

Miniature golf course, Bedford Springs Hotel, Bedford Springs, Pennsylvania. Courtesy of the Library of Congress.

dio executives feared the movie industry would suffer if couples continued to hit the mini-links instead of buying movie tickets.

The urge for self-improvement sparked a sudden explosion of health and fitness fads during the 1920s, including dieting and bodybuilding. Weight-conscious Americans, particularly young women, began counting calories and dieting, or "reducing," as it was then known, both as a way to maintain proper health and to conform to the new slimmer standards of American beauty embodied by the boyish-figured flapper. Meanwhile, a bodybuilding fad erupted among men and teenaged boys. One of the decade's chief promoters of bodybuilding was Bernarr Macfadden, the so-called "Father of Physical Culture," who publicized his gospel of exercise, health, and fitness in his monthly magazine titled *Muscle Builder*. The most famous bodybuilding guru of the 1920s, however, was Charles Atlas, an Italian immigrant born Angelo Siciliano, who developed what he called his "Dynamic Tension" program—a total-fitness method of muscle building that pitted one muscle against another. Atlas claimed that he had used this program to transform himself from a 97-pound weakling into a muscle-bound he-man. In 1922, Atlas won the title of "Most Perfectly Developed Man" at a Madison Square Garden competition, and two years later, after being inundated with requests, he began marketing mail-order courses of his "Dynamic Tension" program in the back pages of pulp magazines and other male-oriented periodicals. As a result, tens of thousands of American men and boys joined the bodybuilding craze during the 1920s.

Self-improvement impulses transcended the physical to include the psychological as well. Millions of Americans became infatuated with the teachings of Emile Coué, a French pharmacist turned psychotherapist who made highly publicized lecture tours of the United States in 1923 and again in 1924. The author of the best-selling *Self-Mastery Through Conscious Autosuggestion* (1922), Coué promoted the idea that people could improve their mental health and happiness through a self-hypnosis program that focused on the repetition of the daily affirmation, "Day by day, in every way, I am getting better and better."[9] The psychosexual theories of Austrian psychoanalyst Sigmund Freud also captivated the nation. Freud's influential *The Interpretation of Dreams* (1900), a study of how the unconscious mind revealed itself in dreams, was widely cited, although seldom read or even vaguely understood by many Americans during the 1920s. Freudianism became a fad, and such terms as *repression, sublimation,* and *complex* entered people's everyday vocabulary. Conservative critics, however, worried that Freudianism encouraged sexual promiscuity and licentious behavior among young adults.

An obsession with Egyptian, Asian, and other seemingly "exotic" world cultures also exerted a strong influence on American popular culture and produced fleeting fads. In 1922, for example, the spectacular archaeological discovery and excavation of Pharaoh King Tutankhamen's tomb inspired an Egyptian craze in the United States. The iconography associated with King Tut influenced not only the styles of American clothing, jewelry, cosmetics, and hairstyles but also architecture, music, and motion pictures. Soon women were wearing designer jewelry decorated with hieroglyphics and shaped like scarab beetles and lotus flowers. In 1923, the musical team of Billy Jones and Ernest Hare recorded the novelty song "Old King Tut (In Old King Tutankhamen's Day)." The discovery of King Tut's tomb also inspired the architectural design and interior décor of Grauman's Egyptian Theatre, built in Hollywood in 1922, which featured massive Egyptian columns in the forecourt, hieroglyphics, and even huge dog-headed Egyptian god statues. Grauman's Chinese Theater, which opened one block away in 1927, offered moviegoers a taste of exotic Orientalism, with its ornate architecture resembling a giant red pagoda, complete with sculptures of huge silver dragons on the interior ceilings.

Middle Eastern and Hawaiian culture also enjoyed widespread popularity in the United States during the early to mid-1920s. Tens of thousands of Americans strummed easy-to-play Hawaiian ukuleles and sang Tin Pan Alley ditties about the Hawaiian Islands. Other foreign cultures, particularly those of Turkey and the Middle East, likewise inspired national obsessions. Fraternal organizations, for example, adopted many supposedly exotic symbols and motifs, such as fezzes, as part of their initiation ceremonies, official uniforms, and lodge decor. Hollywood silent film heartthrob Rudolph Valentino's 1921 movie *The Sheik* and its 1926 sequel, *The Son of the Sheik*, also tapped into—and helped to fuel—the American craze for Middle Eastern exoticism during the Jazz Age.

SPORTS

During the 1920s, watching and following college and professional sports became, for the first time in American history, the pervasive, all-consuming pastime that we know today. The growing middle class, who enjoyed larger paychecks and shorter workweeks, found themselves with enough leisure time and disposable income to follow and even to play sports. Radio broadcasts of the World Series, college bowl games, prizefights, and horse races, as well as newspaper sports columns and daily box scores, boosted the popularity of the nation's mass spectator sports and transformed Babe Ruth, Red Grange, Jack Dempsey, and Gertrude Ederle into national celebrities. During the 1920s, sports mushroomed into a huge industry, and press agents, sports promoters, sportswriters, radio announcers, chambers of commerce, and various media outlets all found new ways to make money by promoting athletic events. Millions of Americans not only watched sports and cheered for their hometown heroes, but they also played. Individual sports such as golf and tennis skyrocketed in popularity as both men and women flooded the thousands of newly constructed golf courses and tennis courts. Cities and even small towns built municipal athletic complexes that attracted whole families to their swimming and recreation facilities. Popular wisdom conceded that exercise was as beneficial for women as it was for men, and so this ardent enthusiasm for athletics was by no means limited to men and boys.

During the 1920s, the popularity of sports grew spectacularly, but most professional athletes did not command the enormous prestige or whopping salaries they do today. Rather, Americans worshiped amateur athletes who provided admirable models of athletic fitness, moral character, and honorable spirit. Because they seemed to play for the sheer enjoyment and thrill of the sport, rather than for crass monetary reward, amateur athletes such as golfer Bobby Jones, tennis champion Helen Wills, and swimmer Johnny Weismuller became American idols. Over the course of the 1920s, however, hundreds of amateur and college athletes succumbed to the allure of large salaries promised by professional sports clubs. Fans often responded quite negatively to these amateurs who turned professional, believing they had "sold out" and thus compromised the purity of their sport. Interestingly, professional baseball never seemed to be troubled by this stigma that plagued other professional sports leagues.

Baseball

Major League Baseball (MLB) rose to prominence as the national pastime during the 1920s, but at the dawn of the decade the sport received a punishing blow, as the "Black Sox scandal" deeply shook Americans' faith in the game. In September 1920, eight members of the Chicago White Sox baseball club—including star outfielder Joe "Shoeless Joe" Jackson, one of the game's greatest hitters—were indicted for conspiring to throw the 1919 World Series against the Cincinnati Reds in exchange for a sizable payoff. During the 1921 trial in Chicago, the signed confessions and other evidence against the eight teammates mysteriously vanished, thus adding another level of intrigue and corruption to the scandal. Due to lack of evidence, the White Sox players were acquitted of intent to defraud. However, the newly installed first commissioner of baseball, Judge Kennesaw Mountain Landis, believing that he had to do something dramatic to repair the damaged credibility of professional baseball, banned all eight White Sox ballplayers from the game for life.

Perhaps in part because of Commissioner Landis' fiat, the "Black Sox scandal" that hung over professional baseball dissipated relatively quickly. Baseball soon became a more exciting game than ever, due primarily to the influence of legendary slugger George Herman "Babe" Ruth and the thrill of dramatic home run hitting. In earlier decades (the so-called "Dead Ball Era"), pitching had dominated the game. Few extra base hits and even fewer home runs kept scores low and strategy confined to singles hitting, bunts, hit-and-run plays, and base stealing. But when Babe Ruth crushed 29 home runs for the Boston Red Sox in 1919 and then followed with an unbelievable 54 home runs for the New York Yankees the next year, baseball fans began to favor these exciting, high-scoring games dominated by power hitters.

Major League Baseball itself contributed to the rise of the home runs by making a number of rule changes that increased the batter's advantage against the pitcher. Beginning in 1920, pitchers were forbidden from scuffing baseballs or altering them with tobacco juice, saliva, mud, grease, or other foreign substances that made a pitched ball move erratically in the air and thus more difficult for batters to hit. As a result of this rule change, pitchers could no longer rely on a host of formerly legal pitches that employed "doctored" baseballs, such as the spitball, the shine ball, the mud ball, and the licorice ball. The frequent substitution of new baseballs into a game also contributed to the explosion of offense. In 1920, Cleveland Indian shortstop Roy Chapman was struck in the head and killed by a pitched ball. It was believed that Chapman had trouble seeing the ball because it was so soiled. In the wake of this tragic accident, the league instructed umpires to replace dirty baseballs with clean white ones. This steady rotation of new baseballs made it easier for batters to see, and therefore hit, the ball. The many new baseball stadiums constructed in the 1920s (including Yankee Stadium, completed in 1923, which held 62,000 fans and was—and still is—known as "the House that Ruth Built") gave long-ball hitters an edge by enclosing the outfields with fences and bleachers. As a result of this fast-paced, high-scoring style of play, average annual attendance at Major League Baseball games leaped from less than 6 million during the 1910s to more than 9 million during the 1920s. Player salaries also increased—especially for those players who could please the crowds by smashing balls into the bleachers. While superstars like New York Yankee outfielder Babe Ruth could earn $100,000 or more through salary, bonuses, and product endorsements, average players earned between $4,000 and $10,000 a year—a very respectable wage.

Babe Ruth was, beyond question, the most celebrated baseball player during the 1920s and arguably in all of baseball history. He began his career as a pitcher with two remarkable seasons with the Boston Red Sox, but after he was traded to the New York Yankees in 1920, he went on an unforgettable streak of record-breaking power hitting, including pounding 60 home runs in 1927—a record that stood until New York Yankee outfielder Roger Maris broke it in 1961. Nicknamed alternately "the Sultan of Swat," "the Bambino," or simply "the Babe," Ruth was one of the highest-paid sports heroes of the decade. Besides his baseball salary, Ruth raked in tremendous sums from his personal appearances and endorsements of sporting equipment, breakfast cereals, candy bars, and even underwear. In 1926, he spent 12 weeks on a nationwide vaudeville tour, earning an astonishing salary of more than $8,000 a week. He also appeared in at least three Hollywood films between 1920 and 1931: *Heading Home*, *Play Ball with Babe Ruth*, and *How Babe Ruth Hits a Home Run*.

Batting third, Ruth anchored the lineup of the New York Yankees—the most dominant club of the decade—including the hard-hitting 1927 team. Nicknamed "Murderers' Row," the 1927 Yankee lineup included such stars as first baseman Lou Gehrig, second baseman Tony Lazzeri, and outfielders Earle Combs and Bob Meusel. Under manager Miller Huggins, the Yankees won six American League pennants and three World Series (1923, 1927, and 1928) during the 1920s. But Ruth and his Yankee teammates were far from the only baseball stars of the decade. Detroit outfielder Ty Cobb, a ferocious, hard-nosed competitor who had

Team photo of the 1926 New York Yankees, American League Champions. Babe Ruth is standing in the center of the back row. Courtesy of the Library of Congress.

a lifetime batting average of .366, enjoyed a remarkable career that spanned 24 years (1904–1928). Never particularly adept at hitting home runs, Cobb made his mark with clutch singles and smart, aggressive base running. His career record of 892 stolen bases stood until 1977. Other baseball heroes of the 1920s included Cleveland Indians outfielder Tristram "Tris" Speaker, Pittsburgh Pirates third baseman Harold "Pie" Traynor, and St. Louis Cardinals infielder Rogers Hornsby.

Not all baseball stars of the 1920s played for Major League Baseball teams, however. Until 1947, strict practices of racial segregation prohibited African Americans from joining professional baseball, regardless of their skills. As a result, black baseball players had played in loosely organized professional leagues of their own since the 1890s. In 1920 Andrew "Rube" Foster, the owner and manager of the Chicago American Giants, founded the National Negro Baseball League (NNBL). The NNBL proved to be a remarkable success, and despite the difficulties posed by segregated hotels and passenger trains, along with the high fees for the use of white-owned ballparks, the NNLB drew more than 400,000 spectators during the 1923 season. Salaries for African-American players compared poorly to those of white Major League Baseball players, but the stars of the all-black league, such as pitcher Leroy "Satchel" Paige and catcher Josh Gibson, could earn as much as $1,000 a month. Major League Baseball did not begin to recognize these great black athletes until the 1970s, when a few superstars of the NNLB were inducted into the National Baseball Hall of Fame in Cooperstown, New York, but baseball fans of the 1920s—especially African-American fans—knew just how talented these players were.

Boxing

Prior to World War I, boxing was considered to be a disreputable, lowbrow sport that attracted primarily gamblers, drinkers, and rowdies. In 1920, prizefighting was legal in only two states, New York and New Jersey, but over the next 10 years, many state legislatures lifted the bans and restrictions on boxing, and state commissioners sought to sanitize this traditionally notorious sport. Boxing soon won widespread popularity throughout the nation, and, before long, matches began to attract fans from all classes of American society. Boxing promoters such as George "Tex" Rickard publicized big matches to such an extent that gate receipts occasionally topped $1 million. Boxing became tremendously profitable not only for talented prizefighters but also for fight promoters and others affiliated with the sport.

One significant reason that boxing rose to prominence so quickly during the 1920s was the abundance of exciting boxing champions in virtually every weight class. Lightweight Benny Leonard, welterweight Edward "Mickey" Walker, and middleweights Harry Greb and Theodore "Tiger" Flowers (the first black middleweight champion) are considered by sports historians to be among the finest boxers in history, and they generated a large fan following during the 1920s. The heavyweight boxing division attracted the most attention of all. Two talented fighters dominated heavyweight boxing in the 1920s: Jack Dempsey and Gene Tunney. In 1921, Dempsey fought in the first $1 million match (nicknamed "the Battle of the Century") against a French war hero named Georges Carpentier, and in 1927, Dempsey's famous bout with Tunney generated a $2 million gate—a record that would stand for half a century. Dempsey held the heavyweight championship title for seven years (1919–1926), until Tunney finally unseated him in 1926. Tunney retained his title until Jack Sharkey, another great heavyweight of the 1920s, defeated him in 1928.

Boxing fans of the Jazz Age found the Jack Dempsey–Gene Tunney rivalry and the considerable ballyhoo surrounding it tremendously exciting. Dempsey, whom sportswriters cast as a working-class hero, had spent most of his teen years riding the rails and living in hobo jungles. He was comparatively short for a heavyweight—only about six feet tall—but he fought so brutally that he was nicknamed "the Manassa Mauler" (after his hometown of Manassa, Colorado). Dempsey's advantageous alliance with promoter Tex Rickard propelled him to prominence in the boxing world. When Rickard arranged for Dempsey to fight the world heavyweight champion Jess Willard in 1919, the relatively unknown Dempsey surprised boxing fans by knocking out Willard in the first round. Dempsey successfully defended his championship title until a 1926 match in Philadelphia, billed as "the Second Battle of the Century," when a promising young boxer named "Gentleman" Gene Tunney beat him in a 10-round unanimous decision. Tunney, the former light-heavyweight champion, was a handsome, educated man and a decorated ex-Marine. The following year, in 1927, more than 100,000 spectators at Chicago's Soldier Field witnessed the highly publicized rematch, which Dempsey was strongly favored to win. During the seventh round, Dempsey knocked Tunney to the canvas with a vicious combination of punches. Instead of retreating to a neutral corner and allowing the referee to begin the count, Dempsey stood excitedly over the prone Tunney, ready to pounce again if he managed to struggle to his feet. This delayed the start of the 10-count by at least four seconds, and when the referee finally got to "nine," Tunney rose to his feet. This now-famous "Long Count" resulted in Dempsey's eventual defeat, as the match went the full 10 rounds and the judges again unanimously declared Tunney the heavyweight champion of the world.

Football

Prior to World War I, college football was an exciting but decidedly minor sport, with fewer than 1,000 athletes across the country belonging to college football squads. But when college and university enrollments nearly doubled during the 1920s, the popularity of college football rose dramatically. Universities that boasted strong football programs and enthusiastic alumni (with deep pockets) built enormous stadiums to promote their teams. Yale University's new stadium held 75,000 spectators, Stanford University's seated more than 86,000, and the University of Michigan's accommodated nearly 102,000. College football quickly became a large and powerful economic force, and dozens of other universities and colleges constructed new football stadiums that held between 60,000 and 80,000 fans, in the hope of keeping up with ever-increasing demand for tickets. Ticket receipts for college football actually exceeded those for Major League Baseball during much of the 1920s, and these revenues supported smaller athletic programs such as lacrosse and gymnastics, repaid bondholders who had funded new stadiums, and paid coaches exorbitant salaries. In 1927 alone, more than 30 million spectators across the country paid more than $50 million for college football tickets.

College football attracted huge numbers of fans and revenue dollars during the 1920s for several reasons. The sport had recently evolved from a strictly running game to a faster, more electrifying passing game that satisfied fans' appetite for excitement and drama. Furthermore, the focus of college football had expanded beyond the eastern schools of the Ivy League, which had long been considered the pinnacle of gridiron competition, to include large midwestern universities such as Notre Dame, Michigan, Illinois, and many others that were bursting with talent. Famed coach Knute Rockne led his Notre Dame squad to tremendous heights during the decade, including an undefeated 1924 season and a Rose Bowl victory, and he had the good fortune to coach superstar halfback George Gipp in 1920 and the phenomenal backfield nicknamed the "Four Horsemen of Notre Dame" (quarterback Harry Stuhldreher, fullback Elmer Layden, and halfbacks Jim Crowley and Don Miller) from 1922 to 1924. These top-level college football players rose to become national celebrities—even heroes—and their high profiles, enhanced by extensive radio and newspaper coverage, in turn boosted the popularity of the game. The extensive radio broadcasting of college games and the newsreels of game highlights, which were shown in movie theaters nationwide, also contributed to the sport's growing fan base.

Perhaps the best-known college football player of the 1920s and certainly one of the most talented was a young halfback from Wheaton, Illinois, named Harold "Red" Grange, whom sportswriter Grantland Rice of the *New York Herald Tribune* dubbed "the Galloping Ghost." At the University of Illinois, where he starred as a three-time All-American (1923–1925), Grange first captured national attention in 1924, when he rushed for 263 yards to score four touchdowns in the first 12 minutes of a game against the University of Michigan. The following year, he became the first athlete featured on the cover of *Time* magazine. In 1925, the day after playing his final college game, Grange signed a lucrative contract with the professional Chicago Bears football team guaranteeing him an annual salary of at least $100,000. Many fans felt betrayed by Grange's eager leap into professional football because, they believed, he had placed financial gain above the pure love of football. But even the critics could not resist the excitement he generated on the professional football field. Grange immediately began luring hundreds of thousands of fans to pro games and, as a result, he almost single-handedly jump-started a stagnant National Football League. Never one to shy away from additional publicity, Grange parlayed his stardom on the gridiron into stardom on the silver screen by appearing in two Hollywood films and a 12-episode movie serial about college football titled *The Galloping Ghost* (1931).

Professional football had existed since the 1890s, but before Red Grange and other superstars began to revitalize it during the mid-1920s, the sport suffered from a lack of organization, direction, and fan support. Players drifted from team to team, and very few spectators were willing to pay to watch struggling, upstart teams that appeared one year and vanished the next. In 1920, the American Professional Football Association (APFA) was founded, in part to provide the nation's fragmented collection of professional teams a stronger sense of organization and leadership. Jim Thorpe, a former Olympic athlete and football star, was elected the association's president, and Stanley Cofall, former Notre Dame football great, became the vice president. Eleven teams paid the APFA a mere $100 apiece to join the league. In 1922, this fledgling association was renamed the National Football League (NFL), and several of the original 11 franchises relocated from small towns in Ohio, Illinois, and Indiana to somewhat larger markets in Green Bay, Detroit, Buffalo, and Cincinnati. Nonetheless, professional football continued to limp along until 1925, when Red Grange joined the Chicago Bears. Spurred on by the tremendous exposure generated by Grange, other NFL teams began to recruit more heavily from the pool of talented college players, and fans gradually came to see professional football as an exciting spectator sport.

Golf

Golf, which had long been considered a game for the moneyed elite, enjoyed a surge in popularity during the 1920s among the middle classes. In 1920, approximately 500,000 recreational golfers converged on the local links each weekend to play a round or two; this figure increased dramatically as the decade went on. Golf also became an increasingly popular spectator sport, and fans attended tournaments and followed their favorite golfers in the newspaper like never before. Unlike today, the greatest public acclaim for golfers was reserved not for professional players but for amateurs, and professional golf never achieved the level of acceptance that professional football and baseball did during the decade. In fact, professionals were considered almost a class of servants, whose responsibilities included giving golf lessons, making and repairing clubs, working in the pro shop, and generally serving the needs of country club members. The most prestigious golf tournaments were reserved for amateurs who played merely for the sheer enjoyment and the love of the sport.

Three fantastic players led American golf during the 1920s: Walter Hagen, Gene Sarazen, and Bobby Jones. In 1922, Walter Hagen became the first American to win the celebrated British Open tournament. Hagen, a professional golfer, consistently agitated for including professionals in the major tournaments—a controversial position in the 1920s. Gene Sarazen won the U.S. Open in 1922 as an amateur, before turning professional. He became the first golfer to win all four major tournaments: the U.S. Open (1922), the British Open (1932), the Professional Golfers' Association (PGA) Championship (1922, 1923, and 1933), and the Masters (1935). The most famous and beloved golfer during the 1920s was Bobby Jones, who competed as an amateur throughout his entire career. Jones dominated the sport between 1923 and 1930, during which time he won 13 of the 21 national championship tournaments he entered. He hated to practice and sometimes went several months without ever picking up his clubs, and he played in only 52 tournaments altogether. In 1930, at the age of 28, Jones became the first player to win the Grand Slam (by winning the British Amateur, the British Open, the U.S. Open, and the U.S. Amateur all in the same year). Later that same year, believing that competitive golf held no more challenges for him, Jones shocked the sports world by retiring while at the pinnacle of his game. In retirement, he designed golf clubs for A. G. Spalding and Company and helped draw up plans for the Augusta National golf course, which began hosting the Masters Tournament in 1934. A member of the World Golf Hall of Fame, Jones is considered by many sports historians to be the greatest golfer of all time.

Tennis

Like golf, tennis enjoyed a tremendous surge in popularity during the 1920s. Middle-class men and women took lessons or casually played the game, which, again like golf, had long been seen as the domain of the wealthy. Tennis fans also supported amateur tennis, which was seen as far more honorable and pure than the materialistic arena of professional tennis, and many esteemed tournaments barred professional players from competing. Both men and women tennis stars captured the public's attention during the Jazz Age, particularly Bill Tilden and Helen Wills, the so-called king and queen of American tennis.

Helen Wills, a middle-class Californian, began her tennis career not under the tutelage of private coaches but by playing rugged, athletic matches on public dirt courts. She won the U.S. tennis championship in 1924 and again in 1925, and in 1926 she played in a highly publicized match against French superstar Suzanne Lenglen, then considered the best female player in the world. Wills lost the match but returned from France determined to improve her game. Between 1927 and 1933, Wills was virtually unbeatable. She won eight Wimbledon tournaments, seven U.S. championships, and four French championships, and during those six years she never once lost a set in singles competition.

William "Big Bill" Tilden occupied a similarly dominant position in men's tennis during the 1920s. Tilden, the son of a wealthy Philadelphia family, began playing tennis when he was just a child, but he didn't develop a real talent for the game until he was in his twenties. He cultivated a tennis game based on powerful serves and drives as well as on style, finesse, and grace. He became known for his remarkable sportsmanship, and if he believed he had received an undeserved call, he would botch his next shot intentionally in order to rectify the error. In 1920, Tilden defeated the defending Wimbledon champion three sets to one to become the first American to win the men's singles title. He took home the trophy again in 1921 and 1930. He also won seven U.S. Open Singles Championships (1920–1925, 1929), and in 1925 accomplished the astounding feat of winning 56 consecutive games over two tournaments. A vocal advocate for amateur athletics, Tilden surprised the world in 1930 when he forfeited his amateur status in order to make a series of Hollywood motion pictures. He began playing tennis on the professional circuit the following year and continued to tour until his death in 1953.

Basketball

Sports fans of the 1920s would likely be astonished at the tremendous popularity of both college and professional basketball today. Basketball during the "golden age" of sports was little more than a sidelight—it would not begin to succeed on a large scale until the mid-1930s. Although basketball was invented in 1891, its rules still had not been widely codified by the 1920s, and so college teams struggled over conflicting interpretations of the sport's most basic elements. The same referees generally officiated whenever a team played at home, and because rules were interpreted differently on each court, visiting teams seldom won. These disorganized and often unruly games generated low scores and even lower fan interest. A handful of eastern colleges, such as New York University and the University of Pennsylvania, were considered strong basketball schools, but nationwide, college basketball was a decidedly minor sport. The national championship tournament, which was established at the end of the 1920 season, was perhaps the only glimmer of national recognition that college basketball received.

Professional basketball, on the other hand, was somewhat more popular during the 1920s, but it, too, lagged far behind baseball, football, and other professional sports in terms of fans and revenue. Professional basketball was an extremely rough, highly unorganized game. Players operated essentially as free agents, signing on with whichever team offered the biggest paychecks per game and often changing their allegiances several times each season. This constant shifting of players from team to team effectively prevented the development of any sort of real team cohesion or strategy. Basketball's disorganized style of play changed abruptly in 1918, when manager Jim Furey hired a head coach and assembled a roster of players called the "Original Celtics," based in

New York City, and then required them to sign contracts for the entire season in exchange for a guaranteed annual salary. The Original Celtics, the first genuine professional basketball team, dominated the sport throughout the 1920s. Because they played together for the whole season, the athletes were able to develop plays and strategies that other teams could not match. The Original Celtics played a grueling schedule, often booking games every day of the week and two games on Sundays throughout the winter. During the 1922–1923 season, the Original Celtics compiled a 204–11 record; in 1924–1925 they went 134–6, and the following year won 90 and lost only 12 games. Their overwhelming success helped to bolster the national reputation of professional basketball and inspired other managers to sign similar contracts with their players. By the end of the 1920s, basketball had markedly increased in both professionalism and popularity.

Like professional baseball, professional basketball was strictly segregated during the 1920s, but all-black club teams did flourish in large cities. Early all-black club teams that garnered substantial fan support include the Smart Set Athletic Club of Brooklyn, New York, the St. Christopher's Club of New Jersey, and the Loendi Club of Pittsburgh. In 1922, Caribbean native Robert L. Douglass founded the Harlem Renaissance Big 5, a team of talented African-American basketball players who took their name from the Renaissance Casino ballroom in Harlem. The "Rens," as they were known, toured the country during the 1920s and 1930s, playing against black and white teams and usually winning. In 1927, five years after the Rens got their start, team owner Abe Saperstein took his Chicago-based black basketball team, known as the Savoy Big Five, and renamed them the Harlem Globetrotters. The Globetrotters dazzled fans by combining their considerable basketball skills with astounding tricks and comedy routines. Like the Rens, the Globetrotters barnstormed across the nation playing exhibition games and entertaining crowds—a tradition that this world-renowned team has continued until the present.

Swimming

Competitive swimming claimed several genuine champions during the 1920s, and their widespread fame led tens of thousands of Americans to take up swimming at public beaches and municipal pools throughout the nation. In 1926, 19-year-old Gertrude Ederle made headlines around the world when she became the first woman to swim the English Channel. She completed the 21-mile swim in 14 hours and 31 minutes—a time that bested the men's record by nearly two hours. The feat earned her lasting fame and a stupendous ticker-tape parade when she returned to

New York City. Ederle also won a gold and two bronze medals at the 1924 Olympics in Paris. Most notable among competitive swimmers was Johnny Weissmuller, who never lost an individual freestyle race throughout his amateur swimming career. In 1921, in his first meet, Weissmuller won the first Amateur Athletic Union (AAU) championship in the 50-yard freestyle. Soon he became known by such monikers as "the Human Hydroplane" and "the Prince of the Waves." Weissmuller maintained his winning streak until 1929, when he retired from competitive swimming. In between, he won three gold medals at the 1924 Olympics and two more at the 1928 Olympics in Amsterdam. Overall, Weissmuller won 52 national championships and 67 world championships, and set 51 world records in various swimming categories. After giving up competitive swimming, he won fame in his second career as an actor playing Tarzan in Hollywood movies. For 17 years, Weissmuller portrayed the celebrated wild man of the jungle in a dozen different films, beginning, in 1932, with *Tarzan, the Ape Man*.

Horse Racing

Prior to World War I, horse racing, the so-called "Sport of Kings," did not enjoy widespread popularity in the United States. Considered either a hobby for the privileged elite or a magnet for crooks and gamblers, horse racing was avoided or simply ignored by most middle-class Americans. But between 1919 and 1920, a powerful chestnut thoroughbred named Man o' War attracted the attention and admiration of millions of Americans when he compiled an incredible track record of 20 wins and only one loss (in 1919 to a horse named, appropriately enough, Upset). The beauty, speed, and near invincibility of Man o' War made him such a beloved figure that he is credited with helping to popularize the previously minor, marginal sport of horse racing among the general public. Although his career ended after only two years of competitive racing, in his retirement he sired horses that won dozens of races during the 1920s and 1930s. When, in the late 1920s, network radio began to broadcast major horse races over the airwaves, fans across the country became even more enamored with the Preakness, the Kentucky Derby, the Belmont, and other exciting high-stakes horse races.

Auto Racing

Automobile racing experienced its first surge of widespread popularity during the 1920s, as racecar drivers and their teams invented new ways to soup up their engines and streamline their vehicles. The first recorded auto race in the United States occurred in Chicago in 1895, with the

Auto racing, Washington, D.C., circa 1922. Courtesy of the Library of Congress.

winner of the 54-mile race averaging a plodding 7.5 miles per hour. As cars got faster and the number of auto racing fans grew, closed-circuit speedways, such as the Indianapolis Motor Speedway (built in 1909), were constructed. By the 1920s, racing cars and motor speedways had improved considerably from the early days of racing, but even then winning speeds seem modest by today's standards. In 1920, Gaston Chevrolet won the Indianapolis 500 with an average speed of just under 89 mph. By the late 1920s, average winning speeds began to approach 100 mph. However, specially built cars designed expressly to break land-speed records dazzled racing fans with their awesome displays of power. In 1904, an automobile first broke the 100 mph barrier, and in 1927, British driver H.O.D. Seagrave pushed the land-speed record to more than 200 mph. Despite British dominance in the sport during the 1920s, Americans claimed their own auto racing superstars. In 1921, driver Jimmy Murphy became the first American to win a major European race, the French Grand Prix, driving an American-built Dusenberg automobile. The following year he won the Indianapolis 500 and was the national champion racecar driver in 1922 and 1924, before he was killed in a car crash in late 1924.

CONCLUSION

The 1920s witnessed significant changes both in the ways that Americans filled their leisure hours and in the variety of commercial recreational activities available to them. Technological advances led to new pastimes ranging from pogo-sticking to auto racing and also created more efficient methods of mass production by which automobiles, sports equipment, toys, and other products were manufactured for American consumers. The vast network of media outlets, including radio stations, movie theaters, and magazines and newspapers, contributed to the wide assortment of popular pastimes by introducing the latest entertainment crazes and sports heroes to the American public with lightning speed. Most importantly, as the nation made the transition from a rural, agrarian society to an urban, industrial one, popular attitudes toward leisure and recreation changed. Rather than being reserved for the wealthy, leisure activities and sports became increasingly affordable to tens of millions of ordinary Americans, and favorite pastimes occupied an important part of their daily lives. People planned their days around attending a baseball game, joining friends for a game of mahjong, or taking a date to play miniature golf. Engaging in recreational activities or short-lived fads thus became one more way that adults and children could participate in the nation's brash new Jazz Age popular culture.

8

Literature

Today, students of American literature remember the 1920s as a decade of innovative, experimental, modernist writing. Indeed, many important writers and poets found their first audiences during the 1920s, including F. Scott Fitzgerald, Ernest Hemingway, William Faulkner, T. S. Eliot, Ezra Pound, and e. e. cummings. African-American writers such as Langston Hughes, Zora Neale Hurston, and Claude McKay also entered the literary scene, in a movement now known as the Harlem Renaissance. All these writers influenced American letters for decades to come and are still heralded as some of the greatest novelists and poets America has ever produced. However, most Americans readers during the 1920s preferred mainstream popular literature written by authors who have now been forgotten or, at least, fallen out of fashion. Readers' tastes varied from popular best-selling fiction to serious works of non-fiction to splashy pulp magazines. One thing is for certain, though—Americans *were* reading in the 1920s. Almost 95 percent of Americans were literate, and enormous quantities of fiction, poetry, and drama were published and read during the 1920s. Along with automobiles, motion pictures, and radio, popular books and magazines occupied an extremely important place in the everyday lives of millions of Americans.

BOOKS

Best-Selling Novels

Although dozens of literary masterpieces were published during the 1920s, most readers weren't dashing out to the corner bookshop to buy

T. S. Eliot's *The Waste Land* (1922) or William Faulkner's *The Sound and the Fury* (1929). Popular literary tastes ran toward romance novels, historical fiction, westerns, crime stories, and other, more traditional literary genres. Authors who combined romance, history, and intrigue in their novels often attracted a large fan following that would last, in some cases, for decades. Among the best-selling fiction writers of the 1920s were Sinclair Lewis, Zane Grey, Edna Ferber, Dorothy Canfield, Booth Tarkington, Temple Bailey, Edith Wharton, Edith Atkinson, Anita Loos, and E. M. Hull.

The advent of subscription book clubs in the 1920s boosted the careers of many popular writers and brought millions of books into American homes. In 1926, Harry Scherman started the Book-of-the-Month Club, which became an immediate hit among regular book buyers. Members enjoyed receiving a novel each month that had been selected by literary "experts," and the success of this club spawned a number of rival organizations, including the Literary Guild, founded in 1927. Subscription book clubs attracted tens of thousands of members and influenced, to some degree, the titles that made the best-seller lists (which were compiled by the *New York Times* and *Publishers Weekly*, among others). The Book-of-the-Month Club's first selection, in April 1926, was the British writer Sylvia Townsend Warner's debut novel, *Lolly Willowes* (1926), a story about an unmarried woman in post–World War I Britain.

The 1920s also marked an age when a considerable number of women writers attracted wide fan bases of primarily women readers. Novelists such as Edna Ferber, Temple Bailey, Gene Stratton-Porter, Mary Roberts Rinehart, and Kathleen Norris churned out novel after novel over the course of the decade, regularly topping the book-sales charts and delighting their large and loyal readership. Many of these novels feature sexually liberated heroines who had adopted the radical, freethinking philosophies commonly associated with the rebellious flapper. For example, Diana Mayo, the sensual heroine in E. M. Hull's *The Sheik* (1921), and Lorelei Lee, the sexy gold-digger in Anita Loos' *Gentlemen Prefer Blondes* (serialized in *Harper's Bazaar* in 1925), each embody certain aspects of the "New Woman," who could live an independent life and enjoy sex just as much as men. These heroines, though, were perhaps more exceptionally liberated than the typical fictional protagonists of the day. The majority of popular women's novels center on young women who had adopted the trappings of flapperdom: bobbed hair, short skirts, makeup, slang, even cigarettes and alcohol. But by the conclusion of the story, they turn out to be old-fashioned girls who want to settle down and become devoted wives and mothers. Time after time, the wild young women outgrow their rebellious flapper "phase" after they meet Mr. Right and learn, sometimes through hard experience, what really matters in life. Like real-life women, fictional heroines often appeared to be more liberated and rebellious than they actually were.

BEST-SELLING WRITERS

Sinclair Lewis

Sinclair Lewis was, by most accounts, the best example of an American writer who managed to appeal to both general audiences and literary critics of the 1920s. A prolific novelist, playwright, satirist, and social critic, Lewis became, in 1930, the first American to receive the Nobel Prize in literature. He was nominated for the Pulitzer Prize for *Main Street* (1920) and *Babbitt* (1922) and won it for *Arrowsmith* (1925). He declined the award, however, claiming that it was intended to honor a novel that celebrated American wholesomeness, and his novel did no such thing. Indeed, much of Lewis' fiction satirized what he saw as America's preoccupation with crass materialism, and he pointedly ridiculed how unbending conformity to small-town ideals could stunt one's potential. Audiences responded enthusiastically to Lewis' biting social commentary, and a number of his popular novels were made into movies, including *Main Street* in 1923, *Babbitt* in 1924 and 1934, and *Arrowsmith* in 1931.

Lewis published two books during the 1910s, but it was not until the 1920s that he achieved his greatest literary success. *Main Street*, the top-selling novel in 1921, traces the story of Carol Kennicott, a freethinking modern woman who finds herself in constant conflict with the expectations of the local townspeople of Gopher Prairie (a town based loosely on Lewis' own hometown of Sauk Centre, Minnesota). After marrying the young town doctor and settling down in his hometown, she attempts to bring what she considers beauty, art, and other forms of cosmopolitan "culture" to the community. Carol's efforts are frustrated by the pettiness of the townspeople, and through her story Lewis mercilessly satirizes the narrow-mindedness of small-town life and attacks the unyielding conformity and dulled intellect of its residents.

Lewis' next novel, *Babbitt*, considered by many critics to be his finest work, made the best-seller lists in both 1922 and 1923. The novel focuses on real estate agent George F. Babbitt, a modern-day slave to consumerism, advertising, and social status, who resides in the midwestern town of Zenith, a slightly larger version of Gopher Prairie. Babbitt takes such inordinate pride in his middle-class home, his automobile, and his zealous Zenith "boosterism" that the term *Babbittry* soon became synonymous with unthinking conformity and shallow, materialistic values. Lewis' next best-seller, *Arrowsmith*, depicts the life of a medical doctor caught between idealism and commercialism. *Elmer Gantry*, which hit the top sales charts in 1927, attacks hypocritical ministers and loosely recalls the story of famous evangelist Aimee Semple McPherson, a real-life Pentecostal preacher whose supposed kidnapping in 1926 fueled rumors of an illicit tryst with a married man. Lewis's final best-seller of the decade, *Dodsworth* (1929), centers on the millionaire Sam Dodsworth, a captain of American industry, and his crumbling marriage. Although Lewis continued to publish novels for the next 15 years (he wrote 22 in all), he never again duplicated his literary successes of the 1920s.

Zane Grey

Perhaps the single most popular author in America during the post–World War I years was Zane Grey, although he never garnered the critical acclaim that Sinclair Lewis did. A prolific writer of westerns, Grey penned more than 60 novels in which he presented the landscape of the American West as a moral battleground that had the power either to destroy or to redeem his characters. His stories usually dealt with settlers, cowboys, desperadoes, Indians, cattle drives, family feuds, and other familiar aspects of Western lore and legend. Grey began publishing his work as early as 1904, but he did not break through to widespread popular acclaim until the release of *Riders of the Purple Sage* (1912), which sold over 2 million copies and was adapted for motion pictures three times. During the 1920s, Grey hit the best-seller lists with *The Man of the Forest* (1920), *The Mysterious Rider* (1921), *To the Last Man* (1922), *The Wanderer of the Wasteland* (1923), and *The Call of the Canyon* (1924), all of which were adapted for the silver screen. Grey sold over 17 million copies of his novels during his lifetime, and some estimates suggest that more than 100 films have been based on his stories.

Edna Ferber

Like Grey, Edna Ferber also became a celebrated writer during the 1920s. Although she began publishing novels in 1911, her first best-seller, *So Big* (1924), solidified her popular success. The inspirational story of Selina DeJong, a young woman struggling to raise her son on a small farm outside Chicago, *So Big* won the Pulitzer Prize in 1925 and was immediately made into a silent film (other movie adaptations followed in 1932 and 1953). In fact, a number of Ferber's novels were translated into popular movies during the 1920s. *Show Boat* (1926), the story of three generations of the Hawks family on board the Mississippi riverboat *The Cotton Blossom*, was made into several films, a successful musical, and a radio program. *Cimarron* (1929), a western dealing with the opening of the Oklahoma Territory, was filmed for the first time in 1931. While Ferber was, by all accounts, a popular novelist, literary critics appreciated her writing style far more than that of most other popular writers of the 1920s.

Rafael Sabatini

Although today it is relatively unusual for a foreign writer to hit the American best-seller lists, it was much more common in the early decades of the twentieth century. For example, American readers loved the works of novelist Rafael Sabatini, who was born in Italy in 1875 to an Italian father and an English mother. Sabatini spoke several languages fluently but began writing short stories and romances in English around the turn of the century. For nearly the next three decades he published, on average, one book a year. His adventure novel of the French Revolution, *Scaramouche* (1921), and his thrilling pirate story, *Captain Blood* (1922), were international best-sellers that were also adapted as films, which further established Sabatini's reputation in the United States. After the success of these two books, publishers re-issued many of Sabatini's earlier novels, and they too climbed the best-seller lists. *The Sea Hawk,* originally published in 1915, reached the American best-seller charts in 1923; *Mistress Wilding,* originally published in 1910, became an American favorite in 1924. Sabatini visited the United States only once, on a book tour during the 1930s. Nevertheless, American readers never seemed to tire of his romantic adventure stories.

Gene Stratton-Porter

Gene Stratton-Porter, an early American feminist, naturalist, and photographer, was also a popular novelist during the 1920s. Stratton-Porter wrote primarily moralistic and romantic novels that chronicled the lives of noble and pure-hearted but often poor, crippled, or otherwise disadvantaged characters. In 1903, she published her first novel, *The Song of the Cardinal*, and during the 1920s she wrote two best-sellers, *Her Father's Daughter* (1921), a story of two very different girls raised as sisters, and the posthumously published *The Keeper of the Bees* (1925), a tale of an injured American soldier who finds renewed meaning in his life by helping others. Critics ridiculed her sentimental stories even as millions of Americans eagerly devoured her works. Stratton-Porter died in 1924 from injuries sustained when a trolley car collided with her limousine; by the time of her death, she had sold more than 10 million copies of her books.

Mary Roberts Rinehart

Mary Roberts Rinehart was a tremendously popular mystery and detective writer during the 1920s. One of her books produced the famous whodunit phrase, "The butler did it," and in her heyday she was more famous than her chief rival, the British writer Agatha Christie. *The Circular Staircase* (1908), the first of Rinehart's many mystery novels, established her as a leading writer of the genre; in 1920 this novel was adapted into a film titled *The Bat*. In 1914, she wrote two novellas in which she introduced readers to Hilda Adams, a nurse (popularly known as Miss Pinkerton) who also worked undercover for the police. This character returned in Rinehart's 1932 popular novel *Miss Pinkerton*. In the 1920s, however, Rinehart wrote primarily romantic fiction, not murder mysteries. Readers loved *A Poor Wise Man* (1920), *The Breaking Point* (1922), and the suspenseful *Lost Ecstasy* (1927), but, as was the case with the works of many popular writers, literary critics panned her best-selling novels.

Non-Fiction Best-Sellers

Non-fiction titles also captured the imagination of American readers during the 1920s. Several historical studies, particularly military ones, hit the non-fiction best-seller lists during the decade, including Philip Gibbs' *Now It Can Be Told* (1920), H. G. Wells' *The Outline of History* (1920), and Hendrik Van Loon's *The Story of Mankind* (1921). Bruce Barton, a veteran salesman and advertiser, published his best-selling *The Man Nobody Knows* (1925), which portrayed Jesus Christ as a dynamic salesman who, with his staff of 12 managers, founded a highly successful global organization called Christianity. Then, as now, diet and health guidebooks also sold well. Dr. Lulu Hunt Peters' *Diet and Health, With Key to the Calories* was originally published in 1918, and by 1922 it had already gone through 16 editions. *Diet and Health* ranked among the best-selling non-fiction books every year between 1922 and 1926, the first American diet book to do so. Cookbooks were also big sellers during the 1920s. For example, Fannie Farmer's *The Boston Cooking-School Cook Book* made the best-seller list between 1924 and 1926. Hundreds of thousands of readers also sought help from Emily Post's *Etiquette in Society, in Business, in Politics and at Home* (1922), which offered advice on what was considered well-mannered and appropriate social behavior. *Etiquette* has remained a favorite on American bookshelves; it is still in print and has gone into its sixteenth revised edition.

Although self-help books occupy large sections of bookstores today, they were a relatively new phenomenon in the 1920s. Emile Coué, a French psychotherapist, published the first popular self-help book in America, *Self-Mastery Through Conscious Autosuggestion* (1922). He posited that self-suggestion could boost confidence and motivation and recommended that his followers chant to themselves 20 times, twice each day, the optimistic mantra: "Day by day, in every way, I am getting better and better."[1] His theory took America and England by storm, and Coué soon founded institutes specifically to teach his principles.

Perhaps the most unusual non-fiction best-seller of the 1920s was not a traditional book at all. In 1924, the fledgling publishing team of Simon and Schuster brought out their first book: a slim volume called *The Cross Word Puzzle Book*, which came with a pencil attached by a string. This was the first book devoted to these popular word puzzles, and although booksellers initially balked at stocking this unconventional volume, it sold hundreds of thousands of copies, sparked a national craze for crossword puzzles, and ensured Simon and Schuster's lasting financial success.

MAGAZINES

American readers purchased popular magazines in record numbers during the 1920s. Magazine publishing had received an enormous boost when, in 1879, Congress decided to offer magazine publishers a lower rate (second-class mail) to send periodicals through the U.S. mail, but American magazines' circulation numbers did not climb into the millions until the 1920s. *The Saturday Evening Post*, *Literary Digest*, and *Ladies' Home Journal*, while founded earlier than the 1920s, attracted enthusiastic audiences with their articles on everything from fashion to romance to business. Literally hundreds of new magazines devoted to almost every imaginable topic were founded in the 1920s, including several that still exist today.

General Audience Magazines

In February 1922, DeWitt and Lila Wallace began publishing *Reader's Digest*, a compilation of news, entertainment articles, and fiction that had been culled from other magazines, abridged (in some cases), and reprinted. The magazine was cleverly marketed to readers as a convenient way to manage the overwhelming amount of information that had become available in the modern age. *Time*, the nation's first weekly newsmagazine, debuted in March 1923. Its founders, Yale graduates Henry Luce and Briton Hadden, believed that American readers needed a magazine that covered a broad range of general news, from international affairs and science to religion and business developments. *Time*'s relatively short, easy-to-read articles enabled busy readers to stay abreast of their fast-changing world, and the magazine's early foray into radio advertising (in 1926) helped boost its weekly circulation to nearly 200,000 readers by the end of the decade. *The Saturday Evening Post* also emerged as one of the more popular magazines in the 1920s. Editor-in-chief George Horace Lorimer appealed to a wide readership by hiring some of America's most talented writers and illustrators, including Sinclair Lewis, Ring Lardner, F. Scott Fitzgerald, and Norman Rockwell. During the 1920s, *The Saturday Evening Post* ranked as a national and international institution and has since been considered by many readers and historians to be an accurate reflection of the pro-business and consumerist values of white middle-class Americans. *Life,* primarily a humor magazine, also delighted readers with book and theater reviews, verse, sketches, light articles, and illustrations by some of the finest artists of the decade. Originally founded in 1883, *Life* had become, by the 1920s, a common sight on the coffee tables of middle-class Americans. All humor magazines struggled during the Great Depression, however, and in 1936, the faltering magazine was sold to Time, Inc., which reinvented *Life* as a photojournalism magazine.

Women's Magazines

A number of periodicals were specifically marketed to middle-class women during the 1920s, including *Good Housekeeping, The Delineator, McCall's,* and *Women's Home Companion*. These magazines featured short stories and serialized novels, recipes, dress patterns, household tips, and advertisements. Other popular women's magazines, such as *Harper's Bazaar* and *Vogue,* focused primarily on clothing and fashion. The undisputed giant among women's magazines, however, was *Ladies' Home Journal,* which, in 1904, became the first American magazine to reach a circulation of 1 million readers. *Ladies' Home Journal* targeted a readership of married, white, middle-class women who took their roles as wife, mother, and homemaker very seriously. *Ladies' Home Journal* offered its devoted readers short stories, household and decorating tips, recipes, and advertisements for products such as cosmetics, clothing, food, appliances, and other items that were seen as part of the woman's domain. As a matter of principle, it refused to run advertisements for alcohol, tobacco, playing cards, patent medicine, or other products considered of questionable moral value.

Smart Magazines

Another periodical genre that found a receptive audience in the 1920s was the so-called smart magazines, such as *The Smart Set: A Magazine of Cleverness* (1900; founded by William D'Alton Mann), *Vanity Fair* (1913; founded by Condé Nast), *American Mercury* (1923; founded by H. L.

Cover of *Life* magazine, illustrated by John Held Jr., February 18, 1926. Courtesy of the Library of Congress.

Mencken and George Jean Nathan), and *The New Yorker* (1925; founded by Harold Ross). These witty and entertaining periodicals catered primarily to educated, middle- and upper-middle-class readers. Amid articles about restaurants, fashion, theater, art, and other topics, smart magazines published early works by F. Scott Fitzgerald, Dorothy Parker, Theodore Dreiser, Eugene O'Neill, and Edna St. Vincent Millay. Although indisputably commercial ventures, smart magazines managed to walk a fine line between the highbrow magazines such as *The Atlantic Monthly* and *Harper's Monthly* and the more highly commercialized, broad-based magazines such as *The Saturday Evening Post* and *Life*. Smart magazines appealed largely to those who wanted to read more intellectual material than the mass-circulated periodical giants could provide.

Little Magazines

Small, non-profit literary magazines of the 1920s, such as *Poetry: A Magazine of Verse* (founded 1912), *The Little Review* (1914), *The Dial* (1917), *Broom* (1921), *The Fugitive* (1922), *Transition* (1927), and *Hound and Horn* (1927), were known as "little magazines." The magazines themselves were usually full-sized; it was their limited circulations that marked them as "little." Although many of them were founded in earlier decades, these magazines experienced a renaissance in popularity in the 1920s. Editors of little magazines were usually willing to publish avant-garde and experimental literature and were receptive to new authors and innovative literary styles. They were often the first to publish the work of important modern writers and critics, such as T. S. Eliot, Gertrude Stein, William Carlos Williams, Marianne Moore, and James Joyce. Because commercial success was not a primary objective of these periodicals, little magazines tended to generate small circulations and often went out of business after releasing only a handful of issues.

Pulp Magazines

Pulp magazines, a periodical genre that flourished between the 1920s and the 1940s, were lurid, thrilling, mass-produced fiction magazines. Pulp magazine covers were made of smooth, shiny paper stamped with colorful and evocative pictures of beautiful women, hard-nosed detectives, rugged cowboys, and even monsters from outer space. Inside, the stories were printed on cheap, porous "pulp" paper, which kept publishing costs down and which suggested the nickname by which this magazine genre became known. The inside pages were extremely fragile—they yellowed and began to disintegrate within months (which makes many of these magazines tremendously valuable to collectors today). Only black ink was used inside the magazine, but many stories were lavishly illustrated with line drawings. Pulp magazines ranged in price from 5 to 25 cents—less than half the price of a typical periodical—and attracted huge numbers of avid readers from all walks of life but particularly from the working classes, who had little disposable income to spend on expensive magazines or books.

The pulp magazine industry began in 1896, when Frank Munsey published an all-fiction issue of *The Argosy*. By the 1920s, hundreds of pulp magazines were being published, some lasting for years, others vanishing after only an issue or two. Pulp magazine publishing was a fast-paced, trendy business that tried to keep up with the changing tastes of its readers. Some pulp magazines enjoyed large subscription circulations, but most of them survived because readers picked them up regularly from newsstands and drugstores. Most pulp magazines can be classified into a handful of general categories, but there were always a few magazines that defied easy categorization and appealed to a narrow target audience, including *Secret Service Stories* (1927), *Firefighters* (1929), *Gangster Stories* (1929), and *Railroad Man's Magazine* (1929).

Crime fiction and detective story magazines attracted particularly large numbers of readers during the 1920s. *Detective Story Magazine* (1915) was the first fiction pulp to dedicate itself to this particular genre of story, and it soon spawned dozens of imitators. In 1920, H. L. Mencken and George Jean Nathan, the editors of the sophisticated but unprofitable magazine *The Smart Set*, introduced the highly successful *Black Mask* to the field of detective and mystery pulp fiction. Several famous detective fiction writers, including Dashiell Hammett, Raymond Chandler, and Erle Stanley Gardner, received their literary start by publishing in *Black Mask* and other detective pulps. Hard-boiled private eyes such as Race Williams and Sam Spade were born in the pages of these magazines, and Hammett's *The Maltese Falcon* first ran as a 65,000-word, five-part serial novel in *Black Mask* (from September 1929 to January 1930). By the end of the 1920s, dozens of pulps, including *Real Detective Tales and Mystery Stories* (1925), *Clues* (1926), *Crime Mysteries* (1927), and *Detective Fiction Weekly* (1928), featured crime and detective stories.

While detective pulps attempted to mirror real-life stories, other genres of pulps abandoned all sense of reality. Audiences fascinated by stories of horror, fantasy, and the supernatural had only to reach for *Weird Tales* (1923), *Ghost Stories* (1926), or *Tales of Magic and Mystery* (1927) to get a taste of the fantastic and the bizarre. *Weird Tales*, for example, contained stories of horror and the supernatural with fantastic titles and even more imaginative writing. These magazines launched the literary careers of a number of well-known American authors, including H. P. Lovecraft, Robert E. Howard, Ray Bradbury, Edmond Hamilton, and other fantasy writers. In 1928, *Weird Tales* also published the first story by the then-14-year-old Thomas Lanier "Tennessee" Williams, who went on to become a celebrated American playwright. Science fiction—then called "scientification"—found outlets in publications such as *Amazing Stories* (1926), *Science Wonder Stories* (1929), and *Air Wonder Stories* (1929). *Amazing Stories* also fostered the formation of some of the earliest science-fiction fan clubs. The magazine published a readers' column that included the mailing addresses of its correspondents. Soon, science fiction enthusiasts began contacting one another directly and started to form fan clubs across the nation.

For those interested in exciting adventures in exotic locations, pulp magazines such as *The Argosy* (1882), *Adventure* (1910), and *Action Stories* (1921), offered stories about strapping he-men engaged in thrilling situations in the South Sea Islands, the Amazon, or any number of other far-off locales around the world. *The Argosy* actually began as a general fiction magazine, but in the 1920s its focus shifted primarily to adventure stories. The top adventure magazines always strove for as much realism as possible and often hired real-life travelers and explorers to contribute their most exciting tales. Edgar Rice Burroughs, one of the most popular pulp writers, contributed his famous *Tarzan of the Apes*, in its entirety, to the October 1912 issue of the adventure pulp *All-Story Magazine* (1905). This inspired a national Tarzan craze that lasted throughout much of the 1920s, even though by that time Burroughs had gone on to write hundreds of other adventure tales. *Adventure*, which cost a quarter (five cents more than most of its competitors), cleverly advertised a sort of "membership" that supplied each reader with an identification card. If the reader were killed or injured while carrying the card, according to the magazine's publicity, someone coming upon the body could contact the magazine, which would then contact the person's next of kin. This became a tremendously successful marketing ploy, and some of these card-carriers eventually formed the Adventurers' Club of New York.

Several pulp magazines commemorated the drama, tragedy, and heroism of World War I. Publications such as *War Stories* (1926), *Battle Stories* (1927), *Over the Top* (1928), *Under Fire* (1928), and *Soldier Stories* (1929) all glorified the military engagements of the Great War and cashed in on a sense of nostalgia that certain Americans felt for the first war of the modern industrial age. Combat soldiers were not the only stars of this genre, however. Other titles such as *Air Stories* (1927), *Aces* (1928), *Wings* (1928), *Flying Aces* (1928), and *Air Trails* (1928) showcased stories about aerial combat, while *Navy Stories* (1929), and *Submarine Stories* (1929) concentrated on tales about maritime warfare.

Western and cowboy pulps, including *Western Story Magazine* (1919), *The Frontier* (1924), *Cowboy Stories* (1925), *West* (1926), and *Wild West Weekly* (1927), attempted to satisfy American readers' apparently insatiable appetite for adventure stories about cowboys, outlaws, and frontiersmen. Some western pulps, including the 15-cent *Western Story Magazine*,

Cover of *Weird Tales: The Unique Magazine*, April 1924. Courtesy of the Library of Congress.

sold as many as 500,000 copies a week. Many of the writers for these pulps had never actually *seen* the American West, but they made up for their lack of personal experience with library research and colorful imaginations, and few readers seemed to know the difference. Stories ranged from nostalgic, pastoral recollections of pioneer life to tales about the violent, gunslinging world of horse thieves and Indian attacks.

Despite all the testosterone-driven stories of warfare and adventure, stories about love and romance also played an important role in the pulp magazine industry. For the most part, these love pulps targeted a female readership, and titles such as *Love Story Magazine* (1921), *Lover's Lane* (1923), *Love Romances* (1926), and *Heart Throbs* (1928) satisfied their readers' desires for passionate, idealistic tales of romance. During the 1920s, women apparently found these stories exciting and even racy, yet they seem remarkably tame by today's standards. The female protagonists were inevitably positive and appealing characters who, after a series of trials and setbacks, usually ended up either engaged or married to their true love. Female authors wrote most of these stories, though some critics claim that at least a handful of male writers adopted female pseudonyms and contributed their work to these lucrative pulps. A few love story magazines, such as *Ranch Romances* (1924) and *Western Romances* (1929), blended genres in order to tap in to the widespread popularity of cowboy stories. In fact, *Ranch Romances* was still in publication in the early 1970s—nearly 20 years after most pulps had disappeared.

Sex pulps—a sensational spin-off of the love story pulps—also flourished during the 1920s. These magazines typically sprinkled their stories with obvious sexual innuendos, lengthy descriptions of beautiful, semiclad women, and racy "true confessions" stories. Although Americans of every background purchased these titillating publications, sex pulps were primarily targeted toward working-class male audiences and were usually sold under the counter at cigar stores, as opposed to the newsstands, where most other pulps were available. To dodge the authorities during a decade when various "blue laws" were intended to limit, if not eliminate, the trade in sexual literature, these magazines relied on such euphemistic titles as *Snappy Stories* (1912), *Pep Stories* (1916), and *Saucy Stories* (1916), the latter of which, like *Black Mask* and the sex magazine *Parisienne* (1915), was edited by H. L. Mencken and George Jean Nathan. These pulps also included sex-advice columns, book reviews, humorous pieces, letters from readers, and advertisements for lingerie and sex merchandise such as performance-enhancing tablets and breast-augmentation products.

One important sub-genre of the sex pulps was true-confession magazines, which started with the founding of *True Story Magazine* in 1919 by Bernarr Macfadden. By the mid-1920s, monthly sales of *True Story Magazine* reached 2 million, making it one of the best-selling pulps. Ordinary people, not professional writers, supposedly wrote for true-confession magazines, which were characterized by first-person accounts of shocking rendezvous and scandalous encounters. Among the most famous titles were *True Confessions*, *True Experience*, *True Romance*, and *Secrets*. Clearly, publishers saw a lucrative market in selling these explicit stories, and many young readers confessed that these magazines were their first introduction to sex education.

Pulp publishers searched for any area of interest that might possibly be developed into another magazine. They tried to market tales about safari and big-game hunting in *Wild Game Stories* (1926), adventures that took place on or near blimps in *Zeppelin Stories* (1929), and even accounts of making big money fast in the poorly timed *Wall Street Stories* (1929). Perhaps the single greatest contribution of pulp magazines to American popular culture was their role as literary springboards that launched the careers of many significant American authors, including Dashiell Hammett, Zane Grey, Edgar Rice Burroughs, Ray Bradbury, and Raymond Chandler.

MODERNIST FICTION

Some of the best-known American literature produced during the 1920s now falls under the category of "modernism," which is a general term used to describe works of art or literature that in some way address the perceived breakdown of traditional society and culture under the pressures of modernity. Modernism actually traces its roots to Europe and was inspired, in part, by the devastating and alienating effects of World War I. During the early twentieth century, modernism exerted a profound influence on literature as well as painting, sculpture, music, dance, film, and drama. Modernist literature could take a number of forms, from the dense, allusive poetry of T. S. Eliot to the sparse, minimalist dialogue of Ernest Hemingway. Unlike Victorian literature, whose plots typically contain a coherent beginning, middle, and end, modernist literature is usually composed of various narrative fragments. Modernist stories and poems omit many details and explanations, often end without resolution, and challenge readers to interpret for themselves a work's ultimate meaning. A common effect of this fragmented style of writing is that the work often appears to lack continuity, a unified plot, or easily identifiable heroic figures. Not surprisingly, then, most American readers of the 1920s passed over great modernist works of fiction and instead reached for their favorite Zane Grey western or Mary Roberts Rinehart mystery.

The 1920s nonetheless saw an incredible outpouring of modernist literary works, many of which are now considered American classics.

Mississippi-born novelist William Faulkner, one of the foremost modernist writers, wrote magazine stories and published his first two novels, *Soldier's Pay* (1926) and *Mosquitoes* (1927), during the decade, to little popular acclaim. In 1929, Faulkner released *The Sound and the Fury*, a modernist masterpiece in which he experimented with language, psychology, and point of view, but even this now-celebrated novel was not particularly well received in its time. Novelist and short-story writer Ernest Hemingway fared considerably better during the 1920s. His first novel, *The Sun Also Rises* (1926), catapulted him to international celebrity and resulted in a wave of American tourists traveling to Spain to see the Pamplona bullfights that he so glamorously immortalized in the book. Hemingway soon became known for his distinctive writing style, which was characterized in part by short, stripped-down sentences in which much was left unsaid, yet still allowed careful readers to comprehend exactly what the characters meant.

F. Scott Fitzgerald

F. Scott Fitzgerald, the darling of the American literary scene during the 1920s, managed to bridge the gap between popular fiction and serious literature to become a genuine celebrity. Then, as now, his name was often associated with the hedonism of all-night partying and carousing during the Jazz Age, an era that he himself named. Fitzgerald commanded high prices for his short stories, which he frequently placed in *The Saturday Evening Post*, *The Smart Set*, and other magazines. He solidified his reputation with his first novel, *This Side of Paradise* (1920), which portrayed the flamboyant exploits of self-indulgent, pleasure-seeking, college-age youth. He followed with three collections of short stories—*Flappers and Philosophers* (1921), *Tales of the Jazz Age* (1922), and *All the Sad Young Men* (1926)—and two more novels—*The Beautiful and Damned* (1922) and his best-known work, *The Great Gatsby* (1925). This latter novel, set against the backdrop of extravagant parties and powerful underworld figures, tells the tragic story of millionaire Jay Gatsby's futile attempt to turn back the clock and win the heart of his former sweetheart. Scott and his beautiful wife Zelda (Sayre) Fitzgerald, also a talented writer and artist, were heralded as the couple that most personified the mood of the 1920s—they were a fun-loving, irreverent, adventuresome pair who loved to party and to spend money recklessly. The 1930s saw Zelda succumb to mental illness and Scott wrestle with debilitating alcoholism, but they are remembered not for their darker periods so much as for their dazzling celebrity and insightful chronicles of the social trends of the Jazz Age.

Scott and Zelda Fitzgerald on their honeymoon, 1920. Courtesy of the Library of Congress.

POETRY

The 1920s marked an important period in the development of American poetry. To be sure, ordinary Americans reached for the poetry of Marianne Moore, e. e. cummings, Carl Sandburg, and Hart Crane far less often than for Sinclair Lewis' novels or the Book-of-the-Month Club's latest selection, but these poets made significant and enduring contributions to American literature. The American poetry scene was remarkably diverse in the 1920s. Modernist poets such as Ezra Pound, T. S. Eliot, Amy Lowell, Wallace Stevens, and William Carlos Williams developed innovative verse forms and techniques (such as free verse and imagism), while more traditional poets such as Robert Frost, Edna St. Vincent Millay, and Edward Arlington Robinson sold many more copies of their books and pleased many more critics. The most acclaimed poet of the 1920s was Edward Arlington Robinson, who won the Pulitzer Prize three times during the decade: *Collected Poems* won in 1922, *The Man Who Died Twice* won in 1925, and *Tristram* won in 1928. Other Pulitzer Prize-winning poets include Amy Lowell for *What's O'Clock* in 1926, Leonora Speyer for *Fiddler's Farewell* in 1927, and Stephen Vincent Benet for *John Brown's Body* in 1929. Poet Conrad Aiken, winner of the Pulitzer Prize in 1930 for his *Selected Poems* (1929), edited and published the *Selected Poems of Emily Dickinson* in 1924 and effectively launched her posthumous literary reputation.

Robert Frost ranked as one of the most popular American poets during the 1920s, in part because he wrote what appeared to be folksy, traditional poems that many readers found accessible. Unlike the deliberately difficult poems of Pound and Eliot, Frost's poems immortalized a rural American countryside that appealed to many who struggled to keep up with fast-paced modern life. His poems evoked nostalgic scenes of the farms, forests, and country people of New England that readers found a refreshing change from their increasingly urban surroundings. In 1924, Frost won the Pulitzer Prize for his *New Hampshire: A Poem with Notes and Grace Notes*.

Edna St. Vincent Millay, the first woman poet to win a Pulitzer Prize (for *The Ballad of the Harp Weaver* in 1923), became famous during the 1920s as much for her bohemian lifestyle in Greenwich Village, New York, as for her poems. Although she wrote about seemingly "old-fashioned" subjects, such as nature, romantic love, death, and even poetry itself, she also dealt candidly with issues of sexuality, rebellion, and the liberated woman. Her outspokenness, as well as her combining of traditional verse forms with quintessentially modern sensibilities, garnered her a larger audience than most other American poets of the decade enjoyed.

THE HARLEM RENAISSANCE

The Harlem Renaissance, sometimes called the Negro Renaissance or the New Negro Movement, describes the period roughly between the end of World War I and the onset of the Great Depression, during which African Americans produced a vast number of literary, musical, and artistic works. The artists associated with the Harlem Renaissance attempted to promote racial consciousness and black pride by creating new images of African Americans and by celebrating their blues and folklore traditions, in order ultimately to destroy old racist stereotypes. The works they created were, for the most part, confident, positive, and optimistic about the future of black Americans.

Between 1915 and 1918, approximately 500,000 African Americans left the South for Harlem and other northern urban-industrial centers as part of the Great Migration. At least another 700,000 black southerners followed during the 1920s.[2] These families left their homes to make new lives for themselves in the North, where, they believed, they would find greater freedom and better job opportunities than were generally available in the Jim Crow South. Thousands of black families crowded into Harlem, a large neighborhood in upper Manhattan loosely defined in the 1920s as the area between 110th and 155th Streets. This dramatic population shift transformed Harlem into the capital of African-American culture during the 1920s, as New York City's black population soared from more than 152,000 in 1920 to nearly 328,000 by 1929.[3] Black people from the American South, the West Indies, and even Africa crowded into the neighborhood, competing for jobs and living space. Harlem became an important cultural crossroads, and talented writers such as Langston Hughes, Countee Cullen, Claude McKay, Jessie Fauset, and Zora Neale Hurston were only a few of the hundreds of young African Americans who flocked to Harlem to join the growing colony of black intellectuals fueling the Harlem Renaissance.

During the 1920s, writers including Hughes, Hurston, McKay, Cullen, Fauset, Jean Toomer, Walter White, Rudolph Fisher, Nella Larsen, and Wallace Thurman produced poems, novels, short stories, essays, and plays that encouraged readers to appreciate African-American culture and its folk roots. African-American journals such as *The Crisis*, *The Messenger*, and *Opportunity* further contributed to the development of African-American artistic, cultural, and political expression by publishing essays, articles, and stories by black writers. In 1925, Alain Locke, an African-American philosopher, critic, and editor, published *The New Negro*, the first literary anthology of the Harlem Renaissance. Contributors included McKay, Hughes, Toomer, Cullen, W.E.B. Du Bois, James Weldon Johnson, Gwendolyn Bennett, and Arna Bontemps. The essays, stories, poems, drama, and art contained in this volume gave voice to the African-American cultural revolution that was taking place not just in Harlem but in metropolitan black communities across the country.

White Americans were also involved, to a certain degree, in the Harlem Renaissance. Black culture fascinated many white people, who believed that it was inherently exotic, primitive, and exciting. Wealthy white New Yorkers and tourists came to Harlem in droves during the 1920s, "slumming," as they called it, in jazz cabarets and speakeasies. White readers regularly purchased books written by Harlem Renaissance authors, and white writers frequently penned laudatory introductions to these volumes. A number of white writers even incorporated what they believed to be African-American themes of exoticism and sensuality into their own writing, most notably playwright Eugene O'Neill, who wrote *The Emperor Jones* (1920) and *All God's Chillun Got Wings* (1924), and novelist Carl Van Vechten, whose 1926 *Nigger Heaven* sparked considerable controversy among both black and white readers. Some wealthy white patrons participated more directly in the Harlem Renaissance by providing living expenses and small stipends to black writers, thus allowing them to pursue their art without having to hold down regular jobs at the same time.

By most accounts, the heyday of the Harlem Renaissance ended with the stock market crash of October 1929. The money that once supported these writers and artists evaporated as the nation sank into dire financial straits. Today, however, works from the 1920s such as Hughes' poem "The Negro Speaks of Rivers" (1921), Toomer's experimental *Cane* (1923), McKay's novel *Home to Harlem* (1928), and Larsen's novellas *Quicksand* (1928) and *Passing* (1929) remind us of the enduring power of these voices from the Harlem Renaissance.

THE FUGITIVES

Not all Americans embraced the technological, ideological, and literary advances that characterized the 1920s. A group of a dozen or so white writers and intellectuals centered around Vanderbilt University in Nashville, Tennessee, spearheaded a fleetingly popular "southern renaissance" that decried the newly emerging modern age as one of godlessness, dehumanization, and crass capitalism. Collectively known as the "Fugitives" or the "Agrarians," these literary men, including Robert Penn Warren, Allen Tate, John Crowe Ransom, and Donald Davidson, published their work in a journal called *The Fugitive*, which appeared between 1922 and 1925. Then, in 1930, the Fugitives published their manifesto, *I'll Take My Stand: The South and the Agrarian Tradition*, authored by "Twelve Southerners." In this anthology, the 12 authors glorified the rural folk culture of the American South and bemoaned the loss of tradition, religion, and community that, they believed, had been sacrificed to northern urban culture, widespread industrialization, and mass consumerism.

The Fugitives' vehement defense of southern traditions and values had been prompted, in large measure, by the disparaging media coverage of the famous 1925 Scopes trial in Dayton, Tennessee. Many of the more than 100 reporters who covered the trial depicted the South as a land full of backward, Bible-thumping, moronic country yokels. H. L. Mencken, reporting for the *Baltimore Sun*, seemed to take particular glee in describing the anti-evolution Tennesseans as "gaping primates" who "sweated freely, and were not debauched by the refinements of the toilet." To Mencken, southerners represented "bigotry, ignorance, hatred, superstition, every sort of blackness that the human heart is capable of."[4] Enraged by what they felt was an unfair portrayal, the Fugitives tried to articulate their beliefs that the North had destroyed the South's economy and racial order during the Civil War and that the modern, industrial "New South" had been irrevocably corrupted by northern business interests. The Fugitives' writings condemned the trends of modern society and art and indicted the modern urban-industrial society that had, by the 1920s, already displaced much of the traditional folk culture of the American South.

NEWSPAPERS

During the 1920s, Americans possessed a seemingly insatiable appetite for news, and the more than 2,000 dailies that were published during the decade did their best to satisfy their readers' interests in current events. In 1920, an estimated 27 million Americans regularly read newspapers; 10 years later, that number had climbed to almost 40 million.[5] But as circulation skyrocketed, the overall number of American newspapers declined. Giant newspaper chains, the largest of which were owned by William Randolph Hearst and the Scripps-Howard chain (led by E. W. Scripps and Roy W. Howard), began acquiring and then consolidating small-town papers across the nation. The central office of each syndicate provided its chain of newspapers with common stories, columns, editorials, and features written for a national audience. Thus, many newspapers during the 1920s shifted their focus from covering exclusively local news to following more national and international events. Some critics complained about this "standardization" of American newspapers and the decline of local news coverage, but the widespread availability of Hollywood gossip, box scores, comic strips, and financial news appealed to many readers across the nation.

While serious journalism thrived during the 1920s, tabloid journalism (sometimes disparagingly called "jazz journalism") emerged as the newspaper industry's equivalent of the lucrative pulp magazines. Rather than reporting on significant newsworthy events, tabloid journalists concentrated on sensational stories about celebrities, murder trials, sex scandals, and public tragedies. When silent screen legend Fatty Arbuckle was charged with raping and murdering a young actress in 1921, when evangelist Aimee Semple McPherson claimed to have escaped from kidnappers in 1926, and when millionaire bootlegger George Remus shot his wife in 1927, the tabloids screamed about it in the headlines for weeks. Tabloid newspapers, which were only half the size of regular newspapers and full of photographs, began when Joseph Medill Patterson launched the New York *Illustrated Daily News* in 1919 (later the *New York Daily News*). By 1924, his paper had garnered a circulation of 750,000 customers—the largest newspaper circulation in the nation. Rival tabloids soon emerged, including William Randolph Hearst's New York *Daily Mirror* (1924) and Bernarr Macfadden's *New York Evening Graphic* (1924), nicknamed the "Evening Pornographic" for its lurid illustrations and photographs. The *Evening Graphic* became particularly famous for its unabashed use of "composographs," or photographs superimposed on one another to create an entirely new (and often ludicrous) image. For example, after film sensation Rudolph Valentino died in 1926, the tabloid ran a "photograph" of Valentino in heaven, standing next to his deceased Italian countryman, opera star Enrico Caruso, who had died in 1921. Because of their immense profitability, tabloid newspapers soon spread beyond New York City, but all could be characterized by their shocking headlines and lurid stories of sex, scandals, violent crimes, sports, and gossip.

CONCLUSION

Books, magazines, and newspapers certainly were not new during the 1920s, but their role in disseminating popular notions about behavior, fashion, and popular taste increased dramatically. Accounts of the 1920s that emphasize the development of radio and motion pictures sometimes overlook the important influence that books, magazines, and newspapers exerted on American popular culture. However, millions of ordinary Americans regularly devoured enormous quantities of reading material that varied widely in terms of both content and quality. The *New York Times* sold well, but more people were drawn to the sensational tabloids full of lurid tales and scandalous gossip. Subscription book clubs helped to boost sales of popular fiction, and tens of thousands of readers found great satisfaction in both serious non-fiction and more trendy diet and self-help books. Most readers of the era ignored innovative modernist writers such as Faulkner and Hemingway, but they never failed to buy romance and mystery novels as well as all varieties of cheap, entertaining pulp magazines. While many authors of the 1920s have long been forgotten, at least a few of them survive in today's anthologies of great American literature.

9
Music

The 1920s marked a watershed era in the development of American popular music, both in the ways that music was disseminated and in the ways that music actually sounded. Since the 1890s, professional songwriting and music-publishing firms had produced most of the popular music that Americans enjoyed, primarily in the form of sheet music, but during the 1920s, venues such as commercial radio, phonograph records, Broadway musicals, and sound motion pictures played an increasingly significant role in delivering the latest popular songs to far-flung audiences. The decade also witnessed the emergence of whole new genres of indigenous American music, most notably jazz, which is often considered the greatest American art form. Jazz ranked as the nation's most popular music during the 1920s and reflected the expanding African-American influence on mainstream culture. Jazz was not the only great American sound of the era, however. During the 1920s, record companies also began to record blues and hillbilly music in an effort to develop new ethnic and regional consumer markets. The commercial success of these genres suggests the enormous diversity of American musical tastes during the decade.

AMERICAN POPULAR MUSIC

Tin Pan Alley

Since the 1890s, New York City's Tin Pan Alley had reigned as the undisputed capital of the American popular music industry and did so until its demise during the 1950s. Originally, the nickname "Tin Pan

Alley" designated an actual business district in Manhattan (West 28th Street between Broadway and Fifth Avenue) where dozens of songwriting and sheet-music-publishing firms maintained their offices at the turn of the century. By the 1920s, however, "Tin Pan Alley" had emerged as a generic term for the popular songwriting and music-publishing industry, as well as a synonym for the commercial music it produced. Collectively, the songwriting and music-publishing firms employed hundreds of full-time composers and lyricists to furnish the American public with a virtually endless supply of songs.

Songwriting and music-publishing firms produced more new songs during the 1920s than during any other decade in the history of Tin Pan Alley. Stylistically, many of these songs featured the syncopated rhythms commonly found in jazz and consisted of a series of stanzas, each of which was followed by a chorus, usually of 32 bars with four, eight-bar phrases (AABA). A considerable number of these popular songs exemplified the spirit of reckless abandon and frivolity that is commonly associated with the 1920s. Such peppy novelty numbers as "Ain't We Got Fun" (1921) and "Yes! We Have No Bananas" (1923) enjoyed spectacular but short-lived success on the best-selling record charts. Tin Pan Alley songwriting and music-publishing firms were also quick to cash in on—and at the same time helped to fuel—the latest musical crazes. Dozens of popular songs, for example, traded on the current vogue for jazz and blues, such as "Jazz Me Blues" (1921) and "Wabash Blues" (1921). Other numbers, such as "Charleston" (1923), "Black Bottom" (1926), "The Varsity Drag" (1927), and "Doin' the Raccoon" (1928), emerged as national hits largely because of their association with a particular dance.

A number of talented and commercially successful Tin Pan Alley songwriters stand out during the 1920s, including Irving Berlin, who composed both the music and the lyrics to more than 1,500 songs during his lifetime. Although best known for his classic songs "God Bless America" (1939) and "White Christmas" (1942), Berlin composed a string of hits during the 1920s, among them "All by Myself" (1921), "Blue Skies" (1927), and "Marie" (1928). Another critically acclaimed songwriter of the decade was George Gershwin, who composed the music for the stage revues *George White Scandals* (1921–1924) and, during the mid- to late 1920s, collaborated with his lyricist brother Ira on several memorable Broadway songs, including "Fascinatin' Rhythm" (1924) and "Someone to Watch Over Me" (1925). Jerome Kern, one of the most prolific songwriters of the 1920s, also achieved his greatest commercial success as a composer for Broadway musicals, including the shows *Sally* (1920), *Sunny* (1925), and *Show Boat* (1927). Among the other prominent popular songwriters of the 1920s were Vincent Youmans, Gus Kahn, Walter Donaldson, Bud DeSylva, Hoagy Carmichael, Richard Rodgers, Lorenz Hart, Oscar Hammerstein II, and Cole Porter.

FORMS OF MUSIC DISTRIBUTION

Sheet Music

Throughout the 1920s, published sheet music represented one of the most important commercial outlets for disseminating American music and therefore one of Tin Pan Alley's primary sources of revenue. Typically, sheet music consisted of four or five pages of musical notation scored for voice and piano (and sometimes even ukulele) and wrapped in colorful, attractive covers. Sheet music was sold at music stores, 5-and-10-cent chain stores, and even through mail-order catalogs, usually for about 25 or 30 cents. However, as radio and phonograph ownership became more widespread, sheet music sales declined, and phonograph recordings routinely began to outsell sheet music. Increasingly, music became something that Americans listened to on radios and Victrolas rather than something they performed themselves, a trend that has accelerated in the decades since the Jazz Age.

Phonograph Records

Although phonograph recordings had existed since the 1890s, the 1920s marked the first decade in which record sales grew large enough to attract the attention of Tin Pan Alley. By 1920, Victor, Columbia, Edison, and some 200 other independent companies were manufacturing phonographs and phonograph records and cylinders for the American market. Most of these recordings were issued on 12-inch, 78 rpm (revolutions per minute) discs that contained one three-minute selection on each side and generally sold for between 35 and 75 cents. In 1922, annual record sales peaked at 110 million discs (more than four times the number of records sold in 1914).[1] Beginning in 1920, the entertainment trade daily *Variety* published a Top Ten records chart to track the sales of phonograph records. A smash hit record might sell 2 million or more copies, and by the mid-1920s, the sale of phonograph records had replaced the sale of sheet music as the gauge used to measure the commercial success of a popular song. Additionally, as a result of sound recordings, popular songs became associated not just with particular performers but also with particular performances, such as Al Jolson's definitive recording of "Sonny Boy" (1928).

"Hello Lindy" sheet music, 1927. Courtesy of the State Historical Society of Missouri, Columbia.

Commercial Radio

Commercial radio, like phonograph records, exerted a tremendous influence on American popular music during the Jazz Age. Beginning in 1920, popular music broadcasts formed the core of radio programming, and stations generally broadcast live studio performances, as opposed to the "canned music" of phonograph records. By 1924, many stations were also airing so-called "remote" broadcasts of musical programs from locations such as opera houses, concert halls, and hotel ballrooms. During the highly experimental era of the early 1920s, radio stations broadcast a wide variety of musical entertainers, and as late as the mid-1920s, it was still not uncommon for radio listeners to hear eclectic daily programming that might include a pianist, an opera tenor, a classical violinist, an old-time string band, a glee club, a Hawaiian guitarist, and a jazz dance band all on one station.

With the formation of the National Broadcasting Company (NBC, in 1926) and of the Columbia Broadcasting System (CBS, in 1927), the range of popular music heard over the nation's airwaves became narrower and more standardized. Network radio typically featured corporate-sponsored musical programs, such as *The Palmolive Hour*, *The Goodrich Silvertown Orchestra*, and *The Voice of Firestone*, which originated in the network's main studios in New York City. As affiliated stations across the country began carrying the network's national programs, these network shows crowded out local programming and reduced the radio opportunities of amateur singers and musicians. Music companies, however, did not care if major recording stars supplanted local talent. By 1930, an estimated 51 million listeners tuned in each night to listen to radio programs, and when they heard a pop song they liked, they often purchased the phonograph recording, the sheet music, or both.

Radio transformed both home entertainment and the ways in which Americans listened to music. Middle-class homemakers tuned in to the radio during the day while performing household chores, and entire families gathered around their radio sets for an evening of entertainment. Tin Pan Alley quickly seized upon the enormous potential of radio to catapult its latest songs into nationwide hits. As early as 1923, music-publishing firms employed "song-pluggers"—professional musicians who would perform a new song on the radio over and over again, hoping that the listening audience would like it enough to buy it. Commercial radio also sparked national crazes for certain songs and sometimes helped to make musicians into overnight celebrities. In 1923, for example, Wendell Hall, an ambitious staff musician on Chicago's KYW, turned his "It Ain't Gonna Rain No Mo' " into a 2-million selling hit record by relentlessly bombarding his radio audience with the song.

Broadway Musicals and Revues

During the 1920s, Broadway theater eclipsed the vaudeville stage as the most important live performance venue for showcasing popular songs. As many as 50 musical shows opened each season on Broadway during the decade, and many of these shows helped to popularize Tin Pan Alley songs among the American public. Among the most commercially successful musicals and musical comedies were *Lady, Be Good!* (1924), *No, No, Nannette* (1925), *A Connecticut Yankee* (1927), *Show Boat* (1927), and *Good News* (1927), all of which featured catchy songs that soon became major hits. A series of all-black musicals and revues also produced a number of hit songs. Among the best known of these shows were Eubie Blake and Noble Sissle's *Shuffle Along* (1921), which included "I'm Just Wild About Harry," and James P. Johnson and Cecil Mack's *Runnin' Wild* (1923), which introduced the song "Charleston" and the popular dance by that name. Musical revues (musical variety shows consisting of a series of unrelated song-and-dance numbers) were also highly celebrated, and some of the most famous were the annual *Ziegfeld Follies*, *George White Scandals*, and Earl Carroll's *Vanities*. These revues introduced dozens of hit songs during the 1920s, such as "My Man" (1921), "Second Hand Rose" (1921), "Three O'Clock in the Morning" (1921), and "My Blue Heaven" (1927), to name only a few. African-American revues also spawned hit songs, such as Jimmy McHugh and Dorothy Fields' *Blackbirds of 1928*, which popularized "I Can't Give You Anything But Love," and Andy Razaf and Fats Waller's *Hot Chocolates* (1929), which introduced "Ain't Misbehavin'."

Hollywood Motion Pictures

Beginning in the mid-1920s, Tin Pan Alley publishing firms also increasingly produced songs and music for motion pictures. Theme songs written expressly for a particular movie became common during the last half of the 1920s. One of the earliest successful movie theme songs was "Charmaine," scored for theater orchestras to accompany the Fox Film Corporation's silent feature *What Price Glory?* (1926). Although songwriters seldom bothered to compose music for the silent cinema, the overwhelming success of the first feature-length "talkie," Warner Brothers' *The Jazz Singer* (1927), starring Al Jolson, demonstrated that the movies could provide an important venue for popularizing new Tin Pan Alley songs. By 1929, with motion pictures attracting audiences of nearly 100 million moviegoers a week, Hollywood studios began to integrate popular music more directly into their movies by producing lavish, big-budget musicals, such as Metro-Goldwyn-Mayer's *The Broadway Melody*

(1929), which was the first musical to win the Academy Award for Best Picture.

POPULAR BANDS AND MUSICIANS

Dance Bands

Given the immense popularity of dancing during the 1920s, it is not surprising that dance bands flourished. Unquestionably, Paul Whiteman and His Orchestra reigned as the most popular dance band of the 1920s, and bandleader Whiteman became known as "the King of Jazz." His first recording, "Whispering" (1920), which sold more than 2 million copies, made him a national celebrity. Over the next nine years, his orchestra reeled off an astonishing string of 28 Number One hits and another 108 Top Ten recordings, a record unmatched during the Jazz Age. A shrewd businessman, Whiteman parlayed his enormous popularity into a cottage industry by franchising his dance music. By 1930, he was operating 11 official Paul Whiteman bands in New York City and some 57 others across the nation. Other popular dance bands of the 1920s included Isham Jones and His Rainbow Orchestra, Ted Lewis and His Band, Fred Waring and His Pennsylvanians, and Guy Lombardo with His Royal Canadians, as well as "all-girl" dance orchestras such as the Twelve Vampires and Babe Egan's Hollywood Red Heads. Most of these ensembles performed as the regular house bands at nationally renowned hotels and ballrooms in New York, Chicago, Los Angeles, and other major cities. By necessity, these bands could perform a wide range of music, including arrangements of Tin Pan Alley songs, jazz instrumentals, symphonic compositions, and occasionally waltzes and tangos. They often performed over the radio via "remote" broadcasts that reached millions of Americans, and they recorded their most popular songs for major record companies. By 1929, according to *Variety*, more than 700 dance bands were touring throughout the nation, playing one-night shows in hotels, cafés, vaudeville theaters, and dance halls.

Singing Stars

Although dance bands dominated the music of the Jazz Age, a number of individual singers also emerged as national celebrities during the 1920s. Most of them had begun their careers on the vaudeville circuit, and the most popular among them also branched into radio, records, and film. Undisputedly, the nation's greatest pop star of the 1920s was Al Jolson, a veteran vaudeville singer, dancer, and all-around showman who billed himself as "the World's Greatest Entertainer." Jolson first won national acclaim in 1911 in the Broadway revue *La Belle Paree* at the Winter Garden Theatre, where his dramatic, booming singing style and extraordinary stage presence catapulted him to stardom. During the 1920s, he appeared in a string of musical revues such as *Bombo* (1921) and *Big Boy* (1925), in which he often portrayed a blundering blackface character named Gus. Jolson recorded a dozen Number One hits during the decade, including his best-known songs "Swanee" (1920), "Toot, Toot, Tootsie (Goo'bye)" (1922), "California, Here I Come!" (1924), "Sonny Boy" (1928), and "My Mammy" (1928). During the late 1920s, he became one of Hollywood's biggest box-office attractions as a result of his starring roles in Warner Brothers' pioneering "talkies," *The Jazz Singer* (1927) and *The Singing Fool* (1929). Although his popularity declined during the Great Depression, Jolson is considered today to be one of the greatest popular entertainers of the twentieth century.

Eddie Cantor, whose large, expressive doe eyes earned him the nickname "Banjo Eyes," also ranked among the most popular male singers of the 1920s. Beginning his vaudeville career at the age of 15, Cantor emerged as a major pop idol as a result of his starring roles in a string of producer Florenz Ziegfeld's celebrated *Ziegfeld Follies* (1917–1919, 1923, and 1927) and the Broadway musical comedies *Kid Boots* (1923) and *Whoopee* (1928), in which he introduced "Makin' Whoopee" (1928), a comical song about the shortcomings of marriage. Cantor went on to star in the film versions of *Kid Boots* (1926) and *Whoopee* (1930) and became one of the leading stars of stage and screen during the late 1920s.

Another one of the more popular vocalists of the Jazz Age was Cliff Edwards, who performed under the stage name "Ukulele Ike." Although best known for voicing the character of Jiminy Cricket and for singing the Academy Award-winning song "When You Wish Upon a Star" in the Disney animated film *Pinocchio* (1940), Edwards was also a major vaudeville and Broadway entertainer of the 1920s. He scored his first major success in George Gershwin's *Lady, Be Good!* (1924), in which he and Fred and Adele Astaire stopped the show with their rendition of "Fascinatin' Rhythm." Edwards established himself as a film star in 1929 in the motion picture *The Hollywood Revue of 1929*, in which he introduced another big hit, "Singin' in the Rain." Among the many other popular male singers of the 1920s were the musicals teams of Gus Van and Joe Schenck and of Billy Jones and Ernest Hare (who performed together on radio as "the Happiness Boys").

A number of women entertainers, many of whom also began their careers in vaudeville, emerged as popular singing stars during the 1920s. One of the most celebrated female entertainers was Sophie Tucker, a vaudeville and Broadway singer known for her racy, sexually suggestive songs and perhaps best remembered for her signature song, "Some of These Days" (1927). Her other well-known number, "I'm the Last of the

Red Hot Mamas" (1929), which she introduced in her talking motion picture debut, Warner Brothers' *Honky Tonk* (1929), won her the stage billing, "the Last of the Red Hot Mamas." Among the other popular women entertainers of the 1920s was comedian and singer Fanny Brice, who starred in virtually every one of the annual *Ziegfeld Follies* produced between 1910 and 1923. Later, Brice's life served as the basis for the Broadway musical *Funny Girl* (1964) and the Oscar-winning Hollywood film of that same title (1968), starring Barbra Streisand. During the late 1920s, Helen Kane achieved success for her roles in such Broadway musicals as *A Night in Spain* (1927) and *Good Boy* (1928), in which she introduced what became her theme song, "I Wanna Be Loved By You." Known as the "Boop-Boop-A-Doop Girl," Kane is remembered for her distinctive little-girl voice and as the inspiration for Betty Boop, an animated cartoon character introduced by Fleisher Studio in 1930.

Crooners and Torch Singers

As electric amplification technology became more advanced, new styles of singing emerged. Prior to the mid-1920s, most recording artists came out of vaudeville, where they typically sang in a loud, robust style so that their voices could reach the back rows of large theaters, but the introduction of sensitive electric microphones in 1925 led to the development of a more intimate, hushed style of singing known as crooning. Crooner Gene Austin recorded one of the biggest hits of the decade, "My Blue Heaven" (1927), which sold more than 5 million copies and dominated the Number One spot on the record charts for 13 weeks. Other prominent crooners included Jack Smith, Nick Lucas, and Rudy Vallee. The rough equivalent for women performers was called torch singing. Torch songs were, by definition, sad, sentimental songs about heartbreak and failed romance. Usually, the singer still "carried the torch" for an ex-lover, hence the nickname for the entire genre. These songs were sung slowly, intimately, and, like crooning, with the assistance of electric microphones. One of the best-known torch singers of the 1920s was Helen Morgan, star of the Broadway musical *Show Boat* (1927), whose signature song was the self-pitying "Why Was I Born?" (1929). Morgan's sorrowful, sultry voice came to define torch singing in the late 1920s. Other acclaimed torch singers of the 1920s included Ruth Etting and Libby Holman, both of whom also starred in a number of popular Broadway musicals.

JAZZ

Although initially considered little more than a passing musical fad when it was first recorded in 1917, jazz became the most influential form of American popular music during the 1920s. Jazz combined elements of a wide range of music, including ragtime compositions, brass-band marches, minstrel numbers, and, to a lesser degree, blues songs. Ragtime, the precursor to jazz, shared many stylistic similarities with jazz, particularly the use of "ragged," or syncopated, rhythms, that is, accenting the off-beat of rhythms. Jazz, however, differed markedly from ragtime in several important respects. Classical ragtime was essentially a composed music that stressed the performance of published musical works in precisely the way in which they had been written. Jazz, in contrast, was an unwritten, polyphonic music characterized, at least originally, by blues accents and collective improvisation, in which musicians each embellished the melody. Early jazz bands featured cornets, clarinets, trombones, drums, and sometimes even banjos, violins, and pianos. Originally, the term *ragtime* was used to describe this new dynamic, musical synthesis, but by the mid-1910s, it was being called *jass* or *jazz*, a word allegedly derived from southern black vernacular speech that (like *rock 'n' roll*) referred to the act of sexual intercourse.

Jazz emerged in the mid-1890s among African-American and creole musicians in New Orleans as well as other Gulf Coast cities and towns. During the first two decades of the twentieth century, this music spread throughout the United States as a result of the migration of New Orleans musicians to New York City, Chicago, Kansas City, Los Angeles, and other urban centers in search of work and to escape Jim Crow segregation. Some jazz musicians performed on steamboats up and down the Mississippi River or in vaudeville shows on the all-black musical circuit managed by the Theater Owners' Booking Agency (TOBA). By the early 1920s, Chicago had emerged as the nation's jazz center, although jazz dance bands were also appearing in dance halls, nightclubs, and speakeasies in many East and West Coast cities. By then, jazz had spread throughout the United States and was attracting growing audiences of both black and white listeners.

The enormous popularity of jazz provided new opportunities for African-American musicians to make records, occasionally perform on radio, and find regular work playing for live audiences. In 1917, a five-piece ensemble of white New Orleans musicians who called themselves the Original Dixieland Jazz Band recorded "Livery Stable Blues" and "Dixie Jass Band One Step," which music historians consider the first jazz recordings. But largely as a result of the racism and discriminatory practices of the recording industry, African-American musicians did not make any jazz recordings until 1922, when New Orleans creole trombonist Edward "Kid" Ory and his band, the Creole Orchestra, cut "Ory's Creole Trombone" and "Society Blues" in Los Angeles. Beginning in 1923, record companies scrambled to record popular jazz bands of both races whose music would please American music buyers. During the remaining years of the 1920s, record companies issued thousands of jazz recordings, including those of such legendary African-American jazz ensembles as King Oliver and the Creole Jazz Band, Clarence Williams' Blue Five, Louis Armstrong and His Hot Five (and His Hot Seven), Fletcher Henderson and His Orchestra, and Bennie Moten's Kansas City Orchestra. The rising popularity of radio also helped to disseminate jazz music throughout the United States. As early as 1921, white dance bands such as Vincent Lopez and His Orchestra and the Coon-Sanders Nighthawks, whose repertoires included a smattering of jazz numbers, were appearing on the radio. But African-American musicians were, with few exceptions, largely excluded from performing on early commercial radio.

Hot Jazz

Beginning in the early 1920s, small African-American bands pioneered a dynamic, emotionally charged musical style known as "hot jazz" that differed from the classic New Orleans jazz. Hot jazz, which peaked between 1925 and 1929, typically featured fast-paced individual solos and hard-driving, swinging rhythms. King Oliver's Creole Jazz Band, which performed at the Lincoln Gardens Café on Chicago's South Side, ranked as one of the important hot jazz bands of the 1920s. Led by cornetist Joe "King" Oliver, the Creole Jazz Band featured some of the finest New Orleans jazz musicians, including Oliver's young protégé, cornetist Louis Armstrong, who joined the band in 1922. In 1923, the Creole Jazz Band made some three dozen classic recordings that stand out as the most important collection of early recorded jazz, including "Dipper Mouth Blues" and "High Society Rag." Another leading exponent of hot jazz was the flamboyant New Orleans creole pianist Ferdinand "Jelly Roll" Morton, one of the earliest jazz composers and arrangers, who began playing piano as a teenager in the brothels of Storyville, New Orleans' notorious red-light district. In 1922, Morton moved to Chicago, and then relocated again, in 1926, to New York City. There, between 1926 and 1930, Morton recorded more than 50 selections with his band, the Red Hot Peppers, including "Black Bottom Stomp" (1926) and "Original Jelly Roll Blues" (1926).

In the late 1920s, dozens of talented jazz musicians migrated from Chicago, Kansas City, and other musical hotbeds to New York City, where most of the major recording companies were located. Consequently, New York City replaced Chicago as the nation's premier jazz center. Pianist Fletcher Henderson, who was sometimes billed as "the Colored King of Jazz," led one of the most popular African-American jazz bands working in Manhattan during the 1920s. Between 1924 and 1934, Henderson and His Orchestra performed as the house band at the

St. Louis Cotton Club Band, circa 1925. Courtesy of the Missouri Historical Society, St. Louis.

prestigious Roseland Ballroom in Times Square. Henderson's Orchestra produced a smooth, sophisticated sound and ranked as one of the most commercially successful black bands of the decade, recording such hit numbers as "Gulf Coast Blues" (1923), "Carolina" (1925), and "Dinah" (1926). In 1928, Henderson began arranging jazz numbers, and he is recognized by jazz historians as one of the first arrangers of what became known in the 1930s as swing music.

With the advent of National Prohibition, Harlem nightclubs and cabarets, located above 125th Street in Manhattan, began to attract wealthy white partygoers and tourists who wanted to drink, dance, and hear "exotic" African-American music. In 1929, *Variety* listed 11 major nightclubs in Harlem that catered to predominantly white crowds, including Small's Paradise, Connie's Inn, and the Cotton Club. These swanky nightclubs and cabarets employed hundreds of African-American jazz musicians during the late 1920s, including bandleader Edward "Duke" Ellington, a formally trained pianist and the preeminent composer of jazz music. Between 1927 and 1931, Ellington's Orchestra performed as the house band at the Cotton Club, a segregated, white-patrons-only nightclub owned by a syndicate of mobsters and decorated to resemble a lavish antebellum southern plantation. Ellington forged a popular jazz style that came to be known as the "Jungle Sound" and recorded a series of his own compositions with his orchestra, including "Black and Tan Fantasy" (1927), "Creole Love Call" (1927), and "Mood Indigo" (1930). In 1929, Ellington appeared in *Black and Tan*, the first of more than a dozen Hollywood films he would make. After the onset of the Great Depression, Ellington was among the relatively small number of hot jazz musicians who were able to make a successful transition to swing music during the 1930s. Indeed, his "It Don't Mean a Thing (If It Ain't Got That Swing)" (1932) came to define the swing era.

By far the greatest jazz musician of the 1920s was Louis Armstrong, a New Orleans-born cornetist and trumpeter whose inventive solos and technical brilliance marked the pinnacle of hot jazz. In 1922, Armstrong moved to Chicago to play with King Oliver's Creole Jazz Band, but two years later, at his wife's urging, he left the band to join Fletcher Henderson's Orchestra in New York City. There, during his 13-month stint with the band, he dazzled audiences with his innovative solos and swinging rhythms. Between 1925 and 1928, Armstrong recorded a series of 65 selections for OKeh Records as the leader of his own bands, the Hot Five and the Hot Seven. Among these songs are such classics as "Heebie Jeebies" (1926), "Potato Head Blues" (1927), and "West End Blues" (1928). By the end of the 1920s, Armstrong had emerged as the most influential jazz musician in the nation, and today jazz critics consider these recordings to be among the greatest of all time.

During the 1920s, a number of white jazz musicians also influenced the development of the genre. As early as the 1910s, black jazz bands had inspired a host of young, white, middle-class imitators to take up jazz music, including cornet player Bix Beiderbecke, clarinetist Benny Goodman, trombonist Irving "Miff" Mole, soprano saxophonist Milton "Mezz" Mezzrow, guitarist Eddie Lang, violinist Joe Venuti, and trombonist Jack Teagarden. Aspiring white musicians assembled jazz combos and played in a hot style similar to that of African-American jazzmen. Among the most important of these white jazz bands were the Original Memphis Five, the Wolverines, Red Nichols and His Five Pennies, the Jean Goldkette Orchestra, and a group informally known as the Austin High Gang (named for the Chicago school many of them attended). As a result of their concerts and recordings, many of these white bands enjoyed great commercial success and, in turn, inspired a new generation of jazz musicians.

Sweet Jazz

Although African-American musicians continued to be the principal innovators of jazz during the 1920s, most Americans would have heard a diluted, commercial form of the music called "sweet jazz," performed primarily by all-white orchestras. In contrast to hot jazz, sweet jazz featured slower tempos and less improvisation and was generally more appealing to the musical tastes of middlebrow white Americans. The greatest exponent of sweet jazz was bandleader Paul Whiteman, who, perhaps more than any other musical figure, was responsible for the enormous popularity of jazz dance music during the 1920s. His band performed carefully arranged compositions that, although they included syncopated rhythms and blues accents, remained respectable and genteel. Indeed, Whiteman sought to refine jazz and make it more commercially accessible to mainstream white audiences—in his words to "remove the stigma of barbaric strains and jungle cacophony" and to "make a lady of jazz."[2] Whiteman's Orchestra, which sometimes contained as many as 30 musicians, featured some of the legendary white jazz soloists of the 1920s, including Tommy Dorsey, Frankie Trumbauer, Joe Venuti, Eddie Lang, and Bix Beiderbecke. Although jazz critics usually disparage his music, Whiteman nonetheless played a significant role in the growing acceptance of jazz within mainstream American popular culture during the 1920s.

Jazz and the Nation's Morals

Despite its enormous popularity, not all Americans shared an enthusiasm for jazz. In fact, many highbrow music critics and conservative Americans considered jazz a serious threat to the nation's moral and social fabric. They blamed jazz for the supposedly rebellious behavior of the younger generation, and argued that this music led to everything from immorality and out-of-wedlock pregnancies to criminal activities and dementia. "Moral disaster," predicted the *New York American*, "is coming to hundreds of young American girls through the pathological, nerve-irritating, sex-exciting music of jazz orchestras."[3] Anne Shaw Faulkner, president of the General Federation of Women's Clubs, posed the question: "Does Jazz Put the Sin in Syncopation?" Her 1921 article, which appeared in *Ladies' Home Journal*, attributed the "immoral conditions among our young people" to jazz and attacked this popular sound as "an evil influence on the young people of today."[4] Automobile tycoon Henry Ford likewise condemned jazz music and the modern dances such as the Charleston that often accompanied it. Jazz, he believed, was nothing more than "monkey talk, jungle squeals, grunts and squeaks and gasps suggestive of cave love," and his newspaper, the *Dearborn Independent*, regularly published attacks on what he called "moron music."[5] Despite these dire pronouncements, jazz enjoyed enormous commercial success and profoundly influenced mainstream American musical tastes throughout the Roaring Twenties.

BLUES MUSIC

Another influential form of African-American music that rose to prominence during the 1920s was the blues. Although it remains difficult to pinpoint an exact origin, the blues emerged sometime around the turn of the twentieth century and evolved from a variety of traditional black musical forms, including field hollers, work songs, ballads, and rags. The Mississippi Delta is often considered the cradle of the blues, but different regional styles of blues music developed simultaneously in East Texas and the Carolina Piedmont and then spread throughout the nation during the 1910s and 1920s. The blues is a distinctive African-American secular music that contains several central elements. Blues music ordinarily contains "blue" notes, which are essentially flattened third and seventh notes (played slightly below their true pitch), and the most common form of the music is the 12-bar blues, containing a series of three-line stanzas. The second line of the stanza repeats the first, and the third line consists of an improvised, rhyming comment on the preceding two (an AAB rhyme scheme), such as in the following example, a stanza from Sleepy John Estes' 1929 recording of "Diving Duck Blues":

> Now if the river was whiskey and I was a diving duck,
> Now if the river was whiskey and I was a diving duck,
> I would dive to the bottom, never would come up.[6]

Early folk blues reflected a variety of experiences of African-American life during segregation and often spoke of work, rambling, crime, gambling, alcohol, imprisonment, disasters, and hard times. Above all, the blues commented on the universal themes of troubled love relationships and sexual desire. Although the blues often conveyed a sense of overwhelming melancholy and resignation, many blues songs were high-spirited, rollicking party numbers intended for social dancing. Indeed, far from being simply about misery and sadness, the blues encompassed the full range of human emotions.

W. C. Handy, the first great popularizer of the blues, was one of the earliest composers to write and publish commercial songs inspired by folk blues. His early compositions, notably "Memphis Blues" (1912) and "St. Louis Blues" (1914), earned him the title "Father of the Blues." The tremendous sales of Handy's sheet music sparked a national mania for blues songs around World War I, and Tin Pan Alley tunesmiths, eager to cash in on this craze, churned out dozens of commercial songs bearing the name "blues." Although most of these, in fact, were not technically blues songs, some of the more authentic ones did help to introduce this African-American music to millions of white listeners. In 1926, Handy published his edited collection titled *Blues: An Anthology* (1926), one of the earliest studies to discuss the significant influence of the folk blues tradition on American jazz, popular, and classical music. The book not only celebrated the rich cultural heritage of African-American musical traditions but also contributed to the growing interest in the blues and black folk culture generally.

Vaudeville Blues

Prior to 1920, the recording industry had virtually ignored African-American music fans, and those recordings by black singers and musicians that were available consisted largely of racist "coon" songs, comedy monologues, dance numbers, and spirituals. But beginning in the 1920s, companies began to record and market blues music specifically for African-American consumers. In 1920, Mamie Smith, accompanied by her band, the Jazz Hounds, recorded "Crazy Blues" for OKeh Records, marking the advent of commercial blues recordings. "Crazy Blues" sold 75,000 copies in the first month of its release, and its surprising success convinced OKeh, Columbia, Paramount, and other white-owned record companies that a lucrative market existed among African-American record buyers for what the industry soon came to call "race records." Within a few years, most of the great vaudeville blues singers (also known as classic blues singers) had made commercial recordings, including Clara Smith, Ethel Waters, Sara Martin, Bertha "Sippie" Wallace, and Victoria Spivey.

Vaudeville blues singers were almost exclusively women, and as veterans of the vaudeville stage, most of them sang in a popular, light operatic style rather than in the soulful, expressive vocal style commonly associated with authentic blues singing. Small jazz combos usually provided the backup accompaniment for vaudeville blues singers, and many of the premier musicians of the 1920s performed on these recordings, including Louis Armstrong, Fletcher Henderson, and Coleman Hawkins. Professional black songwriters such as W. C. Handy, Clarence Williams, and Perry Bradford composed dozens of new "blues" songs for successful female singers, but many of these amounted to little more than commercial pop songs that included the word "blues" in the title.

One of the most influential vaudeville blues singers of the 1920s was Gertrude "Ma" Rainey, a flamboyant dresser who flaunted expensive beaded gowns, a necklace made of $20 gold pieces, and ostentatious diamond earrings and rings. A longtime performer on the southern minstrel show circuit, Rainey made her first recordings for Paramount Records in 1923. Billed as "the Mother of the Blues," she recorded more than 100 songs over the next five years, including "Boll Weevil Blues" (1923), "Jealous Hearted Blues" (1924), and "Ma Rainey's Black Bottom"

Blues singer Bessie Smith. Courtesy of the Southern Folklife Collection, University of North Carolina at Chapel Hill.

(1927). More so than other vaudeville blues singers, she sang in a raw, expressive style that was deeply influenced by southern folk blues, and she remained one of the preeminent vaudeville blues singers throughout the 1920s.

Rainey's young protégé, Bessie Smith, emerged as an even greater vaudeville blues star. Smith's first record, "Gulf Coast Blues," coupled with "Downhearted Blues," made in 1923 for Columbia, sold 780,000 copies in its first six months on the market. Within two years, she became the nation's highest-paid African-American entertainer. Billed as "the Empress of the Blues," she went on to record more than 150 songs for Columbia between 1923 and 1931, on which she was often accompanied by the greatest jazz musicians of the age, including Louis Armstrong, who played cornet on her classic rendition of "St. Louis Blues" (1925). Her other famous songs include " 'Taint Nobody's Bizness If I Do" (1923), "Empty Bed Blues" (1928), and "Nobody Knows You When You Down and Out" (1929). In 1929, Smith starred in *St. Louis Blues*, one of the first all-black talking films. With her expressive, soulful phrasing, she remained the biggest blues star of the 1920s, and today she is unquestionably considered by music historians to be the greatest vaudeville blues singer of all time.

Country Blues

In 1924, as a result of the enormous popularity of vaudeville blues, music companies also began to record country blues. In contrast to the pop vocal styles of most vaudeville blues singers, country bluesmen sang and performed in ways that more closely resembled the authentic folk blues that emerged around the turn of the twentieth century. Solo guitarists often sang and performed country blues by employing a call-and-response interaction in which an instrumental riff "answered" the human voice. Unlike vaudeville blues vocalists, country blues singers were almost exclusively men. Most were self-taught musicians who entertained on a semi-professional basis at local dances, barbecues, fish fries, and other social gatherings.

One of the most influential country bluesmen to record during the 1920s was Blind Lemon Jefferson, a one-time itinerant street musician from Dallas who made his first recordings in 1926. Jefferson soon emerged as the leading exponent of the East Texas blues style and became the most commercially successful country blues singer of the late 1920s. He recorded almost 100 songs, including such classics as "Black Snake Moan" (1927), "Matchbox Blues" (1927), and "See That My Grave Is Kept Clean" (1928), before freezing to death in a Chicago snowstorm in 1929. Charlie Patton, the other great country bluesman of the 1920s, epitomized the Mississippi Delta blues tradition. Called "the Father of the Delta Blues," Patton recorded nearly 70 songs for Paramount between 1929 and his death from a heart attack in 1934, including his signature song "Pony Blues" (1929), as well as "Down the Dirt Road Blues" (1929), "Green River Blues" (1929), and "Spoonful Blues" (1929). Other famous country bluesmen who recorded during the 1920s include Texas Alexander, Mississippi John Hurt, Blind Willie McTell, Frank Stokes, Sleepy John Estes, and Blind Blake.

Throughout the late 1920s, as the blues craze intensified, many of the nation's leading record companies, particularly OKeh, Paramount, and Columbia, issued hundreds of race records specifically intended for an African-American market. Between 1927 and 1930, the peak years of blues recording, companies released some 500 race records a year and advertised them extensively in the *Chicago Defender* and other black newspapers. In 1927 alone, African-American record buyers purchased an estimated 10 million records (most of which cost 75 cents). But the commercial recording of the blues, like almost all other musical genres, drastically declined after the onset of the Great Depression.

HILLBILLY MUSIC

Another popular sound of the American South that first appeared on commercial radio and records during the 1920s was hillbilly music (sometimes called "old-time music"), the forerunner of modern country music. First broadcast and recorded in 1922, hillbilly music consisted chiefly of the vernacular music of ordinary white southerners, particularly amateur and semi-professional musicians from the southeastern United States. These musicians incorporated a remarkably wide range of musical influences into their sound, including traditional British ballads, fiddle tunes, sentimental pop songs of the 1890s, gospel numbers, blues songs, cowboy songs, and even versions of the latest Tin Pan Alley hits. Increasingly, though, the demand for fresh, unrecorded material led them to compose new hillbilly songs for release on radio and records.

Radio Barn Dances

During the 1920s, radio stations in the South and Midwest built one of their largest listening audiences around hillbilly music. As early as 1922, Atlanta's WSB began airing short live programs of old-time music performed by local fiddlers and string bands. Not until the following year did WBAP, Fort Worth, Texas, launch what is considered the first "barn dance"—a variety program of old-time fiddlers, singing cowboys, and string bands. Other radio stations across the South and Midwest soon followed suit, airing their own live barn dances on Saturday nights.

One such popular program was Chicago WLS' *The National Barn Dance* (originally, *WLS Barn Dance*), which premiered in 1924. Even more famous was Nashville WSM's *The Grand Ole Opry* (originally, before 1927, *WSM Barn Dance*), which first aired in 1925. Among *The Grand Old Opry*'s biggest stars during the 1920s were fiddler Uncle Jimmy Thompson, banjoist Uncle Dave Macon (billed as "the Dixie Dewdrop"), and black harmonica player DeFord Bailey ("the Harmonica Wizard"), as well as outrageously named string bands such as Dr. Humphrey Bate and His Possum Hunters and the Binkley Brothers' Dixie Clodhoppers. To enhance the program's rural image, WSM radio director George D. Hay required his musicians to wear rustic costumes of straw hats, checkered work shirts, and denim overalls for the live studio audiences. By the end of the 1920s, *The Grand Ole Opry* had emerged as a country music institution, and it remains on the air today, making it the longest-running radio show in American broadcasting history.

Hillbilly Recordings

Although record companies made a few experimental recordings of hillbilly musicians as early as 1922, it was not until the following year that an Atlanta musician and radio star nicknamed Fiddlin' John Carson made the first commercially successful hillbilly record. Although he was not the first old-time musician to record, the brisk sales of his debut disc, "The Little Old Log Cabin in the Lane," coupled with "The Old Hen Cackled and the Rooster's Going to Crow," for OKeh Records, alerted music industry executives to the potential market for this style of white southern grassroots music. Carson's commercial success marked the advent of the hillbilly recording industry, and, over the next few years, Columbia, Victor, and other companies began to record similar old-time music at dozens of field sessions in Atlanta, Memphis, Dallas, New Orleans, and other southern cities. By 1927, record companies were issuing more than a thousand new hillbilly records a year.

Although it often looked nostalgically to the past, hillbilly music also reflected the contemporary experiences of modern Americans. Many hillbilly recordings were topical songs that chronicled and critiqued significant current events, such as train wrecks, tornados, murders, or social trends. One of the best-known topical songs of the 1920s was Blind Alfred Reed's "Why Do You Bob Your Hair, Girls?" (1927), which accused fashionable young flappers who cropped their hair short of being unchristian. But the greatest interpreter of topical hillbilly songs was Vernon Dalhart, a light opera singer by training, whose 1924 record, "The Prisoner's Song," paired with "The Wreck of the Old 97," became the first hillbilly disc to sell an astonishing 1 million copies. One of the most prolific recording artists of the 1920s, Dalhart went on to make more

The Talking Machine World, New York, June 15, 1924

FIDDLIN' JOHN CARSON
Seven times Champion Fiddler of Georgia and the King of Them All!

HENRY WHITTER
The novelty entertainer from the sky country.

Fiddlin' John Carson
and
Henry Whitter
Exclusive Artists

THESE two mountaineers were discovered by OKeh! Seeing the recording possibilities in their quaint style and their "Old Time Pieces" OKeh recorded some of their selections and at the same time uncovered a brand new field for record sales.

It is noteworthy that in the annual "Fiddlin' Contests" held in the South, and against the best there was, Fiddlin' John Carson was seven times awarded the championship.

Another mountain star is Henry Whitter. Throughout his native hills he is acclaimed the most novel entertainer for he plays a harmonica and a guitar at the same time and never misses a note and in between accompanies himself when he sings those quaint, "Old Time Pieces."

The craze for this "Hill Country Music" has spread to thousands of communities north, east and west as well as in the south and the fame of these artists is ever increasing. And this again gives OKeh Dealers another new field discovered, originated and made possible by the manufacturers of

OKeh Records

The Records of Quality

Manufactured by

GENERAL PHONOGRAPH CORPORATION, NEW YORK

OTTO HEINEMAN, President

Advertisement for OKeh Records, *The Talking Machine World*, June 15, 1924. Courtesy of the Southern Folklife Collection, University of North Carolina at Chapel Hill.

than a thousand old-time recordings between 1924 and 1933, many of them topical songs about highly publicized national disasters, tragedies, and current news events, including "The Death of Floyd Collins" (1925), "The John T. Scopes Trial" (1925), "There's a New Star in Heaven Tonight (Rudolph Valentino)" (1926), and "Lindbergh (The Eagle of the U.S.A.)" (1927). During the 1920s, Dalhart was one of the few hillbilly singers to achieve crossover success by reaching a broad record-buying audience.

Hillbilly Stringbands

Originally, most hillbilly musicians who made it onto commercial records were solo artists or duos, but beginning in 1925, string bands emerged as the most commonly recorded ensembles on hillbilly records. String bands usually consisted of a fiddler (sometimes two), a guitarist, a banjo player, perhaps a mandolin player, or some combination of these. One of the most influential and commercially successful string bands of the 1920s was Charlie Poole and the North Carolina Ramblers, whose first release—"Don't Let Your Deal Go Down Blues," coupled with "Can I Sleep in Your Barn Tonight, Mister?" (1925)—sold 102,000 copies in an age when hillbilly record sales of 30,000 or more was rare. Over the next five years, the North Carolina Ramblers recorded more than 80 selections, including such classics as "White House Blues" (1926) and "If the River Was Whiskey" (1930). Another best-selling string band of the 1920s was the Atlanta-based Skillet Lickers, led by fiddler and comic showman Gid Tanner. The Skillet Lickers recorded nearly 90 selections for Columbia between 1926 and 1931, among them such hits as "Bully of the Town" (1926), "It's a Long Way to Tipperary" (1927), and "Soldier's Joy" (1929). Unlike the North Carolina Ramblers, who featured a distinctive, tightly knit sound, the Skillet Lickers performed in a loose, wildly exuberant style that was perfectly suited for rural forms of dancing.

The First Stars of Hillbilly Music

The first bona fide star of hillbilly music was Jimmie Rodgers of Mississippi, the so-called "Father of Country Music," who sang songs that embodied the rough-and-rowdy ways of hoboes, drifters, and gamblers. A former railroad brakeman, he scored his first hit record with "Blue Yodel (T for Texas)" (1927), which sold more than 1 million copies. Over the next five years, he recorded over 100 songs, including the country standards "Waiting for a Train" (1928), "Daddy and Home" (1928), and "In the Jailhouse Now" (1928), as well as a series of 12 classic "blue yodels." In 1929, he appeared in *The Singing Brakeman* (1929), a film short that showcased his singing abilities. Billed as "the Singing Brakeman" and "America's Blue Yodeler," Rodgers was largely responsible for transforming old-time music from an instrumentalist genre to one dominated by vocalists. Before he died in 1933 at the age of 35 from tuberculosis, Rodgers sold an estimated 6 million records, and his tremendous commercial success spawned a host of imitators, including Gene Autry, Jimmie Davis, and Ernest Tubb, who mimicked his loose, blues-inflected singing and covered his then-current hits.

The other major hillbilly act of the 1920s was the Carter Family, whom music critics today honor with the title "the First Family of Country Music." The Carters consisted of bass singer A. P. Carter, his wife, Sara, who sang lead and played autoharp (and sometimes second guitar), and her cousin, Maybelle, who played guitar. Between 1927 and 1941, the trio recorded more than 300 songs, including literally dozens of numbers that are now considered country music classics, such as "Keep on the Sunny Side" (1928), "Wildwood Flower" (1928), and "Wabash Cannonball" (1929). Although they recorded a diverse range of songs, the Carters especially favored late-nineteenth-century sentimental ballads, parlor songs, and traditional mountain folk songs. Besides popularizing a host of American folk songs and ballads, the group also exerted a significant influence on the musical development of hillbilly music, particularly with their haunting close harmonies and Maybelle's signature guitar style.

HAWAIIAN MUSIC

During the 1920s, a Hawaiian music craze swept the nation. Since at least 1905, music companies had recorded and sold Hawaiian music in the continental United States, but the first widespread exposure that many Americans had to this music came in 1915 at the Panama–Pacific International Exposition held in San Francisco. There, at the Hawaiian Pavilion, mainlanders could hear the lilting tropical melodies of ukuleles and Hawaiian guitars (Hawaiian guitar is an instrumental style in which the guitar is played on the seated performer's lap and is fretted by sliding a knife, steel bar, or other metal object on the strings). Throughout the 1920s, Hawaiian musicians such as steel guitarist Sol Hoopii and ukulele virtuoso Bennie Nawahi (billed as "King of the Ukulele") toured the continental United States in vaudeville shows and revues, and music companies greatly expanded their catalogs of Hawaiian recordings in order to cash in on the public's fascination with this exotic sound. Tin Pan Alley songwriters also seized upon the fad for Hawaiian music. Between 1915 and 1929, they wrote hundreds of novelty numbers about the alluring beauty and charms of Hawaiian life, including "Hello, Hawaii, How Are You?" (1915), "Oh, How She Could Yacki Hacki Wicki Wacki Woo" (1916), "Hula Hula Dream Girl" (1924), and "That Aloha Waltz" (1928).

The Ukulele Craze

The Hawaiian music craze of the 1920s inspired tens of thousands of would-be musicians to take up the ukulele. Inexpensive, portable, and relatively easy to play, ukuleles became one of the most popular instruments for home entertaining among middle-class Americans. Although some ukuleles, such as those produced by the C. F. Martin Company, were finely crafted, professional-quality instruments, most of the instruments manufactured by mainland companies were inexpensive, mass-produced models of varying quality. The 1927 catalog of the Sears, Roebuck and Company, for example, offered 17 different models of ukuleles and ukulele-banjos, ranging in price from $1.73 to $12.45.[7] Correspondence courses and music schools offered lessons in the ukulele and Hawaiian guitar, and amateur musicians formed hundreds of ukulele and Hawaiian guitar clubs. Likewise, music-publishing companies churned out affordable ukulele instructional booklets and song collections, such as *New Standard Ukelele Song Book* (1925) and *Wolff's Complete Ukulele Instruction Course* (1928). The nationwide mania for Hawaiian music and ukuleles waned in the late 1920s, but the music and instruments of the Hawaiian Islands did exert a brief but considerable influence on Jazz Age popular music.

FOREIGN-LANGUAGE RECORDINGS

Between 1890 and 1914, more than 17 million immigrants, most of them from Eastern and Southern Europe, flooded into the United States.[8] As they became more prosperous and began purchasing phonographs, immigrants emerged as a profitable consumer market for the fledgling American recording industry. Since the late 1890s, record companies had targeted this immigrant market by selling foreign-language recordings of Old World folk songs, dances, and instrumental selections to ethnic communities within the United States. During the 1920s, major record companies, such as Columbia and Victor, issued thousands of foreign-language recordings for as many as 30 different ethnic groups, from Albanians to West Indians and even the Hopi Indians of the American Southwest. Mexican records accounted for the single largest group of ethnic recordings, but Italian, Irish, Polish, Hebrew-Yiddish, Hungarian, German, Russian, and Greek recordings also sold well. These recordings helped to preserve and maintain an ethnic identity and collective memory of the Old World for immigrants displaced, either by choice or circumstance, from their country of origin. Although far from recognizable household names to native-born Americans, entertainers such as Ukrainian fiddler Pawlo Humeniuk, Finnish-American accordionist Antti Kosola, and Polish singer Wladyslaw Ochrymowicz emerged as influential cultural figures and icons of ethnic pride among the foreign-born communities of New York City, Chicago, Boston, and other large American cities.

CLASSICAL MUSIC

The 1920s signaled the advent of serious American contributions to the European-dominated field of classical music. Prior to 1920, American composers had produced few operas, symphonies, or chamber music pieces to rival those of the great European composers. However, the 1920s saw the emergence of several influential American composers, most notably Charles Ives, Aaron Copeland, Virgil Thomson, John Alden Carpenter, and William Grant Still, many of whom experimented with fusing the dynamic sounds of jazz and blues with the art music of European tradition. Despite the flowering of American classical music, operatic and symphonic works exerted only limited influence on the nation's popular culture during the Jazz Age.

One of the most significant contacts middle-class Americans had with classical masterworks came through Paul Whiteman, the bandleader of the most commercially successful dance orchestra of the 1920s. A classically trained musician, Whiteman combined elements of modern jazz and classical music to create a synthesis called "symphonic jazz." With the assistance of his arranger, pianist Ferde Grofé, Whiteman sought to break down the imposing cultural barriers between high and low art by combing classical music and jazz. Whiteman's most celebrated concert, "An Experiment in Modern Music," at New York City's Aeolian Hall in 1924, featured performances of popular songs, jazz instrumentals, and classical selections. This legendary concert included the critically acclaimed premiere of songwriter and pianist George Gershwin's jazz concerto, *Rhapsody in Blue*, which became an immediate sensation. Following the success of this performance, Whiteman staged a series of experimental concerts between 1925 and 1938, showcasing selections of popular music, jazz, and classical works. Although best known for his Tin Pan Alley songs and Broadway musical revues, Gershwin went on to compose several other celebrated classical works, including *Concerto in F for Piano and Orchestra* (1925), *Three Preludes for Piano* (1926), *An American in Paris* (1928), and *Porgy and Bess* (1935), before his sudden death in 1937 at the age of 38.

Classical music delighted tens of thousands of opera aficionados and concertgoers during the 1920s, but most ordinary Americans' exposure to the great European classical works came from phonograph recordings and radio broadcasts. Many of the best-selling classical discs of the 1920s

Composer George Gershwin. Courtesy of the Library of Congress.

appeared on Victor's prestigious Red Seal label, whose records cost as much as $7 apiece (or almost 10 times as much as the company's pop records). During the 1920s, Victor spent millions of dollars advertising its premium-priced classical records and recruited some of the greatest international stars of symphonic music and grand opera to make recordings, including Russian pianist Sergei Rachmaninoff, Italian conductor Arturo Toscanini, and, before his untimely death in 1921 at the age of 48, Italian tenor Enrico Caruso, longtime star of the New York Metropolitan Opera. Classical recordings sold relatively well, primarily to upper- and upper-middle-class Americans, some of whom purchased these records more for their cultural prestige than for any appreciation of high art. Even as record sales declined after the advent of commercial radio, Victor managed to sell an average of more than 5 million copies of its Red Seal records each year throughout the decade.

Radio networks prominently featured classical music programming and brought the music of nationally distinguished opera companies and symphony orchestras into millions of American homes. In 1921, Chicago station KYW inaugurated weekly broadcasts of the Chicago Grand Opera Company, the first such company to have its productions regularly aired on radio. Soon, other stations began to carry operatic programs. Dozens of symphony orchestras, such as the Boston Symphony Orchestra and the New York Philharmonic Orchestra, also appeared on network radio during the late 1920s. NBC in particular boasted a strong schedule of classical concert programs, including *General Motors Concerts* and *Mobil Oil Concerts*. Musical education programs such as NBC's *The Music Appreciation Hour*, which premiered in 1928, introduced millions of American radio listeners to classical music. Hosted by Dr. Walter Damrosch, the longtime conductor of the New York Symphony Orchestra, this influential radio show combined classical music performances with simple, down-to-earth explanations in order to foster greater appreciation for this music. By the end of the 1920s, radio listeners in remote rural areas and small towns could hear the nation's leading symphony orchestras interpret the masterpieces of Beethoven, Brahms, and Wagner. Despite the infiltration of classical music into ordinary Americans' lives, most record buyers and radio listeners gravitated more toward jazz and popular music than they did toward operas and symphonies. In fact, during the 1920s George Gershwin was virtually the only composer to bridge the gulf between the middlebrow songs of Tin Pan Alley and the high-art symphonic works of Carnegie Hall.

CONCLUSION

American popular music underwent a revolutionary transformation during the 1920s. Prior to 1920, the most important commercial forces for disseminating American popular music were vaudeville shows and published sheet music. But beginning in the early 1920s, phonograph records, Broadway musicals, commercial radio, and sound motion pictures all helped to distribute Tin Pan Alley, jazz, blues, hillbilly, and other kinds of music to American listeners. Tragically, the Great Depression hit the commercial music industry with a punishing force, and by 1932, annual record sales had plummeted to only 6 million discs. Additionally, several record companies, among them OKeh and Paramount, went bankrupt. While the recording industry struggled through hard times, commercial radio enjoyed a huge upswing in popularity, since radio could provide listeners with music that was cheaper and more vibrant than the "canned music" of phonograph records.

During the 1920s, Louis Armstrong, Duke Ellington, and other jazz musicians transformed the American music scene by making African-American musical styles a dominant force in the twentieth-century entertainment industry. Beginning around World War I, white dance bands, Tin Pan Alley songwriters, and even American classical composers adapted the syncopated rhythms and blues accents of jazz into their music. The 1920s also marked the peak years of several other popular musical sounds, including orchestral dance music, vaudeville blues, hillbilly music, and foreign-language numbers. Most significantly, the accelerated fusion and musical exchange that resulted between African-American and white popular sounds laid the groundwork for the emergence of a number of new musical genres in the decades to come, most notably rock 'n' roll in the mid-1950s.

10
Performing Arts

American performing arts grew spectacularly during the 1920s. Although vaudeville theater declined dramatically in popularity, other fields, especially commercial radio and Hollywood motion pictures, attracted audiences in unprecedented numbers. Americans who had sufficient disposable income spent lavishly on the performing arts, and even the poorest people managed to scrape together the occasional dime to buy a movie ticket or see a vaudeville show. Socializing, especially among those Americans in their teens and twenties, frequently revolved around various performing arts, as young men often escorted their dates to motion pictures, vaudeville shows, theater performances, or nightclub acts. Groups of friends would gather together at "radio parties" to listen to their favorite programs. And young people, who learned the latest dance steps from movies, vaudeville shows, or cabaret acts, would go to parties or clubs to imitate the lively, sometimes acrobatic moves that they had seen on the stage or the screen.

VAUDEVILLE THEATER

Vaudeville theater ranked as the single most popular form of American theatrical entertainment in the first decades of the twentieth century and launched the careers of many great comedic performers, including Abbott and Costello, George Burns and Gracie Allen, the Marx Brothers, Jack Benny, Edgar Bergen, and even "Mr. Television" himself, Milton Berle. Vaudeville shows, whose heyday spanned the years between 1890 and 1920, were essentially variety programs that featured a series of song-and-dance numbers, magicians, comics, minstrel acts, exotic dancers, trained animals, sports celebrities, and abbreviated versions of full-length dramatic or comic plays. Singing and dancing acts anchored every show, but successful vaudeville also relied on more unusual specialty acts, such as mind readers, escape artists, roller skaters, high divers, contortionists, strong men, freaks, living statues, and acrobats. Some of the more famous radio and film stars of the 1920s who began their careers as specialty vaudeville performers include comedians W. C. Fields, who juggled while cracking jokes, and Will Rogers, who performed elaborate rope tricks. Big-time vaudeville shows frequently featured celebrities whose personal appearances dramatically boosted ticket sales. Silent film star Douglas Fairbanks, baseball sensation Babe Ruth, temperance reformer Carry Nation, and handicapped educator Helen Keller all delighted vaudeville audiences and at the same time collected enormous paychecks. Risqué vaudeville numbers were rare, as most theater owners catered to audiences of both men and women and thus did not want to risk offending any ticket holders. Many vaudeville theaters offered two performances a day, with average ticket prices running between 10 and 50 cents. Other theaters scheduled "continuous performances," which allowed audience members to enter at any time and to leave when they began to see the same acts reappear.

American vaudeville theater appealed to a wide variety of audiences in both urban and rural areas. Wealthy spectators took in vaudeville shows performed in opulent urban theaters, while less well-heeled patrons enjoyed similar but usually lesser-grade shows staged in considerably shabbier venues. In their cross-country travels, vaudevillians performed the most up-to-date pop songs, told the latest jokes, wore the most stylish clothing, and employed the most current slang expressions, thus linking audiences across the United States to the most recent trends in America's fast-changing popular culture. Vaudevillians also drew upon and perpetuated long-standing racial and ethnic stereotypes, including the Irish "mick," the Jewish "hebe," the rural white "rube," and, of course, the unsophisticated, watermelon-eating black "coon." In fact, many vaudeville bills featured African-American performers who actually accentuated their skin color by performing in blackface.

Playing the vaudeville circuit was hard work, and wages and working conditions varied widely. Career vaudevillians often toured for 40 or more weeks each year, performing one-night stands on rural stages or appearing for a week or two at a time in the major metropolitan theaters. Salaries ranged from as low as $15 a week for performing in small-town dives, to upwards of $1,500 a week for headlining at the nation's finer urban venues. In 1925, for example, popular bandleader Paul Whiteman earned a whopping $7,000 a week for an engagement at New York City's Hippodrome. Among the other big vaudeville headliners during the 1920s were Al Jolson, Eddie Cantor, Nora Bayes, Cliff Edwards, and

Fanny Brice, all of whom commanded high fees for their performances. The most prestigious, though not the best-paying, vaudeville theater in the country was the luxurious Palace Theatre, located in New York City on the corner of Broadway and 47th Street. Entertainers who performed well at the Palace could expect first-rate bookings to follow, since dozens of talent scouts and agents attended each Monday matinee—the first performance of the week—and would offer lucrative contracts to the acts that most impressed them.

A typical vaudeville bill included about eight or nine acts, but various theaters might book more or fewer performers in any given week. The order in which these acts appeared was carefully chosen, and each slot carried certain levels of prestige and rates of pay. The first and last slots on the bill were generally reserved for the least talented and lowest-paid performers. The final performance before the intermission was usually a big-name act—a sure-fire crowd pleaser whom the audience could discuss during the break. The penultimate spot on the program was almost always reserved for the top-billed headliner, or star of the show—usually a popular singer or comedian, who also enjoyed the nicest dressing room and the highest salary.[1] In lesser venues, bandleaders or comedians were sometimes hired to act as the master of ceremonies, bantering with the audience throughout the show and helping to "sell" some of the less popular or less talented acts.

While African Americans regularly performed in white vaudeville theaters, audiences remained largely segregated, especially in the South. Typically, African Americans were not permitted to buy tickets for performances in white theaters, though sometimes a special section in the balcony would be reserved for black patrons. However, all-black vaudeville troupes played to enthusiastic audiences in African-American theaters throughout the South and Midwest. These black troupes booked their performance schedules through a management agency called the Theatre Owners' Booking Association, or TOBA, which some African-American vaudevillians claimed was an acronym for "Tough on Black Asses." Exhausting schedules, poor backstage amenities, and pitiful wages made working on the TOBA circuit particularly difficult. However, many of the greatest African-American entertainers of the Jazz Age, such as Ethel Waters, Gertrude "Ma" Rainey, Bessie Smith, and Bill "Bojangles" Robinson, advanced their careers by performing throughout the South and Midwest on the TOBA circuit.

Although it was the single most popular form of American entertainment prior to World War I, vaudeville theater diminished considerably in popularity during the 1920s, largely due to the intense competition from nightclubs, radio programs, and especially motion pictures. In fact, motion pictures and vaudeville shows became such fierce competitors that, by the mid-1920s, most vaudeville houses offered "combination" shows that interspersed live entertainment with short films. By 1926, all but around 630 of the nation's once-flourishing 21,000 vaudeville theaters had been converted into motion picture houses. Toward the end of the decade, in a desperate attempt to salvage vaudeville, some theater owners dropped their standard "two-a-day" performance schedule to offer five performances a day, which drained performers and used up material faster than ever. Furthermore, Hollywood studios lured away the most talented vaudeville performers to act in motion pictures. Vaudeville theater struggled to keep pace with the latest trends in popular entertainment, but by the end of the Roaring Twenties it was clearly in decline. Vaudeville limped along as an entertainment industry until the 1940s, but it never again attained the dominance it enjoyed during the years surrounding World War I.

THEATER

Broadway Drama

While vaudeville dwindled in popularity during the 1920s, American theater enjoyed an exciting decade of innovative productions. Then, as now, New York City's famous Broadway reigned as the epicenter of American theater, and during the decade the Broadway theater district experienced a surge of expansion. Between 1924 and 1929, 26 new theaters opened, bringing the total number of theaters to 66. Meanwhile, Broadway introduced audiences to hundreds of tragedies, sex farces, musicals, and experimental shows. During the 1927–1928 season alone, for example, 264 different productions opened on Broadway, and over the course of the decade, an average of 225 new shows were produced every year—a total that has never been equaled. Of course, not every New York City resident or tourist could afford to attend a Broadway show. Theater tickets sometimes cost as much as $3.50—more than 10 times the price of an average movie ticket. Audiences for theatrical productions—even for hit shows—could not compare to the enormous numbers of people who regularly bought movie tickets or tuned in devotedly to their favorite radio programs. But hit Broadway songs were broadcast widely on commercial radio, and Hollywood studios adapted many popular theatrical productions for the silver screen, thereby boosting the influence and attraction of Broadway theater.

During the 1920s, just as today, critically acclaimed productions did not always attract the largest audiences. The longest-running Broadway play of the decade proved to be a silly comedy called *Abie's Irish Rose*, which opened in 1922 and closed in 1927 after an amazing run of 2,327 performances. The story, written by Anne Nichols, revolves around a "mixed" marriage between Abie Levy, a Jew, and Rosemary Murphy, an Irish Catholic. Despite bitter antagonism between their families, Abie and Rosemary wed, and soon Rosemary becomes pregnant. The farcical debate about whether the couple's first child should be raised Jewish or Catholic occupies much of the rest of the play, and the issue is conveniently resolved when Rosemary gives birth to twins. Critics almost universally panned *Abie's Irish Rose,* but that didn't keep tens of thousands of theatergoers from delighting in the shallow plot and predictable jokes.

Of course, not all Broadway theater relied on such flimsy material. In fact, during the 1920s, Broadway became a lightning rod for serious controversy. Issues of censorship had plagued the American theater before, but during the 1920s these battles escalated dramatically. Religious leaders, conservative politicians, reform organizations, and even newspaper magnate William Randolph Hearst railed vociferously against theatrical depictions of content they deemed immoral, including prostitution, white slavery, and homosexuality. Eugene O'Neill's *Desire Under the Elms* (1924) and Sidney Howard's *They Knew What They Wanted* (1924), among others, prompted organizations such as the Actors' Association for Clean Plays and the Society for the Suppression of Vice to lodge formal complaints alleging that these performances were indecent and should therefore be shut down. In 1927, the New York state legislature stepped in to prevent "indecent" theater productions by passing the Wales Padlock Law. This law gave police broad powers to arrest the producers, playwrights, and actors involved in a production that appeared to be morally offensive. Under this law (which was not repealed until 1967), if a court subsequently declared the play obscene, the theater could be closed for up to a year.

While many important dramatists found audiences for their work during the 1920s, including Avery Hopwood, Elmer Rice, and Maxwell Anderson, the most talented and influential American playwright of the decade was Eugene O'Neill. The son of a popular romantic actor, O'Neill accompanied his family on theatrical tours when he was a child. He began writing plays in 1913, and his first major production of the 1920s, *Beyond the Horizon* (1920), won the Pulitzer Prize. Other successes quickly followed: *The Emperor Jones* (1920), *Anna Christie* (1921, which also won the Pulitzer Prize), *The Hairy Ape* (1922), *All God's Chillun Got Wings* (1924), *Desire Under the Elms* (1924), *The Great God Brown* (1926), and *Strange Interlude* (1928). O'Neill experimented boldly in his plays by dramatizing the emotions and memories of his characters and finding new ways to express these feelings onstage. He sacrificed realism to achieve a more emotional effect—sometimes his characters wore masks or addressed the audience directly. At other times, he had two actors play the same character, or he introduced ghosts or choruses into the story. Several of his plays feature main characters who undergo an experience so intense that they psychologically deteriorate into their primitive, chaotic selves.

Serious dramatic theater experienced a renaissance during the 1920s. In the years surrounding World War I, more than 100 plays about the war appeared on Broadway, the most famous perhaps being *What Price Glory* (1924), by Maxwell Anderson and Laurence Stallings. Other serious plays tackled the controversial issues of racism, women's rights, big business, the Red Scare, and other central concerns of modern American life. Only during the 1920s can it be said that experimental dramas appeared on Broadway with any regularity, and many playwrights dabbled in non-realistic portrayals of human experience as a matter of course. Despite the substantial success of "serious theater" during this decade, many theatergoers shunned Broadway's gritty portrayals of the horrors of war or soul-searching forays into the subconscious. What they preferred to see was a beautiful, funny, fantastical world of song and dance into which they could escape for a few hours—the world of musical theater.

Musical Theater

More so than any other kind of theatrical production, Americans audiences of the 1920s were drawn to the spectacle and showmanship of musical theater. The popularity of musicals may have evolved from the well-loved vaudeville shows that had toured the nation for the previous few decades. Then again, audiences may have responded to the extravagant sets, glamorous costumes, and elaborate dance numbers that characterized many of the big musical productions. Or perhaps ticket buyers longed to escape to a world where people spontaneously burst into song and happy endings were almost inevitable. Whatever the reason, musicals became steady favorites during the decade and paved the way for the lavish Hollywood movie musicals of the late 1920s and 1930s.

Most Broadway musicals emphasized great music and memorable dance routines far more than coherent, well-developed plotlines. For example, *No, No, Nanette* (1925), one of the most popular musicals of the decade, featured a forgettable story line but some unforgettable hit songs by composer Vincent Youmans and lyricist Irving Caesar, including "Tea for Two" and "I Want to Be Happy." Occasionally, though, big-budget musicals did take on more sophisticated, complicated plots. *Show Boat* (1927), based on Edna Ferber's 1926 novel of the same name, tackled the sensitive issues of racism and miscegenation. It also featured a tremendous musical score, written by composer Jerome Kern and lyricist Oscar Hammerstein II, which included such classic songs as "Ol' Man River" and "Make Believe." In 1921, *Shuffle Along* made Broadway history as the first musical of the decade to be written, produced, directed, and performed entirely by African Americans. Its score offered the hit songs "Love Will Find a Way" and "I'm Just Wild About Harry," by composer Eubie Blake and lyricist Noble Sissle. *Shuffle Along* gave a number of talented black performers, including Florence Mills, Josephine Baker, and Paul Robeson, their first big break in show business. It also opened the door for other black musicals to appear on Broadway. Many hit musicals of the 1920s were quickly adapted to the silver screen, thus bringing their catchy songs and new dance steps to a broader national audience.

Musical Revues

Along with the perennially popular musical theater, light musical revues—theatrical performances consisting of a series of unconnected musical acts—remained audience favorites throughout the 1920s. Perhaps the most famous and best-loved theatrical revue of the day was *The Ziegfeld Follies*, produced by Chicago native Florenz Ziegfeld Jr. Ziegfeld began his long and successful career in entertainment in the 1890s, producing hit Broadway musicals with memorable scores and lavishly dressed chorus girls. His greatest success came, however, with the production of *The Ziegfeld Follies* (prior to 1911 simply called *The Follies*), an annual Broadway revue based on the famous Parisian *Folies Bergère*. *The Ziegfeld Follies*, essentially a sophisticated variety show, featured a rotating cast of singers, dancers, and comedians who spoofed the social and political "follies" of the day. Ziegfeld staged his first *Follies* in 1907, and over the next 24 years he produced a new show every year. *The Ziegfeld Follies* were inordinately expensive productions, and Ziegfeld constantly changed his roster of stars and songs to keep the show fresh and to encourage repeat customers. One aspect of the revue, however, remained constant: the chorus line of stunning young women known as the "Follies Girls"—long-legged women dressed in gorgeous but scanty costumes who made the *Follies* famous. Changes in popular taste, including Americans' insatiable love for the new talking motion pictures, caused the revue to falter in the late 1920s, and Ziegfeld produced his final *Follies* in 1931.

While *The Ziegfeld Follies* was by far the largest, most elaborate, and most popular of the Broadway revues of the 1920s, a number of other shows competed for a share of ticket receipts. *The George White Scandals* (1919–1939), produced by George White, featured such major stars as singer Rudy Vallee and dancer Ann Pennington. Between 1912 and 1924, J. J. Shubert produced annual versions of *The Passing Show*—a revue that shamelessly copied the format of *The Ziegfeld Follies* and featured headliners such as dancers Adele and Fred Astaire, singer Marilyn Miller, and comics Ed Wynn and Willie and Eugene Howard. John Murray Anderson staged a popular revue series called *The Greenwich Village Follies*

(1919–1928), which became so successful that it eventually moved uptown to Broadway. And, with his *Vanities* (1923–1927) and *Sketch Books* (1929) revues, Earl Carroll gave New York audiences some of its bawdiest shows, including off-color comedy acts and nearly naked chorus girls.

Revues featuring African-American casts also flourished, including *Runnin' Wild* (1923), the *Plantation Revue* (1922), and *Hot Chocolates* (1929). The most popular African-American revue was the *Blackbirds* series, produced and directed by the white impresario Lew Leslie. *Blackbirds*, which premiered in 1926, introduced a series of popular hit songs by composer Jimmy McHugh and lyricist Dorothy Fields, including "I Can't Give You Anything But Love" (1928), "Diga Diga Do" (1928), and "Doin' the New Low Down" (1928). Black performers often traded on then-popular racist caricatures of the country bumpkin "Jim Crow," the knife-wielding urban "Zip Coon," and undomesticated children, referred to as "pickanninies" or "picks." Although these images seem offensive to our current sensibilities, African-American performers of the 1920s understood that the success of a show depended on pleasing white audiences, who demanded familiar, hackneyed—and therefore "safe"—portrayals of African Americans.

DANCE

Dancing during the 1920s, in terms of American popular culture, primarily referred to popular dance. Professional, academic dance such as ballet did not exert much cultural influence, and in fact little high-quality ballet was performed in the United States during the decade, except by touring foreign dance troupes. The fledgling genre of modern dance was just beginning to attract audiences, largely due to the influential Denishawn School of Dance, founded in 1915 by Ruth St. Denis and her husband, Ted Shawn. Two of Denishawn's most famous and talented students, Doris Humphrey and Martha Graham, introduced dance lovers of the 1920s to the creative choreography of modern dance. Some critics found this style of dance exhilarating and liberating, while others found it confusing and even ugly. Modern dance did make great strides toward being accepted and appreciated during the 1920s, but the American public was far more enamored with popular dance.

Popular Dance

Social dancing at nightclubs, dance halls, speakeasies, and in private homes became an all-consuming activity during the 1920s. Dancing's widespread appeal is easy to understand—it was inexpensive, needed little if any special equipment (or even talent), and, above all, it was fun to do and to watch. Furthermore, the availability of hit records, the increasing affordability of radios, the popularity of vaudeville and Broadway musicals, and the ever-increasing influence of Hollywood movies combined to offer Americans unprecedented access to trendy, danceable music and models of great dancers and dances. For example, the brother-and-sister dance team of Fred and Adele Astaire helped to popularize tap dancing in the Broadway musicals of the 1920s, and chorus line dancers, vaudevillians, Broadway entertainers, and movie stars all taught the American public how to fox-trot, shimmy, and tango. Being a good dancer became one avenue to popularity, particularly among high school and college-age youth, so many young people (and even older adults) actually enrolled in dance lessons at local studios. For those too shy or embarrassed to attend dance classes, Arthur Murray invented a correspondence course that taught customers the steps to the latest popular dances by using a lesson book with footprint diagrams and accompanying instructions. By 1925, an estimated 5 million people had learned to dance in their own homes using the footprint maps they received in the mail. Later that year, Murray opened his first studio, on East 43rd Street in New York City, and he began to franchise his dance studios in 1938.

Rather than turn to professional instructors, most social dancers improved their skills by diligently and enthusiastically imitating the dancers they saw on the movie screen or the vaudeville stage. One of the first new dance trends of the decade was the tango, sparked in part by the handsome film star Rudolph Valentino, who performed this classic Latin-American dance in the sexy opening scene of *The Four Horsemen of the Apocalypse* (1921). The early 1920s also witnessed the rise of the shimmy, which Gilda Gray popularized in *The Ziegfeld Follies of 1922*, but nothing better symbolized the carefree spirit and ebullience of the Jazz Age than the Charleston, a high-stepping version of the fox-trot that became a nationwide craze between 1923 and 1926. Although its origins remain uncertain, the Charleston was probably based upon a dance step popularized by African Americans in Charleston, South Carolina. Dancer Elizabeth Welch introduced it to the American public in the 1923 all-black musical revue *Runnin' Wild*, which featured songs by James P. Johnson and Cecil Mack, including their celebrated tune "Charleston." The Charleston, which could be danced solo, with a partner, or as a group, soon took the dancing public by storm. Hotel ballrooms, cabarets, and dance halls across the nation staged Charleston contests, and Tin Pan Alley songwriters turned out dozens of new Charleston songs, such as "I'm Gonna Charleston Back to Charleston" (1925) and "Charleston Baby of Mine" (1925), for dance-mad Americans.

The Black Bottom, which eventually eclipsed the Charleston in pop-

A Charleston dance contest, St. Louis, Missouri, 1925. Courtesy of the Missouri Historical Society, St. Louis.

ularity, was another wildly popular dance of the Jazz Age. First introduced in the all-black musical *Dinah* (1923), the Black Bottom did not become a national sensation until 1926, when white dancer Ann Pennington performed it in *The George White Scandals of 1926*. Other dance crazes followed, including the varsity drag (introduced in the 1927 Broadway musical *Good News*), the collegiate (also known as the collegiate shag), and the raccoon (popularized by the 1928 song "Doin' the Raccoon"). Another social dance of the 1920s was the Lindy hop, first made popular by George "Shorty" Snowden at a 1928 dance marathon. This swing dance, named for aviator Charles Lindbergh, rose to even greater popularity during the Big Band Era of the 1930s and 1940s. But the perennial favorite dance of the 1920s remained the fox-trot, which had been introduced—and perhaps invented—by the nationally known dance team of Irene and Vernon Castle during the 1910s.

Many of these new dances, like the jazz music associated with them, disturbed clergymen, social workers, and older, conservative Americans, who considered them to be degenerate and immoral. Some of these dances required couples to cling to each other with their cheeks and bodies touching, and some, such as the shimmy and the Black Bottom, were explicitly sexual. "Social dancing," warned one evangelist, writing in the *Portland Oregonian*, "is the first and easiest step toward hell."[2] Automobile mogul Henry Ford also believed that modern dances such as the Charleston and the Black Bottom, along with jazz music, corrupted America's youth. To combat this moral decline, Ford tried to revive old-time fiddling and square dancing, both of which he believed embodied the wholesome, conservative values he wanted to encourage. In 1926, he staged a national fiddling contest through his Ford dealerships, offering cash prizes and automobiles to the winners. He also engaged 200 dance instructors to teach square dances, polkas, and waltzes to his employees and their families. As a result, fiddling and square-dancing did witness a brief popular revival. Even so, millions of Americans continued to shake the shimmy, step the Charleston, and do the raccoon throughout the Roaring Twenties.

HOLLYWOOD MOTION PICTURES

During the 1920s, Americans who sought thrills, melodrama, and escape found an outlet in Hollywood motion pictures. After World War I, movies replaced vaudeville theater as the single most popular form of commercial entertainment, and going to the movies became a common form of everyday recreation. By the mid-1920s, nearly every small town counted at least one theater among its downtown businesses, and major cities such as New York and Chicago boasted hundreds of them. In 1928, the nation contained an estimated 28,000 movie theaters, which charged moviegoers 10–50 cents for a ticket. Movie theaters sometimes offered an entire afternoon's or evening's entertainment, which might include a newsreel, perhaps a comedy short or two, and then the feature attraction. Since films contained no synchronized sound until the advent of the so-called "talkies" in 1927, actors and actresses conveyed emotions through pantomime acting, while a minimal number of printed intertitles between the scenes conveyed written dialogue and helped to explain the plot. Most neighborhood theaters featured a pianist or organist who supplied music to accompany the film. In the grand movie palaces, large orchestras, which might contain as many as 100 members, set the mood and heightened the drama unfolding onscreen.

During the 1920s, the Hollywood motion picture companies developed the so-called studio system, which soon helped to expand moviemaking into the fifth largest industry in the United States. Under this system, a handful of studios—Metro-Goldwyn-Mayer (MGM), Paramount Pictures, Fox Film Corporation, Warner Brothers, and RKO Pictures—controlled every aspect of the production, distribution, and exhibition of

Opening night at Grauman's Chinese Theater, Los Angeles, 1927.
Courtesy of the Library of Congress.

their own films. These giant studios, nicknamed the "Big Five," owned and operated nationwide networks of movie theaters that screened only films produced by their parent company. The studios also created a subsidiary market for their movies by employing the "block booking system," which required independent theater owners to show all of a particular studio's films if they wanted to show any of them. This system guaranteed the giant studios reliable outlets for exhibiting even their low-budget films and generated annual profits that ran into the tens of millions of dollars.

During the 1920s, the American motion picture industry matured into the enormously influential commercial industry that we recognize today. Then, as now, it was headquartered in Hollywood, California, and the surrounding suburbs, where studios benefited from the area's warm, sunny climate and diverse landscape for location shooting. Prior to World War I, studios produced films that were intended chiefly to entertain urban working-class audiences. Although director D. W. Griffith's epic films *The Birth of a Nation* (1915) and *Intolerance* (1916) stand out as obvious exceptions, movies of the 1910s typically consisted of only one or two reels of film (each reel usually ran for less than 10 minutes) and were often shot in just a few days. As a result, these "shorts," as they were called, devoted little attention to character or plot development. As the industry expanded after World War I, however, Hollywood began to market its films primarily to middle-class Americans. To attract this clientele, studios produced a greater number of big-budget epic movies with glamorous stars, sophisticated camera shots, complex plots, better-developed characters, and elaborate costuming and sets. MGM's epic *Ben-Hur: A Tale of Christ* (1925), for example, which was filmed in both Italy and southern California, cost a record $4.5 million to make. Feature films such as *Ben-Hur* usually ran between one and two-and-a-half hours, and while most were shot in black-and-white, a few of them, such as *The Black Pirate* (1926), used an early version of Technicolor. These blockbuster films of the 1920s increasingly celebrated the nation's newfound fascination with glamour, sex appeal, exoticism, and urbanity, and American audiences loved them. By 1922, Americans purchased an average of 40 million movie tickets each week.

No other commercial entertainment exerted a more profound influence on American popular culture than did Hollywood motion pictures, especially when it came to what historian Frederick Lewis Allen called the nation's "revolution in manners and morals."[3] Based upon the movies they saw, Americans copied the hairstyles, clothing, speech, and behavior of their favorite actors or actresses. Hollywood films not only dictated many of the nation's fads and fashions during the 1920s but also helped to fuel mass consumption and taught millions of young people about dating and sex. "Goodness knows," remarked one college coed, "you learn plenty about love from the movies."[4] While most movie fans relished the racy images and stories that appeared onscreen, some Americans, of course, were greatly disturbed by the decadence and loose morals they believed the movie industry was encouraging.

Censorship and the Hays Office

Since the advent of nickelodeons during the 1890s, America's moral guardians saw motion pictures as a potentially dangerous influence. During the 1910s and 1920s, conservative and religious critics increasingly condemned what they perceived as Hollywood's salacious, offensive, or immoral themes and images. Additionally, a series of spectacular scandals, among them the mysterious slaying of director William Desmond Taylor and the manslaughter trial of silent film comedian Roscoe "Fatty" Arbuckle, seriously damaged the reputation of the Hollywood motion picture industry. Studio executives decided that the only way to avert the very real threat of federal regulation would be to develop their own stringent system of self-regulation. In December

1921, they invited William H. "Will" Hays, the former chairman of the Republican National Committee and the current postmaster general of the United States, to become the director of the organization soon to be called the Motion Picture Producers and Distributors of America (MPPDA). Hays sought to impose an industry-wide code that would help to clean up Hollywood's tarnished public image and to restore the integrity of American cinema. In 1922, he proved he meant business by banning Arbuckle from appearing in Hollywood movies (Hays lifted the ban later that same year, though) and blacklisting a group of some 200 actors and actresses who had questionable reputations. His radical reforms, strict code of censorship, and powerful leadership soon caused his organization to be nicknamed the Hays Office.

Hays' reform efforts also took the form of a 1924 resolution passed by the MPPDA that essentially pledged to promote clean, moral films and a list, promulgated in 1927, known as "Don'ts" and "Be Carefuls," that informed studio producers what movie content the MPPDA deemed morally appropriate. The "Don'ts" list outlined 11 subjects that were absolutely forbidden in films: profanity, nudity, drug trafficking, sex perversion, white slavery, miscegenation, venereal disease, scenes of childbirth, portrayals of children's sex organs, ridicule of the clergy, and willful offense to any nation, race, or creed. The second part of the list warned moviemakers that they must use prudence, discretion, and good taste if addressing any of the 25 enumerated "Be Carefuls," which included any scenes containing the American flag, the use of firearms, arson, theft, robbery, safecracking, dynamiting, murder, smuggling, hangings or other methods of execution, sedition, cruelty to children and animals, rape or attempted rape, surgical operations, drug use, prostitution, the seduction of girls, and "excessive or lustful kissing."[5] While the Hays Office possessed no legal control over Hollywood moviemakers during the 1920s, it refused to promote or distribute any film that did not conform to its standards. As a result of these reforms, Hays managed to stabilize the industry and ward off government intervention, and in 1930, the MPPDA promulgated even stricter self-censorship guidelines known as the Motion Picture Production Code.

Silent Film Genres and Stars

Through mass production methods, Hollywood studios managed to release a combined average of around a thousand movies each year throughout the 1920s. These motion pictures encompassed a wide variety of film genres, but the most popular were biblical epics, melodramas, romances, historical adventures, westerns, and comedies. Cecil B. DeMille, the single most influential director of the decade, directed and produced two great biblical epics, *The Ten Commandments* (1923) and *The*

King of Kings (1927). He also made a series of lurid melodramas with such suggestive titles as *Why Change Your Wife?* (1920), *The Forbidden Fruit* (1921), and *The Affairs of Anatol* (1921), which frankly addressed themes of sexual desire, infidelity, divorce, and other problems plaguing modern married couples. Moviegoers flocked to see romances, especially the box-office hit *Flesh and the Devil* (1927), which starred John Gilbert and Greta Garbo, one of the Jazz Age's greatest pairs of screen lovers. Garbo, a Swedish émigré who came to the United States in 1925, established herself as a mysterious, sultry sex symbol in a series of Hollywood films, including *The Temptress* (1926), *The Mysterious Lady* (1928), and *A Woman of Affairs* (1929). Other romantic leading men and women included Rudolph Valentino, John Barrymore, Charles Farrell, Gloria Swanson, Clara Bow, and Janet Gaynor.

Some motion pictures of the 1920s tackled important social and cultural issues, such as World War I films like King Vidor's *The Big Parade* (1925) and Raoul Walsh's *What Price Glory?* (1926), but most box-office attractions consisted of escapist entertainment. Several classic westerns were produced during the 1920s, such as John Ford's *The Iron Horse* (1924) and Victor Fleming's *The Virginian* (1929), starring Gary Cooper, one of Hollywood's rising leading men. In addition, studios churned out dozens of popular serial westerns, which often featured "cliffhanger" endings and starred, among others, William S. Hart, Hoot Gibson, Tom Mix, and Ken Maynard. Many of the smaller independent studios produced dozens of low-budget horror films and science fiction thrillers. By the late 1920s, gangster films increasingly captivated moviegoers, reflecting the nation's fascination with crime, corruption, and gangland warfare.

Another popular film genre of the 1920s was slapstick comedy, which traded on sight gags, acrobatic stunts, and physical comedy, often made even more ridiculous by wildly exaggerated acting styles. Harold Lloyd, one of the most successful silent film comedians and best known for his trademark horn-rimmed glasses and straw hat, typically portrayed an innocent "everyman" who was forever getting into improbable, but funny, situations. His comedic masterpiece, *Safety Last* (1923), features a spectacular scene in which he dangles from the hands of an enormous clock eight stories above the city street below (Lloyd actually did most of his own stunt work, including this scene). Another great film comedian was Buster Keaton, known as "the Great Stone Face" for his deadpan, stoic expressions. During the 1920s, Keaton wrote, directed, and starred in a series of classic comedies, most notably *The Three Ages* (1923), *Sherlock, Jr.* (1924), *The Navigator* (1924), and—the film for which he is best known—the Civil War comedy *The General* (1926). The 1920s also saw the screen debut of two of the most influential comedy teams of all time. In 1927, Stan Laurel and Oliver Hardy starred in *Slipping Wives*,

Charlie Chaplin in a scene from *The Circus*, 1928. Courtesy of the Library of Congress.

the first of the 105 comedies the duo would eventually make, and the Marx Brothers, who began their career in vaudeville around 1912, shot their first feature-length film, *The Cocoanuts*, in 1929. Ironically, of all the Hollywood film genres of the 1920s, slapstick comedies often contained the most biting criticisms of America's political conservatism and crass materialism.

By nearly every account, the greatest genius of silent film comedy was the British-born Charlie Chaplin. One of the biggest international celebrities of the 1920s, Chaplin wrote, produced, directed, starred in—and sometimes even composed the musical scores for—some of the most critically acclaimed comedies in the history of American cinema. A former London vaudevillian, he began working in 1914 as an actor and director in dozens of one- and two-reel comedy shorts for a series of Hollywood movie studios, and within four years he had become one of the highest paid film stars in the United States. In 1921, Chaplin directed and starred in his first feature-length film, *The Kid*, which also launched child star Jackie Coogan's career. *The Gold Rush* (1925), widely considered by cinema historians to be one of the greatest films of all time, contains two classic Chaplin routines. In one scene, snowbound and starving in an

Alaskan blizzard, he dines on a Thanksgiving feast consisting of a boiled boot, and in the other, he entertains the girl he loves with a pair of dancing dinner rolls stuck on the ends of forks. Chaplin's many responsibilities on the movie set drastically reduced the number of films he could produce. So, too, did his meticulousness as a filmmaker. As a result, Chaplin made only five feature films during the 1920s, the last of which, *The Circus* (1928), took him two years to complete.

All the comedies Chaplin made during the 1920s featured him in the role of his signature character, "the Little Tramp," whom he had introduced in *Kid Auto Races at Venice* (1914). One of the most recognizable film characters of all time, his kindhearted tramp sported a toothbrush mustache, an ill-fitting suit and baggy trousers, oversized shoes, bowler hat, and a bamboo cane. Chaplin was a master of making audiences laugh, but through this innocent, trusting character, he also leveled some of the most strident social criticism seen in American film. Indeed, in the guise of a tramp—a social outsider—Chaplin safely challenged those capitalist values of respectability, industriousness, and self-control that dominated modern American life during the 1920s and 1930s. For almost a decade after the advent of talkies, Chaplin continued to make silent films, including *City Lights* (1931) and *Modern Times* (1936), which contain only synchronized music, sound effects, and sparse dialogue (Chaplin himself has no spoken lines). He did not make his first wholly sound picture until *The Great Dictator* (1940), a savage satire of Adolf Hitler. Even today, Chaplin is still regarded by cultural historians as one of the greatest film comedians and entertainers of the twentieth century.

While dozens of white film stars flourished during the 1920s, African-American directors, actors, and actresses found it exceedingly difficult to break into Hollywood's studio system. Throughout the first decades of the twentieth century, the major studios almost completely ignored African-American themes and audiences, but during the late 1920s, African-American actors and actresses did begin to land occasional roles in mainstream films. Still, most of these roles consisted of stereotypical bit parts as butlers, maids, and "plantation darkies." Often, black actors played comical buffoons, shiftless ne'er-do-wells, or chicken thieves, which represented then-current racist caricatures of African Americans. For example, during the late 1920s and early 1930s, Stepin Fetchit emerged as the first bona fide black Hollywood star, but he did so largely by portraying dim-witted, shuffling "coon" characters. Late in the 1920s, several Hollywood studios exhibited a new but limited wave of interest in exploring the African-American experience. In 1929, for example, Fox released the critically acclaimed *Hearts in Dixie*, an experimental talking film featuring an all-black cast, and MGM followed with *Hallelujah!* (1929), another early all-black feature film.

Despite Hollywood's racist, exclusionary practices, African-American cinema did succeed during the 1920s. Shut out by white-controlled studios, black actors and actresses found work in low-budget "race pictures" produced for African-American audiences. Most of these movies addressed themes of African-American life and racial issues seldom depicted in mainstream Hollywood movies. Small, independent black film companies, many of them founded in the late 1910s and early 1920s, produced the bulk of these movies, which featured all-black casts of actors and actresses, including Edna Morton, billed as "the Colored Mary Pickford," and Lorenzo Tucker, "the Black Valentino." The most famous director and producer of race pictures was the pioneering African-American filmmaker Oscar Micheaux. Micheaux, a pulp fiction writer, founded his own production company in 1918 in order to make a movie based on a novel he had written titled *The Homesteader* (1917). In 1920, he released one of his best-remembered melodramas, *Within Our Gates*, which tackled the controversial subject of lynching. Throughout the 1920s, he made more than a dozen feature films, including *The House Behind The Cedars* (1923), an adaptation of Charles W. Chesnutt's novel, and *Body and Soul* (1924), the first film of actor Paul Robeson.

The Hollywood Star System

During the 1920s, the fledgling Hollywood star system matured into a full-blown cultural phenomenon. Studios aggressively promoted their film stars in order to capitalize on the nation's fascination with celebrities of all kinds. Consequently, millions of moviegoers came to idolize the glamorous stars of the silver screen. For fans who wanted to know more about their idols, more than 25 mass-circulation magazines, such as *Motion Picture*, *Screenland*, and *Photoplay*, offered the latest Hollywood news, scandals, and gossip. Studio publicists kept their celebrities in the headlines by issuing torrents of press releases, staging publicity stunts, and scheduling interviews and personal appearances. Studio executives understood perfectly well that the more publicity an actor or actress could generate, the more movie tickets Americans would purchase. In May 1929, in one of the industry's many efforts at self-promotion, the Academy of Motion Picture Arts and Sciences (founded in 1927) hosted the first Academy Awards ceremony at a banquet in Hollywood's Roosevelt Hotel. Those awards, which honored the films produced during 1927 and 1928, went to Emil Jannings for Best Actor, Janet Gaynor for Best Actress, and the blockbuster war epic *Wings* for Best Picture. Unlike today, the Academy Award winners were announced in advance, so the actual ceremony held few surprises.

Hollywood's glamorous stars ranked among the most admired celebrities of the Jazz Age. One of the nation's most popular actresses was the diminutive, golden-curled Mary Pickford, who was known as

"America's Sweetheart." Pickford often starred in wholesome melodramas such as *Pollyanna* (1920) and *Sparrows* (1926), in both of which she portrayed innocent young girls (even through she herself turned 30 in 1923). Pickford's dashing, athletic husband, Douglas Fairbanks, whom she married in 1920, starred in a series of swashbuckling historical adventures, including *The Mark of Zorro* (1920), *The Three Musketeers* (1921), *Robin Hood* (1922), and *The Thief of Baghdad* (1924). Lon Chaney, billed as "the Man of a Thousand Faces," thrilled moviegoers with his grotesque characterizations of the monstrous hunchback Quasimodo in *The Hunchback of Notre Dame* (1923) and the horribly disfigured composer Erik in *The Phantom of the Opera* (1925), one of the earliest American horror films. One of the biggest box-office draws of the 1920s was a German shepherd named Rin Tin Tin, whom an American officer had found as a puppy in Western Europe during World War I. Beginning in 1922, Rin Tin Tin appeared in a series of popular serials and feature films before his death in 1932 at the age of 13.

By far the most celebrated romantic lead of the 1920s was Rudolph Valentino, an Italian immigrant—billed as "the Great Lover"—who emerged as one of Hollywood's first great male sex symbols. His darkly handsome (though androgynous) good looks and his sexy Latin exoticism captivated millions of female moviegoers, who were said literally to swoon and faint at the sight of him. After his breakthrough lead performance in *The Four Horsemen of the Apocalypse* (1921), Valentino went on to star in more than a dozen movies, including his most famous, *The Sheik* (1921), before he died suddenly in 1926 at the age of 31. Clara Bow, the greatest female sex symbol of the decade, broke into the film industry in 1921 by winning a national contest sponsored by *Motion Picture* magazine. Over the next six years, she played a series of flappers in such movies as *Daughters of Pleasure* (1924), *Dancing Mothers* (1926), and *Mantrap* (1926), before becoming a silent screen sensation in *It* (1927), an adaptation of British writer Elinor Glyn's popular novella. "It" was a euphemism for sexual attraction and self-confidence, and Clara Bow had plenty of both. With her curly, bobbed red hair, translucent white skin, and scarlet pouting "bee-stung" lips, she became the epitome of the sexy Jazz Age flapper and was known as the "It Girl" for the rest of her film career.

The Advent of the "Talkies"

Throughout the first half of the 1920s, Hollywood produced only silent films, but in 1926, the introduction of synchronized sound revolutionized the industry. The most sensational early talking motion picture, though not the first, was Warner Brothers' feature film *The Jazz Singer*, released in October 1927. Although the film featured synchronized sound in only

Actress Clara Bow. Courtesy of the Library of Congress.

six musical numbers and in one snippet of dialogue—its star Al Jolson's famous line, "Wait a minute! Wait a minute! You ain't heard nothing yet"—*The Jazz Singer* demonstrated the enormous potential of this new technology and whetted movie audiences' appetite for talkies.[6] Studios continued to produce silent films into the 1930s, but talking films represented the film industry's future, and by mid-1928, some 300 theaters across the nation were already wired to exhibit sound films. The advent of sound motion pictures boosted ticket sales. By 1930, American moviegoers were purchasing an estimated 100 million tickets each week—at a time when the nation's population stood at approximately 123 million people.[7]

RADIO

Although amateur radio operators had been broadcasting on a limited scale since at least 1909, it was not until the 1920s that radio emerged as a powerful and broadly appealing commercial mass medium. On November 4, 1920, KDKA, in East Pittsburgh, Pennsylvania, became one of the first stations in the nation to begin regularly scheduled radio broadcasts when it carried the results of the presidential election between Warren G. Harding and James M. Cox. Although only a few thousand listeners owned radio receivers at the time, this historic election-night broadcast is widely considered the birth of commercial broadcasting in the United States. Over the course of the next few years, commercial radio underwent phenomenal growth. The number of licensed radio stations operating in the United States jumped from four at the beginning of 1922 to 576 by the end of that year.[8] Americans eagerly embraced this new medium, and the sale of radios and radio equipment soared from $1 million in 1920 to $400 million in 1925.[9]

The advent of network broadcasting transformed radio into a truly national medium and supplanted much local programming. In 1926, the Radio Corporation of America (RCA) formed the nation's first radio network, the National Broadcasting Company (NBC), which actually operated two networks: NBC-Blue and NBC-Red. Originally, NBC linked 24 affiliate stations located between New York and Kansas City, but by the end of 1928, its almost 70 affiliated stations were broadcasting coast-to-coast. The Columbia Broadcasting System (CBS), established in 1927, soon created its own network of 49 affiliate stations. Before the creation of national networks, local programs that showcased local talent and reflected local interests dominated radio broadcasting. Increasingly, though, as the influence of the networks grew, radio listeners across the nation heard many of the same programs and personalities. Network radio programs carried corporate-sponsored shows, such as *The Eveready Hour*, *The Majestic Theater of the Air*, and *The Voice of Firestone*, many of which featured such national celebrities as Eddie Cantor, Vaughn De Leath, Wendell Hall, and Will Rogers. These network shows crowded out many of the local personalities and performers who had once provided the bulk of radio entertainment. As a result, network radio accelerated the homogenization of American popular culture, since now radio listeners in small-town Missouri could enjoy many of the same programs heard by people in California, North Carolina, and New York. By 1929, commercial radio had developed into a large-scale industry consisting of three national networks and some 618 stations.

As a powerful and influential modern mass medium, radio had a tremendous impact on American popular culture. Radio influenced how people spent their leisure hours, what products they purchased, how they voted, how they talked, and even how they understood their world. Although listening to radio was essentially a private activity conducted in one's home, in many ways this new medium inspired a variety of social activities. Neighbors and friends often gathered around a family's receiver in the evening for what were called "radio parties." Groups of young people rolled up the rug, moved the furniture out of the way, and danced to the latest jazz sounds. Families tuned in on Sunday mornings to listen to nationally famous preachers and church services. Indeed, many listeners actually scheduled their daily activities around their favorite radio shows. By 1929, according to one survey, more than 33 percent of American families owned a radio set, and of those, a reported 80 percent listened to their sets daily.[10] Thus, less than a decade after its advent, commercial radio had become an integral part of everyday life for millions of Americans.

In the early days of radio, music had constituted the single most popular form of station programming, occupying approximately 70 percent of all airtime by 1925, according to one study.[11] Rather than recorded music, stations generally featured live music performed in the studios by singers and musicians. By 1924, many stations also aired so-called "remote" broadcasts (that is, those made from locations outside of the radio studio) of bands and orchestras performing in opera houses, concert halls, and hotel ballrooms. Throughout much of the decade, classical music programs, such as *The Atwater-Kent Hour* and *The Voice of Firestone*, dominated the airwaves, but eventually popular music, particularly jazz, filled daily broadcasting schedules. Among the dozens of network shows that featured pop music were *The A&P Gypsies*, *The Ipana Troubadors*, and *The Goodrich Silvertown Orchestra*.

Radio stations required significant resources to finance their operating costs, and with the advent of paid radio commercials on WEAF, New York, in 1922, commercial advertising soon emerged as the primary means of raising revenue. Radio stations provided stores and manufacturers the opportunity to advertise their merchandise to an entire community of listeners. The most common form of radio advertising involved corporate sponsorship of popular programs, often musical shows. The companies then included their product's name in the title of the show, such as *The Happiness Boys* (named for a candy manufacturer), *The Clicquot Club Eskimos* (named for a ginger ale maker), and *The Gold Dust Twins* (named for a scouring powder manufacturer). Network radio, on which national corporations advertised their brand-name products, generated enormous advertising revenues, reaching an estimated $40 million by 1929. In fact, between 1928 and 1934, as the number of newspaper and magazine ads declined, radio advertising leaped 316 percent.[12]

Besides musical programs and advertisements, radio also provided tens of millions of Americans with local and national news, market reports, weather forecasts, political speeches, public lectures, sports scores, household hints, and dinner recipes. Broadcasts of sporting events boosted the popularity of college and professional sports and turned athletes such as Babe Ruth, Jack Dempsey, and Red Grange into national heroes. Even broadcasters, particularly NBC sportscaster Graham McNamee and CBS news commentator H. V. Kaltenborn, became celebrities.

Special news events, such as the 1925 Scopes trial, which Chicago's WGN covered live via remote broadcasts from Dayton, Tennessee, also formed an important part of broadcasting. An estimated audience of 30 million radio fans, for example, listened to NBC's extensive coverage of Charles Lindbergh's celebrated return to the United States after his historic 1927 transatlantic flight, but most listeners didn't turn on their radio sets only to hear coverage of special events. Rather, radio became a regular part of their everyday routines. Countless Americans arose each morning, switched on the radio, and performed their daily calisthenics to radio exercise programs, and millions of housewives tuned in during the day to homemaker shows, cooking programs, and home economics lectures as they performed their household chores.

By the late 1920s, radio networks offered more innovative and sophisticated programs, including westerns, detective shows, soap operas, comedies, children's shows, romances, and variety shows. Particularly popular were serial comedies and dramas, which featured a cast of characters involved in an ongoing story line. In August 1929, NBC launched *Amos 'n' Andy*, a 15-minute weekday show that is widely considered to be the first serial program on network radio. This program, which was sponsored by Pepsodent Toothpaste, starred Freeman Gosden and Charles Correll, two white vaudevillians. It recounted the adventures of the title characters, a scheming Amos Jones (played by Gosden), and a buffoonish, manipulative Andrew H. "Andy" Brown (played by Correll), black southern migrants living in Chicago who were obsessed with money-making schemes. Gosden and Correll wrote the scripts and performed all of the characters (sometimes as many as 10 different people in a single scene), and the show's roster of minor characters eventually reached into the hundreds. The actors played the uneducated Amos and Andy using a pseudo-black dialect often filled with malapropisms and mispronunciations—"I'se regusted," for instance, for "I'm disgusted."

Despite its racist, stereotypical characterizations, *Amos 'n' Andy* was an immediate sensation, and historians credit the show's popularity for a 23 percent surge in radio sales in 1929. Restaurants piped in the nightly episodes over loudspeakers in order to appease their customers, and movie theaters scheduled the showing of films around the program. After being petitioned by their employees, the managers of 40 textile mills in Charlotte, North Carolina, agreed to end their shifts 15 minutes early so that workers could listen to *Amos 'n' Andy*. The show proved so popular that expressions regularly used on the program—such as "holy mackerel," "check and double-check," and "ain't dat sumpin?"—became popular catchphrases. Within a few years, the show had spawned a syndicated comic strip, a series of phonograph recordings, a candy bar, two books, and a motion picture. In 1931, at the height of the show's popularity, an estimated 40 million fans tuned in each night, or roughly 60 percent of all radio listeners. *Amos 'n' Andy* remained on the air until 1955, despite mounting protests from the National Association for the Advancement of Colored People (NAACP), and the show was also translated into a short-lived CBS television series during the early 1950s.

CONCLUSION

During the 1920s, Americans increasingly relied on mass commercial entertainment to occupy their leisure hours. Vaudeville shows, Broadway musicals, and other live performances introduced new pop songs and dances, while hotel ballrooms, dance halls, nightclubs, and speakeasies offered a dance-mad nation the opportunity to try out the latest steps. Even more influential were network radio programs and Hollywood motion pictures, which united millions of fans in their adoration of Eddie Cantor, Will Rogers, Charlie Chaplin, Clara Bow, and Amos and Andy. Of course, not every citizen enjoyed equal access to commercial entertainment. Some exclusive performances, such as operas, ballets, or Broadway shows, were typically restricted to those affluent white urban residents who could afford expensive tickets, but, for the most part, access to most forms of commercial entertainment was comparatively democratic. People from all walks of life could attend a movie western, dance to a hit jazz song, or listen to a favorite radio comedy.

Meanwhile, motion pictures and radio in particular contributed to the standardization of American popular culture by quickly disseminating the latest songs, dances, fads, and catchphrases across the nation. Radio sets brought entertainment and information directly into millions of American homes, from uptown Manhattan apartments to isolated South Dakota farmhouses, and by the end of the 1920s, listeners across the United States could enjoy many of the same serial dramas, comedy shows, and musical-variety programs. Even small towns of only a few thousand residents usually contained at least one movie theater, where audiences collectively gasped at Harold Lloyd's daredevil stunts, laughed at Charlie Chaplin's slapstick comedies, and hummed along to Al Jolson's show-stopping songs. In short, radio and motion pictures exerted an inestimable impact on the standardization of 1920s American popular culture. Through these media, Americans from every region, racial and ethnic group, and income level shared common experiences that helped to bring a diverse nation of people closer together.

11
Travel and Recreation

"All Roads End at Key West, Florida—The Paradise of America," announced one colorful travel brochure from 1929. "The Ozarks: 'The Land of a Million Smiles,' " promised another. "Yosemite," read a third, "California's All-Year Playground."[1] During the 1920s, Americans were bombarded with advertisements describing wonderful, scenic vacationlands, as well as newer, faster modes of transportation to help them get there. With more leisure time and disposable income, middle-class families traveled farther from their homes to visit seaside resorts, national parks, historic sites, and campgrounds. Railroad and bus lines reached virtually every corner of the United States, and the increasing affordability of automobiles and the nation's expanding network of roads and highways allowed middle-class and even many working-class Americans opportunities to enjoy a Sunday joyride, a weekend of auto-camping, or a driving vacation to the Grand Canyon. By the end of the decade, commercial passenger airlines made long-distance travel faster than ever before. America became a truly mobile society during the 1920s, and a wide array of new businesses—from motels and roadside restaurants to automobile associations and car insurance companies—sprang up to cater to the needs and whims of tens of millions of enthusiastic travelers.

MOTOR VEHICLE TRAVEL

Automobiles

Arguably, no technological advancement transformed American life during the Jazz Age more than the automobile. Although primitive, gasoline-powered "horseless carriages" had been manufactured in the United States since the mid-1890s, the 1920s marked the first decade in which automobile ownership became common among ordinary Americans. Prior to World War I, automobiles were generally unreliable and too expensive for all but the most affluent, but by the 1920s automobiles were more dependable and, as a result of mass production and new credit plans, more affordable. In 1910, 458,000 passenger cars traversed the nation's roadways. Only a decade later, that number had soared to 8 million. By 1930, automobile registrations had almost quadrupled to 23 million. Meanwhile, the estimated number of total miles that Americans drove each year leaped from 122 billion in 1925 to 206 billion in 1930.[2] By the end of the 1920s, automobiles had become, in the words of sociologists Robert S. Lynd and Helen Merrell Lynd, "an accepted essential of normal living," and half of all American families owned at least one motor vehicle.[3]

Henry Ford and the Model T

The individual most responsible for putting so many Americans behind the wheel was Henry Ford, a self-taught mechanical wizard who became the world's foremost automobile manufacturer. In 1903, when he founded the Ford Motor Company, most of the nation's automobile manufacturers were still producing expensive, laboriously hand-assembled vehicles, but Ford's dream was to design and manufacture an automobile for the American masses. "I am going to democratize the automobile," he declared. "When I'm through everybody will be able to afford one, and about everybody will have one."[4] In 1908, Ford introduced the sturdy, dependable Model T, a four-cylinder, 20-horsepower automobile that sold for $850. His Model T was the first car designed for a mass market, and over the next 19 years, his company produced more than 15 million of these "Tin Lizzies."

In 1909, the Ford Motor Company produced more than 12,000 Model Ts, but the factory still struggled to keep pace with the flood of orders. So Ford and his engineers experimented with more efficient methods of mass production at the company's 65-acre Highland Park Plant near Detroit, Michigan. In 1913, Ford incorporated "scientific management" techniques into his production line, creating a system based on interchangeable parts and a division of labor in which each employee repeatedly performed only small, simple tasks that minimized time and effort. Ford also installed new, more efficient equipment, including moving assembly lines, which allowed the chassis and other automobile parts to flow continuously from one station to the next through the factory. These new methods of mass production, which became known as "Fordism," dramatically reduced the time and cost of producing automobiles.

In 1913, the Ford Motor Company was able to produce more than 182,000 Model T cars. Three years later, annual production approached 580,000. By 1920, half of all cars on the road were Model Ts, and a single car took only an hour and a half to build from start to finish, as opposed to the 14 hours it took in 1913.[5]

Ford's mass production methods revolutionized the automobile industry and transformed his company into the largest automobile manufacturer in the world. Ford realized that, by accepting a smaller profit margin on a larger volume of sales, he could reap enormous profits, and through his revolutionary business strategy, he was able to slash the price of his automobiles. In 1909, the Model T sold for $950, but the price steadily dropped until, in 1925, one of his new cars cost only $290.[6] As a result, middle-class and even many working-class Americans could now purchase their own Model Ts. Consequently, Ford became a national hero and one of the most celebrated men in 1920s America.

The Automobile Industry

As other car companies copied Ford's efficient methods of mass production, automobile manufacturing grew into one of the nation's largest and most important industries. In 1920, slightly more than 100 automobile manufacturing companies crowded the U.S. market, but the so-called "Big Three" of Ford, General Motors, and Chrysler accounted for more than 70 percent of all of new car sales. Unlike Ford, whose enormous success rested upon the utilitarian Model T, other U.S. manufacturers concentrated on producing more modern, luxurious automobiles that offered an array of newfangled accessories such as self-starters, fuel gauges, and car radios (available as early as 1923). By 1927, General Motors was producing 72 different models of Cadillacs, Buicks, and Chevrolets, each of which could be purchased with an assortment of useful features and in a wide selection of eye-catching colors. Smaller companies, such as Packard, Reo, Nash, Pierce-Arrow, and Hudson, also commanded a respectable share of the market by providing expensive, high-quality automobiles to wealthier drivers. As the automobile market became saturated, though, many smaller companies went bankrupt or merged with larger corporations. Although the number of manufacturers had fallen to only 44 by 1929, annual automobile production reached 5.3 million in the United States—a figure not surpassed for another 20 years.[7]

Automobile manufacturers generated enormous sales during the 1920s through a brilliant marketing strategy of planned obsolescence, sophisticated advertising, and seductive installment plans. Manufacturers unveiled a new line of automobile models each year, in order to encourage consumers to trade in their old cars and purchase newer ones that were faster, offered more options, and, above all, incorporated the most modern designs available. The automobile companies poured millions of dollars into mass-circulation magazine and newspaper advertisements to promote their newest models. Ads not only highlighted the technical aspects and special features of a particular car but also emphasized such intangibles as the pleasures of driving, the spirit of adventure, and the freedoms that automobiles offered. For example, the famous "Somewhere West of Laramie" campaign, introduced in 1926 to advertise the Jordan Playboy sports car, appealed to female consumers by using romantic imagery of the liberated woman and the American West. Affordable credit plans also encouraged consumers to purchase automobiles, even if they could not pay in cash. Ford and General Motors financed their own car sales, while smaller companies engaged independent finance companies and banks to provide credit to their customers. As a result of such easy-term financing, 75 percent of all automobile sales by 1925 were purchased on deferred-payment credit plans.

The Ford Motor Company continued to dominate the auto industry during the early 1920s, but, facing fierce competition from other firms, its share of the market slipped in the mid-1920s. While General Motors and other companies designed new car models every year, Ford stubbornly refused to revamp his aging Tin Lizzie, which had remained virtually unchanged since 1908. Many consumers chose to purchase secondhand Chevrolets, which were more stylish and comfortable, for a few hundred dollars more rather than purchase a new Model T. In 1927, as a result of slumping sales, Ford introduced a new automobile, the Model A, which proved to be a great success. Nevertheless, General Motors overtook the Ford Motor Company as the leader of the automobile industry in the late 1920s.

Automobiles and American Prosperity

Automobile production played a significant role in fueling the nation's booming economy by stimulating the growth and development of a network of related industries, including steel, petroleum, glass, and rubber manufacturing. Throughout the 1920s, motorists consumed approximately 90 percent of the nation's gasoline and petroleum products, and automobile manufacturers used 80 percent of the rubber, 75 percent of the plate glass, and 20 percent of the steel.[8] Tractors and motorized trucks, an offshoot of the automobile industry, revolutionized agriculture. The number of gasoline-powered tractors in use in the United States jumped from 246,000 in 1920 to 920,000 in 1930, and the expanded use of motorized farming equipment dramatically boosted the nation's agricultural production.[9]

Soaring automobile sales also accelerated the expansion and development of America's highways, and government spending on massive road-building projects pumped tens of millions of dollars into the American economy during the 1920s. Since the first decade of the twentieth century, automobile clubs and trucking companies had lobbied federal and state governments to build better roads. In 1921, Congress passed the Federal Highway Act, which provided the states with matching federal funds in order to finance the construction of a national network of two-lane, hard-surface roads. By 1927, the national highway system totaled more than 96,000 miles, and several transcontinental highways bisected the nation, including U.S. Route 30, which stretched from Atlantic City, New Jersey, to Astoria, Oregon, and U.S. Route 66, known as "the Main Street of America," which ran from Chicago to Santa Monica, California. Automobile travel also stimulated the construction of bridges, tunnels, bypasses, and other structures designed to improve the flow of traffic on the nation's roadways. For example, the Holland Tunnel, an 8,558-foot automobile thoroughfare that ran under the Hudson River and connected New York and New Jersey, opened in 1927. On its first day, more than 51,000 motorists paid the 50-cent toll to pass through what was then the world's longest underwater tunnel.

Meanwhile, an entire roadside service industry of filling stations, garages, camping grounds, motels, and restaurants sprang up across the nation to serve the needs of motorists. Between 1921 and 1929, for example, the number of drive-in gas stations ballooned from 12,000 to 143,000.[10] Other commercial businesses also emerged that catered to American motorists. The American Automobile Association (AAA), founded in 1902, was supplying its members with road maps and touring information as early as 1907, and, beginning in 1915, the organization provided emergency roadside assistance to stranded motorists. *American Motorist* (AAA's official magazine), *Motor Camper and Tourist*, and other auto-related magazines published articles and advertisements about engine maintenance, driving tours, auto-camping, and other related topics. Insurance companies began selling auto insurance policies, and in 1927, Massachusetts became the first state to pass a law requiring all drivers to carry car insurance. Automobile rental companies, which emerged around World War I, catered to traveling salesmen and to those who could not afford to buy their own automobile. In 1923, John D. Hertz, the owner of a Chicago taxicab company, established the Hertz Drive-Ur-Self Company, the forerunner of Hertz Rent-a-Car.

On the downside, automobiles created a perplexing array of unanticipated consequences. Traffic jams, parking problems, and speeding tickets became common annoyances. Increased levels of congestion, noise, and air pollution plagued city dwellers. Automobile travel also contributed to the destruction of the rural countryside, as motorists tossed tin cans and trash along the roads, and gaudy billboards and

The Red Hat gasoline station, Columbia, Missouri. Courtesy of the State Historical Society of Missouri, Columbia.

roadway businesses diminished the natural scenic beauty of the countryside. In 1928, Kenneth Roberts provided this description of a stretch of U.S. 1 in Maine: "The road inland from Bar Harbor to Bangor, which winds through magnificent forests, past lakes and rolling mountains and little old New England farmhouses, is decorated with steadily increasing reminders to ask for Magooslum's Maine-Made Mayonnaise, Smoke Oakum Cigars, and vote for Muddle for Sheriff, to say nothing of using B. O. tobacco, visiting Fuss' overnight camps, buying a nice pair of four-dollar shoes from Buzzard's, picking up a Boston bag at Roorback-Skillet Company's Bangor store and attending a Lion's meeting while in the city."[11] The rapidly increasing number of cars on the road brought about a tragic upsurge in motor vehicle accidents. The death toll from automobile accidents reached 32,900 (most of them pedestrians) in 1930 alone.[12]

Automobiles and American Life

Mass ownership of automobiles dramatically transformed everyday life during the 1920s by providing Americans with greater mobility and spurring the expansion and development of middle-class suburbs. Many businessmen and other white-collar professionals chose to reside in the suburbs, away from downtown congestion, and commute each day to work. Shopping centers that catered to these suburban families also sprang up; the nation's first such suburban shopping center, Country Club Plaza, opened in Kansas City, Missouri, in 1923. Motor vehicles broke down the isolation of rural life, enabling farm families to make frequent trips to town in order to shop, visit relatives, or take in a picture show. As they did, many of the nation's rural crossroad stores, churches, and one-room schoolhouses vanished, unable to compete with the attractions of town.

Automobiles created new leisure activities for middle-class Americans. Cars made it possible to travel long distances relatively easily (by 1925, for example, motorists could cover about 200 miles in an average day), and unlike railroads, automobiles allowed travelers to determine their own departure times, routes, and rates of speed. On weekends, families motored into the countryside to go camping, picnicking, sightseeing, or visiting. Family automobile vacations, unknown only a few decades earlier, became a common facet of middle-class American life. Young Americans used automobiles to escape parental authority, especially when it came to dating and courtship. As a result, dating moved, as the title of one historical study put it, "from the front porch to the back seat."[13] Driving around for the sheer pleasure of it, called "joy-riding," became a popular pastime. Originally, though, driving was strictly a fair-weather pursuit, since most automobiles were open-topped touring cars. But beginning in 1923, when sales of closed cars surpassed those of open-tops, driving became a year-round, though often cold and drafty, activity.

For millions of Americans, automobiles represented the new freedoms of the modern age, but for many others, they came to symbolize the nation's crumbling moral standards. During the 1920s, conservative politicians, religious leaders, and social workers condemned the automobile for eroding the cohesion of American families and morally corrupting the nation's youth. Automobiles bred fears about increased rates of premarital sexual activity among young people, since many believed, as one juvenile court judge put it, that the car was fast becoming "a house of prostitution on wheels."[14] Ministers also thundered about "the desecration of the Sabbath," as some members of their congregations went out for Sunday drives rather than attend church services. Most middle-class Americans, however, had become too attached to their automobiles to be swayed by such condemnatory pronouncements.

The Automobile and American Popular Culture

Beginning around 1900, automobiles regularly cropped up as the subject of songs, theater shows, motion pictures, magazines, comic strips, joke books, and children's toys. Tin Pan Alley songwriters composed hundreds of novelty numbers about automobiles, including "In My Merry Oldsmobile" (1905) and "Otto, You Ought to Take Me in Your Auto" (1905), and more than 60 popular song titles specifically mentioned Henry Ford and his Model T. Hillbilly and blues artists also contributed auto-related songs, among them Fiddlin' John Carson's "My Ford Sedan" (1929) and Frank Hutchison's "Chevrolet Six" (1929). During the 1910s and 1920s, the Model T inspired a series of joke books that poked fun at Ford's humble rattletraps. Broadway comedies such as *Six Cylinder Love* (1921) and *Nervous Wreck* (1923) featured plots that revolved around the automobile. Noted illustrator John Held Jr. immortalized flappers and their sporty roadsters in the caricatures he drew for the covers of *Life* and *Judge* magazines. Automobiles featured prominently in Hollywood motion pictures, especially gangster films and slapstick comedies. Mack Sennett's *Keystone Kops* serials, for example, depicted a troupe of bumbling policemen who chased criminals (and narrowly dodged locomotives and pedestrians) in their overloaded Ford patrol wagon. A bumper crop of children's toys, such as cast-iron cars, trucks, buses, taxicabs, and fire engines, became favorite playthings for American boys. One mechanical wind-up toy called "Pinched," advertised in the 1927 Sears, Roebuck and Company catalog, consisted of a motorist who speeds around a circular highway until a motorcycle policeman suddenly "stops him and 'pinches' him."[15] All of these cultural artifacts reflect the automobile's pervasive influence on American popular culture during the 1920s.

PUBLIC TRANSPORTATION

Buses

Bus companies, like rental car companies, emerged in the 1910s in order to serve America's growing public transportation needs. Originally, bus lines were designed to transport groups of workers over short distances. For example, in 1914, Eric Wickman began shuttling iron miners back and forth to work in his first "bus"—a seven-passenger Hupmobile—between Hibbing and Alice, Minnesota. Wickman soon commissioned the construction of more "buses"—elongated auto bodies welded onto truck frames—and hired additional drivers. In 1915, he and two partners formed the Mesaba Transportation Company in Hibbing, which went through a series of company names before becoming, in 1930, Greyhound Bus Lines—the most successful bus company in American history.

By the mid-1920s, networks of inter-city bus lines across the United States carried travelers from city to city when few other forms of public

A bus, circa 1925. Courtesy of the State Historical Society of Missouri, Columbia.

transportation were available. Local bus service also expanded, as passengers and commuters began to take buses across town or back and forth to work. Originally, most of these "buses" consisted of customized automobiles and trucks, but as the demand grew, automobile manufacturers began producing specially designed multi-passenger vehicles for mass transit. By 1925, at least 3,600 different bus companies operated more than 21,000 vehicles across nearly a quarter of a million miles of America's roads.[16] By 1930, an estimated 41,000 buses navigated the nation's roadways. For a one-way fare of $72, passengers in 1928 could actually travel by bus from Los Angeles to New York, stopping at 132 towns during the grueling five-and-a-half day trip. Although buses proved popular among business travelers, factory workers, and lower-income families who did not own their own cars, buses did not appeal widely to tourists, who much preferred driving their own cars or taking trains. Well-to-do travelers did make one exception when it came to bus travel: sightseeing trips. Tourists visiting new locales often indulged in scenic bus rides, glad to let the driver negotiate what was, for them, unfamiliar terrain, while they relaxed and enjoyed the sights.

Taxicabs

An important spin-off of the automobile industry, at least in urban areas, was the taxicab business. Of course, vehicles-for-hire had been available since the days of horse-drawn hacks and jitneys, but the advent of gasoline-powered motor vehicles led to the dramatic expansion of the taxicab industry, and thousands of independent owners and operators pressed their private autos into makeshift service as cabs during the 1910s and 1920s. Major automobile manufacturers also recognized the potential profits to be earned through taxi fares, and by the 1920s, Ford and General Motors operated extensive fleets of taxicabs in major urban centers across the United States. In 1915, two Chicago businessmen named Walden W. Shaw and John D. Hertz formed the Yellow Cab Company, the nation's largest and oldest taxicab company. This pioneering company operated specially designed taxis that were painted bright yellow in order to make them stand out on busy streets. A Russian immigrant named Morris Markin likewise adopted this strategy when, in 1922, he founded the Checkered Cab Manufacturing Company in Kalamazoo, Michigan. Soon, his distinctive yellow and black taxis became common sights on the streets of many American cities.

Streetcars

Since the 1890s, urban dwellers had relied heavily on public streetcars to transport them around their cities. In 1917, 80,000 electric trolleys traversed 45,000 miles of track in cities and towns nationwide, carrying riders to work, ballparks, department stores, amusement parks, and virtually anywhere else they cared to go. Streetcars were an affordable means of mass transit, and factory workers and other low-wage employees especially depended upon them for their daily commutes. By 1923, however, ridership had begun to dwindle. Most cities failed to give streetcars the right-of-way over private cars, and the hundreds of autos that drove onto the trolley tracks slowed streetcar service and frustrated passengers. Others abandoned trolleys to ride subways (in major metropolitan areas such as New York and Boston) or city buses, which offered more flexible service than trolleys. As the automobile reached new heights of popularity and affordability, more and more middle-class Americans preferred to drive their own cars rather than take streetcars. Although trolleys continued to service metropolitan areas, their popularity waned throughout the 1920s.

VACATIONS

Vacations were nothing new in the 1920s, especially for members of the upper and middle classes, but the sheer number of Americans who vacationed rose considerably during the decade. One-day excursions to amusements parks, the seashore, or the countryside were common recreational activities, but vacations of a week or more, spent either at a single location or touring about in an automobile, became increasingly frequent. Chambers of commerce, tourism agencies, travel brochures, billboards, and advertisements trumpeted the beautiful beaches of Florida, the excitement of Atlantic City, the awe-inspiring majesty of the Grand Canyon, and the restfulness and fun visitors could experience at countless other destinations. Americans eagerly packed their bags and ventured to new places, thrilled to see new sights and experience, for a few days, a break from their everyday routines.

Of course, vacationing depended largely on two factors: sufficient time off from work to make a trip feasible and enough disposable income to spend on travel, accommodations, and other related expenses. These two factors were within reach of many salaried middle-class employees in the 1920s, who increasingly enjoyed the benefits of short paid vacations. By the end of the decade, an estimated 80 percent of white-collar workers received at least some paid vacation time from their employers. By most standards, these treasured vacation days led to modest journeys, for few middle-class Americans had the means to take steamship cruises to Europe or other faraway locales. Rather, they spent their vacations taking inexpensive trips, such as visiting relatives, fishing, camping, or touring a portion of the United States. Owning a car meant that one could "see the world" at one's own pace, and taking along picnic meals, tents, and camping gear made such simple trips both enjoyable and affordable.

While paid vacations became increasingly common among middle-class Americans, the same benefits were seldom extended to the working classes. In large part, this bias evolved from the notion that industrial workers did not "need" vacations, since only those who worked with their minds, not their muscles, suffered the sort of mental strain and emotional tension that vacations could alleviate. Men employed in automobile factories, textile mills, or meatpacking plants could rest on Sundays and, went this logic, feel refreshed again by Monday morning. Furthermore, blue-collar wage earners seldom actually worked for a solid year, owing largely to work stoppages or layoffs during slow seasons. Thus, employers believed that their workers already enjoyed plenty of time off (though this was, of course, at the employees' own expense and through no expressed desire of their own).

Not surprisingly, working-class Americans seldom had either the financial resources or the time to take extended vacations. Their families depended too much on every paycheck, and the great majority of factories, mines, and mills did not provide paid vacations to their laborers. Thus, the working classes spent their leisure hours on more local pursuits. Men might join fraternal organizations, attend prizefights or cockfights, or watch baseball games. Husbands and wives might go to the movies, a dance hall, or a vaudeville show, and whole families might spend a weekend afternoon picnicking, going to an amusement park, or swimming at a public beach. For the most part, vacationing remained beyond the reach of industrial laborers and their families.

A small minority of blue-collar workers, however, did enjoy paid vacations during the 1920s. One study revealed that in 1930, as many as 10 percent of wage earners received paid vacation time from their employers.[17] A few progressive business owners realized that providing paid vacations to their employees increased efficiency, promoted loyalty, reduced turnover, and boosted morale. Many of the companies that furnished paid time off made certain to guide their employees in choosing the "best" vacations, since idle workers with money in their pockets, employers feared, might drink and carouse the whole time and return to work exhausted and in ill health. Thus, many companies aggressively encouraged camping trips and other low-cost, outdoor vacations where, presumably, workers could get into less trouble. Some firms even established their own summer camps, where workers could vacation for little or no money and at the same time be supervised by company-employed recreational directors and social workers.

Auto-camping

Since the mid-1910s, "auto-camping," as it was known, appealed to millions of Americans as an enjoyable way to escape the daily pressures of modern life. Camping provided opportunities for outdoor adventure and communing with nature, and, after the initial outlay for a tent and other equipment, it was a comparatively inexpensive pastime. During the 1920s, a flood of auto-camping accounts and guides—including Elon Jessup's *The Motor Camping Book* (1921), Melville Ferguson's *Motor Camping on Western Trails* (1925), and Frederic F. Van de Water's *The Family Flivvers to Frisco* (1927)—inspired hundreds of thousands of families to pursue this form of recreation. Even President Warren G. Harding took a break from his political duties to join avid outdoorsmen Henry Ford, Thomas A. Edison, and Harvey Firestone on a highly publicized camping trip in 1921.

Since the earliest days of auto-camping, motorists had customized their cars and trucks by adding sleeping compartments and other gadgets to outfit them for outdoor living. During the mid-1910s and 1920s, specialized camping trailers appeared on the market, such as the Automobile Telescope Touring Apartment, first manufactured in 1916, which folded out into a bed, kitchen, and shower. Other motorists pulled trailers, or "trailer coaches," introduced in the mid-1920s, which served as both sleeping and cooking quarters. These trailer owners often referred to themselves as "tin can tourists," a nickname that had originally been applied to all campers because of the provisions they ate and the "Tin Lizzies" many of them drove. Camping equipment manufacturers, such as Coleman, L. L. Bean, and Eddie Bauer, also produced extensive lines of collapsible beds, portable stoves, folding chairs, ice chests, and other outdoor gear designed to make life on the road more comfortable.

Originally, motorists simply pitched tents and set up campsites along the roadside, often without obtaining the permission of the property owner. But by 1920, cities and towns along well-traveled tourist routes had begun to establish municipal camping grounds to capture tourist dollars and, at the same time, to prevent campers from damaging private property. These campgrounds, which were funded by local taxes, were open to all travelers, and the better ones offered free access to toilets and showers, electric lights, firewood, potable water, and a community kitchen. One of the most famous was called Overland Park in Denver, Colorado, a 160-acre, 800-campsite facility located on the shores of the Platte River. Along with the standard facilities, it boasted many additional amenities (all of which came with a price tag), such as a community clubhouse, restaurant, grocery store, barbershop, gas station and garage, dance hall, laundry, movie theater, and children's playground. By 1925, however, many of these municipal campgrounds began to charge entrance and registration fees, as well as to impose stricter regulations and time limits, in order to discourage "undesirable" hoboes and transients from squatting at these campsites.

As the number of free municipal campgrounds dwindled, small entrepreneurs began to establish private campgrounds that charged entrance fees, called auto-camps, many of which went by homey, unpretentious names such as "U Wanna Kum Back" and "Dew Drop Inn." Another offshoot of campgrounds, cabin camps rented small, sparsely furnished cabins to travelers so they did not have to contend with pitching tents and camping outdoors. Although the cabins at many of these roadside businesses were little more than shacks, some of the better facilities featured clean, comfortable buildings and the additional amenities of community rest rooms and showers, gasoline stations, grocery stores, lunch counters, and recreation halls. Most of these roadside cabin camps were located in the South and Southwest, where the warm climate made tourism a year-round industry. Although hotels continued to accommodate most travelers and tourists, cabin camps attracted tens of thousands of visitors each year who desired something cheaper than a hotel and more comfortable than a campsite.

Motels

Like auto-camps and cabin camps, motels first emerged as a thrifty alternative to hotels. Although motels date to at least the 1910s, the first to use the term was the Milestone Mo-Tel, which opened in San Luis Obispo, California, in 1925. Soon *motel* became a generic term to describe a wide variety of roadside accommodations. As opposed to hotels, which were located in downtown urban centers or at country resorts, motels consisted of a number of small cottages clustered around a main office building. Roadside motels catered to middle-class families who chose affordability and convenience over luxury. Motels did not generally feature a main lobby area, so road-weary tourists had no fear of looking unpresentable in front of other guests. Motel patrons carried their own bags in from the car, so there was no need to tip a bellboy. And since few motels offered room service, families could feel free to eat their picnic meals in the privacy of their own room or perhaps drive to an affordable roadside eatery. By 1928, there were an estimated 3,000 motels across the nation, a figure that climbed to almost 10,000 by 1935.[18] The late 1920s also marked the advent of commercial motel chains in the United States. One early motel chain, the Alamo Plaza Tourist Court, opened its first outlet in Waco, Texas, in 1929. That same year, the Pierce Petroleum Corporation built a chain of five 40-room hotels in the Midwest along U.S. Route 66.

TRAVEL DESTINATIONS

Resort cities and towns—including Atlantic City, New Jersey; Newport, Rhode Island; Mackinac Island, Michigan; Palm Beach, Florida; and Niagara Falls, New York—lured millions of vacationers to their hotels, beaches, and boardwalks each year. Resorts provided vacationers plenty of opportunities to loaf and relax as well as to swim, sunbathe, gamble, hunt, fish, dance, play tennis or other sports, listen to band concerts, and walk around looking at the scenery and, of course, the other guests. Racial segregation, anti-Semitism, and other forms of prejudice, however, prevented members of certain minority groups from staying at these desirable vacation spots. Some African Americans responded to this lack of accessibility by opening their own hotels, boardinghouses, and restaurants in established resort areas and then catering to a black middle-class clientele. Others, unwilling to risk unpleasant confrontations, frequented separate vacation destinations altogether. Black seaside resorts sprang up, for example, in Wilmington, North Carolina; Martha's Vineyard, Massachusetts; Sag Harbor, New York; and Highland Beach, Virginia. Jewish vacationers, also unwelcome at many resorts, established their own vacation getaways in the Catskill Mountains of New York and the Poconos of Pennsylvania. Despite the increasing overall numbers of vacationers, the 1920s saw little racial integration at the exclusive resorts.

While resorts appealed to those vacationers who could afford them,

An automobile driving along a mountain road. Courtesy of the State Historical Society of Missouri, Columbia.

far more Americans chose to "rough it" in the fresh air and scenic beauty of the nation's less-populated areas. For many, this involved a trek to one of the western national parks. In 1916, President Woodrow Wilson signed a bill creating the National Park Service, a division of the Department of the Interior, which was charged with the dual mission of conserving the natural resources and beauty of the nation's parks and, at the same time, providing ways for travelers to enjoy these protected public lands. Under this mandate, the Park Service authorized the limited construction of roadways and hotel accommodations within the boundaries of national parks. A vigorous publicity campaign followed, encouraging visitors to travel, by car or by train, to such stunning and unspoiled destinations as Yellowstone National Park (Wyoming), Yosemite National Park (California), Grand Canyon National Park (Arizona), and Glacier National Park (Montana). In 1917, approximately 55,000 automobiles entered the national parks, but by 1926 that number had mushroomed to 400,000.[19] Railways also accommodated thousands of guests seeking respite in the western national parks. For example, between 1921 and 1925, the Yosemite Valley Railroad sold an average of 20,000 tickets annually, and by 1930, five different railroads carried passengers into Yellowstone National Park. Some well-to-do visitors stayed in hotels and inns inside the parks, but the vast majority pitched their tents in designated campgrounds. Conservationists feared the imminent and perhaps permanent destruction of these protected areas, due to the parks' increasing commercialization and subsequent overuse by hundreds of thousands of tourists, but carefully designed networks of roads and buildings did protect and conserve most of these wild public lands.

For those who sought an attractive destination in the East, Florida offered vacationers beautiful beaches, sunny weather, and plenty of amusements. Despite devastating hurricanes and the infamous Florida land boom and bust of the early 1920s, the tourist industry still successfully touted the state as a tropical playground. By 1925, more than a half-million tourists each year motored to Florida, and resorts in Miami Beach, Sarasota, Coral Gables, and Key West attracted visitors from all over the United States. These resort cities boasted luxurious hotels, exclusive shopping districts, and extensive opportunities for golfing, boating, fishing, tennis, and other forms of outdoor recreation. Furthermore, the lenient attitude toward drinking and gambling that prevailed in these resort communities convinced many fun-loving tourists that they had discovered the perfect vacation destination.

TRAIN TRAVEL

Since at least the 1880s, locomotives had formed the principal means of long-distance transportation in the United States, and they remained so until automobiles and trucks eclipsed them in the mid-1920s. In 1920, trains were still the preferred means of inter-city passenger travel and, equally important, the primary method of hauling freight. A transcontinental rail line had existed since 1869, and by 1900 trains reached nearly every sizable city in the nation, with more than 190,000 miles of track in use. Train travel in the United States peaked in 1920, when a record 1.2 billion passengers purchased rail tickets.

Railroad company advertisements stressed the fine amenities and services that they provided their passengers. Dining cars allowed travelers to relax, socialize, and watch the scenery, all the while enjoying an exquisite menu that rivaled those of the nation's best hotels and restaurants. Smoking lounges, hair salons, café cars, and observation cars helped passengers to while away the long hours of an extended journey. Sleeper cars, most of which were owned and operated by the Pullman Company, offered guests private quarters attended by conscientious porters, but such comforts were reserved for first-class passengers only. For coach-class passengers, traveling by train during the 1920s could be hot and dirty, particularly during the summer months, since air-conditioning was nonexistent on parlor cars and dirt and cinders inevitably blew through open windows. Coach passengers could not always access dining cars, and therefore had to pack their own box lunches, eat at depots when the train stopped, or rely on the vendors who walked the train cars selling candy, cigarettes, and sandwiches. Despite the undeniable convenience of train travel, it was not necessarily comfortable, and a cross-country train trip could take a week or even longer.

By 1920, locomotives had become such an integral part of the nation's transportation industry that few could have predicted that the railroad industry would suffer such a steep decline. By 1929, though, the popularity of automobiles had drastically reduced the number of passengers opting for rail travel (by then, private automobiles carried five times as many passengers as did trains).[20] While some long-distance travelers still preferred the ease and convenience of the train, others chose to stay in control of their departure time, route, and rate of travel by driving themselves. Motor vehicles also siphoned off some of the railroad's lucrative shipping trade. While trains did transport millions of new automobiles to dealerships nationwide, thus adding to their collective freight, over-the-road trucking quickly captured a considerable segment of the shipping industry that the railroads had dominated, unchallenged, for almost half a century.

OCEAN TRAVEL

For American tourists, the only way to reach Europe during the 1920s was to book passage on an ocean liner. The world's great steamships symbolized glamour, luxury, and high-seas adventure, and during the Jazz Age, Henry Ford, Charlie Chaplin, F. Scott Fitzgerald, and dozens of other famous millionaires, politicians, and celebrities sailed to Europe in high style and elegance on these grand floating palaces. And for the millions of European immigrants who crowded onto them between the 1890s and the 1920s, these ships came to represent the opportunity to build better lives in the United States.

After the end of World War I, the demand for transatlantic passenger service grew as the British Isles and continental Europe once again opened to American tourism. During the 1920s, approximately 80 companies operated dozens of ships that provided weekly express service between New York harbor and various European ports. Among the great North Atlantic liners of the decade were Cunard Line's *Aquitania*, White Star Line's *Leviathan*, the North German Lloyd Line's *Bremen*, and the French Line's *Île de France*. These mammoth ships sometimes approached 1,000 feet in length and topped 50,000 gross tons. Large ocean liners could carry as many as 3,350 passengers, the majority of whom were booked in third- and fourth-class accommodations. Averaging speeds of around 27 knots, the fastest of these powerful ships could make a transatlantic crossing in four or five days.

The great ocean liners such as the *Aquitania* and the *Île de France* transported first-class passengers across the North Atlantic in state-of-the-art comfort, elegance, and opulence. On most such ships, as much as three-quarters of the onboard space was reserved for some 700 first-class passengers. Wealthy travelers enjoyed world-class dining, well-appointed staterooms, and quality recreation and entertainment, including playing golf, ballroom dancing, soaking in the spa, or working out in the gymnasium. An enormous service staff of physicians, nurses, activities directors, chefs, waiters, valets, maids, tailors, and shoeshine boys catered to a first-class passenger's every need.

Most steamship passengers, however, could not afford first-class travel. Rather, they purchased far more affordable third- and fourth-class tickets that provided just basic accommodations. These passengers occupied less desirable cabins in the bowels of the ship, and sometimes as many as 2,700 steerage passengers would be crowded into as little as one-fifth of the ship's entire space. But because the United States severely restricted immigration during the 1920s, the number of steerage tickets sold on ocean liners dropped dramatically. In response to this reduction in immigrant fares, foreign shipping lines sought to appeal to middle-class American passengers by creating economical "cabin-class" and "tourist-class" rates. Shipping lines recruited some of best graphic artists and illustrators to promote steamship travel through modern, stylish advertising materials. These colorful posters, magazine advertisements, and brochures did succeed in enticing well-off Americans to travel to France, Italy, Spain, England, and other European nations. Of course, sailing aboard ocean liners was an experience largely reserved for the upper classes, who could spend several weeks or months touring various Old World destinations. Some middle-class travelers did splurge on a once-in-a-lifetime "grand tour" of Europe, often to celebrate a honeymoon, wedding anniversary, college graduation, or retirement, but transatlantic travel remained quite uncommon among ordinary Americans.

AIR TRAVEL

During World War I, American aircraft technology developed rapidly, as a result of the use of planes for combat and reconnaissance, but after the war ended, anyone with a few hundred dollars could purchase and then fly (or try to fly) a surplus military biplane. At the time no regulatory system existed to oversee U.S. aviation—no examinations or licenses for pilots, no safety certificates for the planes themselves. Ex-fighter pilots (and more than a few self-taught fliers) bought these discarded planes, fixed them up, and made a little money by barnstorming from town to town, thrilling county fairgoers at air shows by offering $5 rides and performing daredevil stunts such as flying upside down and "barrel-rolling" in midair. These stunt flights were made even more spectacular by the death-defying feats of "wing-walkers" who, standing on the wings of a biplane in flight, hit golf balls, turned cartwheels, or even parachuted safely to the ground. Between county fairs, self-employed pilots often took odd jobs crop dusting, skywriting, assisting with aerial mapping, ferrying passengers short distances, or even smuggling illegal liquor. Full-fledged commercial airlines, with regular routes, schedules, and employees, did not yet exist, and as one underemployed flier wryly commented, the most dangerous aspect of being a professional pilot in the early 1920s was "the risk of starving to death."[21]

The earliest commercial passenger airlines used seaplanes, outfitted with pontoon landing gear, to ferry tourists between coastal resort towns. Because seaplanes flew low over the water and could land at any time, they were commonly considered safer than regular planes. One of the first air passenger services was established in 1914 to shuttle tourists between St. Petersburg and Tampa, Florida. Other passenger airlines soon inaugurated short-distance service between New York and Atlantic City, Chicago and Detroit, Miami and Nassau, and Key West and Havana, delighting tourists eager to experience the novelty of flight. Most of these companies were only seasonal operations, and, since most biplanes could accommodate only one passenger at a time, they failed to be very profitable.

Airmail

During the late 1910s and early 1920s, the fledgling aviation industry received an enormous boost from the U.S. Post Office. In 1918, army

Charles Lindbergh standing next to his plane, *Spirit of St. Louis*. Courtesy of the State Historical Society of Missouri, Columbia.

pilots began flying daily airmail service between New York City, Philadelphia, and Washington, D.C., and, two years later, the Post Office initiated coast-to-coast airmail service. However, the use of planes did little to accelerate mail delivery, since pilots could fly only during daylight hours, and just a tiny percentage of mail made it off the trains and onto planes in the first place. But as the Post Office developed more airfields, better routes, lighted runways, minimum pilot standards, and regular aircraft inspections, the nation's aviation system improved dramatically. By 1924, airmail could travel from New York to San Francisco in just over 29 hours—an astonishing feat.

The increasing efficiency of American aviation worried the powerful railroad owners, who generated millions of dollars in revenue by transporting mail on trains. In 1925, Congress passed the Air Mail Act, introduced by Representative Clyde Kelly, a Pennsylvania Republican who represented the special interests of the railroads. This piece of legislation, also known as the Kelly Act, required the Post Office to cut the army out of the airmail business by allowing only private airline companies (which could be owned by the railroads) to bid for airmail contracts.

These competitive contracts essentially subsidized the commercial aviation industry and made carrying the mail profitable enough to allow airlines to grow and expand. In 1926, the first privately contracted planes began carrying mail, and the following year, the government relinquished all airmail responsibilities to these private contractors. That year, aviation companies such as Boeing Air Transport, National Air Transport, and even the Ford Motor Company began to carry cargo as well as to offer a few regularly scheduled passenger seats aboard their mail planes.

The passage of the Air Commerce Act of 1926 also benefited commercial airlines. This act compelled the Department of Commerce to oversee a system of federal regulation that required pilots and crew members to pass certifying examinations, aircraft to be inspected regularly and issued registration numbers, and air traffic rules to be enforced. The Department of Commerce was also charged with investigating accidents, producing aerial maps, and constructing more lighted airstrips. All of these changes helped to professionalize further the civilian aviation industry and, subsequently, to reduce the number of aircraft accidents. They also made shipping cargo increasingly lucrative for airlines, but full-blown passenger travel was not yet economically feasible. In 1926, only 5,800 passengers traveled by air, compared to the nearly 1 billion who traveled by rail.[22]

Charles Lindbergh

Although airline passenger service was extremely limited until the late 1920s, the commercial aviation industry received an enormous boost from Charles A. Lindbergh's historic 1927 transatlantic flight, a feat as awe-inspiring, at the time, as was the astronauts' moon landing in 1969. In 1919, a French hotelier offered a $25,000 prize to the first pilot or team of pilots who could complete a non-stop transatlantic flight between the United States and France. Several aviators attempted to claim the prize, including four groups in 1927 alone, but each flight ended in disappointment or disaster, including the deaths of at least six pilots. In 1927, a former barnstormer and airmail pilot named Charles A. Lindbergh made his bid for the prize, flying solo in his single-engine monoplane, *Spirit of St. Louis*. On Friday, May 20, 1927, he taxied down the runway at Roosevelt Field on Long Island, New York. When he landed 33½ hours later at Paris' Le Bourget Aerodrome, Lindbergh could not have envisioned the mass hysteria with which the world, and particularly the United States, would celebrate his unforgettable achievement. A shy, introverted Minnesotan who dreaded the glare of the media spotlight, Lindbergh was shocked and dismayed to find that his flight had catapulted him to a level of unsurpassed international celebrity. President Calvin Coolidge dispatched the navy cruiser *USS Memphis* to retrieve the nation's newly minted hero, and upon his return, 4 million fans turned out for a ticker-tape parade in New York City to celebrate his accomplishment. Literally overnight Lindbergh, the unknown pilot, became "Lucky Lindy," the national hero.

More than any other figure of the 1920s, Lindbergh became an object of American hero worship. Interestingly, though, his celebrity arose from two separate but equally compelling ideas about what his historic flight actually meant. First, Lindbergh embodied the courageous individualism and pioneer spirit that many Americans associated with the founding and settlement of the United States. That he had flown across the Atlantic *alone* seemed, to many observers, the most compelling element of his story. For them, his feat conclusively demonstrated that even in an increasingly bureaucratic and mechanized modern age, the individual human spirit could still triumph. Second, and somewhat paradoxically, for many Americans Lindbergh symbolized all the wonders and progress of the Machine Age. He and his airplane together represented the pinnacle of the nation's achievements in science and technology. President Coolidge himself congratulated Lindbergh for flying a plane constructed of materials and parts produced by more than 100 different companies, as if to acknowledge that the *Spirit of St. Louis* itself was the result of the research, development, and labor of countless industrious American engineers and workers.

The Rise of Commercial Airlines

After Lindbergh's historic achievement, the possibilities of flight captured the American imagination like never before. Huge audiences continued to attend air shows to gasp at the spectacular acrobatic feats of stunt pilots and wing walkers. Tens of thousands of children unwrapped model airplanes and toy gliders around the Christmas tree. Suddenly, ordinary Americans wanted to experience flight for themselves. The commercial airline industry, happy to accommodate, purchased fleets of larger, more powerful planes and expanded their passenger services and routes. In 1926, American aircraft manufacturers, including Boeing, Ryan, Curtiss-Wright, and even Ford, had produced a collective total of only about 1,000 airplanes, but in 1929 that figure reached 6,200. Meanwhile, the number of airline passengers soared from 5,800 in 1926 to 417,000 in 1930.[23] By 1929, airline passengers could travel coast-to-coast by flying during the day and riding trains at night (night flight was still deemed unsafe for passenger planes). For around $400, for example, a traveler could purchase a ticket on the transcontinental "Lindbergh Line"—an exhausting two-day adventure that required passengers to ride from New York to Ohio aboard a sleeper train, then in the morning

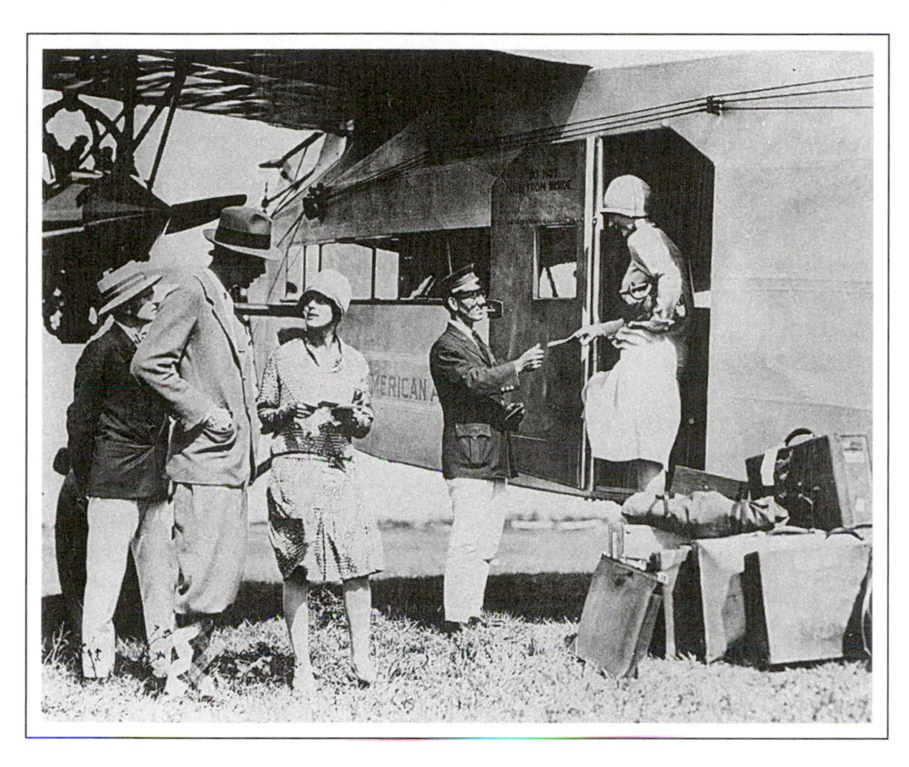

Passengers boarding a Pan-American airplane, circa 1928. Courtesy of the Archives and Special Collections, University of Miami Library, Coral Gables, Florida.

board a Ford Tri-Motor monoplane and fly to Oklahoma, then board another overnight train to New Mexico, and then the next day fly to Los Angeles. Dozens of small carriers, operating only a few planes each, flew thousands of passengers along much shorter routes. Through a series of mergers and acquisitions, though, four major carriers emerged by the end of the 1920s to dominate long-distance air travel: American Airways, Eastern Air Lines, United Airlines, and Transcontinental and Western Air (later Trans-World Airlines). A fifth, Pan-American, was the only American airline to win contracts for mail routes between the United States and Mexico, Central America, and the Caribbean. By 1930, Pan-Am served 20 countries and ranked as the largest commercial airline in the world.

Air travel in the 1920s was, in most cases, far from luxurious. Airplane engines and propellers were irritatingly noisy, flights were often bumpy, and long trips left travelers stiff and sore. Cabins were neither pressurized nor heated, so flying at high altitudes meant passengers endured freezing temperatures, and flying too high for too long caused many passengers to faint. Many suffered terrible airsickness, and while some opened the windows and stuck their heads out to vomit into the skies, others simply threw up in the cabin. In fact, the industry's first flight attendants, hired by Boeing Air Transport for its regular passenger routes in 1930, were actually trained nurses. Since airmail contracts—not passenger tickets—still generated the bulk of commercial airline companies' revenues in the late 1920s, airlines did not yet offer the comfortable seats, decent meals, and other amenities that improved travel conditions for passengers in later decades.

Dirigibles

Few Americans during the 1920s actually traveled on dirigibles, but the U.S. government was intrigued by the military possibilities of these airships and experimented with them throughout the decade. The German military had successfully used lighter-than-air craft in reconnaissance missions and bombing raids during World War I, and so, hoping to follow this example, the U.S. Navy purchased its first dirigible from Great Britain in 1920. The ship promptly crashed on a test run in August 1921, killing 44 crewmen. Unfortunately, other dirigible disasters followed, including the crash of the Italian-built *Roma*, purchased by the U.S. Army in 1920, which plummeted to the ground on its maiden American flight and killed 34. Early dirigibles were filled with hydrogen, which was highly flammable and therefore extremely dangerous. To make dirigibles safer, aeronautical engineers designed aircraft that used non-flammable (but far more expensive) helium. In 1923, the U.S. Navy launched its first helium-filled dirigible, the American-built *Shenandoah*, but even replacing hydrogen with helium could not avert catastrophes. In 1925, after dozens of flights, the *Shenandoah* crashed during a thunderstorm over Ohio and killed 14 of its 43 crew members. This widely publicized tragedy inspired the composition of at least three different songs, including the most famous, "Wreck of the *Shenandoah*," which hillbilly singer Vernon Dalhart recorded in 1925. While proponents of lighter-than-air ships highlighted their quiet, smooth rides and fuel economy, the general public remained justifiably wary of these enormous airships.

A few companies, most notably the Goodyear Tire and Rubber Company, recognized the potential of the airship not as a military bomber or passenger ship but as a brilliant modern advertising vehicle. In 1925, Goodyear commissioned its first blimp, christened *The Pilgrim*—a soft-hulled, inflatable craft that differed from a dirigible, which has a rigid exterior hull. Goodyear's helium-filled blimp, with the company's name emblazoned on its side, began a tradition of airborne public relations that endures to this day. Commercial passenger travel on lighter-than-air craft would not become available in the United States until the 1930s, and even then it was accessible to only the wealthiest travelers. In 1937, the dramatic *Hindenburg* disaster, which killed 36 passengers and crewmen, in Lakehurst, New Jersey, spelled the end of dirigibles as a viable means of commercial transportation.

CONCLUSION

Some of the most revolutionary and far-reaching changes in American popular culture during the 1920s arose from the increased mobility of ordinary citizens. In previous generations, Americans had been a largely provincial people. While travel was certainly possible, most people lived and died within 20 miles of their birthplace. The rise of the automobile meant, in essence, that people were no longer bound by geography but by the limits of their own desires and pocketbooks. Of course, owning an automobile did not necessarily mean that one immediately moved away from one's hometown, but traveling—whether across town to work or across the country to faraway vacation spots—gave millions of Americans a new sense of freedom and control. The increasing popularity of vacations, too, whether to rustic campgrounds or exclusive resorts, allowed middle-class and even many working-class Americans to participate in worlds far different from their own and to see parts of the United States that they might have only read about. Countless tourists carefully pasted penny postcards, photographs, and other souvenirs into their scrapbooks, commemorating and preserving the vacation memories they would long cherish. The passion for traveling and vacationing that so gripped Americans during the 1920s continues to this day.

The 1920s

12
Visual Arts

After 1900, several artistic movements, including Cubism, Dadaism, and Surrealism, gathered momentum in Europe and eventually spread across the Atlantic to play a limited but significant role in shaping the American art world. By the 1920s, American visual arts, especially painting and sculpture, had entered the era of modernism, as evidenced by the opening of New York's Museum of Modern Art in 1929. Although many artists gravitated toward more traditional landscape, portrait, and still-life scenes, some artists created avant-garde works that attempted to capture the realities of the modern world. Of course, not every form of visual art was considered fine art. Comic strips and animated cartoons, for example, were hardly thought of as art—at least during the 1920s. Even photography was not commonly deemed a legitimate art form. While painting and sculpture remained confined to the high art world of museums and gallery exhibitions, vernacular art forms such as comic strips, magazine illustrations, and even commercial photography reached broad audiences of ordinary Americans during the 1920s.

MODERNIST MOVEMENTS

A number of European artistic movements in the early years of the twentieth century influenced American modern art during the 1920s. While few American artists actively participated in these foreign movements, in many cases those artists who were exposed to modern European art learned to see their own art (and their own world) in new ways. Cubism, perhaps the most influential artistic movement in twentieth-century art, began in France in the late 1900s and flourished throughout the 1910s and into the early 1920s. Cubist art emphasized shifting viewpoints, focused on geometric shapes (including cubes), and rendered three-dimensional objects in terms of flat, two-dimensional planes. The Dadaist movement also influenced American art of the 1920s. Rejecting conventional styles of representation, Dadaists instead sought new ways to express their ideas and shock their audiences. The Philadelphia-born artist and photographer Man Ray is the only American who played a significant role in the evolution of Dadaism, but other American artists absorbed some of the unorthodox techniques and philosophies of the movement. Surrealism, another international intellectual and artistic movement, originated in the nihilistic ideas of the Dadaists but also found inspiration in the psychoanalytic theories of Sigmund Freud and the political ideology of Karl Marx. Surrealist paintings were full of confusing, startling images and unexpected juxtapositions that seem, in some cases, to mirror an irrational, dreamlike reality or the workings of the unconscious mind. Surrealism flourished overseas, but Americans made few important contributions to this movement during the 1920s.

The most important introduction of European modernism to American audiences occurred in 1913, when the International Exhibition of Modern Art, better known as the Armory Show, was held at the 69th Regiment Armory in New York City. The exhibit, which then traveled to the Art Institute of Chicago and finally to Copley Hall in Boston, assembled more than 1,300 works of art by contemporary European and American artists and was intended both to stimulate the American art market and to introduce American audiences to influential and radical works of European modernism. Among the pieces exhibited were Impressionist, Post-Impressionist, Fauvist, and Cubist works by such artists as Henri Matisse, Marcel Duchamp, Paul Cézanne, Vincent Van Gogh, Pablo Picasso, Vasily Kandinsky, and Paul Gauguin. The approximately 300,000 people who attended the show were amazed and, in many cases, shocked by the modernist art they saw. This was not technically the first exhibit of modern art in America, but it was by far the largest in scope and significance. Despite relentless ridicule by critics and near-riots by art fans (particularly in Boston), the Armory Show reverberated in American art circles for decades to come. Modern art had arrived in America.

AMERICAN SCHOOLS OF ART

During the 1920s, many American artists, including Oscar Bluemner, Arthur Dove, Marsden Hartley, John Marin, Elie Nadelman, and Max Weber, experimented with techniques borrowed from the European modernists. However, not all American artists sought direction from their colleagues overseas. New schools of distinctly American art emerged, several of which soundly rejected the notion that Europeans had monopolized new methods of artistic expression. Rather, these American artists found in their native country the inspiration to create powerful and bold artistic styles.

The Ashcan School

Robert Henri, an innovative American painter of the 1920s who, as a young man, had studied art in Europe, founded one of the most important new schools of American art. Henri's New York art school placed him at the center of a group of urban realist painters who called themselves "the Eight." The group consisted of Henri, John Sloan, William J. Glackens, Everett Shinn, George Luks, Arthur B. Davies, Ernest Lawson, and Maurice Prendergast. Sloan, Glackens, Luks, and Shinn had formerly worked as newspaper illustrators and cartoonists, and their journalistic background served them well, for Henri encouraged his students to draw their subject matter not from idealized landscapes or romantic scenes but instead from the vibrant and colorful city life they saw around them. These painters became known as members of the "Ashcan school," a disparaging term coined by critic Holger Cahill in 1934, so named because these artists rejected classical themes in order to paint scenes of ordinary street life and working people. Art historians also refer to this group as the New York Realists, and at the time these painters were considered rebels for their unorthodox subject matter. Many of their paintings unapologetically featured slum dwellers, street urchins, prostitutes, immigrants, and vaudevillians. For the most part, Ashcan painters did not depict such lowbrow, everyday scenes for the purposes of social criticism, but rather because immigrants and street people appeared to be interesting, colorful characters. The Ashcan painters gained fame for chronicling New York City street life with bold strokes and realistic detail, and they made it clear that American painters need not look only to Europe for inspiration.

Two prominent painters closely associated with the Ashcan school were George Bellows and Edward Hopper. Bellows, who also studied under Robert Henri, is best remembered for his vivid paintings of boxing matches. Prior to 1920, boxing (or prizefighting, as it was known), was considered highly disreputable, and in most states it was actually illegal to charge admission to watch a prizefight. Bellows painted a number of boxing scenes in the 1900s and 1910s that captured the illicit, underground nature of these events. In 1923, after boxing had been legalized in New York and had actually become a fashionable mass spectator sport, the *New York Evening Journal* commissioned Bellows to paint the much-ballyhooed heavyweight championship bout between Jack Dempsey and Argentinean challenger Luis Firpo. Bellows' famous *Dempsey and*

Firpo (1924) depicted the dramatic moment in the first round of their 1923 fight at the Polo Grounds when Firpo knocked Dempsey out of the ring and onto a desk full of sportswriters (Dempsey returned to the ring and retained the heavyweight belt by knocking Firpo out in the second round). Edward Hopper, another of Robert Henri's students, launched his artistic career as an illustrator for magazines such as *Adventure* and *Scribner's*, but he hated this kind of work and longed to focus on his painting. His first one-man exhibition as a painter, in 1920, met with little acclaim, but by the mid-1920s, his reputation as an accomplished watercolorist had begun to grow. Hopper's *House by the Railroad* (1925), depicting a solitary house standing starkly alongside the railroad tracks, is now considered an American classic, and it holds the distinction of being the first painting acquired by the Museum of Modern Art. Much of Hopper's work in the 1920s was realistic and personal and had not yet taken on many of the dark and lonely qualities for which he is often remembered.

American Scene Painting

American Scene painting, another form of American realism rooted in the tradition of the Ashcan school, also found meaningful subject matter in the experience of American life. This indigenous American art movement lasted until the early 1940s, when the onset of World War II effectively brought it to an end. American Scene paintings proved to be exceptionally popular with American audiences during the 1920s and 1930s, who tended to favor realistic styles and familiar, accessible subject matter. American Scene painters captured particular moments in the lives of ordinary Americans; their works often featured rural farm scenes, small-town festivities, or big-city streetscapes. For example, watercolorist Charles Burchfield portrayed commonplace scenes of provincial America in his paintings *House of Mystery* (1924), *Scrap Iron* (1929), and *Rainy Night* (1929–1930). Other important members of this school include Reginald March, Isabel Bishop, and Alexander Brook. Although art historians often identify them as members of the Ashcan school, George Bellows and Edward Hopper are also sometimes associated with the American Scene movement. American Scene painting deeply influenced the Regionalist movement of the 1930s, spearheaded by midwestern painters Thomas Hart Benton, Grant Wood, and John Steuart Curry.

Precisionism

Precisionism, sometimes called Cubist Realism, was another American art movement that peaked during the Jazz Age. *Precisionism* is a term coined in the 1920s to describe a uniquely American painting style that emphasized sharply defined, geometric forms and flat planes. Precisionist painters composed highly structured, somewhat realistic scenes that seldom included human figures. Instead, these paintings typically depicted the skyscrapers, bridges, office buildings, and smokestacks of the modern city or the barns, farmhouses, and agricultural machinery that cluttered the rural landscape. Three of the most significant members of this school were Charles Sheeler, Charles Demuth, and Georgia O'Keeffe. Sheeler, who also became a well-known photographer, was deeply influenced by the European art movements of Cubism and Dadaism. His Precisionist works of the 1920s, including *New York* (1920), *Offices* (1922), and *Upper Deck* (1929), capture the sharp geometry he saw in the modern metropolitan streetscape. Charles Demuth, a native of Lancaster, Pennsylvania, produced a series of large paintings during the 1920s and early 1930s based on the architecture of his hometown. Also influenced by Cubism and Dadaism, Demuth rendered his distinctive industrial landscapes, including his masterpiece, *My Egypt* (1927), an oil painting of a grain elevator, using flat planes, razor-straight lines, and sharply contrasting colors. An even more famous exponent of Precisionism was Georgia O'Keeffe, best remembered for her exquisite portraits of enormous flowers and southwestern landscapes. Her large, close-up paintings of flowers, including *Petunia No. 2* (1924) and *White Flower* (1929), emphasize the organic geometry of the blossoms. O'Keeffe also painted cityscapes during the 1920s, including *New York With Moon* (1925), *City Night* (1926), and *The Shelton With Sunspots* (1926). These paintings combine the flat planes and geometric shapes of Precisionism with abstract elements and photographic characteristics. In fact, O'Keeffe was well versed in the aesthetics of photography, no doubt due in part to her marriage to famous American photographer Alfred Stieglitz.

ART OF THE HARLEM RENAISSANCE

The Harlem Renaissance, or New Negro Movement, of the 1920s witnessed an outpouring of significant artistic works by African Americans. Sculptors Richard Barthé, Augusta Savage, Meta Vaux Warrick Fuller, and May Howard Jackson created busts and other three-dimensional studies, both abstract and representational, in clay, plaster, bronze, wood, and marble. Photographers Richard S. Roberts and James Van Der Zee captured on film images of African Americans in every imaginable context and pose. Innovative black painters and illustrators such as Archibald J. Motley Jr., Palmer Hayden, and William E. Braxton, among many others, explored various artistic styles and, in some cases, expressed on canvas their interpretations of the African-American experience. However, the deeply ingrained racism of American culture prevented many of these talented artists from achieving public recognition at the levels of their white counterparts.

One serious problem that plagued African-American artists during the 1920s was a lack of opportunity to study art and to show their work. Some museums refused to exhibit the work of black artists, and some art schools declined to consider black applicants for scholarships. In 1923, sculptor Augusta Savage brought this discrimination against black artists to the attention of the American public when, after being rejected for a summer art school in France because of her race, she appealed to the press. After her story appeared in newspapers, many editorials and letters followed, and while she never did receive the scholarship, she did other black artists a great service by focusing public scrutiny on this problem. Wealthy white philanthropist William Elmer Harmon, who decried the lack of support available to African-American artists, tried to rectify this unfortunate situation by establishing the Harmon Foundation in 1922. The foundation gave annual awards and cash prizes for African-American achievement in seven categories: literature, fine arts, science, education, industry, religion, and music. In 1928, the Harmon Foundation began to sponsor all-black art exhibits that helped gain more widespread public exposure for the fine work of African-American artists.

Perhaps the best-known African-American painter of the Harlem Renaissance was Aaron Douglas. Douglas was a student of the German artist Winold Reiss, who painted African Americans neither as crude stereotypes nor as white people with dark complexions, but rather as dignified, unique individuals. Reiss encouraged Douglas to incorporate African imagery into his paintings, which he did with great success. His May 1927 cover for the Urban League's magazine *Opportunity*, for example, depicts the proud profile of a long-necked Mangbetu woman with an elaborate African hairstyle. Many of Douglas' works, including this one, feature angular, elongated figures, usually painted in silhouette and often accented by contrasting outlines and radiating circles and waves. Additionally, Douglas illustrated celebrated novels by Countee Cullen, James Weldon Johnson, and Langston Hughes, among others. In 1928, Douglas became the first president of the Harlem Artists Guild, an organization that helped black artists secure federal funding from the Works Progress Administration during the Great Depression.

ILLUSTRATION

The 1920s saw the craft of illustration blossom, as a result of the expansion of book publishing and book clubs, modern advertising and sophisticated ad campaigns, and mass circulation magazines that reached millions of Americans each month. An army of illustrators found work sketching and painting images that could sell products, bring literary characters to life, or capture the mood of the Jazz Age. In fact, many artists and painters who could not make a living in the art world turned to commercial illustration, which, for the most talented and popular artists, could be an extremely lucrative profession. While many of these artists labored in anonymity, a number of them became household names during the 1920s.

Of all the artists and illustrators of the 1920s, nobody better captured the gaiety and freewheeling spirit of the Jazz Age than did illustrator John Held Jr. His images of the long-legged, long-necked, short-skirted flapper and her round-headed, spindle-necked boyfriend adorned the covers and pages of *Life*, *College Humor*, *Judge*, *The New Yorker*, *Cosmopolitan*, and other national magazines. These simple characters, often depicted engaged in such leisure activities as joy-riding, smoking, dancing, or golfing, emphasized the flamboyant, fun-loving world of youth. Held also drew dozens of satirical (and admittedly inaccurate) maps for *The New Yorker* that poked gentle fun at, for example, the plethora of antique shops in a particular location or the thousands of bootleggers and rumrunners that surrounded the nation's borders during National Prohibition. Additionally, he created memorable advertisement illustrations for Van Heusen shirts, Planter's peanuts, and Packard automobiles, among others. Held was an accomplished artist who could draw more than merely his signature flappers and college boys, but it is these images that are most often enlisted to represent the tenor of the Roaring Twenties.

Ralph Barton was another popular illustrator and caricaturist whose images, like Held's, epitomized the energetic spirit of the Jazz Age. Barton's subjects often included movie stars and other celebrities, and his drawings appeared in books and magazines such as *Vanity Fair* and *The New Yorker*. Barton's illustrations for Anita Loos' best-selling book *Gentlemen Prefer Blondes* (1925) brought to life one of the decade's most famous fictional flappers, Lorelei Lee. At times during the 1920s, Barton earned as much as $1,500 for a single drawing, but his tumultuous personal life (he had four failed marriages) coupled with the poor reviews he received for his 1929 book *God's Country*, a satirical history of the United States in drawings, likely contributed to the deep depression that resulted in his suicide in 1931.

Perhaps the most legendary illustrator and painter of the 1920s was Norman Rockwell, who created thousands of images for magazines, posters, advertisements, and calendars during his more than 40-year career. His heralded association with *The Saturday Evening Post* began in 1916, when the magazine purchased its first illustrations from the 21-year-old Rockwell. His first cover appeared on the May 20, 1916 issue, and Rockwell went on to illustrate more than 300 *Saturday Evening Post* covers. Rockwell also worked as the primary illustrator for a series of

Illustrator Ralph Barton. Courtesy of the Library of Congress.

youth magazines that promoted middle-class ideals of American citizenry, including *Boy's Life, Youth's Companion, St. Nicholas,* and *American Boy.* His wholesome, conservative images of white middle-class experiences represented, for generations of citizens, the epitome of mainstream American life.

Other important illustrators of the 1920s included Fred Cooper, Floyd Davis, Maxfield Parrish, Wallace Morgan, and Saul Tepper. N. C. Wyeth illustrated dozens of adventure books, including a new edition of *Robinson Crusoe* (1920), and contributed hundreds of story illustrations to such magazines as *McCall's* and *The Saturday Evening Post.* Rockwell Kent's unique black-and-white works illustrated books, magazines, and advertisements of the 1920s. Neysa McMein painted every cover for *McCall's* magazine between 1924 and 1936, as well as oil portraits of such notables as President Warren Harding, film comedian Charlie Chaplin, and poet Edna St. Vincent Millay. Frederic Gruger, best known for his thousands of illustrations for *The Saturday Evening Post,* also sketched book illustrations for the novels of such celebrated writers as Theodore Dreiser, Edith Wharton, Sinclair Lewis, and F. Scott Fitzgerald. Howard Chandler Christy was noted for his lovely portraits of "Christy girls," and, during World War I, for his navy recruitment and liberty bonds posters. And J. C. Leyendecker became particularly well known for his illustrations of the handsome, well-dressed man in the Arrow Collars and Shirts advertisements.

CARICATURE

After World War I, the popularity of caricature (the comic or satiric portrait of a person based on exaggerated physical traits) grew dramatically. Caricatures of American celebrities filled the pages of mass-circulation newspapers and magazines, and, indeed, *Vanity Fair* routinely commissioned hundreds of these entertaining images of interesting personalities. The popularity of this kind of irreverent, witty drawing during the 1920s was closely related to the rise in the culture of celebrity in general—motion pictures, photography, and magazines made hundreds of faces, from movies stars to athletes to politicians, instantly recognizable to the general public. The success of celebrity caricature depends largely on the audience's familiarity with a subject's appearance—without that shared experience, caricature becomes essentially meaningless. For the millions of Americans who shared a nationwide popular culture, caricatures of such luminaries as Charlie Chaplin, Babe Ruth, and Calvin Coolidge, which captured their personalities and at the same time mocked their celebrity, delighted readers throughout the decade.

Artist Al Hirschfeld became famous for his distinctive line drawings and caricatures of actors and theater performances. He sold his first caricature, of the French actor Sacha Guitry, to the *New York Herald Tribune* in 1926. Hirschfeld's drawings appeared in several newspapers until 1929, when he signed an exclusive contract as a caricaturist for the *New York Times*; his artwork ran in the *Times* for decades. Other caricaturists also specialized in theatrical personalities, including Alex Gard, who, in 1927, began sketching caricatures of hundreds of famous actors. Eventually, these celebrated images decked the walls of Sardi's Manhattan restaurant. Al Freuh, who began drawing cartoons and caricatures in the early years of the twentieth century, published theatrical caricatures throughout the 1920s in the *New York World*, *Life*, and, after 1925, *The New Yorker*. Ralph Barton also became renowned for his theatrical caricatures when, in 1922, he decorated an intermission curtain for the musical revue *The Chauve-Souris* with caricatures of 139 theater stars, drama critics, and recognizable members of New York high society.

Mexican-born Miguel Covarrubias also established a lasting reputation as a caricaturist during the 1920s. Shortly after his 1923 arrival in New York City, Covarrubias' bold caricatures began to appear in newspapers and magazines, especially *Vanity Fair*. In 1925, he published a successful book called *The Prince of Wales and Other Famous Americans*, which collected 66 of his celebrity caricatures and heightened his visibility as an artist. During the mid-1920s, in part due to the influence of his friend Carl Van Vechten, Covarrubias became progressively more interested in African-American culture. In 1927, he published *Negro Drawings*, his famous collection of caricatures of African Americans and scenes of Harlem life. He also designed the set for *La Revue Nègre* (1925), an American musical that opened in Paris, and illustrated Langston Hughes' *The Weary Blues* (1926) and W. C. Handy's *Blues: An Anthology* (1926). Toward the end of the decade, Covarrubias drew fewer celebrity caricatures and more general comic illustrations, but his caricatures survive as a revealing glimpse into the vibrant world of New York in the 1920s.

COMIC STRIPS

Since their origins in the mid-1890s, comic strips have occupied an important place in American popular culture. Historians usually identify the first American comic strip character as Richard Outcault's Yellow Kid, who appeared in a series called *Hogan's Alley* that began running in the *New York World* in 1895. The first modern-day comic strips, which featured a regular cast of characters, sequential panels that established the narrative, and dialogue balloons, include Rudolph Dirks' *Katzenjammer Kids* (1897), Frederick Burr Opper's *Happy Hooligan* (1900), Outcault's *Buster Brown* (1902), and Winsor McCay's *Little Nemo in Slumberland*

Gasoline Alley comic strip by Frank King, 1921. Courtesy of the Library of Congress.

(1905). The popularity of comic strips skyrocketed so rapidly that, by 1924, no less than 84 percent of urban children and teenagers regularly read the Sunday funny papers.[1] Comic strips often dealt with absurd, fantastical situations, such as George Herriman's famous *Krazy Kat* (1916), which followed the obsessive and futile love triangle of a dog, a cat, and a mouse. Sometimes, however, comic strips directly addressed ordinary aspects of American life. For example, the two main characters in Harry "Bud" Fisher's *Mutt and Jeff* (1907) frequently dodged Prohibition laws and dreamed up countless get-rich-quick schemes. Other strips helped Americans to make sense of their fast-changing modern world. For example, *Chicago Tribune* publisher Robert McCormick thought that a comic strip that regularly featured the automobile might make his readers more comfortable with these new contraptions. He asked illustrator Frank King to create such a comic, and the result, the long-running *Gasoline Alley* (1918), initially focused on men's interest in cars. And Martin Branner's *Winnie Winkle the Breadwinner* (1920), which featured a young, single secretary trying to provide for her family and find herself a good husband, marked the advent of a number of strips featuring modern wage-earning women.

Buck Rogers in the 25th Century A.D.

In 1929, when writer Philip Nowland and artist Dick Calkins introduced the first science-fiction comic strip, *Buck Rogers in the 25th Century A.D.*, they effectively launched a craze for science fiction that has not yet abated. Earlier in the 1920s, pulp fiction magazines had begun to explore the area of scientific fiction or "scientification," as it was then called, but when *Buck Rogers* began to appear in newspapers, a much larger audience was exposed to the excitement of outer-space exploits. Its story line followed the adventures of pilot Anthony "Buck" Rogers, who initially was trapped in an abandoned Pennsylvania coal mine where radioactive gases put him into a state of suspended animation that lasted for 500 years. When he awoke in 2419 A.D., he found that Mongols had invaded the United States and that China now controlled the world. The gallant Rogers promptly joined the guerrilla movement and freed his nation from its conquerors, with the help of Wilma Deering, a tireless freedom fighter and Buck's love interest. Rogers went on heroically to face a parade of evil aliens and other adversaries, all the while taking advantage of futuristic technologies such as laser beams, anti-gravity flying belts, robots, ray guns, and atomic weapons. *Buck Rogers* became so popular that it spawned a number of commercial toys and books, as well as a radio program, *Buck Rogers in the 25th Century* (which premiered on CBS in 1932), a television program, and a series of films based on the strip. It also inspired a wave of later science-fiction thrillers, including *Flash Gordon*, *Star Trek*, and *Star Wars*.

Tarzan

Coincidentally, the *Tarzan* comic strip debuted on the very day that the first *Buck Rogers* strip appeared: January 7, 1929. The character of Tarzan, however, was already 17 years old by then. Author Edgar Rice Burroughs published his short novel, *Tarzan of the Apes*, in its entirety in the October 1912 issue of the adventure pulp *All-Story Magazine*. The story follows the unlikely adventures of John Clayton, whose parents, Lord and Lady Greystoke, are marooned on the coast of Africa. Lady Greystoke dies soon after the birth of her son, and Lord Greystoke is later killed by a band of apes. A female ape named Kala adopts the infant

John and names him Tarzan, meaning (supposedly) "white skin." Tarzan, raised by apes yet constantly wrestling with his true identity, starred in more than 20 novels and more than 50 films. When *Tarzan* first premiered as a comic strip, it was essentially a graphic rendering of Burroughs' first novel, with none of the customary dialogue balloons. The text, adapted from the novel, merely ran below the illustrated panels, drawn by Hal Foster. During the 1930s, the *Tarzan* comic strip was changed to incorporate the dialogue and sound effects that readers had come to expect in the funny pages.

Little Orphan Annie

Little Orphan Annie, one of the most popular and enduring comic strips in American popular culture, debuted in 1924 in the *New York Daily News*. Written and illustrated by Harold Gray, *Little Orphan Annie* tracked the adventures of Annie, a spirited orphan girl from New York who is adopted (along with Sandy, her ever-present canine companion) by Oliver "Daddy" Warbucks, a fabulously wealthy, childless tycoon. Unlike many other comic strip characters, Annie did not possess super powers or live in the future, but she had grit, determination, and a cheerful sense of self-reliance that audiences found irresistible. Annie, drawn with curly red hair and empty, pupil-less eyes, introduced her famous catchphrase "Leapin' Lizards!" into the American vernacular. The strip became increasingly political during the 1930s, as the staunchly conservative Gray infused his story lines with attacks on President Franklin D. Roosevelt's New Deal. Annie's popularity launched a popular radio serial in 1930 and a line of toys and merchandise in the 1930s and 1940s.

Popeye

Popeye, America's favorite cartoon sailor man, made his debut in 1929 as a minor character in Elzie Crisler "E. C." Segar's popular comic strip *Thimble Theatre*. *Thimble Theatre*, which first appeared in 1919, followed the adventures of the bizarre Oyl family: Cole and Nana Oyl and their children Castor and Olive. Many of the earliest stories focused on Castor Oyl and Ham Gravy, Olive's boyfriend. In 1929, Segar introduced Popeye in a series of strips that revolved around Castor and Ham's acquisition of a magical bird and their intention to use her powers to win a fortune at a gambling casino. Readers of *Thimble Theatre* soon took to the uncouth, squint-eyed, pipe-smoking sailor. Segar made him into a recurring character and then, finally, the star of the strip, which Segar renamed *Thimble Theatre Starring Popeye*. Other memorable characters also contributed to the strip's enduring popularity, including the hamburger-mooching J. Wellington Wimpy, Alice the Goon, baby

Swee'Pea, and, of course, Bluto and Brutus, Popeye's archenemies and rivals for Olive's affection. Eating canned spinach gave Popeye superhuman strength, a fact that nutritionists credited in the 1930s for dramatically increasing the consumption of the green, leafy vegetable in the United States. His signature phrase "I yam what I yam" is still recognizable, largely due to the later animated television cartoon bearing his name.

ANIMATED CARTOONS

Since the mid-1910s, short, animated cartoons that were often shown before feature films entertained tens of millions of moviegoers across the nation. These cartoon films typically lasted between one and seven minutes; feature-length animated stories did not begin to appear until the 1930s. Many animated cartoons, such as the *Krazy Kat* series and *Keeping Up with the Joneses*, brought to life already-popular comic strip characters. Of course, animated cartoons, like the films they preceded, did not incorporate synchronized sound until the late 1920s. Nevertheless, these silent but amusing anthropomorphic animals and their human counterparts cavorted across the nation's movie screens, captivating children and adults alike with their slapstick comedy and humorous antics.

Felix the Cat

Felix the Cat, created by Otto Messmer and Pat Sullivan, was the first American star of animated cartoons. Felix made his debut in 1919 in *Feline Follies* and went on to appear in approximately 150 short films during the 1920s. Much of Felix's comedy came from his remarkable ability (thanks to the marvels of creative animation) to transform various body parts into useful tools with which he could solve problems. Felix the Cat is an excellent example of early crossover merchandising, for throughout the 1920s his image was licensed to doll companies, toy manufacturers, cigarette companies, and other industries eager to capitalize on his popularity. The famous feline also appeared in a newspaper comic strip called *Felix the Cat*, beginning in 1923, and was the subject of a popular novelty song, "Felix! Felix! Felix the Cat" (1928). But in 1928, at the height of his fame, the introduction of synchronized sound to cartoon animation dealt Felix an awful blow. Felix had succeeded because his creators were so skillful at manipulating silent animation to get a laugh from their audiences. Sullivan and Messmer proved unable to adapt their character effectively to the new technology of sound animation, and Felix's final silent film cartoon, aptly titled *The Last Life*, appeared in 1928.

Despite a few unsuccessful attempts at a talking Felix, the famous cat had disappeared from the silver screen by 1930.

Walt Disney and Mickey Mouse

While he is perhaps best remembered as a remarkable entrepreneur and founder of one of the most successful multi-national companies in American history, Walt Disney actually started out as a struggling illustrator and animator. In 1922, he founded his own animation company in Kansas City, Missouri, called the Laugh-O-Gram Corporation, which specialized in making short, animated fairy tales. When the company went bankrupt in 1923, Disney headed to Los Angeles with his brother, Roy, where they founded the Disney Brothers Studio (later renamed the Walt Disney Company). The Disneys got their start by creating a series of short films based on *Alice in Wonderland*, which juxtaposed a live Alice with a cartoon background and supporting cast of animated characters. This popular series, called *Alice in Cartoonland* (1923–1927), included dozens of popular short films that were released in movie theaters across the country.

In 1927, Disney created a new cartoon character, Oswald the Lucky Rabbit, who starred in more than 20 short animated films, but a New York distributor copyrighted the character and Disney lost control of the rabbit's image. But in 1928, when he created Mickey Mouse, Disney knew enough to copyright the mouse for himself. Disney did not actually draw Mickey Mouse. Rather, his colleague, artist Ub Iwerks, was responsible for illustrating the famous rodent. Mickey Mouse appeared in two 1928 silent cartoons, *Plane Crazy* and *Galloping Gaucho*, but he did not speak in his famous squeaky falsetto voice until *Steamboat Willie*, the first animated cartoon with synchronized sound, was released late that same year. *Steamboat Willie* was an overnight sensation. Audiences were delighted to actually hear Mickey whistle a tune, as well as play the xylophone on a cow's teeth and the bagpipes on a sow's udder. The following year, Disney began work on the *Silly Symphonies* animated series, with the first film released titled *Skeleton Dance* (1929). The Walt Disney Company expanded and flourished throughout the twentieth century, but much of the company's financial success and cultural influence can be traced to the innovative Mickey Mouse cartoons of the late 1920s.

PHOTOGRAPHY

During the 1920s, photographs became more common in newspapers, magazines, and illustrated books than ever before. However, perhaps because of its ubiquity, photography was not then generally considered an important art form. Few art museums collected or exhibited photographs during the 1920s, and photography was largely seen as either the pastime of hobbyists or merely an element of journalism and advertising. Alfred Stieglitz, a talented photographer and influential member of the modern art world, helped to change American's perception of art photography. Stieglitz exhibited art photography in his New York studio, called "291," and nurtured the careers of many art photographers, including that of his wife, Georgia O'Keeffe. By the end of the 1920s, several important art museums had begun to include photographs in their displays, including the Metropolitan Museum of Art and the Museum of Modern Art, and the careers of such famous art photographers as Ansel Adams, Imogen Cunningham, Edward Steichen, Edward Weston, and Man Ray had been launched.

Art photography, however, constituted only a tiny aspect of the world of photography during the 1920s. Amateur photography was far more widespread and, indeed, was an exceptionally popular pastime during the decade. Prior to 1900, photography had rightly earned the reputation of being costly, messy, and difficult—an endeavor best left to professionals or to wealthy hobbyists. Around the turn of the century, though, technological advances helped to democratize photography by making cameras much simpler, lighter, and more efficient, and making film developing easier and cheaper. The Kodak Brownie box camera, the first camera marketed to children, debuted in 1900 and sold for $1, plus 15 cents for film. It soon became clear that many adults also used this simple and affordable camera to record special events and milestones. From 1914 through the mid-1920s, Kodak promoted various models of its popular "Autographic Kodak" folding cameras, which allowed users to write on each negative a short sentence identifying the date, place, and subject of the photograph. Kodak advertising convinced consumers that chronicling the lives of their families and, particularly, their children was an important and necessary endeavor. Not surprisingly, in this era of mass consumerism, sales of photography equipment escalated rapidly, and many Americans eagerly began to snap pictures of events such as birthdays, holidays, family reunions, vacations, and even ordinary weekdays. As Kodak reminded consumers in a nostalgic 1926 advertising campaign, "In the house or out of doors, whenever there's a home story you want to save, your Kodak saves it. Children are always little, and the scenes just as they used to be—in your Kodak album."[2]

Photography enthusiasts often joined camera clubs, which had flourished since the 1890s. Members gathered to discuss the latest camera technologies and development techniques, though by the 1920s most casual photographers chose to have their film developed in labs rather than doing it themselves. Despite the popularity of amateur photography, professional studios also contributed to Americans' family photo albums. By the 1920s, almost every small town in the nation counted at least one studio photographer among its Main Street businesses. Even camera buffs sometimes engaged a studio photographer to chronicle an important family event. These professionals captured weddings, first communions, graduations, and even funerals on film, providing lasting mementos for future generations.

Photojournalism and Commercial Photography

Newspapers and magazines began to incorporate an increasing number of photographs into their pages during the 1920s, and photography was widely recognized as an important medium for documenting the political and social realities of the age. Less concerned with portraying reality were the immensely popular tabloid newspapers, such as the *New York Daily News* and the *New York Evening Graphic*, which filled their pages with photographs of everything from national celebrities to accused criminals to dramatic images of reenacted or fictional events (called "composographs"). Composographs were collages of photographs juxtaposed in such a way that they portrayed events never actually captured on film. Users of this technique often sacrificed realism for sensationalism. For example, when Rudolph Valentino died suddenly in 1926, the *Evening Graphic* published a famous composograph of the deceased film star meeting his fellow countryman, Italian opera star Enrico Caruso, in heaven. Photographs dominated the pages of the tabloids, and often the front page consisted of nothing but pictures and a single headline. Inside, more photographs—some authentic, some fabricated—taught readers to rely on images to tell them a story, and in many cases people came to prefer looking at photos to reading actual text. In 1928, the *New York Daily News* scored a major scoop when it published an illicit photograph of the actual electrocution of Ruth Snyder, a Queens, New York, housewife convicted of murdering her husband. Disobeying the orders of prison officials, a newsman snapped the gruesome image with a hidden camera strapped to his ankle, and when published on the cover of the tabloid on January 13, 1928, the photograph ignited a storm of controversy. Nonetheless, that edition of the *Daily News* sold an extra half-million copies.[3]

Commercial photography in the 1920s followed the lead of photojournalism insofar as advertisers began to realize how receptive the American public was to photographic images, yet it wasn't until the mid- to late 1920s that photography emerged as an important component of modern advertising. In 1925, only about 6 percent of national newspaper ads contained photographs, and advertisers still believed that the best way to attract consumers' attention was through the use of striking artwork and, when possible, bold colors. But by the end of the decade, photography had become increasingly prevalent in newspaper and magazine advertising. Advertising photographers used a variety of artistic techniques, including extreme camera angles, distorting lenses, and artificial backgrounds, to enhance the look of the product and entice consumers into considering its purchase. The fashion industry also began to look toward photography to showcase the latest stylish outfits. And many commercial photographers experimented with retouching photographs or superimposing multiple photographs onto one another in order to create stunning visual effects.

SCULPTURE

Admittedly, sculpture did not capture ordinary Americans' imagination the way that illustrations, cartoons, and photographs did. In many cases, sculpture remained a rarefied art form that was accessible only to urban museumgoers—not exactly a large portion of the population in Jazz Age America. The general public was exposed, however, to a certain amount of outdoor sculpture, often in the form of large bronze statues of Confederate soldiers, famous generals, or presidents. Tourists in Washington, D.C., could visit the impressive Lincoln Memorial, which opened in 1922 and featured Daniel Chester French's sculpture of a seated President Lincoln. One innovative sculptor of the 1920s, however, set his sights on creating artistic sculpture of a scale never before attempted. Gutzon Borglum's work attracted national headlines as he labored to carve and blast mountains into art.

Gutzon Borglum

Gutzon Borglum is best remembered for carving the gigantic portraits of George Washington, Thomas Jefferson, Abraham Lincoln, and Theodore Roosevelt onto the face of South Dakota's Mount Rushmore, but Borglum, an Idaho native born to Danish immigrant parents, sculpted far more than Mount Rushmore. His artistic career actually began in the 1880s, but some of his most memorable work was done during the 1920s. He created numerous public monuments and outdoor statues, including a dramatic bronze figure of Union General Philip Sheridan on horseback (1924), and an enormous bronze casting of 42 life-size figures, horses, and cannons that memorialized American soldiers and sailors, titled *Wars of America* (1926). In 1927, Borglum completed a full-sized marble statue of Georgia's former governor and vice president of the Confederacy, Alexander Stephens, now on display in the U.S. Capitol's Statuary Hall (Borglum also created two other sculptures for this hall). In 1928,

Gutzon Borglum carving the image of Robert E. Lee on the face of Stone Mountain, Georgia, 1924. Courtesy of Special Collections and Archives, Robert W. Woodruff Library, Emory University.

he completed a plaster plaque honoring Nicola Sacco and Bartolomeo Vanzetti, the Italian anarchists who were executed in 1927 after a questionable "Trial of the Century" found them guilty of robbery and murder. The plaque, not cast in bronze until 1938, was later stolen and has never been recovered.

Borglum's first mountain-sized commission came in 1915. That year, the United Daughters of the Confederacy invited Borglum to plan the sculpture that would consume much of the next 10 years of his life: carving the head of Confederate General Robert E. Lee onto the granite face of Stone Mountain near Atlanta, Georgia. Borglum soon expanded the scope of this project to include the images of Confederate President Jefferson Davis and General Stonewall Jackson, as well as a long procession of Confederate soldiers on foot and on horseback. Stone carving on such a massive scale had never before been attempted, and Borglum had to invent several new techniques to turn the mountainside into art. Using a specially designed projector, he devised a way to project an image onto the side of the mountain so that it could then be outlined in paint. He also worked with engineers to develop techniques for dynamiting out pieces of rock without irreparably damaging the sculpture itself. Drilling began in June 1923, and, seven months later, Borglum unveiled the partially completed sculpture of Lee's head at a dramatic dedication ceremony. In the spring of 1924, however, a rift developed between the sculptor and the Stone Mountain Confederate Memorial Association, formed in 1923 to solicit financial support for the project. Borglum was fired from the unfinished project, and his vision of the enormous mountain sculpture was never fully realized (although, in 1970, the carvings of Lee, Jefferson Davis, and Stonewall Jackson were finally completed). Later in 1924, at the invitation of the South Dakota state historian, Borglum traveled to the Black Hills to begin planning his immense sculpture of four U.S. presidents on Mount Rushmore. Carving began in 1927, and although Borglum died in 1941, before he could put the finishing touches on his great sculpted portraits, he did live long enough to see the gigantic visages of George Washington, Thomas Jefferson, Abraham Lincoln, and Theodore Roosevelt emerge from the stone.

CONCLUSION

The visual arts' influence on American popular culture during the 1920s should not be underestimated. Although the majority of ordinary Americans did not have access to, or interest in, art shows, museums, or galleries, modern art did profoundly affect more common forms of visual arts, including, for example, magazine and newspaper illustrations and advertising. The visual arts' influence on popular culture also transcended notions of "fine art" to include more vernacular art forms, such as comic strips and animated cartoons. Millions of Americans followed the day-to-day escapades of Little Orphan Annie in the funny papers and laughed at the silly antics of Felix the Cat in movie theaters. Furthermore, increasing numbers of Americans actually began producing visual art themselves in the form of amateur photography, preserving "Kodak moments" in their family albums and scrapbooks. Despite the elite nature of some modern art, the 1920s witnessed the democratization and increased public accessibility to the visual arts through advertising, newspapers, magazines, and other forms of mass media.

Cost of Products in the 1920s

Price varied over the course of the 1920s, so the figures below represent approximations of what common consumer goods cost. By adjusting for inflation, it is possible to compare prices between the 1920s and today. On average, $1.00 during the 1920s had the purchasing power of about $10.50 in 2003 (the most recent year for which data are available). Conversely, $1.00 in 2003 would have had the buying power of about a dime in the 1920s. For example, a Baby Ruth candy bar cost a nickel during the 1920s. That would translate to about 53 cents in 2003 currency. A new Cadillac, which cost $2,885 in 1920, would cost around $30,293 today. A more accurate measure of 1920s prices would track average prices from year to year, since the U.S. economy changed dramatically between 1920 and 1930. Nevertheless, the list below offers readers a general idea of the cost of certain items during the 1920s.

COSMETICS

Ivory soap: $0.49/12 bars

Phillips Milk of Magnesia: $0.39/bottle

Listerine mouthwash: $0.79/bottle

Colgate toothpaste: $0.25/tube

Odor-o-no deodorant: $0.60

Pepsodent toothbrush: $0.50

Vaseline petroleum jelly: $0.13/4-ounce jar

Bayer aspirin tablets: $0.98/bottle

CLOTHING

Women

Mink coat: $1,750–$2,750

Camel-hair coat: $58.00

Tweed coat: $37.50

Wool jersey skirt and shirt outfit: $17.50

Housedress: $1.98–$3.48

Ladies garters: $0.40–0.60/pair

Silk stockings: $1.00–$6.00/pair

Underwear: $1.00–$3.95

Cloche hat: $1.95–$4.44

Men

Hand-tailored wool tuxedo: $55.00

Arrow broadcloth shirt: $1.95

Linen collars: $1.00/3 collars

Neckties: $0.95–$2.45

BVD suit: $1.30

Dress oxford shoes: $7.75

Waltham wristwatch: $5.00

Peaked cap: $1.25–$1.95

Bathing suit: $5.00

Children

Winter coat: $14.50–$16.50

Three-piece knit baby suit: $2.98

Teen boy's knicker suit: $8.95

Young girl's jersey dress: $2.98

HOME FURNISHINGS AND APPLIANCES

Steinway grand piano: $1,425

Dining room suite: $110–$330

Gas range: $63.50–$93.50

Frigidaire refrigerator: $195–$245

Pop-up toaster: $12.00

Vacuum cleaner: $48.00
Water Witch electric washing machine: $92.00
Upholstered armchair: $24.50–$50.00
Persian rug: $44.00–$55.00
Wool blanket: $9.95

AUTOMOBILES

Cadillac: $2,885 (1920)
Packard: $2,485 (1923)
Rolls-Royce: $10,900 (1923)
Model T Ford: $290 (1925)
Gasoline: $0.18–$0.25/gallon
Dearborn automobile tire: $5.95
Allstate truck tire: $16.45
Champion spark plug: $0.55

FOODSTUFFS

Round steak: $0.37/pound
Pork chops: $0.36/pound
Chicken: $0.47/pound
Bacon: $0.48/pound
Eggs: $0.52/dozen
Milk: $0.28/half-gallon (delivered)
Bread: $0.12/loaf
Flour: $0.28/5 pounds
Butter: $0.56/pound
Sugar: $0.44/5 pounds
Potatoes: $0.36/10 pounds
Oranges: $0.53/dozen
Canned tomatoes: $0.11/can
Campbell's condensed soup: $0.12/can
Kraft cheese: $0.38/pound
Baby Ruth candy bar: $0.05
Coffee: $0.44/pound
Coca-Cola: $0.05/bottle
Canada Dry Ginger Ale: $0.35/bottle
Wrigley's spearmint gum: $0.39/10 packs

ENTERTAINMENT AND SPORTING GOODS

Dinner at the Hotel Vanderbilt in New York City: $2.50

Metropolitan Opera matinee ticket: $1.00–$5.00

Broadway theater ticket (top seat): $3.50

Movie at the Apollo Theater in New York City: $0.50–$1.00

Victrola cabinet phonograph: $125–$250

RCA Radiola radio: $175

Victor record: $0.75

Kodak Brownie box camera: $2.29–$4.49

Winchester Model 94 rifle: $31.98

Louisville Slugger baseball bat: $2.00

Grover Cleveland Alexander baseball glove: $3.39

Football: $1.69–$3.98

Tennis racquet: $10.50

Ouija board: $0.87–$1.00

MISCELLANEOUS DEMOGRAPHIC TRENDS, 1920–1930

U.S. population, 1920: 106,021,537; 1930: 123,202,624

Life expectancy male/female, 1920: 53.6/54.6 years; 1930: 58.1/61.6 years

Births, 1920: 28/1,000 people; 1930: 21/1,000 people

Marriages, 1920: 12/1,000 people; 1930: 9/1,000 people

Divorces, 1920: 1.6/1,000 people; 1930: 1.6/1,000 people

Deaths, 1920: 13/1,000 people; 1930: 11/1,000 people

Unemployment, 1920: 2,132,000; 1930: 4,340,000

Average salary, 1920: $1,236/year; 1930: $1,368/year

U.S. gross national product, 1920: $91.5 billion; 1930: $90.4 billon

Homicides, 1920: 6.8//100,000 people; 1930: 8.8/100,000 people

Suicides, 1920: 10.2/100,000 people; 1930: 15.6/100,000 people

The statistical data presented in this section are compiled from a number of sources, including *Historical Statistics of the United States: Colonial Times to 1970*, Vols. 1 and 2 (Washington, DC: U.S. Bureau of the Census, 1975); Donald B. Dodd, comp., *Historical Statistics of the United States: Two Centuries of the Census, 1790–1990* (Westport, CT: Greenwood Publishing Group, 1993); Scott Derks, *Working Americans: 1880–1999*, Vols. 1–4 (Millerton, NY: Grey House, 2000–2002); and Lois Gordon and Alan Gordon, *The Columbia Chronicles of American Life, 1910–1992* (New York: Columbia University Press, 1995).

Notes

INTRODUCTION

1. Malcolm Cowley and Robert Cowley, eds., *Fitzgerald and the Jazz Age* (New York: Charles Scribner's Sons, 1966), 173.

2. F. Scott Fitzgerald, "Echoes of the Jazz Age," in *Fitzgerald and the Jazz Age*, ed. Cowley and Cowley, 182, 183.

3. David A. Shannon, *Between the Wars: America, 1919–1941*, 2nd ed. (Boston: Houghton Mifflin, 1979), 94.

CHAPTER 1

1. Carl Abbott, *Urban America in the Modern Age: 1920 to the Present* (Arlington Heights, IL: Harlan Davidson, 1987), 17.

2. Roderick Nash, *The Nervous Generation: American Thought, 1917–1930* (Chicago: Rand McNally and Company, 1970), 145.

3. Eric Arnesen, *Black Protest and the Great Migration: A Brief History with Documents* (Boston: Bedford/St. Martin's, 2003), 1.

4. Arthur F. Raper, *The Tragedy of Lynching* (New York: Dover Publications, 1970 [1933]), 25, 27, 481.

5. Robert Grant and Joseph Katz, *The Great Trials of the Twenties: The Watershed Decade in America's Courtrooms* (Rockville Centre, NY: Sarpedon, 1998), 142.

6. Edward Behr, *Prohibition: Thirteen Years That Changed America* (New York: Arcade Publishing, 1996), 87.

7. Robert A. Divine et al., *The American Story* (New York: Longman, 2002), 814.

8. Judith S. Baughman, ed., *American Decades: 1920–1929* (Detroit: Gale Research, 1996), 277.

9. Dorothy M. Brown, *Setting a Course: American Women in the 1920s* (Boston: Twayne Publishers, 1987), 62–63.

10. Winifred D. Wandersee, *Women's Work and Family Values, 1920–1940* (Cambridge, MA: Harvard University Press, 1981), 17.

11. J. Fred MacDonald, *Don't Touch That Dial* (Chicago: Nelson-Hall, 1979), 23.

12. Erica Hanson, *A Cultural History of the United States Through the Decades: The 1920s* (San Diego: Lucent Books, 1999), 98.

CHAPTER 2

1. H. L. Mencken, *The American Language: An Inquiry into the Development of English in the United States* (New York: Alfred A. Knopf, 1989 [1936]), 314–315.

2. Joseph M. Hawes, *Children Between the Wars: American Childhood, 1920–1940* (New York: Twayne Publishers, 1997), 33.

3. David A. Shannon, *Between the Wars: America, 1919–1941*, 2nd ed. (Boston: Houghton Mifflin, 1979), 109.

4. Elliott West, *Growing Up in Twentieth-Century America: A History and Reference Guide* (Westport, CT: Greenwood Press, 1996), 135.

5. Shannon, *Between the Wars*, 111.

6. Dorothy M. Brown, *Setting a Course: Women in the 1920s* (Boston: Twayne Publishers, 1987), 133.

7. Harvey Green, *The Uncertainty of Everyday Life, 1915–1945* (New York: HarperCollins, 1992), 127.

8. West, *Growing Up*, 118–120.

9. F. Scott Fitzgerald, *This Side of Paradise* (New York: Dover Publications, 1996 [1920]), 42.

10. Paula Fass, *The Damned and the Beautiful: American Youth in the 1920's* (New York: Oxford University Press, 1977), 6.

11. John F. Carter Jr., " 'These Wild Young People' by One of Them," *Atlantic Monthly* 126 (September 1920): 301–304.

12. Thomas Hine, *The Rise and Fall of the American Teenager* (New York: Avon Books, 1999), 178–179.

13. Elizabeth Stevenson, *Babbitts and Bohemians: From the Great War to the Great Depression* (New York: Macmillan, 1998 [1967]), 142.

14. Fass, *The Damned and the Beautiful*, 321, 323–324.

15. Mary Beth Norton et al., *A People and a Nation: A History of the United States*, 5th ed. (Boston: Houghton Mifflin, 1998), 709.

16. Robert S. Lynd and Helen Merrell Lynd, *Middletown: A Study in American Culture* (New York: Harcourt Brace, 1929), 267–268.

17. Ibid., 163.

18. Ibid., 242.

19. John Modell, "Dating Becomes the Way of American Youth," in *Growing Up in America: Historical Experiences*, ed. Harvey J. Graff (Detroit: Wayne State University Press, 1987), 454.

CHAPTER 3

1. Editors of Time-Life Books, *This Fabulous Century: Sixty Years of American Life: Volume III, 1920–1930* (New York: Time-Life Books, 1969), 99.

2. Daniel Pope, *The Making of Modern Advertising* (New York: Basic Books, 1983), 26.

3. Judith S. Baughman, ed., *American Decades: 1920–1929* (Detroit: Gale Research, 1996), 298.

4. Roland Marchand, *Advertising the American Dream: Making Way for Modernity, 1920–1940* (Berkeley: University of California Press, 1985), 11–13.

5. Ibid.

6. Jackson Lears, *Fables of Abundance: A Cultural History of Advertising in America* (New York: Basic Books, 1994), 226.

7. George E. Mowry, ed., *The Twenties: Fords, Flappers & Fanatics* (Englewood Cliffs, NJ: Prentice-Hall, 1963), 16–17.

8. Lynn Dumenil, *The Modern Temper: American Culture and Society in the 1920s* (New York: Hill and Wang, 1995), 87–88.

9. Editors of Time-Life Books, *This Fabulous Century*, 125.

10. Marchand, *Advertising the American Dream*, 136, 141, 174.

11. Ibid., 89.

12. Ibid., 15, 181.

13. Ibid., 18–20.

14. Ibid., 102.

15. Ibid., 113, 246.

16. Ibid., 213, 216, 268.

17. Ibid., 81.

18. Ibid., 152.

19. Ibid., 96–100.

20. Frank Presbrey, *The History and Development of Advertising* (New York: Greenwood Press, 1968 [1929]), 483.

21. Susan Smulyan, *Selling Radio: The Commercialization of American Broadcasting, 1920–1934* (Washington, DC: Smithsonian Institution Press, 1994), 91.

CHAPTER 4

1. Ann Douglas, *Terrible Honesty: Mongrel Manhattan in the 1920s* (New York: Farrar, Straus and Giroux, 1995), 436.

2. David A. Shannon, *Between the Wars: America, 1914–1941*, 2nd ed. (Boston: Houghton Mifflin, 1979), 111.

3. Judith S. Baughman, ed., *American Decades: 1920–1929* (Detroit: Gale Research, 1996), 168.

CHAPTER 5

1. Emily Post, *Etiquette in Society, in Business, in Politics and at Home* (New York: Funk and Wagnalls, 1969 [1922]), 540.

2. Alan Mirken, ed., *1927 Edition of the Sears, Roebuck Catalogue* (New York: Bounty Books, 1970 [1927]), 92–103, 220–221.

3. Lynn Dumenil, *The Modern Temper: American Culture and Society in the 1920s* (New York: Hill and Wang, 1995), 141.

CHAPTER 6

1. Richard S. Tedlow, *New and Improved: The Story of Mass Marketing in America* (New York: Basic Books, 1990), 314.

2. Harvey A. Levenstein, *Revolution at the Table: The Transformation of the American Diet* (New York: Oxford University Press, 1988), 182.

3. *Good Housekeeping's Book of Menus, Recipes, and Household Discoveries* (New York: Good Housekeeping, 1924).

4. Hillel Schwartz, *Never Satisfied: A Cultural History of Diets, Fantasies, and Fat* (New York: Free Press, 1986), 182.

5. Ibid.

6. Levenstein, *Revolution at the Table*, 185.

7. Automobile Manufacturers Association, *Automobiles of America* (Detroit: Wayne State University Press, 1968), 249.

8. John Mariani, *America Eats Out: An Illustrated History of Restaurants, Taverns, Coffee Shops, Speakeasies, and Other Establishments That Have Fed Us for 350 Years* (New York: William Morrow and Company, 1991), 122.

9. Ray Broekel, "The Land of the Candy Bar," *American Heritage* 37 (October/November 1986): 75.

10. Andrew Barr, *Drink: A Social History of America* (New York: Carroll and Graf, 1999), 238.

11. William H. Ukers, *All About Coffee*, 2nd ed. (New York: Tea and Coffee Trade Journal Company, 1935 [1922]), 529.

12. John J. Riley, *A History of the American Soft Drink Industry: Bottled Carbonated Beverages, 1807–1957* (Washington, DC: American Bottlers of Carbonated Beverages, 1958), 142.

CHAPTER 7

1. Gary B. Nash et al., *The American People: Creating a Nation and a Society*, Brief 4th ed. (New York: Longman, 2003), 679.

2. Mary Beth Norton et al., *A People and a Nation: A History of the United States*, 5th ed. (Boston: Houghton Mifflin, 1998), 709.

3. Robert S. Lynd and Helen Merrell Lynd, *Middletown: A Study in American Culture* (New York: Harcourt Brace, 1929), 226.

4. Alan Mirken, ed., *1927 Edition of the Sears, Roebuck Catalogue* (New York: Bounty Books, 1970), 594.

5. Editors of Time-Life Books, *Our American Century: The Jazz Age, the 20s* (Alexandria, VA: Time-Life Books, 1998), 176; "Endurance Contests Sweep on in Cycles," *New York Times*, July 27, 1930.

6. Editors of Time-Life Books, *Our American Century*, 176.

7. Ibid., 183.

8. Paul Sann, *Fads, Follies, and Delusions of the American People* (New York: Bonanza Books, 1967), 77.

9. Ibid., 107.

CHAPTER 8

1. Paul Sann, *Fads, Follies, and Delusions of the American People* (New York: Bonanza Books, 1967), 107.

2. Eric Arnesen, *Black Protest and the Great Migration: A Brief History with Documents* (Boston: Bedford/St. Martin's, 2003), 1.

3. Gilbert Osofsky, *Harlem: The Making of a Ghetto, Negro New York, 1890–1930*, 2nd ed. (New York: Harper and Row, 1971), 128.

4. Fred C. Hobson Jr., *Serpent in Eden: H. L. Mencken and the South* (Baton Rogue: Louisiana State University Press, 1978 [1974]), 151.

5. U.S. Bureau of the Census, *Historical Statistics of the United States: Colonial Times to 1970, Part II* (Washington, DC: U.S. Bureau of the Census, 1975), 809.

CHAPTER 9

1. Ian Whitcomb, *After the Ball: Pop Music from Rag to Rock* (New York: Simon and Schuster, 1973), 97; Russell Sanjek, *Pennies from Heaven: The American Popular Music Business in the Twentieth Century* (New York: Da Capo Press, 1996), 27.

2. Geoffrey C. Ward, *Jazz: A History of America's Music* (New York: Alfred A. Knopf, 2000), 99.

3. Ibid., 79.

4. Anne Shaw Faulkner, "Does Jazz Put the Sin in Syncopation?" *Ladies' Home Journal* 38 (August 1921): 16, 34.

5. Burton W. Peretti, *Jazz in American Culture* (Chicago: Ivan R. Dee, 1997), 42.

6. William Barlow, *Looking Up At Down: The Emergence of Blues Culture* (Philadelphia: Temple University Press, 1989), 223.

7. Alan Mirken, ed., *1927 Edition of the Sears, Roebuck Catalogue* (New York: Bounty Books, 1970), 674.

8. Carl Abbott, *Urban America in the Modern Age: 1920 to the Present* (Arlington Heights, IL: Harlan Davidson, 1987), 17.

CHAPTER 10

1. Robert W. Snyder, *The Voice of the City: Vaudeville and Popular Culture in New York* (New York: Oxford University Press, 1989), 66–67.

2. Editors of Time-Life Books, *Our American Century: The Jazz Age, the 20s* (Alexandria, VA: Time-Life Books, 1998), 35.

3. Frederick Lewis Allen, *Only Yesterday: An Informal History of the 1920s* (New York: Harper and Row, 1964 [1931]), 73–101.

4. Stuart A. Kallen, ed., *The Roaring Twenties* (San Diego: Greenhaven Press, 2002), 169.

5. Raymond Moley, *The Hays Office* (Indianapolis: Bobbs-Merrill Company, 1945), 240–241.

6. Andre Millard, *America on Record: A History of Recorded Sound* (New York: Cambridge University Press, 1995), 154.

7. Mary Beth Norton et al., *A People and a Nation: A History of the United States*, 5th ed. (Boston: Houghton Mifflin, 1998), 709.

8. Thomas Streissguth, *The Roaring Twenties: An Eyewitness History* (New York: Facts on File, 2001), 126.

9. Geoffrey Perrett, *America in the Twenties: A History* (New York: Simon and Schuster, 1982), 231.

10. Harvey Green, *The Uncertainty of Everyday Life, 1915–1945* (New York: HarperCollins, 1992), 188.

11. Judith S. Baughman, ed., *American Decades: 1920–1929* (Detroit: Gale Research, 1996), 311.

12. Green, *The Uncertainty of Everyday Life*, 190.

CHAPTER 11

1. John Margolies and Eric Baker, *See the USA: The Art of the American Travel Brochure* (San Francisco: Chronicle Press, 2000), 79, 94–95, 106.

2. Automobile Manufacturers Association, *Automobiles of America* (Detroit: Wayne State University Press, 1968), 249, 250.

3. Robert S. Lynd and Helen Merrell Lynd, *Middletown: A Study in American Culture* (New York: Harcourt Brace, 1929), 253.

4. George Brown Tindall and David E. Shi, *America: A Narrative History*, Vol. 2, 4th ed. (New York: W. W. Norton and Company, 1996), 1134.

5. Gary B. Nash et al., *The American People: Creating a Nation and a Society*, Brief 4th ed. (New York: Longman, 2003), 681.

6. Nelson Lichtenstein et al., *Who Built America? Working People and the Nation's Economy, Politics, Culture, and Society*, Vol. 2 (New York: Worth, 2000), 200.

7. John B. Rae, *The American Automobile: A Brief History* (Chicago: University of Chicago Press, 1965), 105.

8. Ibid., 88.

9. Paul S. Boyer et al., *The Enduring Vision: A History of the American People*, 4th ed. (Boston: Houghton Mifflin, 2000), 689.

10. John Margolies, *Pump and Circumstance: The Glory Days of the Gas Station* (Boston: Bullfinch Press, 1993), 44.

11. Kenneth L. Roberts, "Travels in Billboardia," *The Saturday Evening Post* 201 (October 13, 1928): 186, 189.

12. Stephen W. Sears, *The American Heritage History of the Automobile in America* (New York: American Heritage, 1977), 229.

13. Beth L. Bailey, *From Front Porch to Back Seat: Courtship Rituals in Twentieth-Century America* (Baltimore: Johns Hopkins University Press, 1988).

14. Lynd and Lynd, *Middletown*, 114.

15. Alan Mirken, ed., *1927 Edition of the Sears, Roebuck Catalogue* (New York: Bounty Books, 1970), 594.

16. Margaret Walsh, *Making Connections: The Long-Distance Bus Industry in the USA* (Burlington, VT: Ashgate, 2000), 8.

17. Cindy S. Aron, *Working at Play: A History of Vacations in the United States* (New York: Oxford University Press, 1999), 203.

18. John A. Jakle, Keith A. Sculle, and Jefferson S. Rogers, *The Motel in America* (Baltimore: Johns Hopkins University Press, 1996), 20.

19. John A. Jakle, *The Tourist: Travel in Twentieth-Century North America* (Lincoln: University of Nebraska Press, 1985), 71.
20. G. Freeman Allen, *Railways: Past, Present & Future* (New York: William Morrow and Company, 1982), 185.
21. T. A. Heppenheimer, *Turbulent Skies: The History of Commercial Aviation* (New York: John Wiley and Sons, 1995), 5–6.
22. Ibid., 14.
23. Ibid., 22.

CHAPTER 12

1. Ian Gordon, *Comic Strips and Consumer Culture, 1890–1945* (Washington, DC: Smithsonian Institution Press, 1998), 86.
2. Nancy Martha West, *Kodak and the Lens of Nostalgia* (Charlottesville: University Press of Virginia, 2000), 178.
3. Barbara H. Solomon, ed., *Ain't We Got Fun? Essays, Lyrics, and Stories of the Twenties* (New York: New American Library, 1980), 128.

Further Reading

Albertson, Chris. *Bessie: Empress of the Blues*. New York: Stein and Day, 1972.

Aldcroft, Derek H. *From Versailles to Wall Street, 1919–1929*. Berkeley: University of California Press, 1977.

Alexander, Doris. *Eugene O'Neill's Creative Struggle: The Decisive Decade, 1924–1933*. University Park: Pennsylvania State University Press, 1992.

Allen, Frederick Lewis. *Only Yesterday: An Informal History of the 1920s*. New York: Harper and Row, 1964 [1931].

Anderson, Jervis. *This Was Harlem: A Cultural Portrait, 1900–1950*. New York: Farrar, Straus and Giroux, 1982.

Armitage, Shelley. *John Held, Jr.: Illustrator of the Jazz Age*. Syracuse, NY: Syracuse University Press, 1987.

Arnesen, Eric. *Black Protest and the Great Migration: A Brief History with Documents*. Boston: Bedford/St. Martin's, 2003.

Aron, Cindy S. *Working at Play: A History of Vacations in the United States*. New York: Oxford University Press, 1999.

Asakawa, Gil, and Leland Rucker. *The Toy Book*. New York: Alfred A. Knopf, 1992.

Asinof, Eliot. *1919: America's Loss of Innocence*. New York: D. I. Fine, 1990.

Bailey, Beth L. *From Front Porch to Back Seat: Courtship Rituals in Twentieth-Century America*. Baltimore: Johns Hopkins University Press, 1988.

Barlow, William. *Looking Up at Down: The Emergence of Blues Culture*. Philadelphia: Temple University Press, 1989.

Baughman, Judith S., ed. *American Decades: 1920–1929*. Detroit: Gale Research, 1996.

Belasco, Warren. *Americans on the Road: From Autocamp to Motel, 1910–1945*. Baltimore: Johns Hopkins University Press, 1997.

Benson, Susan Porter. *Counter Cultures: Saleswomen, Managers, and Customers in*

American Department Stores, 1890–1940. Urbana: University of Illinois Press, 1986.

Berg, A. Scott. *Lindbergh*. New York: Putnam, 1998.

Bergreen, Laurence. *Capone: The Man and the Era*. New York: Simon and Schuster, 1994.

———. *Louis Armstrong: An Extravagant Life*. New York: Broadway Books, 1997.

Bernstein, Irving. *The Lean Years: A History of the American Worker, 1920–1933*. Boston: Houghton Mifflin, 1960.

Blum, Stella, ed. *Everyday Fashions of the Twenties, as Pictured in Sears and Other Catalogs*. New York: Dover Publications, 1981.

Botshon, Lisa, and Meredith Goldsmith, eds. *Middlebrow Moderns: Popular American Women Writers of the 1920s*. Boston: Northeastern University Press, 2003.

Braider, Donald. *George Bellows and the Ashcan School of Painting*. Garden City, NY: Doubleday, 1971.

Brinkley, Douglas. *Wheels for the World: Henry Ford, His Company, and a Century of Progress, 1903–2003*. New York: Viking, 2003.

Broekel, Ray. *The Great American Candy Bar Book*. Boston: Houghton Mifflin, 1982.

Brown, Carrie. *Rosie's Mom: Forgotten Women Workers of the First World War*. Boston: Northeastern University Press, 2002.

Brown, Dorothy M. *Setting a Course: Women in the 1920s*. Boston: Twayne Publishers, 1987.

Brown, Milton W. *American Painting from the Armory Show to the Depression*. Princeton, NJ: Princeton University Press, 1955.

Bruccoli, Matthew J. *F. Scott Fitzgerald: A Descriptive Biography*. Pittsburgh: University of Pittsburgh Press, 1987.

Canemaker, John. *Felix: The Twisted Tale of the World's Most Famous Cat*. New York: Pantheon Books, 1991.

Carroll, John M. *Red Grange and the Rise of Modern Football*. Urbana: University of Illinois Press, 1999.

Carter, Paul A. *The Twenties in America*. New York: Crowell, 1968.

Carter, Robin Borglum. *Gutzon Borglum: His Life and Work*. Austin, TX: Eakin Press, 1998.

Chafe, William H. *The Paradox of Change: American Women in the 20th Century*. New York: Oxford University Press, 1991.

Chesler, Ellen. *Woman of Valor: Margaret Sanger and the Birth Control Movement in America*. New York: Anchor Books, 1993.

Clarke, Donald. *The Rise and Fall of Popular Music*. New York: St. Martin's Press, 1995.

Cohen, Lizabeth. *Making a New Deal: Industrial Workers in Chicago, 1919–1939*. Cambridge: Cambridge University Press, 1990.

Conkin, Paul K. *The Southern Agrarians*. Knoxville: University of Tennessee Press, 1988.

Cowan, Ruth Schwartz. *More Work for Mother: The Ironies of Household Technologies from the Open Hearth to the Microwave*. New York: Basic Books, 1983.

Cowley, Malcolm, and Robert Cowley, eds. *Fitzgerald and the Jazz Age*. New York: Charles Scribner's Sons, 1966.

Creamer, Robert W. *Babe: The Legend Comes to Life*. New York: Simon and Schuster, 1992.

Cremin, Lawrence A. *American Education: The Metropolitan Experience, 1876–1980*. New York: Harper and Row, 1988.

Cripps, Thomas. *Slow Fade to Black: The Negro in American Film, 1900–1942*. New York: Oxford University Press, 1993 [1977].

Daniel, Pete. *Deep'n as It Come: The 1927 Mississippi River Flood*. New York: Oxford University Press, 1977.

Dardis, Tom. *Buster Keaton: The Man Who Wouldn't Lie Down*. Minneapolis: University of Minnesota Press, 2002.

Davis, Martin. *The Greatest of Them All: The Legend of Bobby Jones*. Greenwich, CT: American Golfer, 1996.

DeLong, Thomas A. *Pops: Paul Whiteman, King of Jazz*. Piscataway, NJ: New Century, 1983.

D'Emilio, John, and Estelle B. Freedman. *Intimate Matters: A History of Sexuality in America*. New York: Harper and Row, 1988.

Douglas, Ann. *Terrible Honesty: Mongrel Manhattan in the 1920s*. New York: Farrar, Straus and Giroux, 1995.

Douglas, George H. *Skyscrapers: A Social History of the Very Tall Building in America*. Jefferson, NC: McFarland, 1996.

———. *The Smart Magazines: 50 Years of Literary Revelry and High Jinks at Vanity Fair, the New Yorker, Life, Esquire, and the Smart Set*. Hamden, CT: Archon Books, 1991.

Dumenil, Lynn. *The Modern Temper: American Culture and Society in the 1920s*. New York: Hill and Wang, 1995.

Dunning, John. *On the Air: The Encyclopedia of Old-Time Radio*. New York: Oxford University Press, 1998.

DuSablon, Mary Anna. *America's Collectible Cookbooks: The History, the Politics, the Recipes*. Athens: Ohio University Press, 1994.

Editors of Time-Life Books. *Our American Century: The Jazz Age, the 20s*. Alexandria, VA: Time-Life Books, 1998.

Ellsworth, Scott. *Death in a Promised Land: The Tulsa Race Riot of 1921*. Baton Rouge: Louisiana State University Press, 1982.

Ely, Melvin Patrick. *The Adventures of Amos 'n' Andy: A Social History of an American Phenomenon*. New York: Free Press, 1991.

Engelmann, Larry. *The Goddess and the American Girl: The Story of Suzanne Lenglen and Helen Wills*. New York: Oxford University Press, 1988.

Epstein, Daniel M. *Sister Aimee: The Life of Aimee Semple McPherson*. New York: Harcourt Brace Jovanovich, 1993.

Erenberg, Lewis A. *Steppin' Out: New York Nightlife and the Transformation of American Culture*. Chicago: University of Chicago Press, 1981.

Ermoyan, Arpi. *Famous American Illustrators*. New York: Rotovision, 1997.

Ernst, Robert. *Weakness Is a Crime: The Life of Bernarr Macfadden*. Syracuse, NY: Syracuse University Press, 1991.

Evensen, Bruce J. *When Dempsey Fought Tunney: Heroes, Hokum, and Storytelling in the Jazz Age*. Knoxville: University of Tennessee Press, 1996.

Fass, Paula. *The Damned and the Beautiful: American Youth in the 1920's*. New York: Oxford University Press, 1977.

Faulkner, Harold U. *From Versailles to the New Deal: A Chronicle of the Harding-Coolidge-Hoover Era*. New York: United States Publishers Association, 1950.
Feuerlicht, Roberta Strauss. *Justice Crucified: The Story of Sacco and Vanzetti*. New York: McGraw-Hill, 1977.
Finan, Christopher M. *Alfred E. Smith, the Happy Warrior*. New York: Hill and Wang, 2002.
Finch, Christopher. *The Art of Walt Disney: From Mickey Mouse to the Magic Kingdoms*. New York: Abrams, 1995.
Fischler, Stanley I. *Moving Millions: An Inside Look at Mass Transit*. New York: Harper and Row, 1979.
Fite, Gilbert C. *The Farmers' Dilemma, 1919–1929*. Columbus: Ohio State University Press, 1968.
Flink, James J. *The Car Culture*. Cambridge, MA: MIT Press, 1975.
Fox, Richard Wrightman, and T. J. Jackson Lears, eds. *The Culture of Consumption: Critical Essays in American History, 1880–1980*. New York: Pantheon Books, 1983.
Furhman, Candice Jacobson. *Publicity Stunt! Great Staged Events That Made the News*. San Francisco: Chronicle Books, 1989.
Galbraith, John Kenneth. *The Great Crash, 1929*. Boston: Houghton Mifflin, 1997 [1955].
Gilbert, Julie Goldsmith. *Ferber: A Biography*. Garden City, NY: Doubleday, 1978.
Ginger, Ray. *Six Days or Forever? Tennessee vs. John Thomas Scopes*. Boston: Beacon Press, 1958.
Goings, Kenneth W. *Mammy and Uncle Mose: Black Collectibles and American Stereotyping*. Bloomington: Indiana University Press, 1994.
Goldberg, David J. *Discontented America: The United States in the 1920s*. Baltimore: Johns Hopkins University Press, 1999.
Goldman, Herbert G. *Banjo Eyes: Eddie Cantor and the Birth of Modern Stardom*. New York: Oxford University Press, 1997.
———. *Jolson: The Legend Comes to Life*. New York: Oxford University Press, 1988.
Gordon, Ian. *Comic Strips and Consumer Culture, 1890–1945*. Washington, DC: Smithsonian Institution Press, 1998.
Grandinetti, Fred M. *Popeye: An Illustrated History of E. C. Segar's Character in Print, Radio, Television, and Film Appearances, 1929–1993*. Jefferson, NC: McFarland, 1994.
Grant, Robert, and Joseph Katz. *The Great Trials of the Twenties: The Watershed Decade in America's Courtrooms*. Rockville Centre, NY: Sarpedon, 1998.
Green, Harvey. *The Uncertainty of Everyday Life, 1915–1945*. New York: HarperCollins, 1992.
Hackett, Alice Payne. *70 Years of Best Sellers, 1895–1965*. New York: R. R. Bowker, 1967.
Hadlock, Richard. *Jazz Masters of the Twenties*. New York: Da Capo Press, 1988 [1965].
Haining, Peter. *The Classic Era of American Pulp Magazines*. Chicago: Chicago Review Press, 2001.
Harries, Meirion, and Susie Harries. *The Last Days of Innocence: America at War, 1917–1918*. New York: Vintage Books, 1998.

Harrison, Daphne Duval. *Black Pearls: Blues Queens of the 1920s*. New Brunswick, NJ: Rutgers University Press, 1988.

Haskins, Jim. *The Cotton Club*. New York: New American Library, 1977.

Hasse, John Edward. *Beyond Category: The Life and Genius of Duke Ellington*. New York: Simon and Schuster, 1993.

Hawes, Joseph M. *Children Between the Wars: American Childhood, 1920–1940*. New York: Twayne Publishers, 1997.

Hawley, Ellis W. *The Great War and the Search for Modern Order: A History of the American People and Their Institutions, 1917–1933*. New York: St. Martin's Press, 1979.

Heimann, Jim. *Car Hops and Curb Service: A History of American Drive-In Restaurants, 1920–1960*. San Francisco: Chronicle Books, 1996.

Heppenheimer, T. A. *Turbulent Skies: The History of Commercial Aviation*. New York: John Wiley and Sons, 1995.

Herald, Jacqueline. *Fashions of a Decade: The 1920s*. New York: Facts on File, 1991.

Hicks, John D. *Republican Ascendancy, 1921–1933*. New York: Harper and Row, 1960.

Higashi, Sumiko. *Virgins, Vamps, and Flappers: The American Silent Movie Heroine*. Montreal, Quebec: Eden Press Women's Publications, 1978.

Higdon, Hal. *Leopold and Loeb: The Crime of the Century*. Urbana: University of Illinois Press, 1999.

Higham, Charles. *Cecil B. DeMille*. New York: Da Capo Press, 1980 [1973].

Hildebrand, Grant. *Designing for Industry: The Architecture of Albert Kahn*. Cambridge, MA: MIT Press, 1974.

Hill, Daniel Delis. *Advertising to the American Woman, 1900–1990*. Columbus: Ohio State University Press, 2002.

Hillier, Bevis, and Stephen Escritt. *Art Deco Style*. London: Phaidon, 1997.

Hobson, Fred C., Jr. *Serpent in Eden: H. L. Mencken and the South*. Baton Rouge: Louisiana State University Press, 1978 [1974].

Hoffmann, Frank W., and William G. Bailey. *Arts and Entertainment Fads*. New York: Haworth Press, 1990.

———. *Sports and Recreation Fads*. New York: Haworth Press, 1991.

Hoffman, Frederick J. *The Twenties: American Writing in the Postwar Decade*. New York: Viking Press, 1955.

Hogan, David Gerard. *Selling 'em by the Sack: White Castle and the Creation of American Food*. New York: New York University Press, 1997.

Hooker, Clarence. *Life in the Shadows of the Crystal Palace, 1910–1927: Ford Workers in the Model T Era*. Bowling Green, OH: Bowling Green State University Popular Press, 1997.

Isaacs, Neil D. *All the Moves: A History of College Basketball*. New York: Harper and Row, 1984.

Jablonski, Edward. *Gershwin*. Garden City, NY: Doubleday, 1987.

Jackson, Kenneth T. *The Ku Klux Klan in the City, 1915–1930*. New York: Oxford University Press, 1967.

Jakle, John A. *The Tourist: Travel in Twentieth-Century North America*. Lincoln: University of Nebraska Press, 1985.

Jakle, John A., and Keith A. Sculle. *Fast Food: Roadside Restaurants in the Automobile Age*. Baltimore: Johns Hopkins University Press, 1999.

———. *The Gas Station in America.* Baltimore: Johns Hopkins University Press, 1994.

Jakle, John A., Keith A. Sculle, and Jefferson S. Rogers. *The Motel in America.* Baltimore: Johns Hopkins University Press, 1996.

Jasen, David A. *Tin Pan Alley: The Composers, the Songs, the Performers, and Their Times.* New York: Donald I. Fine, 1988.

Kahn, Roger. *A Flame of Pure Fire: Jack Dempsey and the Roaring '20s.* New York: Harcourt Brace, 1999.

Kellner, Bruce. *Carl Van Vechten and the Irreverent Decades.* Norman: University of Oklahoma Press, 1968.

———. *The Last Dandy, Ralph Barton: American Artist, 1891–1931.* Columbia: University of Missouri Press, 1991.

Kennedy, David M. *Over Here: The First World War and American Society.* New York: Oxford University Press, 1980.

Kenney, William Howland. *Recorded Music in American Life: The Phonograph and Popular Memory, 1890–1945.* New York: Oxford University Press, 1999.

Kessler-Harris, Alice. *Out to Work: A History of Wage-Earning Women in the United States.* New York: Oxford University Press, 1982.

Klein, Maury. *Rainbow's End: The Crash of 1929.* New York: Oxford University Press, 2001.

Kobler, John. *Ardent Spirits: The Rise and Fall of Prohibition.* Stillwater: Oklahoma State University Press, 1975.

Korda, Michael. *Making the List: A Cultural History of the American Bestseller, 1900–1999.* New York: Barnes and Noble Books, 2001.

Krasner, David. *A Beautiful Pageant: African American Theatre, Drama, and Performance in the Harlem Renaissance, 1910–1927.* New York: Palgrave Macmillan, 2002.

Larson, Edward J. *Summer for the Gods: The Scopes Trial and America's Continuing Debate over Science and Religion.* Cambridge, MA: Harvard University Press, 1998.

Latham, Angela. *Posing a Threat: Flappers, Chorus Girls, and Other Brazen Performers of the American 1920s.* Hanover, NH: University Press of New England for Wesleyan University Press, 2000.

Laubner, Ellie. *Fashions of the Roaring '20s.* Atglen, PA: Schiffer Publishing Ltd., 1996.

Leach, William. *Land of Desire: Merchants, Power, and the Rise of a New American Culture.* New York: Pantheon Books, 1993.

Lears, Jackson. *Fables of Abundance: A Cultural History of Advertising in America.* New York: Basic Books, 1994.

Leider, Emily W. *Dark Lover: The Life and Death of Rudolph Valentino.* New York: Farrar, Straus and Giroux, 2003.

Lencek, Lena, and Gideon Bosker. *Making Waves: Swimsuits and the Undressing of America.* San Francisco: Chronicle Books, 1989.

Leuchtenburg, William E. *The Perils of Prosperity, 1914–1932.* Chicago: University of Chicago Press, 1993 [1958].

Levenstein, Harvey A. *Revolution at the Table: The Transformation of the American Diet.* New York: Oxford University Press, 1988.

Levine, David O. *The American College and the Culture of Aspiration, 1915–1940*. Ithaca, NY: Cornell University Press, 1986.

Lewis, David Levering. *When Harlem Was in Vogue*. New York: Alfred A. Knopf, 1981.

Lichtman, Allan J. *Prejudice and the Old Politics: The Presidential Election of 1928*. Chapel Hill: University of North Carolina Press, 1979.

Liebs, Chester H. *Main Street to Miracle Mile: American Roadside Architecture*. Baltimore: Johns Hopkins University Press, 1985.

Lingeman, Richard. *Sinclair Lewis: Rebel from Main Street*. New York: Random House, 2002.

Lucic, Karen. *Charles Sheeler and the Cult of the Machine*. Cambridge, MA: Harvard University Press, 1991.

Lynd, Robert S., and Helen Merrell Lynd. *Middletown: A Study in American Culture*. New York: Harcourt Brace, 1929.

MacCann, Richard Dyer, comp. *Films of the 1920s*. Lanham, MD: Scarecrow Press, in association with Image and Idea, 1996.

MacDonald, J. Fred. *Don't Touch That Dial*. Chicago: Nelson-Hall, 1979.

MacLean, Nancy. *Behind the Mask of Chivalry: The Making of the Second Ku Klux Klan*. New York: Oxford University Press, 1994.

Maddocks, Melvin. *The Great Liners*. New York: Time-Life Books, 1978.

Madsen, Axel. *Chanel: A Woman of Her Own*. New York: Henry Holt, 1990.

Malone, Bill C. *Country Music, U.S.A.* Rev. ed. Austin: University of Texas Press, 1985 [1968].

Maltin, Leonard. *Of Mice and Magic: A History of American Animated Cartoons*. New York: McGraw-Hill, 1980.

Marchand, Roland. *Advertising the American Dream: Making Way for Modernity, 1920–1940*. Berkeley: University of California Press, 1985.

Margolies, John. *Pump and Circumstance: The Glory Days of the Gas Station*. Boston: Bullfinch Press, 1993.

Mariani, John. *America Eats Out: An Illustrated History of Restaurants, Taverns, Coffee Shops, Speakeasies, and Other Establishments That Have Fed Us for 350 Years*. New York: William Morrow and Company, 1991.

Marling, Karal Ann. *Norman Rockwell*. New York: Harry N. Abrams, in association with the National Museum of American Art, Smithsonian Institution, 1997.

Marschall, Richard. *America's Greatest Comic-Strip Artists*. New York: Abbeville Press, 1989.

Marsden, George M. *Fundamentalism and American Culture: The Shaping of Twentieth-Century Evangelicalism, 1870–1925*. New York: Oxford University Press, 1980.

Martin, Carol. *Dance Marathons: Performing American Culture in the 1920s and 1930s*. Jackson: University of Mississippi Press, 1994.

Martin, Robert F. *Hero of the Heartland: Billy Sunday and the Transformation of American Society, 1862–1935*. Bloomington: Indiana University Press, 2002.

May, Henry F. *The End of American Innocence: A Study of the First Years of Our Own Time, 1912–1917*. New York: Alfred A. Knopf, 1959.

May, Lary. *Screening Out the Past: The Birth of Mass Culture and the Motion Picture Industry*. New York: Oxford University Press, 1980.

May, Stephen. *Zane Grey: Romancing the West*. Athens: Ohio University Press, 1997.

McAlester, Virginia, and Lee McAlester. *A Field Guide to American Houses*. New York: Alfred A. Knopf, 2000.

Milford, Nancy. *Savage Beauty: The Life of Edna St. Vincent Millay*. New York: Random House, 2001.

Millard, Andre. *America on Record: A History of Recorded Sound*. New York: Cambridge University Press, 1995.

Millington, Roger. *Crossword Puzzles, Their History and Their Cult*. Nashville, TN: T. Nelson, 1975.

Mintz, Steven, and Susan Kellogg. *Domestic Revolutions: A Social History of American Family Life*. New York: Free Press, 1988.

Mirken, Alan, ed. *1927 Edition of the Sears, Roebuck Catalogue*. New York: Bounty Books, 1970.

Mizejewski, Linda. *Ziegfeld Girl: Image and Icon in Culture and Cinema*. Durham, NC: Duke University Press, 1999.

Moore, Leonard J. *Citizen Klansmen: The Ku Klux Klan in Indiana, 1921–1928*. Chapel Hill: University of North Carolina Press, 1991.

Mordden, Ethan. *Make Believe: The Broadway Musical in the 1920s*. New York: Oxford University Press, 1997.

Moriarty, Florence. *True Confessions: Sixty Years of Sin, Suffering, and Sorrow, 1919–1979*. New York: Simon and Schuster, 1979.

Mowry, George E., ed. *The Twenties: Fords, Flappers & Fanatics*. Englewood Cliffs, NJ: Prentice-Hall, 1963.

Murdock, Catherine Gilbert. *Domesticating Drink: Women, Men, and Alcohol in America, 1870–1940*. Baltimore: Johns Hopkins University Press, 1998.

Murray, Robert K. *Red Scare: A Study in National Hysteria, 1919–1920*. Westport, CT: Greenwood Press, 1980 [1955].

Murray, Robert K., and Roger W. Brucker. *Trapped! The Story of Floyd Collins*. Lexington: University Press of Kentucky, 1982 [1979].

Nash, Roderick. *The Nervous Generation: American Thought, 1917–1930*. Chicago: Rand McNally and Company, 1970.

Nathan, Daniel A. *Saying It's So: A Cultural History of the Black Sox Scandal*. Urbana: University of Illinois Press, 2003.

Naylor, David. *Great American Movie Theaters*. Washington, DC: The Preservation Press, 1987.

Neuhaus, Jessamyn. *Manly Meals and Mom's Home Cooking: Cookbooks and Gender in Modern America*. Baltimore: Johns Hopkins University Press, 2003.

O'Brien, Richard. *The Story of American Toys from the Puritans to the Present*. New York: Abbeville Press, 1990.

Ogren, Kathy J. *The Jazz Revolution: Twenties America and the Meaning of Jazz*. New York: Oxford University Press, 1989.

Oja, Carol J. *Making Music Modern: New York in the 1920s*. New York: Oxford University Press, 2000.

Oriard, Michael. *King Football: Sport and Spectacle in the Golden Age of Radio and Newsreels, Movies and Magazines, the Weekly and the Daily Press*. Chapel Hill: University of North Carolina Press, 2001.

Panati, Charles. *Panati's Parade of Fads, Follies, and Manias: The Origins of Our Most Cherished Obsessions*. New York: HarperPerennial, 1991.

Paris, Barry. *Garbo: A Biography*. New York: Alfred A. Knopf, 1995.

Pendergast, Sara, and Tom Pendergast, eds. *Bowling, Beatniks, and Bell-Bottoms: Pop Culture of 20th-Century America*. Detroit: Gale Group, 2002.

Peretti, Burton W. *The Creation of Jazz: Music, Race, and Culture in Urban America*. Urbana: University of Illinois Press, 1992.

———. *Jazz in American Culture*. Chicago: Ivan R. Dee, 1997.

Perrett, Geoffrey. *America in the Twenties: A History*. New York: Simon and Schuster, 1982.

Peterson, Robert W. *Cages to Jump Shots: Pro Basketball's Early Years*. New York: Oxford University Press, 1990.

Porterfield, Nolan. *Jimmie Rodgers: The Life and Times of America's Blue Yodeler*. Urbana: University of Illinois Press, 1992.

Prothro, James W. *The Dollar Decade: Business Ideas in the 1920's*. Baton Rouge: Louisiana State University Press, 1954.

Radway, Janice A. *A Feeling for Books: The Book-of-the-Month Club, Literary Taste, and Middle-Class Desire*. Chapel Hill: University of North Carolina Press, 1997.

Rae, John B. *The American Automobile: A Brief History*. Chicago: University of Chicago Press, 1965.

———. *The Road and Car in American Life*. Cambridge, MA: MIT Press, 1971.

Rampersad, Arnold. *The Life of Langston Hughes: Volume 1, 1902–1941: I, Too, Sing America*. New York: Oxford University Press, 1986.

Reilly, Adam. *Harold Lloyd: The King of Daredevil Comedy*. New York: Macmillan, 1977.

Riverol, Armando R. *Live from Atlantic City: The History of the Miss America Beauty Pageant Before, After and in Spite of Television*. Bowling Green, OH: Bowling Green State University Popular Press, 1992.

Robinson, David. *Chaplin: His Life and Art*. New York: Da Capo Press, 1994.

———. *From Peep Show to Palace: The Birth of American Film*. New York: Columbia University Press, in association with the Library of Congress, 1996.

Robinson, Frank M., and Lawrence Davidson. *Pulp Culture: The Art of Fiction Magazines*. Portland, OR: Collectors Press, 1998.

Roth, Leland M. *A Concise History of American Architecture*. New York: Harper and Row, 1979.

Salmond, John A. *Gastonia 1929: The Story of the Loray Mill Strike*. Chapel Hill: University of North Carolina Press, 1995.

Sanjek, Russell. *Pennies from Heaven: The American Popular Music Business in the Twentieth Century*. New York: Da Capo Press, 1996.

Sann, Paul. *Fads, Follies, and Delusions of the American People*. New York: Bonanza Books, 1967.

———. *The Lawless Decade: A Pictorial History of a Great American Transition: From the World War I Armistice and Prohibition to Repeal and the New Deal*. New York: Bonanza Books, 1957.

Schwartz, Hillel. *Never Satisfied: A Cultural History of Diets, Fantasies, and Fat*. New York: Free Press, 1986.

Sears, Stephen W. *The American Heritage History of the Automobile in America*. New York: American Heritage, 1977.

Shannon, David A. *Between the Wars: America, 1919–1941*. 2nd ed. Boston: Houghton Mifflin, 1979.

Shaw, Arnold. *The Jazz Age: Popular Music in the 1920s*. New York: Oxford University Press, 1987.

Shelton, Suzanne. *Ruth St. Denis: A Biography of the Divine Dancer*. Austin: University of Texas, 1990 [1981].

Singal, Daniel J. *The War Within: From Victorian to Modernist Thought in the South, 1919–1945*. Chapel Hill: University of North Carolina Press, 1982.

Sklar, Robert. *Movie-Made America: A Cultural History of American Movies*. Rev. ed. New York: Vintage Books, 1994 [1975].

Slayton, Robert A. *Empire Statesman: The Rise and Redemption of Al Smith*. New York: Free Press, 2001.

Slide, Anthony. *The Encyclopedia of Vaudeville*. Westport, CT: Greenwood Press, 1994.

Smith, Bruce. *The History of Little Orphan Annie*. New York: Ballantine Books, 1982.

Smith, Richard Norton. *An Uncommon Man: The Triumph of Herbert Hoover*. New York: Simon and Schuster, 1984.

Smulyan, Susan. *Selling Radio: The Commercialization of American Broadcasting, 1920–1934*. Washington, DC: Smithsonian Institution Press, 1994.

Snyder, Robert W. *The Voice of the City: Vaudeville and Popular Culture in New York*. New York: Oxford University Press, 1989.

Solomon, Barbara H., ed. *Ain't We Got Fun? Essays, Lyrics, and Stories of the Twenties*. New York: New American Library, 1980.

Stearns, Marshall, and Jean Stearns. *Jazz Dance: The Story of American Vernacular Dance*. New York: Da Capo Press, 1994 [1968].

Stein, Judith. *The World of Marcus Garvey: Race and Class in Modern Society*. Baton Rouge: Louisiana State University Press, 1986.

Stenn, David. *Clara Bow: Runnin' Wild*. New York: Cooper Square Press, 2000.

Stevenson, Elizabeth. *Babbitts and Bohemians: The American 1920s*. New York: Macmillan, 1967.

Strasser, Susan. *Never Done: A History of American Housework*. New York: Pantheon Books, 1982.

———. *Satisfaction Guaranteed: The Making of the American Mass Market*. New York: Pantheon Books, 1989.

Stratton, David H. *Tempest Over Teapot Dome: The Story of Albert B. Fall*. Norman: University of Oklahoma Press, 1998.

Streissguth, Thomas. *The Roaring Twenties: An Eyewitness History*. New York: Facts on File, 2001.

Taliaferro, John. *Tarzan Forever: The Life of Edgar Rice Burroughs, Creator of Tarzan*. New York: Scribner, 1999.

Tashjian, Dickran. *Skyscraper Primitives: Dada and the American Avant-Garde, 1910–1925*. Middletown, CT: Wesleyan University Press, 1975.

Tchudi, Stephen N. *Soda Poppery: The History of Soft Drinks in America*. New York: Charles Scribner's Sons, 1986.

Teachout, Terry. *The Skeptic: A Life of H. L. Mencken*. New York: HarperCollins, 2002.

Tentler, Leslie Woodcock. *Wage-Earning Women: Industrial Work and Family Life in the United States, 1900–1930*. New York: Oxford University Press, 1979.

Thomas, Gordon. *The Day the Bubble Burst: A Social History of the Wall Street Crash of 1929*. Garden City, NY: Doubleday, 1979.

Trachtenberg, Leo. *The Wonder Team: The True Story of the Incomparable 1927 New York Yankees*. Bowling Green, OH: Bowling Green State University Popular Press, 1995.

Tuttle, William M., Jr. *Race Riot: Chicago in the Red Summer of 1919*. New York: Atheneum, 1970.

van der Linden, F. Robert. *Airlines and Air Mail: The Post Office and the Birth of the Commercial Aviation Industry*. Lexington: University of Kentucky Press, 2002.

Vermilye, Jerry. *The Films of the Twenties*. Secaucus, NJ: Citadel Press, 1985.

Voss, Arthur. *Tilden and Tennis in the Twenties*. Troy, NY: Whitston, 1985.

Wainscott, Ronald H. *The Emergence of the Modern American Theater 1914–1929*. New Haven, CT: Yale University Press, 1997.

Wandersee, Winifred D. *Women's Work and Family Values, 1920–1940*. Cambridge, MA: Harvard University Press, 1981.

Ward, Geoffrey C. *Jazz: A History of America's Music*. New York: Alfred A. Knopf, 2000.

Ward, John W. "The Meaning of Lindbergh's Flight." *American Quarterly* 10 (Spring 1958): 3–16.

Watkins, T. H. *The Hungry Years: America in an Age of Crisis, 1929–1939*. New York: Henry Holt and Company, 1999.

Watts, Steven. *The Magic Kingdom: Walt Disney and the American Way of Life*. Columbia: University of Missouri Press, 2001.

Weinberg, Arthur, and Lila Weinberg. *Clarence Darrow, a Sentimental Rebel*. New York: Putman, 1980.

West, Elliott. *Growing Up in Twentieth-Century America: A History and Reference Guide*. Westport, CT: Greenwood Press, 1996.

Wiebe, Robert H. *The Search for Modern Order, 1877–1920*. New York: Hill and Wang, 1967.

Wik, Reynold M. *Henry Ford and Grass-Roots America*. Ann Arbor: University of Michigan Press, 1972.

Wintz, Cary D. *Black Culture and the Harlem Renaissance*. College Station: Texas A&M University Press, 1996.

Witzel, Michael Karl, and Gyvel Young-Witzel. *Soda Pop! From Miracle Medicine to Pop Culture*. Stillwater, MN: Town Square Books, 1998.

Wolfe, Charles K. *A Good-Natured Riot: The Birth of the Grand Ole Opry*. Nashville: Country Music Foundation Press and Vanderbilt University Press, 1999.

Yallop, David A. *The Day the Laughter Stopped: The True Story of Fatty Arbuckle*. New York: St. Martin's Press, 1976.

Ziegfeld, Richard, and Paulette Ziegfeld. *The Ziegfeld Touch: The Life and Times of Florenz Ziegfeld, Jr*. New York: H. N. Abrams, 1993.

Index

A&P grocery stores, 57, 68, 128
A&P Gypsies, The, 68, 240
A&W, 133
A&W Root Beer, 133, 140
Abie's Irish Rose, 222–223
Academy Awards, 197, 236
Academy of Motion Picture Arts and Sciences, 236. *See also* Academy Awards
Actors' Association for Clean Plays, 223
Adventure, 180
Adventurers' Club of New York, 180
Advertising, 51–72; advertising executives, 54; automobile, 246; celebration of youth, 38, 40–41, 58; clothing, 96, 100; Coca-Cola, 67, 139; cosmetics and beauty products, 40; criticism of, 54, 68, 70–71; food, 56, 58–59, 61, 62, 63, 65, 136–137; growth of, 5, 52–53; household appliances, 56, 61; Kodak cameras, 284; Lucky Strike cigarettes, 53, 61–62; magazines and newspapers in, 55–56, 58, 65–67, 240; racial stereotypes in, 62–63; rise of modern advertising, 53–54; scams and swindles, 71–72; toiletries, 56, 58–59, 60, 65, 66; "Truth-in-Advertising" campaign, 71; women and, 55–62
Advertising strategies: appeal to antimodernism, 58; appeal to insecurities and fears, 58–61; appeal to modernity, 56; bandwagon, 61; celebrity endorsements, 61–62, 96; hard sell/soft sell approaches, 53–54; publicity stunts, 63–65, 149; recapturing youth, 58; scientific information and medical advice, 61; slogans, 56, 62, 63, 67, 134, 139; snob appeal, 61; spokespersons, 61–63
Advertising venues, 51, 52, 65–71; airships, 266; architecture, 66, 82–83, 86–87, 134, 135; billboards, 66, 247–248; comic strips, 66; "commercials" before films, 66; magazines and newspapers, 55–56, 58, 65–67, 240; radio, 63, 66, 67–71, 240; window displays, 66
African Americans: black nationalism, 12; dance, 227–228; films, 235–236; Great Migration, 9, 186–187; hair and skin care products, 108, 109; Harlem Renaissance, 186–188, 273–274; music, 199–209; "New Negro,"

12–13; racial stereotypes, 62–63, 87, 145, 220, 226, 235, 241; segregation, 9, 31, 157, 164, 221, 256; sports, 157–158, 164; stage performances, 196, 220, 221, 224–225, 226, 227, 228; violence against, 9–12
Agrarians, 188
Agriculture, 35–36, 38, 123, 246
Aiken, Conrad, 185
"Ain't Misbehavin'," 196
"Ain't We Got Fun," 42, 192
Air Commerce Act of 1926, 263
Air Mail Act of 1925, 262
Airmail, 261–263, 266
Airplanes and air travel, 261–266
Alamo Plaza Tourist Court, 256
All God's Chillun Got Wings, 187, 223
Allen, Frederick Lewis, xiii, 231
Allen, Ida Bailey, 70, 124, 125
Allen, Roy, 133
All-Story Magazine, 180, 280
Amazing Stories, 180
American Automobile Association (AAA), 247
American Birth Control League, 46
American Girl, 38
American Mercury, 176, 178
American Professional Football Association (APFA), 161
American Scene painting, 272
American Tobacco Company, 53, 62, 81
Amos 'n' Andy, 241–242
Anderson, John Murray, 225
Anderson, Maxwell, 224
Anderson, Walter, 134
Angelus Temple (Los Angeles), 21
Arbuckle, Roscoe "Fatty," 25, 189, 231, 232
Architecture, 73–93; as advertising, 66, 82–83, 86–87; architects, 74, 76, 91–93; Art Deco, 73–74; bungalows, 87–88; churches and temples, 80; Colonial Revival, 88; Egyptian and other foreign influence, 74, 84–85, 86, 153; European influence, 73–75, 83–84, 87, 88, 90; Four-Square, 88; gas stations, 85–86; government buildings, 81–82; industrial, 82, 91; International Style, 74–75; mimetic, 66, 86–87; modern building materials, 75, 76, 82–83; movie palaces, 83–85; residential, 87–90; restaurant, 66, 82–83, 86–87, 134, 135; skyscrapers, 75–80; Spanish Colonial Revival, 88, 90; styles, 73–75, 80, 81, 83–85, 86; university, 80–81
Arden, Elizabeth, 109
Argosy, The, 179, 180
Armory Show. *See* International Exhibition of Modern Art
Armstrong, Louis, xiv, 201, 203, 208
Arrow Collars and Shirts, 113, 277
Arrowsmith, 171–172
Art: American Scene painting, 272; American schools, 270–273; Ashcan school, 271–272; Cubism, 269–270, 273; Dadaism, 270, 273; European influence, 269–270, 273; Harlem Renaissance, 273–274; Modernism, 269–270; painting, 271–274, 277; photography, 283–284; Precisionism, 272–273; sculpture, 81, 273, 286; Surrealism, 270
Art Deco, 73–74
Art expositions, 73–75, 270
Ashcan school, 271–272
Association of Laundry Owners, 56
Astaire, Adele, 198, 225, 227
Astaire, Fred, 198, 225, 227
Atlantic Monthly, 39, 178
Atlas, Charles, 112, 152–153
Augusta National golf course, 162
Aunt Jemima, 63
Aunt Sammy, 70, 125
Austin, Gene, 199
Auto racing, 165–166
Auto-camping, 247, 254–255, 258
Automobiles: criticism of, 249; decline of railroads and, 259; drive-in restaurants and, 133–134; highway construction and, 246–247; impact on daily life, 133–134, 243–244, 247–249, 259; impact on other industries, 246–247; insurance, 247; manufacturing, 244–246; ownership of,

133, 244–245; popular culture and, 137, 249–250, 279–280; racing, 165–166; rental car companies, 247. *See also* Model A Ford; Model T Ford

B. F. Goodrich Company, 68, 240
Babbitt, 171
Baby Ruth candy bars, 65, 136
"Back to Normalcy," 4
Bailey, DeFord, 210
Baker, Josephine, 111, 225
Bara, Theda, 109
Barn dances, 209–210
Barton, Bruce, 55, 174
Barton, Ralph, 275–276, 278
Baseball, 155–158
Basketball, 163–164
Bathing suits, 103–105
"Battle of the Century, The," 158
Bayes, Nora, 220
Beautiful and Damned, The, 184
Beauty pageants, 96, 97, 104
Beiderbecke, Bix, 203, 204
Bellows, George, 271–272
Benet, Stephen Vincent, 185
Ben-Hur: A Tale of Christ, 231
Berlin, Irving, 192
Better Homes & Gardens, 90
Betty Crocker School of the Air, The, 70, 125
Beverages, 14, 67, 68, 122, 125, 138–140
Beyond the Horizon, 223
Bicycles, 146
Big Parade, The, 233
Billboards, 66, 247–248
Birdseye, Clarence, 122
Birth of a Nation, The, 230
Black Bottom (dance), 42, 227–228, 229
"Black Bottom" (song), 192
Black Mask, The, 179, 182
Black nationalism, 12
Black Pirate, The, 231
"Black Sox scandal," 155
"Black Thursday," 26
"Black Tuesday," 26
Blackbirds series, 196, 226
Blake, Eubie, 196, 225
Blanchard, Carrie, 62
Blues: An Anthology, 205–206, 278
Blues music, 205–209
Bobbed hair, 30, 107–108. *See also* Hairstyles
Bodybuilding, 111–112, 152
Boeing Air Transport, 263, 266
Book-of-the-Month Club, 170
Boop, Betty, 199
Bootlegging, 14, 15–17
Borglum, Gutzon, 286–288
Boston Cooking-School Cook Book, The, 124, 174
Bow, Clara, 44, 61, 109, 136–137, 233, 237, 238
Boxing, 158–159, 271–272
Boy Scouts, 37
Bradbury, Ray, 179
Bradley, Alice, 124
Branner, Martin, 280
Brassieres, 105–106
Brice, Fanny, 199, 221
Broadway Melody, The, 196–197
Broadway musicals and revues. *See* Musicals and revues
Brooks, Louise, 107
Brown Derby, 87, 124
Brown of Harvard, 34
Bryan, William Jennings, 21–22
Bubble gum, 137
Buck Rogers in the 25th Century A.D., 280
"Bunion Derby," 149
Burchfield, Charles, 272
Burma Shave shaving cream, 66
Burroughs, Edgar Rice, 180, 280–281
Burt, Harry, 137
Buses, 250–251
Butterfinger candy bar, 136

Caesar, Irving, 224
Caesar salad, 124
Cahill, Holger, 271
Calkins, Dick, 280
Camp Fire Girls of America, 38
Campbell Soup Company, 56, 61
Camping. *See* Auto-camping

Canada Dry Pale Dry Ginger Ale, 140
Candy, 134–137
Cantor, Eddie, 147, 198, 220, 239
Capone, Al "Scarface," 15–17
Captain Blood, 173
Cardini, Caesar, 124
Carnegie, Dale, 55
Carpentier, Georges, 158
Carroll, Earl, 226
Carson, Fiddlin' John, 210–211, 250
Carter, Garnet, 151
Carter, Howard, 74
Carter Family, 213
Cartoonists, 270, 282–283
Cartoons, 282–283
Caruso, Enrico, 189–190, 217
Castle, Irene, 107, 110, 228
Castle, Vernon, 228
Catalina Swimwear, 104
Chandler, Raymond, 179
Chanel, Gabrielle "Coco," 101, 102, 103, 107, 109, 111
Chaney, Lon, 237
Chaplin, Charlie, xiv, 63–64, 234–235
Chapman, Roy, 156
Charleston (dance), 42, 227, 229
"Charleston" (song), 192, 227
"Charleston Baby of Mine," 227
"Charleston Trio," 145
"Charmaine," 196
Checkered Cab Manufacturing Company, 252
Chevrolet, Gaston, 166
Chicago Bears, 160, 161
Chicago Tribune, 279
Chicago Tribune Tower, 75, 76, 91
"Chicken Snatcher," 145
Children: Americanization of, 31–32; cartoons, 282–283; comic strips, 44, 66, 278–282; education, 31–32; fashion, 116–117; labor, 35–36; magazines, 38, 277; organized recreation, 36–38; toys and games, 144–146, 147–148, 151–152, 175, 250
Chocolate. *See* Candy
Christy, Chandler, 277
Chrysler Building, 74, 75, 78–79, 92
Chrysler Corporation, 79, 245
Cigarettes, 41, 53, 61–62
Classical music, 215–217
Cleanliness Institute of New York, 59
Cliquot Club Dry Ginger Ale, 140
Cliquot Club Eskimos, The, 68, 240
Cliquot Club Ginger Ale Company, 68
"Cliquot Foxtrot March, The," 68
Cobb, Robert, 124
Cobb, Ty, 156–157
Coca-Cola, 139, 140
Coca-Cola Company, 67, 139–140
Cocktails, 14, 138
Cocoanuts, The, 234
Cofall, Stanley, 161
Cole, Fred, 104
College, 34
College Humor, 34
Colleges and universities: architecture of, 80–81; college life, 33–35; college students as cultural arbiters, 34–35; enrollment, 32–33, 81; fashion, 114–115; football, 33–34, 159–160; fraternities and sororities, 33; growth of, 81; popular culture and, 34–35, 147, 148
"Collegiate," 34
Collins, Floyd, 24
Columbia Broadcasting System (CBS), 125, 195, 239
Comic strips, 44, 66, 278–282
"Composographs," 189–190, 285
Consumerism, xv, 5–6, 40, 43, 51, 95, 99–100, 128
Contraceptive devices, 45–46
Coogan, Jackie, 63, 234
Cookbooks, 124–125
Cooking, 56, 70, 119–122, 123–125
Coolidge, Calvin, 5, 6, 7, 8, 263–264
Coon Chicken Inns, 87
Cooper, Gary, 233
Correll, Charles, 241
Cosmetics and makeup, 99, 109
Cotton Club, 202
Coué, Emile, 153, 174–175
Country Club Plaza, 249
Covarrubias, Miguel, 278
Crandall, Milton, 148

Crazes. *See* Fads and crazes
"Crazy Blues," 206
Credit plans, 5, 52, 246
Crime, 4–5, 7, 8–9, 10, 12, 14, 15–17, 21–22, 25, 71, 189, 231
Crocker, Betty, 62, 70, 125; Betty Crocker Kitchens, 62
Cross Word Puzzle Book, The, 148, 175
Crossword puzzles, 147–148, 175
Cummings, Alma, 148
Curtis Candy Company, 65, 136

Daily Mirror (New York), 189
Dalhart, Vernon, 24, 210, 212, 266
Damrosch, Walter, 217
Dance: criticism of, 42, 228–229; dance bands, 197, 200–204; marathons, 148–149; modern dance, 226; popular dances, 42, 226–229; popular song and, 192, 227, 228; popularity of, 226–227; sexuality and, 42, 228–229; square dancing, 229
"Dance Derby of the Century, The," 148–149
Dance marathons, 148–149
Darrow, Clarence, 21–22, 25
Dating and courtship, 44–47, 249
Davidson, Donald, 188
"Death of Floyd Collins, The," 24, 212
De Leath, Vaughn, 239
Deering, Wilma, 280
DeMille, Cecil B., 232–233
Dempsey, Jack, 158–159, 271–272
Dempsey and Firpo, 271–272
Demuth, Charles, 273
Department stores, 65, 100
Desire Under the Elms, 223
Detective novels, 174
Dickinson, Emily, 185
Diemer, Walter E., 137
Diet and Health, With Key to the Calories, 127, 174
Dieting, 62, 127–128, 152
Dinah, 228
Dirigibles, 266–267
Disney, Walt, 283
Disney Brothers Studio, 283
"Dixieland Jass Band One Step," 200
"Doin' the Racoon," 192, 228
Douglas, Aaron, 274
Douglass, Robert L., 164
Drama, 187, 222–224, 250
Dubble Bubble gum, 137
Duke, James B., 81
Duke University, 81
Duncan, Donald, 151

Earhart, Amelia, 62
Earl Carroll's *Vanities*, 196, 226
Eberson, John, 85
"Echoes of the Jazz Age," xiii
Eckholm, H. Conrad, 96
Economic depressions, 5, 26
Economy, 5–6, 26
Ederle, Gertrude, 164–165
Education, 31–35
Edward, Prince of Wales, 103, 115
Edwards, Cliff ("Ukulele Ike"), 198, 220
Egyptian craze, 74, 84, 111, 153
Eighteenth Amendment, 13
Electrical appliances, 18, 56, 120–122
Electrification, 18
Ellington, Edward "Duke," 202–203
Elmer Gantry, 172
Empire State Building, 78
Emperor Jones, The, 187, 223
Endurance contests, 147, 148–151
Epperson, Frank, 137
Equal Rights Amendment (ERA), 19–20
Equitable Life Assurance Society, 59–60
Erector sets, 145
Eskimo Pies, 137
Etiquette in Society, in Business, in Politics and at Home, 45, 95, 96, 174
"Eton crop," 107
Eveready Hour, The, 68, 70, 239
Everygirls, 38
"Experiment in Modern Music, An," 215
Exposition Internationale des Arts Décoratifs et Industriels Modernes, 73–74

Fabian, Warner, 43
Fads and crazes, 146–154; bodybuilding, 111–112, 152; Coueism, 153, 174–175; crossword puzzles, 147–148, 175; dance marathons, 148–149; dancing, 42, 148–149, 226–229; dieting, 62, 127–128, 152; Egyptian and Oriental crazes, 74, 84–85, 86, 111, 153–154; endurance contests, 147, 148–151; flagpole sitting, 65, 149–150; Freudianism, 153; mahjong, 147; miniature golf, 151–152; pogo sticks, 151; swimwear, 104; transcontinental races, 149; ukuleles, 153, 213–214; yo-yos, 151
Fairbanks, Douglas, 63, 220, 237
"Fairyland" miniature golf course, 151
Fall, Albert B., 4–5
Farmer, Fannie Merritt, 124, 174
"Fascinatin' Rhythm," 192, 198
Fashion, 95–118; bathing suits, 103–105; brassieres, 105–106; children's fashion, 116–117; corsets, 105; cosmetics and makeup, 99, 109; designers, 96–97, 101–102, 103–104, 106; Egyptian influence, 111, 153; English influence, 112, 115; fashion trendsetters, 29–31, 97, 99, 103, 107, 109, 110, 111, 112, 114–115; French influence, 96–97, 101–102, 103, 107–108, 110; hairstyles, 30, 107–108, 115; men's fashion, 111–116; popular culture and, 96–97; retail clothing, 99–100; standards of feminine beauty, 97, 99, 127; women's fashion, 97–111
Fass, Paula, 39, 41
Faulkner, Anne Shaw, 204
Faulkner, William, 184
Federal Highway Act of 1921, 247
Felix the Cat, 282–283
Ferber, Edna, 172–173, 224
Fetchit, Stepin, 235
Fields, Dorothy, 196, 226
Fields, W. C., 220
Firpo, Luis, 271–272
Fisher, Harry "Bud," 279
Fitzgerald, F. Scott, xiii, 39, 184
Fitzgerald, Zelda, 184
Flagpole sitting, 65, 149–150
Flaming Youth, 43
Flappers, 29–30, 38–39, 99, 237, 250, 275
Flappers and Philosophers, 184
Fleer, Frank H., 137
Fleer Chewing Gum Company, 137
Fleming, Victor, 233
Flores, Pedro, 151
Florida land boom, 72, 258
Food, 119–141; advertisements for, 56, 58, 59, 61, 62–63, 65, 67, 68, 136–137; candy and chocolate, 134–137; canned, 120, 122–123; dieting, 62, 127–128, 152; emergence of standard American diet, 119, 140–141; ethnic, 132–133; frozen, 122; fruits and vegetables, 123–126; ice cream and ice cream bars, 137; impact of National Prohibition on, 129–130, 132–133; meals, 123–124; preparation of, 119–122; restaurants, 129–134; rise of giant corporations, 122; scientific nutrition, 70, 123, 125–126
Football, 33–34, 159–161
Ford, Henry, xiv, 6–7, 204, 229, 244–245, 246, 254
Ford, John, 233
Ford Motor Company, 6–7, 82, 91, 244–246, 263, 264
Foreign-language records, 214–215
Fosdick, Harry Emerson, 20
Foster, Andrew "Rube," 157
Foster, Hal, 281
4-H, 38
"Four Horsemen of Notre Dame, The," 160
Four Horsemen of the Apocalypse, The, 227, 237
Foursquare Gospel, 21
Fox Film Corporation, 196, 229, 235
Fox Theater (San Francisco), 83, 84
Fraternities and sororities, 33
Fremont Canning Company, 125
French, Daniel Chester, 81, 286
Freshman, The, 34

Freud, Sigmund, 153
Freuh, Al, 278
Frost, Robert, 185–186
Frozen foods, 122
Fugitive, The, 178, 188
Fugitives. *See* Agrarians
Fundamentalism, 20–23
Furey, Jim, 163–164
Furnishing the Little House, 90

Galloping Gaucho, 283
Galloping Ghost, The, 160
Games. *See* Toys and games
Garbo, Greta, xiv, 110, 233
Gard, Alex, 278
Gardner, Erle Stanley, 179
Garvey, Marcus, 12
Gas stations, 85–86, 247
Gasoline Alley, 279–280
Gaynor, Janet, 233, 236
Gehrig, Lou, 156
General, The, 233
General Electric refrigerators, 56
General Foods Corporation, 122
General Mills, 70, 122
General Motors, 245, 246
General Motors Concerts, 217
Generation gap, 29, 39–40
Gentlemen Prefer Blondes, 170, 275
George A. Hormel and Company, 122
George White Scandals, The, 192, 196, 225, 228
Gerber Baby Food, 125
Gershwin, George, xiv, 192, 198, 215–217
Gershwin, Ira, 192
Gibson girl, 97, 99, 127
Gilbert, A. C., 145
Gilbert, John, 233
Gillette razor blades, 59
Gipp, George, 160
Girl Scouts of America, 38
Glyn, Elinor, 237
Gold Dust soap powder, 63
Gold Dust Twins, 63, 240
Gold Medal flour, 62, 125
Gold Rush, The, 234–235
Golf, 161–162
Good Housekeeping, 124–125
Good Humor Bars, 137
Good News, 196, 228
Goodhue, Bertram Grosvenor, 81, 88
Goodrich Silvertown Orchestra, The, 68, 195, 240
Goodyear Tire and Rubber Company, 266
Gosden, Freeman, 241
Graham, Martha, 226
Grand Ole Opry, The, 210
Grange, Harold "Red," 61, 136, 160–161
Grauman's Chinese Theater, 63, 65, 85, 153
Grauman's Egyptian Theater, 84, 153
Gray, Gilda, 227
Gray, Harold, 281
Gray, Judd, 25
Great Depression, 26
Great Gatsby, The, 15, 184
Great Migration, 9, 186–187
Greene, Charles Sumner, 88
Greene, Henry Mather, 88
Greenwich Village Follies, The, 225–226
Grey, Zane, 172
Greyhound Bus Lines, 250
Griffith, D. W., 70, 230
Grocery stores, 57, 67, 68, 128
Grofé, Ferde, 215
Gruger, Frederic, 277
Gulick, Charlotte, 38
Gulick, Luther, 38

Hadden, Briton, 175
Hagen, Walter, 161
Hairstyles, 30, 107–108, 115. *See also* Bobbed hair
Hall, Wendell, 195, 239
Hallelujah!, 235
Hall-Mills murder case, 25
Hamburgers, 134
Hammerstein, Oscar, II, 193, 224
Hammett, Dashiell, 179
Handy, W. C., 205–206, 278
Hansburg, George, 151
Happiness Boys, 68–69, 198

Happiness Boys, The (radio program), 68–69, 240
Happiness Candy Stores, 68
Harding, Warren G., 4–5, 239, 254
Hardy, Oliver, 233–234
Hare, Ernest, 68–69, 153, 198
Harlem, 9–10, 186–187, 202–203
Harlem Globetrotters, 164
Harlem Renaissance, 12–13, 186–188, 273–274
Harlem Renaissance Big 5, 164
Harmon, William Elmer, 274
Harmon Foundation, 274
Hawaiian music, 153, 213–214
Hay, George D., 210
Hay, William Howard, 127
Hays, William H. "Will," 232
Hays Office, 231–232
Hearst, William Randolph, 25, 189, 223
Heart Throbs, 43, 182
Hearts in Dixie, 235
Held, John, Jr., 38, 177, 250, 275
Hemingway, Ernest, 183, 184
Henderson, Fletcher, 201–202, 203
Henri, Robert, 271–272
Herriman, George, 279
Hershey, Milton S., 135
Hershey Chocolate Company, 135–136
Hertz, John D., 247, 252
Hertz Drive-Ur-Self Company, 247
Highways, 246–247
Hillbilly music, 209–213
Hillier, Bevis, 74
Hindenburg, The, 267
Hirshfeld, Al, 277–278
Hitchcock, Henry-Russell, 74
Holland Tunnel, 247
"Hollywood Eighteen Day Diet," 127
Hollywood motion pictures. *See* Motion pictures
Homemakers' shows, 70, 125
Honky Tonk, 199
Hood, Raymond M., 74, 76, 91
Hoopii, Sol, 213
Hoover, Herbert, 5, 6, 23, 25–26, 81
Hoover vacuum cleaner, 61
Hopper, Edward, 271, 272
Horse racing, 165
Hot Chocolates, 196, 226
Housekeeper's Half Hour, The, 70
How to Win Friends and Influence People, 55
Howard, Sidney, 223
Howe, George, 74, 76
Howells, John Mead, 76, 91
Huggins, Miller, 156
Hughes, Langston, 187, 188, 278
Hull, E. M., 170
Humphrey, Doris, 226
Hurston, Zora Neale, 187
Hutchison, Frank, 250

"I Love the College Girls," 34
"I Wanna Be Loved By You," 199
Ice cream, 137
I'll Take My Stand, 188
Illustrators, 38, 177, 250, 271, 272, 273, 274–277
"I'm Gonna Charleston Back to Charleston," 227
"I'm Just Wild About Harry," 196, 225
"I'm the Last of the Red Hot Mamas," 198–199
Immigration, 7–9, 31–32, 213–214
Independent Grocers Alliance (IGA), 128
Indianapolis Motor Speedway, 166
Ingram, Edgar Waldo "Billy," 134
Interior design, 90
International Exhibition of Modern Architecture, 74–75
International Exhibition of Modern Art, 270
International Style, 74–75
International Style, The, 74
Interpretation of Dreams, The, 153
Intolerance, 230
Ipana Toothpaste Company, 68
Ipana Troubadours, The, 68, 240
Iron Horse, The, 233
Isaly, William, 137
It (candy bar), 136–137
It (film), 44, 136–137, 237
It (novella), 237

"It Ain't Gonna Rain No Mo'," 195
Ivory soap, 65

J. L. Kraft and Brothers Company, 122
Jackson, Joe "Shoeless Joe," 155
Jackson, Reuben W., 133
Jannings, Emil, 236
Jantzen, Carl, 103–104
Jazz, 199–204, 215
Jazz Age, xiii–xvii, 3, 26
"Jazz journalism," 189
Jazz Singer, The, 196, 198, 237–238
Jefferson, Blind Lemon, 208
Jell-O, 120, 124
Jews, 220, 222–223, 256
"John T. Scopes Trial, The," 211
Johnson, Howard, 133
Johnson, James P., 196, 227
Johnson, Nunnally, 149
Johnson's Baby Powder, 56
Jolson, Al, 196, 197–198, 220, 238
Jones, Billy, 68–69, 153, 162, 198
Jones, Bobby, 115
Jordan Playboy, 246

Kahn, Albert, 74, 82, 91
Kaltenborn, H. V., 240
Kane, Helen, 199
KDKA (East Pittsburgh), 238–239
Keaton, Buster, 233
Keller, Helen, 220
Kellerman, Annette, 103
"Kellerman Suit," 103
Kellogg's Rice Crispies, 122
Kelly, Alvin "Shipwreck," 65, 149
Kelly, Clyde, 262
Kelly Act, 262
Kent, Rockwell, 277
Kern, Jerome, 192, 224
Keystone Kops, 250
Kid, The, 234
King, Frank, 280
King of Kings, The, 232–233
Kirby, J. G., 133
Klondike Bars, 137
Kodak Brownie box camera, 284
Kool-Aid, 140
Krazy Kat, 279, 282
Kroger, 67, 128
Krystal, 134
Ku Klux Klan, 10–11
KYW (Chicago), 195, 217

Labor strikes, 7
Ladies' Home Journal, 58, 176
Lady, Be Good!, 196, 198
Lamb, Thomas W., 85
Landis, Kennesaw Mountain, 155
Lang, Eddie, 203, 204
Larsen, Nella, 187, 188
Laugh-O-Gram Corporation, 283
Laurel, Stan, 233–234
Lazzeri, Tony, 156
Lee, Lorelei, 170, 275
Leisure, 143–167; dancing, 42, 148–149, 226–229; dating and courtship, 44–47, 249; drinking, 41, 138; fads and crazes, 146–154; joy-riding, 249; motion pictures, 41–42, 196, 230–231, 238; popular music, 42; radio, 239–242; reading, 43, 169–170; smoking, 41; sports, 33–34, 154–166; swimming, 103–104, 164; toys and games, 144–146, 147–148, 151–152, 175, 250; youth and, 30, 41–44. *See also* Travel
Lenglen, Suzanne, 162
Leopold, Nathan, 24–25
Leopold and Loeb trial, 24–25
Leslie, Lew, 226
Lewis, Sinclair, 171–172
Leyendecker, J. C., 277
Libby Foods, 62
"Liberty torches," 41. *See also* Cigarettes
Life, 176–177
Lincoln Logs, 145
Lincoln Memorial, 81, 286
Lindbergh, Charles A., xiv, 115, 137, 194, 228, 241, 263–264
"Lindbergh (The Eagle of the U.S.A.)," 212
"Lindbergh Line," 264–265
Lindy hop, 228
Lionel train sets, 146
Listerine mouthwash, 58–60

Literary Guild, 170
Literature, 169–190; book clubs, 170; fiction best-sellers, 169–175; Harlem Renaissance, 186–188; historical novels, 172; modernist fiction, 183–184; mysteries and detective novels, 174; "New Woman" in, 170–171; non-fiction best-sellers, 174–175; westerns, 172–173
Little Orphan Annie, 281
"Livery Stable Blues," 200
Lloyd, Harold, 233
Locke, Alain, 12, 187
Loeb, Richard, 24–25
"Long Count, The," 159
Loos, Anita, 170, 275
Lorimer, George Horace, 176
Love Story Magazine, 43, 182
Lovecraft, H. P., 179
Lowell, Amy, 185
Luce, Henry, 175
Lucky Strike cigarettes, 53, 61–62. *See also* Cigarettes
Lynching, 10, 236
Lynd, Helen Merrell, 143, 244
Lynd, Robert S., 143, 244
Lysol disinfectant, 58

Macfadden, Bernarr, 152, 182
Mack, Cecil, 196, 227
Macon, Uncle Dave, 210
Macy's department store, 65, 100
Macy's Thanksgiving Day Parade, 65
Magazines, 175–183; advertising in, 55–56, 58, 65–67; caricatures in, 277–278; circulation of, 66–67, 175, 176, 178; commercial photography in, 285–286; general audience magazines, 175–176; girls' magazines, 38; illustrations in, 274–277; little magazines, 178; pulp magazines, 43, 178–183, 280; smart magazines, 176–177; women's magazines, 55–56, 67, 124–125, 176, 182
Mahjong, 147
Maiden Form Brassiere Company, 106
Mail-order catalogs, 100
Main Street, 171
Makeup. *See* Cosmetics and makeup
"Makin' Whoopee," 198
Maltese Falcon, The, 179
Man Nobody Knows, The, 55, 174
Man o' War, 165
Mann, William D'Alton, 176
Manners and morals, 29–30, 44–47, 95
Manufacturing: airplanes, 264; automobiles, 5, 244–246; big business and, 5–6; candy and chocolate, 135–137; clothing, 96–97, 99–100; cosmetics and makeup, 109; hair care products, 108; motion pictures, 229–231, 232, 235–236, 237–238; phonograph records, 193, 209, 210–212, 214, 217; processed foods, 122–123; sheet music, 193–194; toys and games, 144–145; ukuleles, 214
Marcel, Grateau, 107
"Marcel waves," 107–108
Marie Barlow Facial Preparations, 40
Markin, Morris, 252
Marks, Percy, 43
Mars, Frank, 136
Mars bars, 136
Mars Candies, 136
Martin, Mary Hale, 62
Marx Brothers, 219, 234
McCormick, Robert R., 76, 279–280
McHugh, Jimmy, 196, 226
McKay, Claude, 187, 188
McMein, Neysa, 277
McNamee, Graham, 240
McPherson, Aimee Semple, 21, 172, 189
"Medical Millennium Diet," 127
Medicine and medical advances, 23–24. *See also* Scientific and technological advances
Mencken, H. L., 22, 29–30, 176, 178, 179, 182, 188
Men's fashion. *See* Fashion
Messmer, Otto, 282
Metro-Goldwyn-Mayer, 196–197, 229, 231, 235
Miami (Florida) *Daily News*, 72
Micheaux, Oscar, 236
Mickey Mouse, 283

Middletown: A Study in American Culture, 143
Milestone Mo-Tel, 256
Milky Way candy bars, 136
Millay, Edna St. Vincent, 186
Milquetoast, Caspar, 44
Mimetic architecture, 66, 86–87
Miniature golf, 151–152
Miss America Pageant, 96, 104
Model A Ford, 246
Model T Ford, 6, 244–245, 246
Modern dance, 226
Modernism, 183–186, 188, 269–270
Montgomery Ward Company, 100
Morgan, Helen, 199
Morton, Ferdinand "Jelly Roll," 201
Motels, 255–256
Motion Picture Producers and Distributors of America (MPPDA), 232
Motion pictures: African-American films, 235–236; attendance, 42, 196; cartoons, 282–283; genres, 232–237; Hays Office, 231–232; motion picture industry, 229–232; movie palaces and theaters, 83–85, 153, 229–230, 238; musicals, 196–197, 198–199; popular music and, 196–197; scandals, 25, 189, 231; sexuality and, 42, 231, 232; silent films, 229, 230–231, 232–237; stars, 233–235, 236–238; studio system, 229–230; talking films, 196–197, 198–199, 237–238; vaudeville and, 221–222; before World War I, 230–231; youth and, 34, 40, 41–42
Motor Camper and Tourist, 247
Mount Rushmore, 286, 288
Movie theaters. *See* Motion pictures
Movies. *See* Motion pictures
Moxie, 140
Munsey, Frank, 179
"Murderers' Row," 156
Murphy, Jim, 166
Murray, Arthur, 227
Museum of Modern Art, 269, 272, 284
Museums, 269, 272, 284
Music, 191–218; African-American influence on, 191, 192, 199–200, 204, 215, 218; blues, 205–209; classical, 215–217; dance bands, 197, 200–204; foreign-language records, 214–215; Hawaiian, 153, 213–214; hillbilly, 209–213; jazz, 199–204, 215; motion pictures and, 196–197, 198; musicals and revues, 192, 196, 198, 224–226, 227–228; phonograph records and, 193, 209, 210–212, 214, 217, 218; popular, 191–199; radio and, 68, 195, 240; sheet music and, 193–194; swing, 202, 203; "symphonic jazz," 215; Tin Pan Alley, 191–199, 213, 227, 250; vocalists, 197–199
Music Appreciation Hour, 217
Musicals and revues, 192, 196, 198, 224–226, 227–228
Mutt and Jeff, 279
"My Blue Heaven," 42, 196, 199
My Egypt, 273
Mystery novels, 174

Nabisco Cream of Wheat, 63
Nast, Condé, 176
Nathan, George Jean, 178, 179, 182
Nation, Carry, 220
National Barn Dance, The, 210
National Broadcasting Company (NBC), 23, 68–69, 70, 125, 195, 217, 239
National Carbon Company, 68
National Football League, 161
National Negro Baseball League, 157–158
National Origins Act of 1924, 8
National Park Service, 257–258
National parks, 257–258
National Prohibition, 13–17, 41, 44, 129–130, 132–133, 138
National Radio Home-Makers' Club, The, 70, 125
Nawahi, Bennie, 213
Nelson, Christian, 137
Neon signs, 66
Nervous Wreck, 250
Neutra, Richard J., 74
"New Negro," 12–13
New Negro, The, 12, 187

New Republic, The, 54
New York Daily News, 189, 281, 285
New York Evening Graphic, 189–190, 285
New York Evening Journal, 271
New York Herald Tribune, 44
New York Realists. *See* Ashcan school
New York Times, 278
New York Yankees, 155, 156
New Yorker, The, 138, 178
Newspapers and tabloids, 24–25, 189–190; advertising in, 65–66, 67, 240; circulation of, 189; comic strips, 44, 66, 278–282; "jazz journalism," 189; photojournalism, 285; sensationalism and, 189–190; sports and, 154, 160
Nichols, Anne, 222
Nigger Heaven, 187
Nineteenth Amendment, 19
No, No, Nannette, 196, 224
Nowland, Philip, 280
Nutrition. *See* Scientific nutrition

Ocean liners, 259–261
Odor-o-no deodorant, 59
O'Keefe, Georgia, 273, 284
"Ol' Man River," 224
"Old King Tut (In Tutankhamen's Day)," 153
Oliver, Joseph "King," 201, 203
Oliver's Creole Jazz Band, 201, 203
Olivieri, Natale, 140
O'Neill, Eugene, 187, 223–224
Only Yesterday, xiii
Opera, 215, 217
"Original Celtics," 163–164
Original Dixieland Jazz Band, 200
Ory, Edward "Kid," 200
Oscar Mayer and Company, 122
Oswald the Lucky Rabbit, 283
Overland Park (Colorado), 255
"Oxford bags," 30, 115
Oyl, Olive, 281–282

Painters, 271–274, 277
Pajeau, Charles, 145
Palmer, A. Mitchell, 7
"Palmer Raids," 7–8
Panama-California Exposition, 88
Pan-American Airlines, 265
Passing Show, The, 225
Patterson, Joseph Medill, 189
Patton, Charlie, 208–209
Payne, Andy, 149
Pennington, Ann, 225, 228
Pepsi-Cola, 140
Perkins, Edward, 140
Peters, Lulu Hunt, 127, 174
"Petting parties," 45
Philadelphia Savings Fund Society Building, 75, 76
Phonograph records, 193, 209, 210–212, 214, 217, 218. *See also* Foreign-language records
Photography, 189–190, 270, 273, 283–286
Pickford, Mary, 63, 236–237
Pierce Arrow, 137, 245
Pig Stand Company, Incorporated, 133–134
Piggly Wiggly, 128
Pilgrim, The, 266
Plane Crazy, 283
Plastic Age, The (film), 34
Plastic Age, The (novel), 43
Playwrights, 222–223
Poets, 185–186
Pogo sticks, 151
Ponzi, Carlo "Charles," 71
Ponzi schemes, 71
Poole, Charlie, and the North Carolina Ramblers, 212
Popeye, 281–282
Popsicles, 137
Post, Emily, 45, 95, 96, 174
Post 40% Bran Flakes, 58, 122
Postum Cereal Company, 62, 122, 139
Postum Food Coffee, 139
Potato chips, 122
Precisionism, 272–273
Presidential administrations. *See* Coolidge, Calvin; Harding, Warren G.; Hoover, Herbert; Roosevelt, Franklin D.

"Prisoner's Song, The," 210
Procter and Gamble, 65
Prohibition. *See* National Prohibition
"Prohibition Suit," 104
Public transportation. *See* Travel
Publicity stunts, 63–65, 149–151
Pulp magazines: adventure stories magazines, 180, 280; beginning of the industry, 179; circulation of, 182; cost of, 179, 180; crime and detective, 179; definition and description of, 178–179; horror and fantasy, 179–181; other titles of, 179, 183; romance and love, 43, 182; science fiction, 180; sex, 43, 182; true confession, 182–183; war, 180; western, 180, 182
Pyle, C. C., 149
Pyramid schemes, 71

Quaker Oats Company, 63
Quota Act of 1921, 8

"Race films," 235–236
"Race records," 206, 209
Race relations, 9–13
Race riots, 9–10
Radio: advertising on, 63, 66, 67–71, 240; audience, 195, 240, 241–242; barn dances, 209–210; commercial sponsorship of, 67–71; criticism of radio advertising, 68, 70–71; daily life and, 195, 239–240; earliest broadcasts, 238–239; formation of networks, 195; homemakers' shows, 70, 125; musical programs, 63, 68–69, 195, 217, 240; personalities, 239, 240, 241–242; program format, 239–242; Scopes trial and, 22, 241; variety shows, 68, 70, 239
Raggedy Ann and Andy, 144
Railroads, 123, 258–259
Rainey, Getrude "Ma," 206, 207, 221
Ransom, John Crowe, 188
Rappe, Virginia, 25
Rastus, 63
Ray, Man, 270, 284
Razaf, Andy, 196
Reader's Digest, 175
Red Scare, 7–8
Red Seal records, 217
Red Summer of 1919, 9
Reed, Blind Alfred, 210
Refrigerators, 56, 120
Religion, 20–23
Remus, George, 15
Rental car companies, 247
Republicans, 4–5
Resorts, 256, 258, 261
Restaurants: architecture of, 82–83, 87; automats, 130; cafeterias, 130; chain, 130–131, 133–134; Chinese, 132; diners, 130; drive-in, 133–134; ethnic, 132–133; franchising of, 133; growth of, 129, 130; hamburger, 134; impact of National Prohibition on, 129–130, 132–133; Italian, 132; lunchrooms, 130; Mexican, 132–133; roadside, 133–134; tearooms, 131–132
Rhapsody in Blue, 215
Rice, Grantland, 160
Rickard, George "Tex," 158, 159
Rin Tin Tin, 237
Rinehart, Mary Roberts, 174
Robeson, Paul, 225, 236
Robinson, Bill "Bojangles," 221
Robinson, Edward Arlington, 185
Rockne, Knute, 160
Rockwell, Norman, 275, 277
Rodgers, Jimmie, 212–213
Roemer, Philip, 124
Rogers, Buck, 280
Rogers, Will, 70, 220, 239
Roosevelt, Franklin D., 5, 17, 281
Rosenthal, Ida Cohen, 106
Ross, Harold, 178
Roxy Theater (New York), 83
Rubenstein, Helena, 109
Runnin' Wild, 196, 226, 227
Russian Tea Room, 132
Ruth, George Herman "Babe," xiv, 136, 155, 156, 220

Saarinen, Eliel, 76
Sabatini, Rafael, 173
Sacco, Nicola, 8–9, 288

Safety Last, 233
Sally, 192
Sanger, Margaret, 46
Sanka coffee, 139
Sarazen, Gene, 161–162
Saturday Evening Post, The, 40–41, 63, 66–67, 139, 149, 176, 275
Saucy Stories, 43, 182
Saunders, Clarence, 128
Savage, Augusta, 274
Scams and swindles, 71–72
Scandals, 4–5, 21, 25, 155, 172, 189–190, 231, 232, 285
Scaramouche, 173
Scherman, Harry, 170
Schnering, Otto, 65
Schubert, J. J., 225
Schuster, Max L., 147, 175
Science fiction, 180, 280
Scientific and technological advances, 23. *See also* Medicine and medical advances
Scientific management, 6, 244–245
Scientific nutrition, 70, 123, 125–126
Scopes, John T., 21–22
Scopes trial, 21–23, 188, 212, 241
Scott tissues, 59
Scripps-Howard newspaper chain, 189
Sculptors, 81, 273, 286–288
Seagrave, H.O.D., 166
Seal, Ethel Davis, 90
Sealex Linoleums, 56
Sears, Roebuck and Company catalog, 96, 100, 102, 145, 214, 250
"Second Battle of the Century, The," 159
Segar, Elzie Crisler "E. C.," 281
Self-Mastery Through Conscious Autosuggestion, 153, 174–175
Self-service grocery stores, 128. *See also* Grocery stores
Sennett, Mack, 250
7-Up, 140
Shannon, David A., xiv
Shaw, Walden W., 252
Shawn, Ted, 226
Sheeler, Charles, 273
Sheik, The (film), 30, 43–44, 115, 154, 237
Sheik, The (novel), 170
Sheiks, 30
Shenandoah, 266
Shimmy, 42, 227
Show Boat (musical), 192, 196, 199, 224
Show Boat (novel), 172, 224
Shuffle Along, 196, 224–225
Siciliano, Angelo. *See* Atlas, Charles
Simon, Richard L., 147, 175
Simon and Schuster, 147, 175
"Since Ma Is Playing Mah Jong," 147
"Singin' in the Rain," 198
Singing Fool, The, 198
Sissle, Noble, 196, 225
Six Cylinder Love, 250
Skyscrapers, 75–80
Slang, 43–44, 171, 241, 281
"Slumming," 187
Smart magazines, 176–177
Smart Set, The, 176, 179
Smith, Alfred E., 5, 136
Smith, Bessie, 207–208, 221
Smith, Mamie, 206
Snappy Stories, 43, 182
Snowden, George "Shorty," 228
Snyder, Albert, 25
Snyder, Ruth, 25, 285
So Big, 172
Society for the Suppression of Vice, 223
Soft drinks, 67, 68, 139–140
"Some of These Days," 198
Son of the Shiek, The, 154
"Sonny Boy," 198
Sororities. *See* Fraternities and sororities
Sound and the Fury, The, 184
Spade, Sam, 179
Speakeasies, 14–15, 44
Speyer, Leonora, 185
Spirit of St. Louis, 263, 264
Spokespersons, 61–63
Sports, 154–166; amateurism and professionalism, 155, 160, 161, 162; auto racing, 165–166; baseball, 155–

158; basketball, 163–164; boxing, 158–159, 271–272; football, 33–34, 159–161; golf, 161–162; horse racing, 165; segregation in, 157–158, 164; swimming, 103–104, 164–165; tennis, 162–163
Square dancing, 229
St. Denis, Ruth, 226
St. Louis Blues (film), 208
"St. Louis Blues" (song), 205, 208
St. Valentine's Day Massacre, 17
Stallings, Laurence, 224
Standard Brands, 122
Steamboat Willie, 283
Stephenson, David C., 10, 12
Stieglitz, Alfred, xiv, 273, 284
Stone Mountain, 287, 288
Stone Mountain Confederate Memorial Association, 288
Stover, Russell, 137
Stratton-Porter, Gene, 173
Streetcars, 252
Strikes. *See* Labor strikes
Style Moderne. *See* Art Deco
Sullivan, Pat, 282
Sun Also Rises, The, 184
Sunday, Billy, 20–21
Swimming, 164–165
Swimwear. *See* Bathing suits
Swing music, 202, 203
"Symphonic jazz," 215

Tabloids. *See* Newspapers and tabloids
Tales of the Jazz Age, 184
Talmadge, Constance, 62
Tango, 42, 227
Tanner, Gid, and the Skillet Lickers, 212
Tarzan (comic strip), 280–281
Tarzan of the Apes (serialized novel), 180, 281–282
Tarzan, the Ape Man (film), 165
Tate, Allen, 188
Taxicabs, 252
Taylor, William Desmond, 231
"Tea for Two," 224
Teapot Dome Scandal, 4–5
Tearooms, 131–132
Television, 23
Ten Commandments, The, 232
Tennis, 162–163
Theater Owners' Booking Agency (TOBA), 200, 221
"There's a New Star in Heaven Tonight (Rudolph Valentino)," 212
They Knew What They Wanted, 223
Thimble Theatre, 281
This Side of Paradise, 39, 184
Thorpe, Jim, 161
Tilden, Bill, 115, 162–163
Time, 175–176
"Tin can tourists," 254–255
Tin Pan Alley, 191–199, 213, 227, 250
Tinkertoys, 145
Toomer, Jean, 187, 188
Tourism, 243, 252–261, 264–266, 267
Toys and games, 144–146, 147–148, 151–152, 175, 250
Travel, 243–267; airplanes, 261–266; auto-camping, 247, 254–255, 258; automobiles, 244–249, 259; buses, 250–251; destinations, 256–258; dirigibles, 266–267; lodging, 255–256; ocean liners, 259–261; railroads, 258–259; rental cars, 247; resorts, 256, 258, 261; streetcars, 252; subways, 252; taxicabs, 252; vacations, 249, 252–254, 267
Trials: Arbuckle, 25, 189, 231; Hall-Mills, 25; Leopold and Loeb, 24–25; Sacco and Vanzetti, 8–9; Scopes, 21–22; Snyder, 25; Stephenson, 10, 12
True Story Magazine, 182–183
"Truth-in-Advertising" campaign, 71
Tucker, Sophie, 198
Tunney, Gene, 158, 159
Tutankhamen, King, 74, 111, 153
Twenty-First Amendment, 17

Ukuleles, 153, 213–214
Ullbeck, Sylvia, 127–128
Universal Negro Improvement Association (UNIA), 12
Universities. *See* Colleges and universities

University of Notre Dame football team, 160
Urbanization, xv, 9–10, 186–187

Vacations, 249, 252–254, 267
Valentino, Rudolph, 30, 43–44, 115, 189–190, 227, 233, 237
Vallee, Rudy, 199, 225
Van Alen, William, 78, 92
Van Vechten, Carl, 187, 278
Vanderbilt University, 188
Vanity Fair, 176
Vanzetti, Bartolomeo, 8–9, 288
Variety, 193
"Varsity Drag, The," 192
Vaudeville, 219–222
Vaudeville blues, 206–208
Velveeta, 122
Victor Talking Machine Company, 193, 215, 217
Vidor, King, 233
Virginian, The, 233
Vogue, 176
Volstead Act, 13

Wales Padlock Law, 223
Walker, A'Lelia, 108
Walker, Madame C. J., 108
Walker College of Hair Culture, 108
Wall Street, 7, 26, 183
Wall Street Stories, 183
Wallace, DeWitt, 175
Wallace, Lila, 175
Waller, Fats, 196
Walsh, Raoul, 233
Warbucks, Daddy, 281
Waring, Fred, and His Pennsylvanians, 34, 197
Warner, Sylvia Townsend, 170
Warner Brothers, 196, 198, 199, 229, 237
Warren, Robert Penn, 188
Washburn-Crosby Company, 62, 70, 125
Waters, Ethel, 206, 221
Wayne, John, 34
WEAF (New York), 63, 68
Webster, T. H., 44
Weird Tales, 179, 181
Weissmuller, Johnny, 165
Welch, Elizabeth, 227
Western novels, 172–173
WGN (Chicago), 22, 241
What Price Glory? (film), 196, 233
What Price Glory? (play), 224
Wheaties, 122
"Whispering," 197
White, George, 225
White Castle, 82–83, 134, 135
White Tower, 134
Whiteman, Paul, 197, 204, 215, 220
Whoopee, 198
"Why Do You Bob Your Hair, Girls?," 210
"Why Was I Born," 199
Wickman, Eric, 250
Williams, Paul Revere, 92
Williams, Thomas Lanier "Tennessee," 179–180
Williams Luxury Shaving Cream, 59
Wills, Helen, 162
Wing walkers, 261
Wings, 236
Winnie Winkle the Breadwinner, 280
Wisconsin Daily Cardinal, 41
Within Our Gates, 236
WLS (Chicago), 210
Woman of Affairs, A, 110
Women: advertising and, 55–62; dieting and, 62, 127–128, 152; drinking and, 14–16; entertainers, 197, 198–199, 206–208, 220–221; fashion, 30, 43, 97–111; flappers, 29–30, 38–39, 99, 237, 250, 275; higher education and, 32–33; homemaking and domestic chores, 18, 56, 70, 119–122, 125; magazines and, 43, 55–56, 67, 124–125, 176, 182; marriage and divorce, 17, 18; politics and suffrage, 19–20; popular images of, 17, 29–30, 280; roles of, 17–20, 29–30; sexuality and, 17, 39, 42, 43, 44–47, 182–183, 231; smoking and, 41; standards of beauty, 97, 99, 127; in the workforce, 18–19, 54, 120; writers, 170–171, 172–174, 185, 186

Wonder Bread, 59, 123
Work, 35–36, 143, 253–254. *See also* Labor strikes
World War I, 39, 135–136, 180, 224, 233, 261
"Wreck of the Old 97, The," 210
"Wreck of the *Shenandoah*," 266
Wright, Frank, 133
Wright, Frank Lloyd, 92–93, 145
Wright, John Lloyd, 145
Writers, 169–174, 176, 178–180, 182–188
WSM (Nashville), 210
Wyeth, N. C., 277

Yankee Stadium, 156
Yellow Cab Company, 252
"Yes! We Have No Bananas," 42, 192
Yoo-Hoo, 140
Youmans, Vincent, 192, 224
Youth, 29–47; celebration of, 34–35, 38, 40–41, 58; clubs and organizations, 36–38; criticism of, 38–39, 204; dancing and, 42; dating and courtship, 44–47, 249; drinking and, 41; fashion, 30, 43; generation gap, 29, 39–40; identity of, 29–31; motion pictures and, 40, 41–42, 231; popular music and, 42; reading, 43, 178–183; sexuality and, 39, 42, 99; slang, 43–44; smoking and, 41; stereotypes of, 29–31
Yo-yos, 151

Zeppelin Stories, 183
Ziegfeld, Florenz, Jr., 198, 225
Ziegfeld Follies, The, 151, 196, 198, 199, 225, 227

About the Authors

KATHLEEN DROWNE is Assistant Professor of English at the University of Missouri, Rolla.

PATRICK HUBER is Assistant Professor of History at the University of Missouri, Rolla.